RE-VISIONING GENDER ĪN
PHILOSOPHY OF RELIGION

INTENSITIES: CONTEMPORARY CONTINENTAL PHILOSOPHY OF RELIGION

Series Editors:
Patrice Haynes and Steven Shakespeare,
both at Liverpool Hope University, UK

This series sits at the forefront of contemporary developments in Continental philosophy of religion, engaging particularly with radical reinterpretations and applications of the Continental canon from Kant to Derrida and beyond but also with significant departures from that tradition. A key area of focus is the emergence of new realist and materialist schools of thought whose potential contribution to philosophy of religion is at an early stage. Rooted in a vibrant tradition of thinking about religion, whilst positioning itself at the cutting edge of emerging agendas, this series has a clear focus on Continental and post-Continental philosophy of religion and complements Ashgate's British Society for Philosophy of Religion series with its more analytic approach.

Other titles in the series:

Intensities
Philosophy, Religion and the Affirmation of Life
Edited by Katharine Sarah Moody and Steven Shakespeare

Re-visioning Gender in Philosophy of Religion

Reason, Love and Epistemic Locatedness

PAMELA SUE ANDERSON
University of Oxford, UK

ASHGATE

Published by
Ashgate Publishing Limited
Wey Court East
Union Road
Farnham
Surrey, GU9 7PT
England

Ashgate Publishing Company
110 Cherry Street
Suite 3-1
Burlington, VT 05401-3818
USA

www.ashgate.com

British Library Cataloguing in Publication Data
Anderson, Pamela Sue.
  Re-visioning gender in philosophy of religion : reason,
  love and epistemic locatedness. – (Intensities)
  1. Religion – Philosophy. 2. Feminist theory. 3. Feminism –
  Religious aspects. 4. Feminist ethics.
  I. Title II. Series
  210.8'2–dc23

Library of Congress Cataloging-in-Publication Data
Anderson, Pamela Sue.
  Re-visioning gender in philosophy of religion : reason, love and epistemic locatedness /
by Pamela Sue Anderson.
    p. cm. — (Intensities)
  Includes bibliographical references (p.   ) and index.
  ISBN 978-0-7546-0784-7 (hardcover) 1. Women and religion. 2. Sex role—Religious
  aspects. 3. Feminism—Religious aspects. 4. Feminist theory. 5. Religion—Philosophy.
  6. Philosophy and religion. I. Title.

  BL458.A55 1993
  210.82—dc23

                                                              2012018440

ISBN 9780754607847 (hbk)
ISBN 9780754607854 (pbk)
ISBN 9781409454120 (ebk – PDF)
ISBN 9781409472322 (ebk – ePUB)

Printed and bound in Great Britain by the
MPG Books Group, UK.

In loving memory of

PJAH

Contents

Preface

I would like to offer a preliminary statement concerning the project of re-visioning gender in philosophy of religion as it will be developed in the present book. First of all, the field of philosophy of religion will serve as the object of this re-visioning. Here re-vision means 'the act of looking back, of seeing with fresh eyes, of entering an old text from a new critical direction'.[1] 'An old text' will be another name for the object of re-vision. In *Re-visioning Gender in Philosophy of Religion*, I have sought to see 'with fresh eyes', as if I am 'entering an old text [of traditional theism]', one which I have taught and studied for more than thirty years, but now 'from a new critical direction' informed by women-philosophers and not only by men in the field. As a woman-philosopher who teaches Anglo-American philosophy of religion, while also writing on topics in Continental philosophy of religion, I am looking back on what can be broadly construed as twentieth-century philosophy of religion.

Second, the idea of re-visioning gender in this field draws on 'the philosophical imaginary'[2] to find clues 'to how we live, how we have been living, how we have been led to imagine ourselves'.[3] This means that I follow Michèle Le Doeuff's close reading of philosophical texts for the imagery, the asides and stories which portray or represent women's lives, as well as the ideas of men and women. Also crucial is the relationship of this imaginary to what is external to, yet still shaping, the philosophical text. Uncovering this philosophical imaginary enables us to see what has been on the margins of philosophical reasoning. Yet note that, according to Le Doeuff, 'the red ink in the margins' of a philosophy text is absolutely necessary to support the philosophical arguments and reasoning of the philosopher/author.[4] Traditionally, the philosophical imaginary has been largely a (male) philosopher's prerogative in determining – often by the content excluded from – philosophical fields of thinking. The critical concern here is the role which gender has played (implicitly) and will play (explicitly) in determining the field of philosophy of religion.

---

[1] Adrienne Rich, 'When We Dead Awaken: Writing as Re-vision'. *College English*, 34, 1, 'Women Writing and Teaching' (October 1972): 18; reprinted in Barbara Gelpi and Albert Gelpi (eds), *Adrienne Rich's Poetry and Prose* (New York and London: W. W. Norton & Company, 1991), p. 167.

[2] Michèle Le Doeuff, *The Philosophical Imaginary*, translated by Colin Gordon (New York and London: Continuum, 2002), pp. 1–20.

[3] Rich, 'When We Dead Awaken', p. 167.

[4] Le Doeuff, *The Philosophical Imaginary*, pp. 57–99.

I do not know exactly what the twentieth-century poet Adrienne Rich had in mind when she created the lines of her 'Diving into the Wreck';[5] but the imagery in this poem helps to capture the twofold, general and specific activities of re-visioning which are set out in this preliminary statement. The image of 'the Wreck' becomes a focus for *Re-visioning Gender in Philosophy of Religion: Reason, Love and Epistemic Locatedness*. Rich identifies the wreck as 'the thing-itself': the thing to which we look back – as if, to an old philosophical text – and from which we look forward – as if, equally, becoming a new text for our lives today. The imagery of 'diving into a wreck' both focuses and opens up exploration of the remains of 'the disaster'; it is as if we (still) need to discover something valuable from the past with potential knowledge for the future of, in my appropriation of 'the wreck', gender in philosophy of religion. Both truth and justice are, as will be discovered in the overall argument of the present book, values necessary to motivate this re-visioning.

With total confidence as a poet and a woman, Rich takes her readers into an imaginary dimension in order for them/us to see with fresh eyes. Her lines of poetry in 'Diving into the Wreck' promises to take each of us with her on an exploratory journey in the first person: '… I came to explore the wreck', to find where re-visioning gender can begin. Starting at a critical distance we move deep into the traditional waters where myths (of gender) have in the past supported (male) philosophers. Rich's poem opens up the productive imagination of the thinker who finds the critical space where 'the wreck' includes original fragments of analytical and creative thoughts. In this manner, the philosopher's imaginary finds it has the power both to trap and to liberate those who follow. So, in the world of the imaginary, the woman-philosopher meets the woman-poet, as Rich says in exploring the wreck, 'the words are purposes … [and] maps'. It is *as if*, in the manner of Rich's attempt to re-vision, we understand that 'the very act of naming [God and "his" attributes] has been till now a male prerogative'.[6] Yet in moving forward we can also learn to see differently and to name new terms for a less patriarchal way into the future.

It follows from what I am saying that Rich's poem does not just introduce us to poetry but also to ourselves and to our philosophical naming of men and women. In the dual activity of reflecting back into the past and looking forward from the past:

> I came to see the damage that was done
> and the treasures that prevail.[7]

---

[5]   Adrienne Rich, *Diving into the Wreck* (New York: W. W. Norton & Company, Inc., 1973), pp. 22–24.

[6]   Rich, 'When We Dead Awaken', p. 167.

[7]   Rich, *Diving into the Wreck*, p. 23.

Appropriating freely the terms of this poem, I link 'the damage that was done' to the upshot of traditional gender norms in philosophy of religion on those of us in the field who have struggled to be heard; and I recognize 'the treasures that prevail' in valuable arguments which have been put forward and often revised by contemporary philosophers of religion. In this way, 'Diving into the Wreck' is meant to resonate with the project of seeking change creatively for philosophy of religion today. To see – *really* see – the treasures in the field requires time and ongoing, critical reflection on both the academic field and the changing concepts which guide one's own life.

Clues from Le Doeuff's philosophical imaginary and Rich's poetic vision of human life can only gradually reveal how we – men and women – live, how we have been living, how we have been led to imagine ourselves. Yet, crucially, we do not only face destruction of the old, but the construction of new insights from philosophical arguments which have perhaps been previously thought to be completely understood with an understanding that was assumed to be timeless.

Rich's poem seeks neither 'the story of the wreck' nor 'the disaster', but 'the thing itself'. We do not seek 'the myth' but the philosophy itself for the twenty-first century. Rich also imagines with the wreck, 'the drowned face always staring', looking 'toward the sun'. She describes 'the evidence of damage', yet she grasps poetically the hopeful fact that 'the drowned face' has 'always' been staring toward 'the sun', and so, to life not death.[8] Despite the damage of tears and 'the disaster' of years, the chapters of this book aim, in re-visioning gender, to grasp, what Rich captures poetically, 'a threadbare beauty'; she describes 'the ribs' of the disaster as still 'curving their assertions'.[9]

This discovery of beauty means equally a discovery of justice; seeking to be just as an undeniably integral feature of beauty is the decisive motivation for the philosophical act of re-visioning gender in this book. Without the attraction of beauty and the assertions of justice, there might be no motivation for change or for new life. It is necessary to become aware of our 'epistemic locatedness', so that the justice of our reasons and the true beauty of our loves can motivate the re-visioning of the social and material conditions of the field.

It is for these, perhaps to some thinkers, ethereal reasons that I have sought not simply to revise the subject matter of philosophy of religion, but to re-vision it. As will be demonstrated in the course of this book, re-visioning gender requires a concern for justice which is at the same motivated by and motivating our attraction to beauty and goodness. As philosophers we, women and men, are attracted to beauty as a reality of our lives and loves – without which, arguably, we could not live – so well. We philosophers are – as women and men – able, if we so choose, to see life afresh and to think anew from a location sensitive to gender in its intersections with a range of social and material variables.

---

[8] Ibid., p. 24.
[9] Ibid.

'Intersectionality'[10] is a current term for the inescapably interrelated categories in the construction of gender. Gender is inescapably formed by, and recognized where it intersects with, a range of social and material categories, including race, religion, ethnicity, class, age and sexual orientation. Masculine or male prerogatives for gender construction of, as in this field, God and 'his' omni-attributes, including omnipotence, omniscience, omnibenevolence, omnipresence and omnitemporality, come from a location which has been fixed by assumptions of the same theistic/atheistic religious framework, yet in fact interlinking with social and material categories. This singular sameness is deceptive, since it can never represent human gender fairly, especially if the gender represented is merely a creation of the divine in the projection of the identity of a singular gender grouping. Kimberlé Crenshaw has been credited with naming intersectionality as the mechanism of gender constructions. Initially Crenshaw wrote about the interlinking of gender and race. However, her own account of the more extensive role of intersectionality in constructions of gender is clear here:

> In mapping the intersections of race and gender, the concept [intersectionality] does engage dominant assumptions that race and gender are essentially separate categories. By tracing the categories to their intersections, I hope to suggest a methodology that will ultimately disrupt the tendencies to see race and gender as exclusive or separable. While the primary intersections that I explore here are between race and gender, the concept can and should be expanded by factoring in issues such as class, sexual orientation, age and color.[11]

Rich has also argued strongly about the need for new concepts, while she is readily aware of dangers in the act of re-vision. Rich's prose summarizes what I have already suggested is at stake in this Preface:

> Until we can understand the assumptions in which we are drenched we cannot know ourselves. And this drive to self-knowledge, for women, is more than a search for identity: it is part of our refusal of the self-destructiveness of male-dominated society. A radical critique of literature [in philosophy of religion], feminist in its impulse, would take the work first of all as a clue to how we live, how we have been living, how we have been led to imagine ourselves, how our language has trapped as well as liberated us, how the very act of naming [God] has been till now a male prerogative, and how we can begin to see and name – and therefore live – afresh. A change in the concept of sexual identity is

---

10   Kimberlé Crenshaw, 'Mapping the Margins: Intersectionality, Identity Politics, and Violence against Women of Color', *Stanford Law Review*, 43 (1991): 1241–1279; Leslie McCall, 'The Complexity of Intersectionality', *Signs*, 30, 3 (Spring 2005): 1771–1800; and Kimberlé Crenshaw, *On Intersectionality: The Essential Writings of Kimberlé Crenshaw* (New York: The New Press, 2012).

11   Crenshaw, 'Mapping the Margins', pp. 1144–1145, footnote 9.

essential if we are not going to see the old political order reassert itself in every new revolution. We need to know the writing of the past, and know it differently than we have ever known it.

...But there is also a difficult and dangerous walking on the ice, as we try to find language and images for the consciousness we are just coming into.[12]

It is to such a difficult and dangerous journey that I chose to commitment myself in *Re-visioning Gender in Philosophy of Religion*. A passion for justice and truth motivated and sustained me as I often knew to be walking on ice.

Acknowledgements

First, I would like to thank Sarah Lloyd for her patient confidence in this project and in me for more than ten years. Second, I would like to thank equally two readers of material for the manuscript which eventually became *Re-visioning Gender in Philosophy of Religion: Reason, Love and Epistemic Locatedness*: Jerome Gellman read the original proposal and a very early version of the material which has gone into this manuscript; and Chad Meister ten years later read a complete draft of the manuscript. Third, during more than a ten-year span when I felt myself 'diving into the wreck' personally and intellectually, I am grateful for all those who read versions of the chapters in this book, but also for friends who believed in me more than I did myself. Fourth, I thank Adrian Moore in particular for his inspiration as a philosopher and as a friend over the decades. Although I myself deviate from 'the philosophical straight and narrow', I owe a huge debt to his work in philosophy and his integrity. Any misunderstandings of his philosophy in this book are my own. Finally, for colleagues at Regent's Park College, Oxford, and for students at the University of Oxford who over the years have become my friends, I am most grateful.

I also acknowledge gratefully each of the publishers who gave their permission for me to revise often substantially and then, to reprint the material making up nine chapters. Specifically, I acknowledge the permission of Oxford University Press, Rodopi, Routledge, Fordham University Press, Springer Publishing (and as was Kluwer Publishing), SCM Press, (Wiley-)Blackwell Publishing for the following:

An earlier version of Chapter 1 appears as 'Feminism and Patriarchy', in Andrew Hass, David Jasper and Elisabeth Jay (eds), *The Oxford Handbook to English Literature and Theology* (Oxford: Oxford University Press, 2007), pp. 810–828.

The original version of Chapter 2 appears as 'Feminism in Philosophy of Religion', in Deane-Peter Baker and Patrick Maxwell (eds), *Explorations in Contemporary Continental Philosophy of Religion* (Amsterdam and New York: Rodopi, 2003), pp. 189–206; and another version is reprinted in Chad

---

[12] Rich, 'When We Dead Awaken', pp. 167–168.

Meister (ed.), *The Philosophy of Religion Reader* (London: Routledge, 2008), pp. 655–670.

An earlier version of Chapter 3 appears as 'Feminism', in Stewart Goetz, Victoria Harrison and Charles Taliaferro (eds), *The Routledge Companion to Theism* (New York and London: Routledge, 2012), Chapter 35.

Chapter 4 draws material from two previously published essays as 'Ineffable Knowledge and Gender', in Philip Goodchild (ed), *Rethinking Philosophy of Religion: Approaches from Continental Philosophy*, series edited by John Caputo (New York: Fordham University Press, 2002), pp. 162–183; and 'Gender and the infinite: On the aspiration to be all there is', *International Journal for Philosophy of Religion*, Issues in Contemporary Philosophy of Religion on the Occasion of the 50th vol., no. 1–3 (December 2001): 191–212.

An earlier version of Chapter 5 appears as '"Moralizing" Love in Philosophy of Religion', in Jerald T. Wallulis and Jeremiah Hackett (eds), *Philosophy of Religion for a New Century* (Dordrecht: Kluwer Academic Publishers, 2004), pp. 227–242.

An earlier version of Chapter 6 appears as 'Redeeming Truth, Restoring Faith in Reason: A Feminist Response to the Postmodern Condition of Nihilism', in Laurence Paul Hemming and Susan Frank Parsons (eds), *Redeeming Truth: Considering Faith and Reason* (London: SCM, 2007), pp. 60–84.

An earlier version of Chapter 7 appears as 'The Urgent Wish: To Be More Life-Giving', in Elaine Graham (ed.), *Grace Jantzen: Redeeming the Present* (Farnham, Surrey: Ashgate Publishing Limited, 2009), pp. 41–54.

An earlier version of Chapter 9 appears as 'Divinity, Incarnation and Inter-subjectivity: On Ethical Formation and Spiritual Practice', *Philosophy Compass* 1/3 (2006): 335–356. [Blackwell online]

An earlier version of Chapter 10 appears as 'A Feminist Perspective', in Chad Meister (ed.), *The Oxford Handbook of Religious Diversity* (Oxford: Oxford University Press, 2011), pp. 405–420.

Warm thanks to Jil Evans for allowing me to use her wonderful painting, *Dutch Opera V*, on the cover of this book and so, to connect Oxford and Minneapolis!

Chapter 1
Re-visioning Gender and the Myths of Patriarchy[1]

Introduction: gendering and re-visioning gender

Gendering is to some degree a hidden process of determining the identities of women and men. Re-visioning gender in this book, as already set out in the Preface, aims to be an act of looking back with open eyes at the gendering process from a new critical direction;[2] that is, looking back with a 'reflective critical openness'[3] to the epistemic locatedness of men and women in philosophy of religion. A central contention of *Re-visioning Gender in Philosophy of Religion: Reason, Love and Epistemic Locatedness* is that the field of philosophy of religion continues to be implicitly and explicitly gendering the moral and religious dimensions of human identities; this includes shaping human emotion, reason and cognition. In this domain of philosophy, the arguments of philosophers of religion concerning human and divine relations are either shaping or accepting (given) exclusive norms of heterosexuality, of femininity and masculinity.

Traditionally Anglo-American philosophers of religion have assumed uncritically that gender has to do with sociology, politics or, possibly, developmental psychology but not with philosophy. Admittedly, discussions of the sexually specific knowledge concerning transgender, bi-sexual, gay and lesbian identities has been increasingly emerging in moral psychology and branches of theology, including moral and pastoral theology, historical and systematic theology. Yet more explicit, philosophical debate about the deep and often ethically damaging gender norms in philosophy of religion is long overdue. With this in mind, the chapters to follow will seek (i) to recognize the process of gendering in western philosophy, even if it

---

[1] Substantially revised material in this chapter comes from 'Feminism and Patriarchy', in Andrew Hass, David Jasper and Elisabeth Jay (eds), *The Oxford Handbook to English Literature and Theology* (Oxford: Oxford University Press, 2007), pp. 810–828.

[2] Adrienne Rich, 'When We Dead Awaken: Writing as Re-vision', in Barbara Charlesworth Gelpi and Albert Gelpi (eds), *Adrienne Rich's Poetry and Prose* (New York and London: W. W. Norton and Company, 1991), p. 167.

[3] For my previous attempt to formulate 'reflective critical openness' as an intellectual virtue, appropriating some earlier ideas from Miranda Fricker, for philosophy of religion, see Pamela Sue Anderson, 'An Epistemological-Ethical Approach to Philosophy of Religion', in Pamela Sue Anderson and Beverley Clack (eds), *Feminist Philosophy of Religion: Critical Readings* (London: Routledge, 2004), pp. 87–92.

is only possible to draw out salient threads of this process; and (ii) to propose the 're-visioning'[4] of gender as it has been functioning in fairly central ways in philosophy of religion.

As introduced already in the Preface, *Re-visioning Gender in Philosophy of Religion* maintains that gender needs to be understood in terms of intersectionality; an adequate understanding of human identity requires a careful interpretation of the intersection of gender with a range of other material and social variables, including age, class, ethnicity, race, religion and sexual orientation. Gender theorists in the past twenty or more years have persuasively demonstrated that 'gender' is not a mere cultural construction as distinct from a biological or natural given of 'sex', or of sexual orientation. Of course, this does not make gender a simple or discrete matter. Instead it is necessary to support ongoing discussions of gender's necessary and multi-faceted intersection with other social and material categories such as religion and race. The intersection of these categories continues to be crucial for understanding ethical, legal, political and religious issues in our global world. This is evident, for example, in the writings of Naomi Zack, as well as Crenshaw's 2012 collection of essays.[5]

Contemporary philosophers of religion tend to hold gender assumptions which have been determined by the social constructions of western patriarchy. Roughly speaking, patriarchal beliefs and norms have constituted gender roles which privilege men over women, father over son, materially or socially privileged fathers over less privileged men, and so on. These roles, in turn, have determined the dominant, heterosexual relations of men and women in the western world. In philosophy of religion, gendering re-enforces both the un-ramified beliefs and those ramified religious beliefs which are most problematic for sex/gender relations;[6] this includes beliefs which have been determined by traditional Christian myths[7] concerning the human and the divine (attributes). The use of 'myth', in this context as also mentioned in the Preface, does not mean a mere falsehood as assumed in more

---

[4]   Rich, 'When We Dead Awaken: Writing as Re-vision', p. 167.

[5]   Naomi Zack, 'Can Third Wave Feminism Be Inclusive? Intersectionality, Its Problems and New Directions', in Linda Martin Alcoff and Eva Feder Kittay (eds), *The Blackwell Guide to Feminist Philosophy* (Oxford: Blackwell Publishing, 2007), pp. 193–207. Also, see Kimberlé Crenshaw, *On Intersectionality: The Essential Writings of Kimberlé Crenshaw* (The New Press, 2012).

[6]   For earlier discussions of the sex/gender distinction, see Pamela Sue Anderson, *A Feminist Philosophy of Religion: the Rationality and Myths of Religious Belief* (Oxford: Blackwell, 1998), pp. 5–13; and 'Gender and the Infinite: On the Aspiration to be All There Is', *International Journal for Philosophy of Religion*, 50 (2002): 4–6.

[7]   For a fuller discussion of different approaches to myth's role in the gendering (of love) in philosophy, see Pamela Sue Anderson, 'Myth and Feminist Philosophy', in Kevin Schilbrack (ed.), *Thinking Through Myths: Philosophical Perspectives* (London and New York: Routledge, 2002), pp. 101–122. An earlier consideration of myth in philosophy and how it could be reconfigured appears in Anderson, *A Feminist Philosophy of Religion*, pp. 3–4, 21–22, 135–143.

everyday conversation. Instead myth is characterized by its plot; its narrative which is often about perennial questions concerning the beginning and end of life (birth and death); its human and divine characters and their most fundamental relationships. Myth has emerged in the histories of humankind to tell stories about the origins of human goodness and evil, human culture and social contracts. Myths are often about human and divine relations concerning procreation and sex; concrete sexual relations are portrayed by variations on a narrative core, accompanied by varying arrangements of often perennial imagery. All of these features come together in myth to help shape the identities of individuals and collectives. For this reason, tradition holds on to its cultural and religious myths, while innovation plays with creating variations on older mythical themes. Some philosophers might imagine that myth and myth-making were left behind with the emergence of ancient Greek philosophy and its rational discourse; but arguably, myth has always accompanied philosophy in constituting the identities of men, women and the divine. In this way, myth has a fundamental role to play in the (implicit) gendering of philosophy of religion, especially since religion relies on myth for sustaining its ritual practices and norms of behaviour, but also, for conceptions of the divine.

If left as it is, without any further qualifications, this and the previous paragraphs could be accused of sweeping and unfair generalizations about gender and patriarchy. However, in order to be clear, the challenge needed to be set out starkly; yet these introductory paragraphs are not meant to be against any particular philosopher. In this book, I would like to appeal to a collective consciousness in carrying out my proposals for re-visioning.

Instead of leaving things as they are, *Re-visioning Gender in Philosophy of Religion* begins with an extended exploration of how we might unearth the obstacle which does not have a precise name in the literature of Europe and in the Anglo-phone world of philosophy. This obstacle is, bluntly stated, 'patriarchy'. The problem is that the patriarchal structures of gender oppression in western philosophy and, more particularly, in theism are not readily visible. Yet once gender oppression is glimpsed, even if the structures of patriarchy are not completely visible, then the reader can begin to understand what is meant here by 'gender' in philosophy of religion, but also by the re-visioning of gender norms.

One critical dimension of the obstacle which needs to be addressed is the normative function of patriarchy in Anglo-American philosophy of religion. This barely perceptible dimension of gender oppression remains deeply embedded in the lives of those women who have been decisively constrained by the rule of the father. Another part of the obstacle is that patriarchy itself as an object of contemporary feminist critiques is not straightforwardly one thing. For this reason, feminist critiques vary according to the different, social and material locations of women and men. Nevertheless, whenever oppressive structures determine philosophical norms and religious beliefs, both the reader and the woman writer can attempt to work out the myths of patriarchy which render women and non-dominant men vulnerable to sexually specific suffering. Indications of these myths can be recognized in the imagery and stories which represent the lives of women and men.

The Nobel prize-winner Toni Morrison captures the imperceptible reality of racial domination with imagery of a fishbowl. Her readers are compelled to imagine the bowl as a transparent structure permitting the ordered life which it contains to exist in a larger world.[8] Her imagery reveals the ways in which apparently invisible structures of domination can suddenly become visible. With Morrison's cogent use of imagery in mind this chapter aims to recognize patriarchy by revealing both the transparent structure of male domination which has contained women's lives and the ways in which feminism has emerged with this revelation. The bare outlines of patriarchy will be made evident in a quick look at a sample of women writers in the history of western 'philosophical theology' (which is another name of what is currently treated as a pre-Enlightenment form of 'philosophy of religion'). These women in philosophical theology remain in some sense at least shaped by Christian patriarchy. The emergence of feminism can be seen when the writer and reader are as if outside that ordered life which privileges father-son relations. This attempt to move outside fixed norms aims to tackle for the non-privileged 'the obstacle which does not speak its name'.[9]

The reality of patriarchy and the emergence of feminism

Feminism and patriarchy form a conceptual pair. Together these two concepts can help men and women come to see what has been the significant reality of a woman's material and social relations to men, to other women and to the impersonal agents of traditional institutions. As long as patriarchy in the most basic sense of father rule justifying the domination of women by men makes up the fundamental structure of societies in various explicit and implicit ways, feminism will have its *raison d'etre*: to enable each woman to become aware of her own capacity to think for herself and to live in a situation of equality with men, other women and institutional agents.

Yet patriarchy exists in different cultural forms, including its different religious forms.[10] Feminism in philosophy of religion also has its various forms, figures

---

[8]   Toni Morrison, *Playing in the Dark: Whiteness and the Literary Imagination* (New York: Vintage Books, A Division of Random House, 1993), pp. 6–17.

[9]   Michèle Le Doeuff, *Hipparchia's Choice: An Essay Concerning Women, Philosophy, Etc.*, trans. Trista Selous with an Epilogue (2006) by the author (New York: Columbia University Press, 2007), p. 28.

[10]   Judith Butler, *Gender Trouble: Feminism and the Subversion of Identity* (New York and London: Routledge, 1990), p. 35. For essays located within or against different cultural and religious forms of patriarchy, see Pamela Sue Anderson (ed.), *New Topics in Feminist Philosophy of Religion: Contestation and Transcendence Incarnate* (Dordrecht, New York and London: Springer, 2010).

and differences; but feminist philosophers are readily aware that contemporary feminists continue to disagree about their own self-definition.[11] Nevertheless, a common feature of every form of feminism is ultimately to remove the patriarchal structures which oppress women's lives; eradicate the structures which devalue women's acting, thinking, feeling and, as will be found in this chapter, writing their own ideas. At the very least, feminist authors in this context would agree that a woman deserves to have her reason, experience, authority, identity and truth-claims given equal consideration to those of every man and every other woman.

In the historical writings of philosophical theology, feminism and patriarchy are found to enable or to inhibit women's own reading and writing. In the useful terms of socialist feminism,[12] women's role, or their lack of a socially significant role, in the production of philosophical and theological works is dialectically related to the material conditions of their lives.[13]

From the seventeenth century at least, women in the English-speaking world are known to have struggled against adverse material conditions in order to write poetry, plays, philosophical essays and correspondences of a significant intellectual nature. As will be discussed here, Virginia Woolf (1882–1941) offers us a classic description of the conditions necessary for a woman to write a literary piece of her own in *A Room of One's Own* (1929). Woolf claims that Aphra Behn (1640–89) is possibly the earliest English woman to prove 'that women could make money by writing'.[14] Behn's contribution to the recognition of patriarchal oppression rests both in her personal struggle to be paid for written work and in her sexually explicit writings of poetry, drama, and especially of the fiction which possibly invented the novel: *Oroonoko, or the Royal Slave.*[15]

Already in her own century Behn's writing is taken up by other women writers. For a notable example, Catharine Cockburn (née Trotter, 1679–1749) writes a verse dramatization of Behn's 'Agnes de Castro' which is performed in 1695 at the theatre in Drury Lane. Highly significant in the present context is that Cockburn and her seventeenth-century predecessor Viscountess Anne Conway (née Finch, 1631–79) both also write philosophical essays on theological topics. Along with her conversation and correspondence with the Cambridge Platonist

---

[11] Anderson, *A Feminist Philosophy of Religion*, pp. 67–70, 230–235; and 'Myth and Feminist Philosophy', pp. 103–120.

[12] For reference to the socialist feminism as just one form of 'feminism', see footnote 24 (below).

[13] For a feminist materialist analysis of women's lives, see Christine Delphy, *Close to Home: A Materialist Analysis of Women's Oppression*, trans. and edited by Diana Leonard (London: Hutchinson, 1984).

[14] Virginia Woolf, *A Room of One's Own* [1929], *Three Guineas* [1938], and 'Professions for Women' [1931], edited with an Introduction and Notes by Michèle Barrett and Appendix (Harmondsworth: Penguin, 1993), p. 59.

[15] Aphra Behn, *Oroonoko, or the Royal Slave*, in *The Histories and Novels of the Late Ingenious Mrs. Behn*, in One Volume (London: S. Briscoe, [1688] 1696).

Henry More (1614–87),[16] Conway develops her own distinctive non-trinitarian and cogent philosophical arguments concerning God, Christ and creation. More himself is the university tutor of Conway's brother and friend of her husband, so someone through whom Anne Conway has indirect access to debates in philosophical theology. As a seventeenth-century woman Conway is certainly not allowed a university education. For a woman of her time to develop her own ideas discursively is doubly difficult, since socially her role as daughter, sister, lover or wife would prevent her direct access to learning, let alone the equality to think and write for herself.[17] It is, then, highly significant that Conway has correspondence with and intellectual respect from More.

Conway's original account of metaphysical change and process, and in particular her argument that 'substance' incorporates body-mind-spirit, can still challenge Christian orthodoxy today and engage modern physicists in timely debates. Conway left a volume of her philosophical writings which More published for her posthumously in Holland; and it has been suggested that this work influenced the metaphysical ideas of the great German eighteenth-century philosopher Gottfried Leibniz (1646–1716).[18] Equally, after her marriage to Reverend Patrick Cockburn, Catharine Cockburn writes well-argued theological essays on such matters as the resurrection (admittedly, defending the view of John Locke, 1632–1704) and on whether God ordains what is good and evil at will or according to the fitness to creation – about which she writes for and is read by certain clergymen of her day.[19]

In addition, Mary Astell (1666–1731) should be recognized as another seventeenth-century woman writer who gains access to, and authority for, writing seriously on theological ideas, in large part, due to her dialogue with a Cambridge Platonist, John Norris (1657–1711). Her letters on both personal and philosophical matters reflect Astell's intellect as a woman, revealing both her self-education and the significant material conditions necessary for her writing. Not unlike Conway, Astell writes on theological matters; and like Behn, she also creates poetry and drama.

---

[16]   On the education of women in philosophy, see Michèle Le Doeuff, *The Philosophical Imaginary,* trans. Colin Gordon (New York and London: Continuum, 2002) pp. 105–108; Anne Conway, 'The Principles of the Most Ancient and Modern Philosophy [extracts]' in Mary Warnock (ed.), *Women Philosophers* (London: J. M. Dent, Everyman, 1996), pp. xxxvi, 5–28; Charles Taliaferro and Alison Teply (eds), *Cambridge Platonist Spirituality* (Mahwah, New Jersey: Paulist Press, 2004), pp. 37–43.

[17]   On the nature of the relationship between the master philosopher and the faithful student who follows (him), and its socially problematic nature for a woman's education, see Le Doeuff, *The Philosophical Imaginary*, pp. 105, 117–120.

[18]   For additional background on, and excerpts from, the writings of Conway and Cockburn, see *Women Philosophers*, pp. xxxv–xxxvii, 3–36. For more of Conway, see Taliaferro and Teply (eds), *Cambridge Platonist Spirituality*, pp. 37–43, 187–192.

[19]   Catherine Cockburn, 'Answer to a question in *The Gentleman's Magazine*' and 'Remarks upon an Inquiry into the origins of human appetites and affections', in Warnock (ed.), *Women Philosophers*, pp. 30–36.

The published essays by Conway, Cockburn and Astell provide significant evidence of the feminism emerging as women and men begin to recognize the oppressive nature of English patriarchy. Moreover, it is extremely important that the writings and ideas of these women are taken seriously enough to be debated by prominent seventeenth- and eighteenth-century theologians and philosophers. None of Behn, Cockburn, Conway or Astell explicitly articulates either a form of feminism or a definition of patriarchy. Yet Astell writes (for instance) in defense of women, especially on the miseries of marriage. In fact, she produces a searing critique of the powerlessness of women within the (patriarchal) marital institution.[20] Astell also proposes a 'Religious Retirement' where Anglican women could retreat to engage in religious observance, learning language and other skills.[21] All of these writings testify to the fact that a seventeenth-century woman in Britain could and did exhibit an awareness of male domination over women in social, theological and literary institutions.

The content of the aforementioned women's writings and the material conditions in which the actual production of their works takes place support the claims of socialist feminism. As already explained, the feminists who call themselves 'socialist' claim that change will come about when the concrete circumstances of women's lives are transformed; and that this transformation will take place when their involvement in producing new works, say, of a literary and theological nature is socially significant enough to change material conditions. However, despite some change at the centre of social life, the feminist struggle against the domination of women by men continued on the margins of eighteenth and nineteenth-century societies. For example, the notable Hannah More (1745–1833), one of the English 'bluestockings', works to ameliorate women's education by writing political tracts and by setting up eleven village schools, with her sisters, after running possibly the most successful girl's school of the eighteenth-century in Bristol. Although the inheritance of More's essays and novels, the seeds for future forms of feminisms, are more significant than any actual social changes to patriarchy in the late eighteenth and early nineteenth centuries, it can be revealing to consider what it means to call her a bluestocking!

'English bluestockings' is the name given to a group of educated, intellectual women who met for intellectual debate and flourished in London in the late eighteenth-century. The description derives from the stockings made from blue worsted rather than silk and seems to go back to the days when men in the Parliament of 1653 would not wear silk and instead wore those blue stockings. The derogatory nature of this label remains as imagery for those who would dress or act in an inappropriate manner, that is, like those who would not appreciate the significance of silk for ceremonial occasions. Michèle Le Doeuff gives a witty, insightful story about the emergence of 'the bluestockings' first in Parliament

---

20   Mary Astell, *Some Reflections on Marriage* [1700] (London: Wm. Parker, 1730).
21   Mary Astell, *A Serious Proposal to the Ladies* (London: R. Wilkin, 1694).

and then later as an epithet for women who met to discuss 'feminist' issues.[22] In fact, Le Doeuff's story implies that perhaps no one ever wore the warm worsted stockings. Instead this imagery becomes a convenient way to refer to those who were thought capable of something highly inappropriate!

Along with the actual historical struggle for feminism to emerge, however gradually, in British intellectual and philosophical-theology circles shaped by patriarchy, it should be understood more broadly that every religious tradition serves as a primary space in which and by means of which gender hierarchy is culturally articulated, reinforced and consolidated in institutional forms. In particular, women's exclusion from the production of significant literary and religious works globally re-enforces culturally specific gender hierarchies in the domination of women by privileging the ideas and images of men. Although English writers and the Christian religion together make up only one great cultural and historical form in the production of sacred and aesthetic texts, they display an unvarying, global ambivalence on the subject of women. This ambivalence means that for every patriarchal text that places well-domesticated womanhood on a religious pedestal, another text (shaped by patriarchy) announces that, if uncontrolled, women are the root of all evil. There is plenty of evidence that this ambivalence concerning a woman in western theological and literary texts continues across various cultures worldwide.[23]

The conceptual pair of feminism and patriarchy initially set out in this chapter supports a material analysis of women, men and the impact of their philosophical, theological and/or literary ideals on social reality. At the same time, it is important to acknowledge the existence of different forms of feminism, often existing side by side.[24] This chapter relies upon, but also adapts, the political distinctions used thirty years ago to describe four different forms of feminism: socialist, radical, liberal, difference (Marxist). In 1983, Alison M. Jaggar gives detailed accounts of these feminist forms in *Feminist Politics and Human Nature*. Amongst feminist philosophers Jaggar's distinctions have become almost classic for teaching feminisms. But the poststructuralist form of feminist is newer than Jaggar's book, so it needs to be added to the other four forms of feminism. These five forms of feminism can, then, be read as waves of a larger feminist movement which have their ups and downs; the different forms return like waves, mixing and disappearing with earlier or later waves only to re-appear sometimes up and other times down. In other words, it has not been the case in recent, at least western, history that

---

[22]   Michèle Le Doeuff, *The Sex of Knowing*, trans. Lorraine Code and Kathryn Hamer (London and New York: Routledge, 2003), pp. 1–4.

[23]   For cross-cultural evidence of this, see Dorota Filipczak, 'Autonomy and Female Spirituality in A Polish Context: Divining a Self', in Pamela Sue Anderson and Beverley Clack (eds), *Feminist Philosophy of Religion: Critical Readings* (London: Routledge, 2004), pp. 210–222.

[24]   Alison M. Jaggar, *Feminist Politics and Human Nature* (Totowa, New Jersey: Rowman & Littlefield Publishers, Inc., 1983).

any form of feminism stops existing. Instead one form may take precedent over another depending upon the location and the period of time; but until there is no longer an obstacle for a woman in relation to everyone else socially and materially the forms of feminism will persist, even while transforming. At this point, it is helpful to list brief descriptions of the different forms of feminisms which appear in the present book.

Socialist feminism, as stated earlier in this chapter, aims to change the concrete circumstances of women's lives; that is, their social and material situations. The 'socialist' feminist assumes that the solidarity and interdependence of men as grounded on a material and economic base enables men to dominate women.

Radical feminism regards patriarchy as an all-pervasive and a-historical system. 'Radical' refers to the belief that patriarchy is deeply rooted, inherently hierarchical and aggressive, existing independently of social changes. A key condition of the radical is: that the shifts from one economic or political structure to another would not make any great difference to women's subjugation.[25]

Liberal feminism is readily seen to participate in a number of the waves of feminism. 'Liberal' describes one of feminism's earliest forms. Liberal feminism is identified by its political agenda to eradicate the social and legal inequalities suffered by women.[26]

Difference feminism, or at least one version of a form stressing sexual difference, identifies women's reproductive function as the primary site of female oppression; the biological family structure is, then, the ground of patriarchal constructions of women as a subordinate class. This use of class for female reproduction is essentially a refinement of a Marxist conception of class oppression which is, then, equated with a biological function of women.[27]

Finally, *poststructuralist feminism* has been taken up and expanded by those contemporary theorists who recognize patriarchy as an ideological structure permeating every aspect of life. Poststructuralists, especially those informed by French psycholinguistics, tend to assume a conception of language as the ground of all meaning and value. According to psycho-linguistic poststructuralism, language is structured by sets of binary terms, including man/woman, rationality/irrationally, omnipotence/impotence, straight/curved, light/dark, etc; these pairs of terms are not simply words, but paired terms with differential values. Binary terms

---

[25] Adrienne Rich, *Of Woman Born: Motherhood as Experience and Institution* (New York and London: W. W. Norton & Company, 1995), pp. 56, 57–58; cf. Anderson, 'Myth and Feminist Philosophy', pp. 103–105.

[26] Mary Wollstonecraft, *A Vindication of the Rights of Woman*, edited with an Introduction by Miriam Brody (Harmondsworth: Penguin Books Ltd., 1992); and William Godwin, *Memoirs of the Author of A Vindication of the Rights of Woman* [1798] (Ontario, Canada: Broadview Press, 2001), especially, pp. 43–44, 72–79.

[27] Michèle Barrett, 'Introduction', *Virginia Woolf: Women and Writing* (London: The Women's Press, 1979); and Barrett, 'Introduction', in Woolf, *A Room of One's Own*, pp. x–xvi.

give meaning to language-users; and, crucially, the second term is always given less value than the first. Poststructuralists seek to confront the binary structure which makes up a text. Taking up these poststructuralist conceptions, feminist deconstructive strategies target the gendered binary constituting the various texts of patriarchal cultures.[28] Later in this chapter, reference will be made to the continuing rise and fall of these different forms of feminism as an ongoing movement with (as yet) unending waves.

Before concluding this chapter a further, critical comment will be given about a cross-current traversing the waves of feminism, that of *postfeminism*. Until then, bear in mind that the common goal of the various forms of feminism is the eradication of patriarchy. But this does not prevent feminism from accompanying patriarchy. Just the reverse is true. Feminism does and, arguably, should exist alongside patriarchy until ideally, the obstacle dissolves and so, the distinction.

The necessary conditions for a woman to have her own ideas

The contemporary French feminist philosopher Michèle Le Doeuff has offered philosophers and cultural critics some intriguing detective work on the problematic conception of woman and on the ideals of divine knowledge which have silenced women within the long tradition of western philosophy. Her standpoint as an outsider to Anglo-American philosophy of religion sheds light on the narrowness of the vision of twentieth-century philosophers in this tradition. But she also notices a cultural narrowness in a woman such as Virginia Woolf who was otherwise crucial in raising British women's consciousness to an awareness of patriarchy in literature, as well as to the material conditions necessary for a woman to be able to write. In a moment, we will return to Le Doeuff's detective work concerning Woolf and the other intellectual women in European history who Woolf could have recognized.

Le Doeuff's special interest in 'the philosophical imaginary' has motivated her to dig into the collective history of literary and philosophical-theological ideas in order to work out how a woman came to produce her own ideas.[29] Crucial here is Le Doeuff's documentation concerning the ways in which philosophical and moral (including theological) conceptions of women have not only prohibited a woman's freedom and authority on matters of truth, reason, good and evil, but

---

[28]   For a range of early examples of French feminism, including the deconstructivists and the poststructural essentialists, see Elaine Marks and Isabelle de Courtivron (eds) *New French Feminisms: An Anthology* (Hemel Hempstead, Hertfordshire: Harvester Wheatsheaf, 1980).

[29]   For her conception of 'the philosophical imaginary', see Michèle Le Doeuff, *The Philosophical Imaginary,* trans. Colin Gordon (London: The Athlone Press, 1989; New York and London: Continuum, 2002), 'Preface: The Shameful Face of Philosophy', pp. 1–20.

have advocated an oppressive form of 'absolute altruism' whereby a woman becomes 'a nothingness in the eyes of the other'.[30]

Insofar as her identity is determined by patriarchal literary and theological traditions, a woman finds it virtually impossible to possess the authority which would be necessary to write with her own integrity of style, to have her own ideas, to write and have them read. Moreover, the conditions necessary for a woman to achieve authority as the recognized author of her own ideas on particular matters in philosophical theology would require the transformation of those moral ideals which portray woman as untrustworthy.[31] Patriarchy is embedded in the philosophical and theological imaginations, shaping the gendered nature of a woman's life, thought and action. What will make a woman author a feminist is not merely being born female: she is a feminist when as a woman standing against the patriarchal norms she allows no one else to think, or write, in her place.

Le Doeuff articulates with concrete stories and imagery the necessary conditions of a woman's literary creativity. Le Doeuff works literally like a detective, trying to uncover cases which make up a latent tradition of women thinkers.[32] For example, she studies the life and legacy of a European woman writer whose work is known to have been translated into the English vernacular in 1521. Christine de Pizan (1364–1430) overcomes the obstacle which generally prevented women from acquiring the necessary conditions to write, that is, the necessary education and material circumstances (according to Woolf, it was place and time) to contribute to women's creativity. In the fourteenth-century, de Pizan not only had to have the self-education, she also had to refute *both* a tradition of Christian theology which conceived women as 'sinful like Eve' *and* a tradition of ancient philosophy which conceived women as 'defective males'. This conception of Eve as representing the sinfulness of all women was exaggerated at the time with a strongly misogynist reading of Paul's teachings in the New Testament on a woman's role in personal and social life; and that conception of women as defective males derives from Aristotle via medieval theologians and from ancient Greek physics. These traditions which silenced women reflect philosophical conceptions that were and are anti-feminist. In overcoming these, de Pizan writes without living in complete submission to a man – whether husband, male confessor or other patriarchal figure – and his

---

[30] Le Doeuff, *Hipparchia's Choice*, p. 280, also see, p. 108. For Le Doeuff's own account of *Déshérences*, translated into English, 'Cast-offs', see Le Doeuff, *The Sex of Knowing*, pp. 1–68.

[31] Wollstonecraft, *A Vindication*, p. 92; Le Doeuff, *The Sex of Knowing*, pp. 46–48, 108–110. For further discussion of the problem in establishing a woman's trustworthiness and truth-telling, see the later sections of Chapter 6.

[32] For her detective work on Christine de Pisan (which is the spelling used by Le Doeuff, but I have followed the spelling of the Penguin edition), see Le Doeuff, *The Sex of Knowing*, pp. ix–x, 135–138. Le Doeuff describes de Pisan as her representative of a literary *epikleroi*, that is, a woman from whom later generations have inherited a certain knowledge and a practical know-how, see *The Sex of Knowing*, pp. 112–118.

God. Moreover, she does not claim a woman's ignorance, weakness and frailty as necessary conditions for her authorship; in other words, she does not give the stamp of authority for her knowledge to a male God. Instead she cultivates certain intellectual virtues.

Careful reading of de Pizan's text renders a startling possibility for this fourteenth-century lady: that (today) she be called a feminist; and that her feminism may have had an unacknowledged impact in the sixteenth-century on women and men in the English-speaking world. On this point, Woolf comes back into Le Doeuff's detective work and the argument of this chapter. Totally unaware of Pizan, or any other woman writer as early as this, Woolf simply dismisses any possibility that a medieval or Renaissance woman could have had the education and material conditions which would have been necessary to write on her own.[33] Despite Woolf's particular lack of imagination and knowledge of this historical period, feminism and patriarchy in English societies may have its earliest origins in reading a woman's writings from outside its cultural boundaries. Now, redressing any such acts of what she calls a woman's 'disinheritance', Le Doeuff digs into the texts of fifteenth-century Europe in order to retrieve a significant feminist inheritance for twenty-first century men and women.

These conditions constitute the sort of women's tradition Woolf sought: that is, women struggling for a feminist literary imagination. The perceptive reader recognizes a paradigmatic figure in Le Doeuff's feminist texts. An older and wiser figure than the Victorian 'Angel in the House',[34] or the medieval Christian 'helpmeet', emerges as if a dissenting angel who is no longer trapped in the house, or fishbowl! This figure enhanced by the philosophical imaginary encourages each individual woman to write; to create her own anecdotes of life with a feminist wit that enables hope for change in the collective historical experiences of women. The aim of this imaginary figure is to convey truth, in a post-Woolfian style, under new, playful imagery and political passion, not unlike the expression of truth which render such feminist classics as *A Room of One's Own*.

The contemporary British feminist Michèle Barrett makes an explicit point about the continuing present day appeals to Woolf's highly significant text: '*A Room of One's Own*, published in 1929, even now remains one of the clearest and most eloquent accounts that we have of women's writing.'[35] Often in a literary critic's account of Woolf's novels, the 'feminist' nature of her creative writing is contested. But in contrast, the feminism of *A Room of One's Own* (1929) and *Three Guineas* (1938) is not so easily contested. In her 1929 text, Woolf argues that the writer is a product of her historical circumstances, and that material conditions have decisive significance for the very possibility of a woman writer.

---

[33]   Woolf, *A Room of One's Own*, p. 38.

[34]   Virginia Woolf, 'Professions for Women' (Lecture for the National Society of Women's Service, 21 January 1931), p. 357; cf. Le Doeuff, *Hipparchia's Choice*, pp. 127–129; *The Sex of Knowing*, pp. 77–78.

[35]   Barrett, 'Introduction', in Woolf, *A Room of One's Own*, p. ix.

Rarely has an argument concerning feminism and patriarchy in English writers been presented more concisely and carefully. Without 'a room of one's own', that is, without the money, education and social circumstances which would allow the right psychological elements for developing the creative process of the literary imagination, women will not be enabled to produce their own writings. This argument remains true at least for feminists who advocate female autonomy.

In addition, the later argument of *Three Guineas* has more significance today than it did when first published in 1938: at that time, the equation of masculinism and militarism was not so easily accepted. Woolf advocates giving three guineas, one to each of three separate funds with particular aims: the first guinea would go to a fund for rebuilding a woman's college; the second guinea to an agency for helping women find employment; and the third guinea would go to prevent war (i.e., the spread of fascism in 1930s Europe) by protecting intellectual and cultural freedoms. The heart of Woolf's argument is that these ostensibly separate funds point to an inseparable concern for women's financial independence; this would be gained through education and employment. So, at that time at least, women's education and employment were not only the essential preconditions for their independence but, according to Woolf's feminism, for the force against war. The connection of these preconditions to political debates (e.g., on war) may not have been (fully) understood in the late 1930s Britain. Yet Woolf's argument is compatible with subsequent feminism in linking the private and public worlds: 'That fear, small, insignificant and private as it is, is connected with the other fear, the public fear, which is neither small nor insignificant, the fear which has led you to ask us to help you prevent war', that is, the tyranny of women's domestic servitude is one and the same as 'the tyrannies and servilities of the other'.[36]

In these terms, present day feminists would (generally) agree that Woolf had the capacity to anticipate the political concerns of future men and women. The crucial element in Woolf's argument is that a lack of an accessible tradition of women writers puts a brake on a woman's imagination and so constrains her own critical reflection on both private and public life. This argument continues to inspire and direct clearly vocal critics, editors and theorists of English writers by and for women.[37] As the political question of war illustrates (in *Three Guineas*), in order to accomplish the common feminist goal of eradicating the tyrannies of

---

[36]   Woolf, *Three Guineas*, p. 270.

[37]   See Barrett, 'Introduction', *Virginia Woolf*; Rosalind Brown-Grant, 'Introduction', Christine de Pizan, *The Book of the City of Ladies*, translated with Notes by Rosalind Brown-Grant (Harmondsworth: Penguin Books Ltd., 1999), in de Pizan, *The Book of the City of Ladies*, p. xvi; Carolyn G. Heilbrun, *Writing A Woman's Life* (London: The Women's Press Ltd., 1989), pp. 13, 15, 30; Le Doeuff, *Hipparchia's Choice*, p. 16; Toril Moi, *Sexual/Textual Politics: Feminist Literary Theory* (London and New York: Routledge, 1988), pp. 1–18; Rich, *Of Woman Born*, pp. xxv, 56n; Patricia Waugh, *Feminine Fictions: Revisiting the Postmodern* (London: Routledge, 1989), pp. 88–125.

patriarchy, female authors need to be allowed to create and develop their own imaginative tradition for the good of both women and men.

In this context, English history and patriarchy together constitute a formidable force for good or evil in (re-)shaping women's lives. Feminism supports the struggles of women to write about human lived experiences, whether spiritual, personal and/or political. Feminists recognize the uniqueness of specific texts by women in the history of English writers, at least since the Middle Ages. Julian of Norwich (1342–after 1416) is said today to be the first woman writer in English who can be identified with certainty.[38] Julian struggles over a number of years to write the 'Short Text' and 'Long Text' of her experience of divine revelations, or 'showings' of divine love.[39] Her medieval culture would have strongly resisted her effort to write and especially to teach as a woman. This resistance would have been justified by appeals to Pauline writings in the New Testament.[40] Moreover, any writing which discussed theological ideas in the vernacular (English) would have been suspect. Consequently, not only would Julian have worked for years on her texts in order to express her ideas well, but also to take care to keep her self-presentation modest. In Chapter 6 of the 'Short Text' of her visions Julian writes:

> … I beg you all for God's sake and advise you all for your own advantage that you stop paying attention to the poor, worldly, sinful creature to whom this vision was shown, and eagerly, attentively, lovingly and humbly contemplate God, who in his gracious love and in his eternal goodness wanted the vision to be generally known to comfort us all. …
>
> But God forbid that you should say or assume that I am a teacher, for that is not what I mean, nor did I ever mean it; I am a woman, ignorant, weak and frail.[41]

Julian's text does not illustrate a woman's writing in a space free of patriarchy. As a woman in all humility she had to defer to the perfect goodness and authority of the patriarchal Christian God. Nevertheless, whatever can be said historically about Julian's theological strategy and literary force in claiming weakness, poverty and sinfulness on her part, while acknowledging the strength, richness and goodness on the part of God, she successfully acquires the time, space and knowledge necessary for her writing *Revelations of Divine Love*. Moreover, in appealing to a God-given vocation, this autobiographical writing appears at the beginning of a now long tradition of women writers who gain authority from a spiritual calling of service to others, from which these women would be otherwise prohibited. Later

---

[38]   A. C. Spearing, 'Introduction', in Julian of Norwich, *Revelations of Divine Love*, trans. Elizabeth Spearing with Notes by A. C. Spearing (London: Penguin Books Ltd., 1998), pp. vii–xx.

[39]   Julian of Norwich, *Revelations of Divine Love*.

[40]   See, for example, I *Corinthians* 11: 3–10, 14: 33–35; also, I *Timothy* 2: 9–15.

[41]   Julian, *Revelations of Divine Love*, pp. 9–10.

examples of similar spiritual appeals by women to a God-given authority are found
in the writings and service of Margery Kempe (1373–1438), or albeit in quite
different cultural circumstances in Margaret Cavendish (1623–73) and Florence
Nightingale (1819–90). Such women writers,[42] who each wrote on theological
matters relevant for philosophy of religion, did consistently and unselfconsciously
submit their ideas to structures of male authority; and as such, none of them can
be identified as explicitly feminist in voicing their own ideas. Yet it can be said
that one by one each of these woman anticipated a still imperceptible feminism.
So it is just possible to claim these women's writings as critical background for
re-visioning gender in philosophy of religion.

'I ask you to write more books … for your good and for the good of the world'[43]

Women writers continue to confront that barely perceptible reality which does
not speak its name.[44] To help detect this reality, Le Doeuff offers an account of
'feminist' knowledge:

> … the term feminist here in its most basic sense … [refers to] someone who
> knows that something is still not right in the relations between a woman and
> everybody else, in other words men, other women, the supposedly impersonal
> agents of institutions, and anyone else: some hitch that is strictly potential, of
> course, simply liable to manifest itself, but which you must learn to identify in
> everyday situations and conversations.[45]

It is crucial to understand that as long as patriarchal structures condition a
woman's life, her relations will not be right. A woman's self-recognition is not
simply a matter of a once-for-all expression of a shared obstacle. Patriarchy is
not an a-temporal structure which all women at any time and in any place can

---

[42]   On the inspirational role of the spiritual autobiographies of such women as Kemp
and Nightingale, see Heilbrun, *Writing A Woman's Life*, pp. 22–24, also, pp. 118–119. In
addition, for historical background on the development of a feminist consciousness through
creativity within, and resistance to, patriarchal traditions, see the references to Margery
Kempe, Margaret Cavendish and Florence Nightingale, in Gerda Lerner, *The Creation of
Feminist Consciousness: From the Middle Ages to Eighteen-Seventy* (New York: Oxford
University Press, 1993), pp. 83–87, 173–174, 179.

[43]   These words from Woolf appear as an epigraph on the otherwise blank page before
the 'Contents' in bell hooks, *Remembered Rapture: The Writer at Work* (London: The
Women's Press, 1999): '… when I ask you to write more books I am urging you to do what
will be for your good and for the good of the world at large'; cf. Woolf, *A Room of One's
Own*, p. 99.

[44]   Le Doeuff, *Hipparchia's Choice*, p. 28; *The Philosophical Imaginary*, pp. 100–128.

[45]   Le Doeuff, *Hipparchia's Choice*, p. 28.

identify as one and the same thing. For example, not all women have experienced the same inner conflict(s) between the virtues of the Victorian angel and the desire for intellectual and social autonomy, when struggling to produce her own ideas. Instead each woman must dig deep in her material and social relations to identify what is wrong in her everyday communication.

Historically, women who have managed to communicate their own ideas under socially and materially oppressive conditions would have struggled personally and politically; but even the smallest glimmers of hope, in communicating the specificities of each woman's relations, added to the creativity of a multi-faceted feminist movement. Although the present sketch cannot consider in detail the wide-ranging impact of the movement of feminism on patriarchal structures, it seeks nevertheless to make sense of the various ways in which feminism gradually emerges in relation to different understandings of patriarchy.[46] Essentially, those women literary figures who have taken up the ultimate goal of feminism, i.e., the eradication of patriarchy, seek their own freedom to think, to write and to gain authority in their lives and relationships. In strong sympathy with this emerging literary tradition the present detective work confirms and continues this process by picturing the movement of feminism as 'our collective historical experience'.[47]

Following Woolf and Le Doeuff, women philosophers today can draw productively on the imagery in women's writings to make sense of this feminist movement but also, of the gendering of their ideas. Woolf begins *The Waves* with the imagery of sun, sea and sky: 'The sun had not yet risen. The sea was indistinguishable from the sky, except that the sea was slightly creased as if a cloth had wrinkles in it. Gradually as the sky whitened a dark line lay on the horizon dividing the sea from the sky.'[48] Le Doeuff carries on her use of imagery:

> The waves of hope rise and fall: 'The grey cloth becomes barred with thick strokes moving, one after another, beneath the surface, following each other, pursuing each other, perpetually. As they neared the shore each bar rose, heaped itself, broke and swept a thin veil of white water across the sand. The wave paused, and then drew out again, sighing.' These opening sentences from Virginia Woolf's *The Waves* might well contain the poetics of our collective historical experience. Successive waves of women have joyfully fought, convinced that once we had at last gained the right to, for example, a job, education, citizen's rights, or a sexuality freed from the chains of reproduction, something fundamental would have changed in the general female condition. A thin veil of white water across the sand: these gains have hardly even yet been gained ... Inward migrations, exoduses, expansions, recessions, fresh waves: whether economic, cultural or

---

[46] Sarah Gamble, 'Post-Feminism', in Sarah Gamble (ed.), *The Routledge Companion to Feminism and Post-Feminism* (London: Routledge, 2001), p. 293.

[47] Le Doeuff, *Hipparchia's Choice*, p. 242.

[48] Virginia Woolf, *The Waves*, edited with an Introduction and Notes by Gillian Beer (Oxford: Oxford World's Classics, Oxford University Press, 1993), p. 3.

political, the waves break more of us than they keep afloat. And even if they did keep us afloat, they would be deceiving us. There are enough ideological or political eddies in the Movement, enough inquiries going adrift, to make sure of that.[49]

In brief, a feminist writing tradition is shaped around the collective history of a movement, the ebb and flow of the imagery and political ideas of each woman writer. Shifts in the philosophical imaginary constantly move feminism either backwards or forwards. The imagery of the waves is a case in point. Woolf as a paradigmatic figure of and for a woman's writing speaks profoundly to her readers, even in this new century, about patriarchy and feminism. Feminist writers can profitably pick up and exploit Woolf's metaphorical and mystical language to express the rise and fall of hope in the feminist movement. The waves of feminism reflect a process within a wider political movement of women historically. This imagery gives expression to the complex patterns and shifts in the historical movement(s) of both the collective and the individual woman.

The moments of vision when Woolf seems at one with creation link women and fiction: the characters in her novels gain virtually mystical moments of insight, reflecting a writer's own efforts to transcend the real contingencies of familial and gendered relationships. Yet, despite the mystical nature of her explorations in *The Waves* and other novels, the author herself rails against Christianity in her letters to her sister Vanessa as she does in her novels as in her political essays.[50] Obviously, her relationship to Christian patriarchy is not one of believer or academic theologian. What is most clear is that she blames the Church for forbidding women's access to education.[51] Nevertheless, to understand her writings, the reader should detect the patriarchal structures of Victorian Anglicanism haunting the self in the figure of Woolf's 'Angel in the House': 'It was she who bothered me and wasted my time and so tormented me that at last I killed her.'[52] Woolf goes on to describe this Victorian angel:

She was intensely sympathetic. She was immensely charming. She was utterly unselfish. She excelled in the difficult arts of family life. She sacrificed herself daily ... [she] preferred to sympathize always with the minds and wishes of others. Above all ... she was pure. Her purity was supposed to be her chief beauty. ... And when I came to write I encountered her with the very first words. The shadow of her wings fell on my page ... she slipped behind me and

---

[49]   Le Doeuff, *Hipparchia's Choice*, pp. 242–244; cf. Woolf, *The Waves*, p. 3.

[50]   Virgina Woolf, *The Letters of Virginia Woolf* 1975–1980, vol. 1, edited by Gillian Beer (Oxford: Oxford University Press, 1992), p. 442; *The Voyage Out* [1915] (Harmondsworth: Penguin, 1992); *Three Guineas*, pp. 205–207.

[51]   For biographical background, see Hermione Lee, *Virginia Woolf* (London: Vintage, 1997), pp. 226–227.

[52]   Woolf, 'Professions for Women', p. 357.

whispered: 'My dear, you are a young woman. You are writing about a book that has been written by a man. Be sympathetic; be tender; flatter; deceive; use all the arts and wiles of our sex. Never let anybody guess that you have a mind of your own. Above all, be pure.'[53]

This angel of Victorian patriarchy captures the female figure imagined, and then, re-enforced by Christianity; that is, by what have been the Christian moral ideals in Anglican theology, while similar moral ideals come into Anglo-American philosophy of religion and its history. Woolf's novels also exhibit a profound longing to (re)turn to a mother-daughter relationship, to reject the destructiveness of patriarchal relations as excavated in mothers, in daughters, in fathers and other men. Consider Clarissa Dalloway preparing for the dinner party in *Mrs Dalloway*, Mrs Ramsey and Lily Briscoe exploring mother-daughter (older-younger woman) roles in *To The Lighthouse*, the woman-man exploration of gender, androgyny, writing and desire in *Orlando*, and Bernard seemingly transcending gender and life/death distinctions in *The Waves*. Upon reflection it becomes clear that each character and each event in Woolf's novels are shaped around a struggle to transcend the bi-gendered roles of women and men who not only seek to understand the Victorian values of Woolf's own upbringing, but the Christian values which continue to determine the patriarchy of contemporary philosophy of religion. Woolf's writings are pivotal in the present context both for her contribution to the philosophical imaginary and for her own significant, true (human) insights from which she draws most profoundly.

A paradigmatic figure for feminism and patriarchy may derive from Woolf, but the re-visioning of gender in philosophy requires a more consistent, feminist writer than Woolf herself. The re-visioning of the gender paradigm for a woman philosopher would have to inspire women and men in philosophy, through the collective characters and stories of a feminist imagination. We need the imagination to experience, reason, feel, seek truth and create new relations between women and men, women and women, mothers and daughters, daughters and fathers, persons and nature, nature and knowledge which cannot be spoken. But this is not to make a (feminist) moral saint of any particular female figure who manages to write philosophy and be recognized as a philosopher.

Feminism does not need moral saints. Woolf herself provokes hotly contested and conflicting interpretations.[54] Some interpretations present Woolf exclusively as a modernist whose primary concern is to shape her writing according to a formal aesthetic. Ironically she has been criticized for failing to be 'shrill', 'strident' or 'angry' as a 'feminist' ought to be.[55] To be too eloquent and too controlled would be to fail to kill the Angel in the House. On such grounds, critics deny that

---

[53] Ibid.

[54] Moi, *Sexual/Textual Politics*, pp. 1–18.

[55] Heilbrun, *Writing A Woman's Life*, pp. 14–15; Lee, *Virginia Woolf*, pp. 476, 520–521; Moi, *Sexual/Textual Politics*, pp. 1–8; Waugh, *Feminine Fictions*, pp. 88–125.

Woolf's writings are consistent, or genuinely feminist at all. Her general hostility to life might be criticized as madness; her hostility to Christianity might be called repressed anger; her preoccupation with her mother, her father, her familial relations verge on the narcissistic; her inner battle with heterosexual emotions/relations could smack of a general dishonesty in failing to confront her own sexuality. Ultimately, a woman's failure to recognize her own self-deception might render not only her art, but her politics self-destructive. Yet where else do we go, if not to an individual woman writer to create a feminist paradigm, to conceive the elements for hope that feminism and patriarchy will one day dissolve?

Despite the contestations of feminist critics, the figure of Woolf becomes a messenger of hope for those women who want to know what is necessary in order to reverse their silencing. Against what Le Doeuff's names 'the mutism' of their own condition under patriarchy, women after Woolf advocate two grounds which will give a woman freedom for self-expression and creativity: (1) material conditions allowing independence of thought and (2) social circumstances allowing time and place away from domestic labours.

Admittedly, creating a messenger of hope out of 'Virginia Woolf' in recognition of persisting forms of patriarchy and in an embrace of feminism will not satisfy, or be acceptable to, her critics. The latter see only weakness, madness and repression in the post-Woolfian literary imagery. Nonetheless, the Woolfian imagery such as the Angel in the House break free, to some degree, from its origin in 1920s and 1930s Britain. Yet Woolf's lack of explicitly directed anger about her own social and material conditions as a writer has provided ground for critics to dismiss the possibility that her writings could direct other women to feminist action. Nevertheless, the present contention is that Woolf's self-expression and literary creativity can become part of – along with the work of such women writers as the others mentioned above – the imagery for a philosophical imaginary that will generate new visions for men and women.

Even if successfully imagined as a messenger of hope, Woolf's imperfections raise a more general question about precisely what categories guide expressions of feminism and patriarchy toward their own ultimate end. To answer this consider a slightly earlier attempt on another continent to confront the walls of patriarchy and imagine the literary struggle out of confinement. The late nineteenth-century American Charlotte Perkins Gilman writes a small masterpiece, 'The Yellow Wallpaper' (1892), portraying a woman's deeply disturbing split-self awareness of confinement by her husband:

> ... for really I wasn't alone a bit! As soon as it was moonlight and that poor thing began to crawl and shake the pattern, I got up and ran to help her. I pulled and she shook, I shook and she pulled, and before morning we had peeled off yards of that paper.[56]

---

[56] Charlotte Perkins Gilman, *The Yellow Wallpaper* (London: Virago Press, 1981), p. 32.

... I kept on creeping just the same, but I looked at him over my shoulder. 'I've got out at last,' said I, 'in spite of you. And I've pulled off most of the paper, so you can't put me back!'

Now why should that man have fainted? But he did, and right across my path by the wall, so that I had to creep over him every time![57]

Gilman captures patriarchy in the imagery of walls, of crawling, shaking, creeping, seeking a way out of the constraining other, finding one's own inner world, however small it may be. Moving against their oppressor enables women writers and their readers to build up a feminist tradition that seeks to imagine and subvert the obstacle of (Christian) patriarchy that does not speak otherwise than through a social imaginary.

The patriarchal containment of a woman physically and mentally is portrayed in a short story. Bi-gendered imagery rests at the heart of stories written by women who struggle to give expression to their oppressive, social and material conditions under patriarchy. In turn, the women authors of exemplary (feminist) texts and readers of their creatively gendered stories make it possible to generate messengers of hope – in subversive figures – not only in fiction, but in social reality. But it is helpful at this point to think back in the century before Gilman and Woolf, to a late eighteenth- and early nineteenth-century mother-daughter pair of women authors.

Aesthetic education and the monstrous sublime

Mary Wollstonecraft (Godwin) (1759–97) and Mary (Godwin) Shelley (1797–1851) enable a bridge across the eighteenth and nineteenth centuries. A political philosopher, if not a feminist in contemporary terms, Wollstonecraft argues persuasively against the prevailing opinion of woman's sexual character for her historical and cultural context. In particular, she responds to both Jean-Jacques Rousseau's account of the moral education of women in *Emile: or, On Education* (1762) and John Milton's portrayal of the first woman, Eve, in *Paradise Lost* (1667). Rousseau's political treatise and Milton's poetic text become the targets of Wollstonecraft's brilliant and energetic rebuttal of the prevailing literary and theological (in fact, political) opinion of a woman's moral nature. Wollstonecraft insists *contra* Rousseau that women were destined just as men were to acquire human virtues, if only given the freedom to have the moral education for these. Of course, this would go against the moral education necessary for women who were to stay at home and prevent the chaos which, it was thought (by Rousseau), would result from their presence in public life. Nevertheless, Wollstonecraft persists in asking, what if women were educated, and then, what if they were to confront Milton's theological reading of woman. While advocating the acquisition of

---

[57]   Ibid., p. 36.

human virtues by women, Wollstonecraft exposes the way in which Milton turns the voice of Eve against herself:

Milton, I grant, was of a very different opinion [to me] ...

'To whom thus Eve with perfect beauty adorn'd.
My author and disposer, what thou bid'st
Unargued I obey; so God ordains;
God is *thy law, thou mine*: to know no more.'

These are exactly the arguments that I have used to children; but I have added, your reason is now gaining strength, and, till it arrives at some degree of maturity, you must look up to me for advice – then you ought to *think* and only rely on God.[58]

The problem (in the above) is that Eve's voice from Milton's magisterial poem resounds in the ears of the woman at the heart of the patriarchal tradition in British literary and philosophical history. Eve's ignorance in submitting to (her) man is based upon an analogy to man's submissive obedience to his God. This patriarchal hierarchy is not easily dismantled. As an implicit, European Christian conception of a woman, Milton's representation of Eve re-enforces the hidden obstacle against a woman's own thinking. This obstacle is repeatedly identified in literature and reality, while the waves of feminism return to force themselves beyond that which obstructs women.[59]

At the end of the eighteenth and beginning of the nineteenth centuries, philosophical readings align beauty with certain feminine virtues and the sublime with masculine ones.[60] Although it may seem surprising that after 1792 when Wollstonecraft published her momentous text on the rights of woman, the values attributed to the beautiful and the sublime rise up against women to cause a significant backlash on ideals of gender. Arguably Enlightenment moral and aesthetic education has a direct impact on conceptions of women and men – often to the detriment of the former. This is also the historical point at which the sublime

---

[58] Wollstonecraft, *A Vindication*, p. 101; cf. John Milton, 'Paradise Lost', in *John Milton: The Major Works*, edited with an Introduction and Notes by Stephen Orgel and Jonathan Goldberg. Oxford World's Classics (Oxford: Oxford University Press, 2003), pp. 355–618, book IV, lines 634–638; Wollstonecraft's italics of Milton's text is reproduced here.

[59] For an extremely witty and wise anecdote about an incredible, contemporary ignorance of Mary Wollstonecraft, see Le Doeuff, *The Sex of Knowing*, pp. 108–110.

[60] Edmund Burke, *A Philosophical Enquiry into the Origin of Our Ideas of the Sublime and Beautiful* [1757] edited by Adam Phillips (Oxford: Oxford University Press, 1990); Immanuel Kant, *Observations on the Feeling of the Beautiful and the Sublime* [1764], trans. John T. Goldthwait (Berkeley: University of California Press, 1960).

becomes associated with the divine – often in place of the beautiful. But then another sudden change – twenty-one years after her mother's death as a result of her own birth – Mary Shelley subverts the theme of submissive female beauty and so undermines the powerful Enlightenment views of the sublime which had become a theological ideal *par excellence*. Before describing Shelley's subversive novel, consider the persuasive aesthetic-theological argument which shifts associations of the divine from the beautiful to the sublime.

The basic argument is initially that whatever God is, or creates, has to be perfect; and, in this case, if God is to fulfill the human desire for perfect fairness, fit or countenance, God has to be the origin and end of perfect beauty. Or, turning this around, man's (*sic*) awareness of design in nature, including human nature, gives grounds for the existence of a perfect being who designed this order. Why, in this light, would late eighteenth-century conceptions of 'man' (*sic*) and God gradually lead theologians from a concern for perfected beauty to a search for the sublime? Essentially the argument becomes, if divine perfection is greater than any human conception of perfect or perfected beauty and is greater than any imitation of natural beauty, then this inexpressible perfection, i.e., maximal greatness, of the divine is best simply named 'the sublime'. It is, then, stressed that, unlike perfect beauty, the sublime is always ultimately inconceivable. And yet, the sublime is, then, associated as much with divine superabundance as it has been with the monstrosity of a negative (terrifying) sublime. What more can be said about the inconceivable and often monstrous sublime before the social imagination, in the ebb and flow of the conceptions of a philosophical imaginary, reverts back to the sublime expressing experiences of perfect beauty in nature?[61] This question has generated plenty of answers, but the question still persists in philosophy and in interdisciplinary debates, especially with feminist critics.

In eighteenth-century Europe, Rousseau's account of the different moral and aesthetic educations of men and women in *Émile* (1762) is given a critical response in Mary Wollstonecraft's *Vindication of the Rights of Woman* (1792). But Wollstonecraft's response is not taken up directly by her own contemporaries; it takes possibly another century before women championed her vindication.[62]

---

[61]   In fact, the relationship between, and at times the equation of, the sublime and the beautiful is once again at the interface of current debates in philosophy, theology and literature; for a contextualizing of this contemporary Kantian interdisciplinary debate in a major essay on Iris Murdoch, Kant and Gerard Manley Hopkins, see by Paul Fiddes, 'The Sublime and the Beautiful: Intersections between Theology and Literature', in Heather Walton (eds.), *Literature and Theology: New Interdisciplinary Spaces* (Farnham, Surrey: Ashgate Publishing Limited, 2011), pp. 127–152. Also, for further discussions of beauty and Iris Murdoch, see Chapter 8.

[62]   For various arguments why this initial lack of positive response to her work and life might have been so, see Valerie Sanders, 'First Wave Feminism', in Sarah Gamble (ed.), *The Routledge Companion to Feminism and Post-Feminism* (London: Routledge, 2001), pp. 16–28. For further background to the reception of Wollstonecraft's (feminist) ideas after her death, see Pamela Clemit and Gina Luria Walker, 'Introduction', in William

Instead, at the time Rousseau's assumptions concerning gender are appropriated by philosophers, including Immanuel Kant's *Observations on the Feeling of the Beautiful and the Sublime* (1764). The latter raises heated gender debates even today about such statements as: 'The fair sex has just as much understanding as the male, but it is a *beautiful understanding* whereas ours should be a *deep understanding,* an expression that signifies identity with the sublime.'[63]

A positive reading of Kant's claim acknowledges a certain level of equality in understanding between the male and female sexes. However, the gender differences between beautiful and deep understandings have unavoidably negative implications when read alongside Kant's assertion that 'The virtue of a woman is a beautiful virtue. That of the male sex should be a noble virtue. Women will avoid the wicked not because it is un-right, but because it is ugly; and virtuous actions mean to them such as are morally beautiful. Nothing of duty, nothing of compulsion, nothing of obligation!'[64] At first glance women seem freed from the constraints of duty. But in Kantian terms this would imply excluding them from moral autonomy, since this autonomy would mean being free to act for the sake of duty alone. Moreover, additional gender connotations differentiate men from women by the former's ability to distance themselves from nature and move closer to the divine. This crucial gender difference shapes later associations of women with nature; and so, women's beauty as a gift of nature becomes increasingly problematic as modern science and technology seek to dominate all of nature as unruly and threatening rather than orderly and nurturing. What began, for some, as gender differences due to education becomes for many post-Enlightenment thinkers entrenched assumptions concerning fixed natural differences between women and men. Kant's gendering of beauty affects subsequent accounts of aesthetic education in profound ways. Even more worrying is that theological accounts of divine greatness as the sublime give further substantial ground to privilege men over women. From Kant to the twentieth-century French postmodernist Jean-Francois Lyotard, the problematic assumption persists that absolute beauty is unobtainable for women while men struggle to re-order the chaotic and corrupting forces of nature.

And yet hope emerges in a significant, ironic form which portrays a monstrous sublime. This upshot[65] of Kant's text implies a decisive lesson: once human desire

---

Godwin, *Memoirs of the Author of A Vindication of the Rights of Woman* (Ontario, Canada: Broadview Press, 2001), pp. 10–42.

[63] Kant, *Observations on the Feeling*, p. 78. For a highly significant philosophical and feminist reading of the gender debates over Kant, 'the unfair sex' and women's relationship to aesthetics, see Christine Battersby, 'Kant and the Unfair Sex', *The Sublime, Terror and Human Difference* (London and New York: Routledge, 2007), pp. 45–67.

[64] Kant, *Observations on the Feeling*, p. 81.

[65] Crucial for a feminist writer's relationship to the history of philosophical and theological ideas are two sorts of readings of canonical texts: the first is the upshot of the text, which is the manner it has been understood by its (current) history; and the second is

and delight go beyond their proper limits, human creations become monstrous. At the extreme the yearning connoisseur of beauty, despite a powerful recognition of un-surpassing beauty, fails tragically to be worthy of this perception. Without the mutual exchange between creator and creature, lover and beloved, monstrous forms of creativity manifest human unworthiness.[66] Instead of harmony, integrity, and splendour, the one-sided endeavour to create human beauty results in the monstrous sublime of death and destruction, 'where by its size it defeats the end that forms its concept'.[67] In contrast to any ideal of the mutual exchange of human love in beauty, the (monstrous) sublime undermines beauty: lifesaving potential is a creative yet fragile intimation of the divine. This monstrosity is powerfully represented in the Enlightenment myth of a new Prometheus in Mary Shelley's *Frankenstein* (1818).[68]

Shelley's story about a man-made creature explores the tragedy and distortions of a scientific man who endeavours to replace divine with human creations, religion with science, and love with technology; the outcome is truly horrific. Shelley learns about a woman's rights and a revised moral ideal from a mother she never knew, and discovers for herself the productivity of the imagination. The brilliant young daughter captures, in her terrifying story of *Frankenstein*, the danger of displacing love. Hence she demonstrates with unforgettable imagery that the Romantic idea of human creativity cannot be sustained without the virtues of mutual love and justice; or, in the words of Frankenstein's monster: 'Cursed creator! Why did you form a monster so hideous that even you turned from me in disgust? God in pity made man beautiful and alluring, after his own image ... but I am solitary and detested.'[69] Virtues, including beauty which accompanies justice as fair countenance, sustained by a perfect order which is transcendent of men and women, would suggest that neither male nor female creativity results in the self-destructiveness of a chaotic and violent nature.[70]

---

the possibility remaining in the text for the philosopher who is persuaded to return to it, to reread that text with fresh eyes; see Le Doeuff, *Hipparchia's Choice*, pp. 168–170.

[66]   This could be usefully put in contrast to Anne Conway's account of the necessary interactions between the changing aspects of creation, see Anne Conway, *The Principles of the Most Ancient and Modern Philosophy* [1670; 1690], edited by Peter Loptson (The Hague, Netherlands: Martin Mijhoff, 1982), pp. 209–210.

[67]   Immanuel Kant, *The Critique of Judgement*, trans. James Creed Meredith (Oxford: Clarendon Press, 1952), p. 100.

[68]   Mary Shelley, *Frankenstein, or the Modern Prometheus* [1818] edited with Introduction and Notes by Marilyn Butler (Oxford and New York: Oxford University Press, World Classics, 1993).

[69]   Ibid., p. 105.

[70]   Chapter 8 (below) will return to this idea of perfection.

Feminist or not

Angel or devil, submissive or strident, anti-feminist or thinking woman, each stark alternative repeats a patriarchal image of a woman's gender type. 'A thin veil of white water across the sand …' the imagery speaks volumes, if we treat the waves as representative of feminism's impact on patriarchy. Feminism has not yet had its last day. At the turn of this century the gender theorist Sarah Gamble takes a strong stand in the debates over feminism and postfeminism:

> post-feminists are [not] wholly misguided in focusing attention upon what feminism has already gained for women. But it's also easy to be too optimistic and to take one's own privileged position as representative, which can lead to the conclusion that the time for feminism is past, and that those who still cling to activist principles are deluded and fanatical.[71]

Two points of caution: (1) it is crucial not to become overly optimistic and ignore the deep ambivalences about women's gender identities which continue to undermine their authority as women and as writers of their own ideas; (2) it is essential that a woman is not afraid to affirm her uniqueness in seeking to write. Instead she could aim at, as Dorota Filipczak argues, 'divining a self'. This divining means to locate herself spiritually and socially in order to enable the autonomous female self to create a spiritual identity within her own political and religious context.[72] Feminism and patriarchy struggle with both creative and destructive forms of language. The challenge is to explore that part of a woman's cognitive and imaginative capacities which constitutes the theologian or philosopher of religion, as much as female or male author.

The paradigmatic figure which has gradually emerged in the previous pages of this chapter is that of a dissenting angel. The post-Woolfian author seeks her own destiny, while appropriating Woolf's ultimate vision of light as it sets the sea ablaze.

> The surface of the sea slowly became transparent and lay rippling and sparkling until the dark stripes were almost rubbed out. Slowly the arm that held the Lamp raised it higher and then higher until a broad flame became visible; an arc of fire burnt on the rim of the horizon, and all around it the sea blazed gold.[73]

Taking up the imagery from the above novel, the reader imagines how years pass until another narrative interlude puts into play the sun, sea, sky and waves. Here it is the end of another day:

---

[71]   Gamble, 'Post-Feminism', p. 53.
[72]   Filipczak, 'Autonomy and Female Spirituality', pp. 210–222.
[73]   Woolf, *The Waves*, pp. 3–4.

The sun was sinking. The hard stone of the day was cracked and light poured through its splinters. Red and gold shot through the waves, in rapid running arrows, feathered with darkness. Erratically rays of light flashed and wandered like signals from sunken islands, or darts shot through laurel groves by shameless, laughing boys. But the waves, as they neared the shore, were robbed of light, and fell in one long concussion, like a wall falling, a wall of grey stone, unpierced by any chink of light.[74]

Thus, even when a feminist light is darkening, metaphor, imagery, narrative and imagination seek to embody human knowledge. Creativity is one path to freedom, to free thinking, writing and feeling. The creation of feminist knowledge(s) gives reality and substance to that part of the mind which exists to be developed. The creation of language and the creation of an inner world threaten to separate one from another, and yet these two dimensions of creativity remains essential for life itself. For the post-Woolfian feminist, mental states are themselves described, or spoken of, by external landscapes. The obstacle that does not speak its name is, nevertheless, shown in concrete practices and concrete exchanges. Myths of patriarchy (as traditional narratives about human and divine, men and women relations) also unearthed in the creation of characters, the structure of narratives, meaning of imagery. In myths and their imagery, glimpses of ineffable truths continue to rise and fall. Feminist creativity, in re-visioning gender, continues to produce messengers of hope for a world freed from oppressive material and social relations. Re-visioning gender is a creative process which, as argued here, should have a role in contemporary philosophy of religion.

Conclusion

The scene has been set for understanding the struggle to transform those damaging gender stereotypes which have been most resistant to change in philosophy of religion: that is, the materially and socially specific obstacle which has had no name in the conscious or unconscious exclusion of women from the field. Instances of gender oppression, or what Miranda Fricker would call 'hermeneutical injustice',[75] may not be nameable; nonetheless, such injustice and such oppression are lived and felt in the damaged done by those who are blind to and blinded by the unfair sexual and gender relations in exclusive 'moral' and religious forms of patriarchy. Fathers may rule, but daughters, mothers and lovers of all sorts have supported these rulers often at the expense of their own lives, as well as the lives of and relations to other marginalized subjects. The problem is not merely that they have been left out of philosophy, but women have been left out of the picture, while still

---

[74]   Ibid., p. 173.
[75]   Miranda Fricker, *Epistemic Injustice: Power and the Ethics of Knowing* (Oxford: Oxford University Press, 2007), pp. 161–169.

propping up the damage done to what could have been a much fuller and richer (conception of) human life.

The next chapter will turn to philosophy of religion and how we might begin to recognize and re-vision gender in contemporary philosophy of religion. This will be followed by a chapter on the recent relations between so-called 'masculinist'[76] theism and difference feminism. Once the patterns of gender exclusions and oppositions in the field become clearer, then feminism in philosophy can function to provide the possibility of philosophers being true to philosophy's self-transforming nature; that is, when it comes to philosophical men and women, their epistemic norms and practices hold the answer to the origin of gender in/justice and fairness, but also to truth.[77] The contention of this book is that by, first, coming to see the gendering process and, second, re-visioning gender in philosophy of religion, it is possible for a discipline that straddles the gap between religious practice and philosophical critique to be thoroughly enriched. Reason, love and epistemic locatedness will play key roles in this transformative process.

---

[76] 'Masculinist' is a term used to designate 'anti-feminist positions' by Grace M. Jantzen, *Becoming Divine: Towards a Feminist Philosophy of Religion* (Manchester: Manchester University Press, 1998), p. 3. I will largely follow Jantzen's use of masculinist in this book.

[77] Miranda Fricker, 'Epistemic Oppression and Epistemic Practice', *Canadian Journal of Philosophy*, supplementary volume, *Civilization and Oppression*, edited by Catherine Wilson (1999): 191–210.

Chapter 2

Gender in Philosophy of Religion[1]

Preliminaries: Gender and injustice

Chapter 1 aimed to present necessary, textual background for re-visioning gender through new reading and writing practices. The history of women writers is full of examples that expose the external and internal process of gendering the author. This gendering shapes the identity of women and men often unwitting but always profoundly. In addition, the previous chapter proposed that gender in western philosophy has generally been determined to a greater or less degree by the dominant patriarchal constructions of heterosexuality, of femininity and masculinity. Without recognizing the process of gendering in philosophy, especially when mixed with traditional religious norms, the ethical dangers of homophobia and misogyny, sexism, ethno-centrism, racism and compulsory sexual norms and practices will continue in the lives of those of us who fail to be critically self-reflexive. This chapter will continue to maintain that the gendering of human-divine relations in philosophy of religion shapes both un-ramified and ramified beliefs of Christian theism. Many of these gendered beliefs in philosophy of religion were originally constituted by Christian myths concerning women, men and divine as opposed to human attributes.[2] In particular, the portrayal of divine ideals, which are humanly unachievable, re-enforces some of the most problematic norms in the gendering of human identity. Men and women who try to achieve the impossible, to 'be' divine, too easily perpetuate gendered forms of domination and injustice.

Chapter 1 sought in particular to demonstrate that, by unearthing the ways in which the myths of Christian patriarchy have historically inhibited and prohibited women from thinking and writing their own ideas about God, God-man, man-man and man-woman, fresh ground can be laid for re-visioning the problematic gender practices in the writing of philosophy of religion. This chapter will aim to show how philosophy's self-definition, including its definition of philosophy of religion,

---

[1]   For a much earlier version of this chapter, see Pamela Sue Anderson, 'Feminism in Philosophy of Religion', in Deane-Peter Baker and Patrick Maxwell (eds), *Explorations in Contemporary Continental Philosophy of Religion* (Amsterdam and New York: Rodopi, 2003), pp. 189–206; and reprinted in Chad Meister (ed.), *The Philosophy of Religion Reader* (London: Routledge, 2008), pp. 655–670.

[2]   For further background on the definition of 'myth' at work here, see Pamela Sue Anderson, 'Myth and Feminist Philosophy', in Kevin Schilbrack (ed.), *Thinking Through Myths: Philosophical Perspectives* (New York and London: Routledge, 2002), pp. 101–120.

is being gradually transformed by an increasing awareness of its own history and locatedness. For some years, I have been arguing that as long as philosophy remains true to one of its most original characteristics, that is, its reflexive nature, then it will inevitably have to recognize the relevant and reciprocally related aspects of its material and social locatedness. These reciprocally related aspects of our locatedness inform our recognition of gender in philosophy.

Epistemic practices and consciousness-raising

In the 1970s, especially, women would have achieved recognition of gender injustice through a collective exercise of consciousness-raising. Once consciously aware of their material and social locatedness each woman and each man, including the male philosopher, would no longer be able to suppose that gender neutrality was the essential epistemic norm for thinking and writing philosophically. Note that consciousness-raising, as practiced by 1970s feminists, assumed a political commitment to change the world as it is/was generally known. Such a political commitment, especially when applied to critical thinking and transformative philosophizing, would encourage the creation of new concepts with which to gain new knowledge and seek justice for all women and men. Consistent with the characterization of feminism as political in recognizing and re-visioning gender bias and injustice, awareness of the social and material aspects of our philosophical locatedness would aim at a transformation of the field and its epistemic practices.[3]

Obviously, any such transformation of philosophy is ambitious; and it would not be straightforward. The challenge is not just to recognize the gender relations which have been 'invisible', but to re-vision gender as an epistemic norm for overcoming injustice. Gender relations, whether personal, political or both in philosophy of religion have traditionally shaped epistemic practices from a privileged (for instance, a white-male; or, a so-called God's eye) position. A serious problem arises when this position has been thought to be a fully rational and unexceptional stance, when it is not. Philosophical rationality, including various forms of logical, theoretical, practical and instrumental reasoning, has too often been too narrowly defined; bracketing out the political, material and social aspects of our lives results in a lack of understanding and/or inadequate knowledge of ourselves and the concepts we live by. A great price has been paid by an innocent

---

[3]   For groundbreaking work on epistemic injustice, see Miranda Fricker, *Epistemic Injustice: Power and the Ethics of Knowing* (Oxford: Oxford University Press, 2007). For part of an ongoing discussion of Fricker's central case of 'hermeneutical injustice' (Fricker, *Epistemic Injustice*, pp. 147–161), in which understanding of a woman's experience fails (or, roughly, her experience is not understood because they is no name for it; hence, this injustice is called 'hermeneutical'), along with the role which 'consciousness-raising' plays in naming the injustice, 'sexual harassment', see Rebecca Mason, 'Two Kinds of Unknowing', *Hypatia: A Journal of Feminist Philosophy*, 26, 2 (Spring 2011): 294–307.

subject when the reciprocally related aspects of her epistemic locatedness have seemed largely irrelevant to the core practices of Anglo-American philosophy (of religion). This so-called irrelevance has been the ground both for a serious lack of understanding and for injustice.

Change in philosophy is never easy; and feminism in philosophy has been strongly resisted, or at least it was in the twentieth-century, by Anglo-American philosophers who have identified themselves with a norm of political neutrality. Women writers have struggled to grasp with the help of the imagination what is wrong in women's relations to philosophy and under laws of 'father rule'. However, gradually the assumption that Anglo-American philosophy of religion is politically neutral, as well as gender-neutral, is beginning to lose some of its ground. Today it would be difficult for many philosophers to deny that thinking and writing in philosophy of religion reflect more than the skills of logical argumentation; philosophical thought and action reveal the values and insights of its most vocal practitioners. Yet by and large, philosophers need to be asked to reflect on the value-laden nature of doing philosophy, if they are to remain true to philosophy's self-definition. A return to the ancient practice of reflection on morality and justice would help each and every philosopher to see anew the strengths and weaknesses in the shape of the field.

In addition to the difficulty of identifying the politics of (patriarchal) philosophy, there is a further difficulty in revealing the role of gender in philosophy. 'Feminism' covers a whole range of different feminist voices and views. So, it is not one thing; and not every 'feminist' would seek to raise a woman's consciousness of her social and material locatedness. Nevertheless, gender in philosophy of religion can be revealed in the reading of a philosophical text; new abilities are found to see what is not immediately visible. For instance, the ability of 'dialoguing with a text',[4] with a singular, critical focus can help to elucidate the gender beliefs in the arguments of a particular philosopher. The point is to start reading and writing somewhere; accept the locatedness of gender norms and beliefs.

A well-known example of elucidating gender in philosophy is the recognition of an ideal: that is, 'the man of reason' who, as Janet Martin Soskice describes, '... in various guises trudges through the works of early *modern philosophy*, [as] a disengaged self in the disenchanted universe'; '... this new agent of *science* gains control, even in his *moral life*, through "disengagement" and objectification [of the surrounding world but also of his own emotions, fears and compulsions ...]'; '... indeed this miracle of self-mastery is a familiar figure in the texts of *spiritual* theology.'[5] This elucidation of gender in philosophy reveals that 'the man of

---

[4] Michèle Le Doeuff, 'Women in Dialogue and in Solitude', *Journal of Romance Studies*, 5/2 (Summer 2005): 1–15.

[5] Janet Martin Soskice, 'Love and Attention', in Pamela Sue Anderson and Beverley Clack (eds), *Feminist Philosophy of Religion: Critical Readings* (London: Routledge, 2004), pp. 200–206, italics added; cf. Genevieve Lloyd, *The Man of Reason: 'Male' and 'Female' in Western Philosophy* (London: Routledge, 1993).

reason' has personified the subject's self-image in various branches of philosophy, including often in philosophy of religion.

The Oxford moral philosopher, Iris Murdoch saw this crucial philosophical construction of gender, even before Soskice or Genevieve Lloyd did.[6] To her credit, Murdoch also saw clearly the link between moral philosophy and religious ideals. The 'man of reason' links moral philosophy and philosophy of religion. In fact, as a branch of philosophy, philosophy of religion touches and crosses other branches, not only moral philosophy, but epistemology, metaphysics, philosophy of science, philosophy of language and philosophy of history. Moreover, feminism in philosophy of religion faces similar problems, issues and struggles as feminism in (almost) any of the other branches of contemporary philosophy.

Norms and beliefs: gender in philosophy of religion

A significant contention of this chapter is that insofar as feminism exposes gender in philosophical texts, it challenges in a deep and fundamental manner philosophy's ideals as these have *both* objectified women and led to self-fulfilling beliefs about the divine; that is, men have been propped up by their ideal of the divine, but also by the gender role given to women. This contention is supported, for example, by Penelope Deutscher's reading of the divine in Augustine's account of relations between men and women, and the divine and man; women and men are equal in terms of their capacity to reason, but men are propped up by the divine toward which they also move.[7]

However, it may be surprising that gender specifically in Anglo-American philosophy of religion was not part of any general concern of twentieth-century philosophers or of feminists. This is true of philosophy and of feminism for equally fundamental reasons; and these reasons have to do with assuming philosophy's gendered ideals as norms for critical thought and action. Precisely, because of its commitment to a distinctive norm of neutrality, twentieth-century Anglo-American philosophy has strongly resisted political, and often religious, commitments. In maintaining norms of critical thinking and concrete action for change, both philosophers and feminists have resisted religious commitments because of the religious traditions supporting past practices uncritically. Nevertheless, a growing awareness that social location and personal commitments do inevitably shape our

---

[6]   The first edition of Lloyd, *Man of Reason*, was published (Minneapolis, MN: University of Minnesota Press) in 1984, while the first edition of the article where Soskice discusses the man of reason, in *Philosophy, Religion and the Spiritual Life* (Cambridge: Cambridge University Press, 59–72) was 1992. However, Murdoch herself much earlier referred to the ideal, 'rational man', or hero, in Iris Murdoch, *The Sovereignty of Good* (London: Routledge & Kegan Paul, 1970), p. 80.

[7]   Penelope Deutscher, *Yielding Gender: Feminism, Deconstruction and the History of Philosophy* (London: Routledge, 1997), pp. 154–168.

philosophical perspectives creates one of the significant horizons for re-visioning gender in philosophy of religion. This means looking at, and challenging, the horizon that has been shaped by certain central and fundamental norms, notably, the divine as the ideal moral agent and the ideal observer. These ideals have, in turn, fixed the gender of other philosophical norms for thinking and acting.[8]

Feminism has given (some) women in philosophy of religion the ethical motivation to transform some of the most traditional aspects of philosophy's self-definition, including those gender norms most resistant to change. Commitments to gender norms reinforced by religious ideals for men and for women should not go unnoticed by philosophers or feminists in that they contain a potentially powerful force for legitimating *either* change *or* the status quo. There is a gap, if not *aporia*, between the truth of what is in reality possible and the present reality. In this sense, feminists and philosophers generally have failed to give attention to their locatedness in the past and present, but especially failed to attend to the epistemic norms of the particular religious traditions to which they are related wittingly or unwittingly.

Feminism in philosophy

Consider the highly impressive collection of philosophy essays published in *The Cambridge Companion to Feminism in Philosophy*. This collection aimed to 'encompass … at least, all of the core subjects commonly taught in Anglophone undergraduate philosophy courses'.[9] Yet it contains no essay, or even a mention of, feminism in philosophy of religion. Even without a survey of philosophy courses in the Anglophone world, there would be little dispute that philosophy of religion has generally existed on the syllabus of undergraduate philosophy courses. So why might it not be included as a core subject area of philosophy in a feminist-philosophy publication? This exclusion is not a simple mistake, or a careless oversight, of the editors. Instead it is a statement about this area of 'philosophy' which tends to be a problem for philosophers, but also often for Christian theologians.

For one thing, analytic philosophy of religion as practised in the Anglophone world is often unwittingly marginalized, or treated as non-core, because it is practised most vocally by conservative, at times aggressively apologetic, theologians. Such dogmatism is a serious problem for philosophers; it is not obviously compatible with the critical spirit of philosophy, or of feminism! For another thing, at least in this context, it is possible that feminists have not been able to imagine that either feminism or philosophy could exist in the subject area of religion. On the one hand, there is the political commitment of feminism that seems to clash, if it is

---

8   Alison Jagger, 'Feminism in Ethics: Moral Justification', in Miranda Fricker and Jennifer Hornsby (eds), *The Cambridge Companion to Feminism in Philosophy* (Cambridge: Cambridge University Press, 2000), pp. 227–228, 239–241.

9   Fricker and Hornsby, *The Cambridge Companion to Feminism in Philosophy*, p. 5.

not totally inconsistent, with a personal religious (or 'private') commitment; and on the other hand, there is once more a generally supposed neutrality of analytic philosophy on matters private.

Nevertheless, it is helpful to recall the claim of the late Margaret Whitford that 'the feminist philosopher' who may be 'a theoretical impossibility ... obstinately insists on existing'.[10] The crucial point is that feminism does actually exist, and seeks to thrive, *in* philosophy of religion. Beverley Clack has given us a significant account of the ways in which feminist philosophy of religion is addressing philosophical issues of lived experience relevant to both those feminists and those philosophers who recognize the necessity in addressing (their own) embodiment critically.[11] An even stronger contention could be made here: that religion responds to a human need to try to understand ourselves, the world around us, and to form theories about the place of human beings in the universe, creating pictures of our relations to others, the world and what might be conceived to be the divine. Ignoring philosophy of religion would, then, imply a failure to recognize how men and women have located themselves, and how this locatedness has objectified women (and some men) in materially and socially specific ways, while creating self-fulfilling beliefs about the divine. This failure hurts both women and relations between men, women and the divine.

In addition, much evidence exists to support a common core of topics for feminism in philosophy of religion and in other branches of philosophy. On this count, several things were initially striking to me about the points of view presented on feminism in philosophy in *The Cambridge Companion to Feminism in Philosophy*. First of all, it was striking to find use made of familiar imagery, that of Neurath's boat, to express the reformist nature of the project of feminism in philosophy. The same imagery was used to introduce the reformist project in the Preface to *A Feminist Philosophy of Religion*[12] as follows: 'Summarizing overall, I intend to supplement contemporary approaches to the philosophy of religion. My approach is reformist, reaching back to rebuild philosophy at the level of fundamental presuppositions.'[13] *A Feminist Philosophy of Religion* also cited the well-known statement by Quine on rebuilding philosophy as follows: 'We can change [the conceptual scheme that we grew up in] bit by bit, plank by plank, though meanwhile there is nothing to carry us along but the evolving conceptual

---

[10] Margaret Whitford, 'The Feminist Philosopher: A Contradiction in Terms?' *Women: A Cultural Review*, 3/2 (Autumn 1992): 112.

[11] Beverley Clack, 'Embodiment and Feminist Philosophy of Religion', *Women's Philosophy Review*, 29, Special Edition: 'Philosophy of Religion' edited by Pamela Sue Anderson and Harriet A. Harris (2002): 46–63.

[12] Pamela Sue Anderson, *A Feminist Philosophy of Religion: the Rationality and Myths of Religious Belief* (Oxford: Blackwell, 1998).

[13] Ibid., pp. x–xi.

scheme itself.'[14] This builds on Quine's claim that philosophers cannot detach themselves completely from their conceptual scheme to achieve an absolutely correct representation of reality. However, this does not imply that philosophers have to give up the search for objectivity or for true belief.

Second, *The Cambridge Companion* draws on the significance of the philosophical imaginary as conceived by Michèle Le Doeuff. The imagery of a boat, or ship on the open sea, mentioned a number of times in *A Feminist Philosophy of Religion*, becomes a critical element of its philosophical imaginary: the imagery plays an equally significant role in the *Cambridge Companion*. Le Doeuff points to the many intertextual connections of the imagery of a ship on the open sea: the imagery moves from the philosophical texts of ancient Greece, to Francis Bacon in sixteenth-century England, to Kant in eighteenth-century Germany, to Neurath and Quine in the last century – and finally, to Le Doeuff's philosophical imaginary. Overall the debt of feminist philosophy remains to Le Doeuff for her reading of the imaginary which is absolutely essential to, but often ignored in the texts of western philosophy. In particular, Le Doeuff encourages women in philosophy to read the texts in the history of western philosophy according to the text's outside and its cultural upshot, but also to read texts fully aware of our present situation so that we allow for the possibilities in new readings of past texts.[15] In this way, feminism in philosophy supports change for a very different future in philosophy.[16]

In addition to reading Quine's imagery in terms of its significance for conceptions of objectivity in the history of modern philosophy, I picked up on the figure of the lone mariner to suggest the ways in which we might transform 'him'. Neurath and Quine create a picture of a mariner, but a lone mariner also appears prior to modern philosophy in the ancient text of Homer's *Odyssey* and later appears in the mid-twentieth-century text of Horkheimer and Adorno, *Dialectic of Enlightenment* (1947). We might say that the cultural upshot of these philosophical texts culminates with the question of the subject in the postmodern debates. However, these past texts not only tell us something about philosophy's past, but they offer us material now for transforming the subjects of philosophy's future. For instance, we find Luce Irigaray miming the possible roles of future female subjects in her *Marine Lover of Friedrich Nietzsche*.[17] Roughly, her mime demonstrates that

---

[14] Willard van Orman Quine, *From a Logical Point of View: Logico-Philosophical Essays* (New York: Harper & Row, 1953), pp. 78–79.

[15] Le Doeuff, *Hipparchia's Choice*, pp. 166–170. For an example of reading Kant's texts with the help of this Le Doeuffian method, see Pamela Sue Anderson, 'Kant's Metaphors for Spatial Locations: Understanding Post-Kantian Space', in Roxana Baiasu, Graham Bird and A. W. Moore (eds), *Contemporary Kantian Metaphysics: New Essays on Space and Time* (New York: Palgrave Macmillan, 2012), pp. 169–196.

[16] Genevieve Lloyd, 'Feminism in History of Philosophy: Appropriating the Past', in Fricker and Hornsby (eds), *The Cambridge Companion to Feminism in Philosophy*, pp. 256–258.

[17] Luce Irigaray, *Marine Lover of Friedrich Nietzsche*, trans. Gillian C. Gill (New York: Columbia University Press, 1991).

in modern philosophy the subject increasingly dissociates himself from 'marine waters', which represent the disorderly turbulent nature of desire, the mysterious forces of embodiment and of material nature; her marine waters symbolize nature as threatening to reason in particular. The result is a paradoxical – in fact, an unsustainable – account of the embodied male philosophical subject who has denied his own relations to nature, to his body and desire. The 'marine lover' offers (us) imagery for exploring new conceptions of relations between male and female subjects for feminism in philosophy. The textual and historical exploration of imagery forces reflection upon our beliefs about the subjects of philosophy and the actual shape of our gendered self-images: we recognize ourselves as materially and socially located, whether women or men in philosophy.

Feminism in philosophy of religion: the missing branch

Stepping back to see the larger picture of contemporary philosophy, the same three reciprocally related issues emerge for feminism in the various branches of philosophy; and yet feminism in philosophy of religion is not often read alongside of feminism in the other branches of philosophy. To demonstrate this similarity and the difference, let us focus on three possible, epistemological frameworks: post-positivist, foundationalist and anti-foundationalist philosophers of religion.

First, we can see a strong methodological similarity between feminism in philosophy of science and feminism in philosophy of religion. Without changing the truth of her account, it is possible to take claims made in Alison Wylie's 'Feminism in Philosophy of Science: Making Sense of Contingency and Constraint' and re-read them in terms of philosophy of religion. Where Wylie writes 'science(s)' and 'philosophy of science', 'religion(s)' and 'philosophy of religion' can be read, without confusion, as follows:

> … feminists see [religion] as an important locus of gender inequality and as a key source of legitimation for this inequality; feminists both within and outside [religion] have developed close critical analyses of the androcentrism they find inherent in the institutions, practices and content of [religion].[18]

Ignorance of feminist critical analyses of androcentrism in western philosophy would suggest the failure to be reflexive about fundamental dimensions of the philosopher's self-image. There is a curious failure of the philosopher to be reflexive about the religious dimensions of this self-image, which have helped to shape practices such as moral reflection in terms of an ideal observer (I will return

---

[18]   Alison Wylie, 'Feminism in Philosophy of Science: Making Sense of Contingency and Constraint', in Fricker and Hornsby (eds), *The Cambridge Companion to Feminism in Philosophy*, p. 166.

to this ideal at the end of this chapter). This leads me to the next set of issues concerning both philosophy of science and philosophy of religion.

Second, we find that feminist critiques and reconstructions of philosophy of religion, like those in philosophy of science, face issues related to the locatedness of the epistemic practices and institutions of religions, as well as their contextual values. In particular, '... feminist engagement[s] with [philosophy of religion] – constructive and critical – raise epistemological questions about ideals of objectivity, the status of evidence and the role of orienting (often unacknowledged) contextual values'.[19] Early in the twentieth-century, philosophy of religion was to a large extent modelled on the positivist methods and values of science. The internal critiques of positivism in the 1960s and 1970s eventually forced scientists and at least some philosophers of religion, and notably certain feminist philosophers, to consider post-positivist research which turned to fine-grained, discipline- and practice-specific studies of belief, acquisition of religious knowledge, knowledge-making practices and methodologies.

Third, feminism in philosophy of religion, like in science, has faced issues raised by certain sorts of philosophical critics, most notably positivist(-like) critics. Echoing the words of Wylie concerning philosophy of science, we easily find that, 'Despite substantial overlap between philosophical and feminist interests in [religion], a number of outspoken critics argue that the very idea of feminist philosophy of [religion] (or, more generally, feminist epistemology) is a contradiction in terms.'[20] For example, a definite sense of contradiction – between the political and the (supposedly) neutral – is implicit in a recent disagreement where an analytic philosopher of religion brackets the feminism in the text of a feminist philosopher of religion, in order to critically assess her methodology. The implicit objection would be that philosophy of religion must stand up methodologically to criticism without relying upon the political commitment of feminism. Appropriating the answer to this objection given by Wylie for philosophy of science, we can see how this works for philosophy of religion as follows:

> In response to objections of this sort, feminist philosophers of [religion can] argue [following philosophers of science] that their critics make a number of highly problematic assumptions about philosophy of religion, or more specifically, the justification of religious belief. Arguments that were well established by the late 1970's such as arguments from the theory-ladenness of evidence, the underdetermination of theory by evidence, and the various perspectives of holism.[21]

---

[19] Ibid.
[20] Ibid.
[21] Ibid.

This makes it clear that the empirical basis of any knowledge-based discipline, whether science or religion, cannot be treated as, in Wylie's words, 'a foundational given in any straightforward sense, and that objectivity cannot be identified with strict value neutrality and the context of independence of epistemic standards'.[22]

Philosophy and (political) neutrality

Such a response could be given to Paul Helm, who is a prominent philosopher of religion apparently in the grip of the assumption of the strict value-neutrality that derived originally from positivist philosophy of science. Helm's manner of criticism of feminist philosophy of religion also exhibits a strong resistance to the reflexive nature of philosophy which would allow for recognition and critique of both its androcentrism and ethnocentrism. Instead Helm not only brackets feminism, apparently to remain philosophically neutral about a methodological issue, in his article, 'The Indispensability of Belief to Religion', but he refuses to try to understand the terms of continental philosophy.[23] Both of these refusals seem to go together, and could be explained by residual positivist assumptions, which allow 'the philosopher' to be unaware of his own sexism and social location.

To be fair, we might readily agree with the view of Miranda Fricker and Jennifer Hornsby in their 'Introduction', in *The Cambridge Companion to Feminism in Philosophy*, that:

> analytic philosophy creates an intellectual climate in which it is especially problematic to acknowledge locatedness. This is surely an important part of the explanation why continental philosophy can seem more hospitable to feminist projects ... [yet] the [feminist] imperative of *social* criticism will ensure that feminist philosophy of any kind is likely to share an affinity with work in the continental tradition ... We believe it is philosophically valuable that work written in the Anglo-American paradigm can produce genuine engagement with questions typically raised in the continental tradition.[24]

It is necessary to consider an area of difficulty in the field: of philosophy of religion; that is, there are increasingly difficult disagreements between 'Continental' philosophy of religion and analytic philosophy of religion.[25] Analytic philosophers

---

[22]   Ibid., pp. 166–167.

[23]   Paul Helm, 'The Indispensability of Belief to Religion', *Religious Studies*, 37 (2001): 75–86.

[24]   Fricker and Hornsby, *Cambridge Companion to Feminism*, p. 8; emphasis added.

[25]   For an engagement with Continental and analytic philosophy, focusing on the different styles of doing philosophy of religion, see Chapter 4 (below). For examples of distinctively Continental philosophy of religion, see Philip Goodchild (ed.), *Rethinking Philosophy of Religion: Approaches from Continental Philosophy*, series edited by John

of religion (and analytic theologians) continue to resist the Continental approach to the field. Yet it is the latter approach and not the former which has been most willing and able to recognize philosophy's material and social locatedness; and so, there are those philosophers who would argue that the Continental approach to philosophy has appeared more amenable to feminism than the analytic approach.

To illustrate the strong antagonism in this difficult area at the interface of Continental and analytic approaches to philosophy of religion, it is revealing to consider the opposing attitudes to the norm of neutrality. In this case, Paul Helm gives voice to the analytic approach and the necessary role of neutrality; and Grace Jantzen is the voice of a Continental feminist philosophy of religion who insists on the impossibility of neutrality in philosophy (roughly, only a masculinist would claim neutrality because he only sees his own point of view). In fact, these two philosophers of religion represent the bi-gender opposition of the masculinist and the feminist.

To see this, first, Helm states

> In *Becoming Divine* Grace Jantzen turns her back on Anglo-American philosophy of religion and the way of doing philosophy which it embodies in favour of certain continental European ways. Jantzen thinks that these ways offer a better prospect for developing a feminist philosophy of religion. [My] paper is not at all concerned with the issue of feminism, but only with the methodological turn that Jantzen makes.[26]

I argue that for her, belief is as indispensable in religion and in the philosophy of religion as it is for the Anglo-American philosophy of religion which she rejects. Further, the only argument she offers for her position is a genetic argument for the origins of religious beliefs.[27]

Second, Jantzen replies as follows:

> [Helm's] article, in fact, is as neat an illustration as I could have wished of exactly my point: the preoccupation of philosophers of religion with beliefs to the exclusion of consideration of issues of gender and justice, while refusing to consider how rationality as they perceive it is constructed upon masculinist desire. Helm briefly acknowledges that there is much more to religion than beliefs ... But in practice his article, like the discipline of which it is a part, proceeds as though that were not so.[28]

Caputo (New York: Fordham University Press, 2002); and Pamela Sue Anderson (ed.), *New Topics in Feminist Philosophy of Religion: Contestations and Transcendence Incarnate* (Dordrecht: London: New York: Springer, 2010).

[26] Helm, 'The Indispensability of Belief to Religion, p. 75.

[27] Ibid.

[28] Grace M. Jantzen, 'What Price Neutrality? A Reply to Paul Helm', *Religious Studies*, 37 (2001): 88.

Such narrowness in the conception of religion and religious practices adds to the lack of interest in philosophy of religion shown by philosophers and feminists working in other branches of philosophy. Jantzen's alternative conception of religion depends upon her qualified use of a psychoanalytic model derived from the Continental tradition, but especially from her particular readings of Luce Irigaray and Adriana Cavarero. Personally, I am not in agreement with this particular use of psychoanalysis for feminism in philosophy; my disagreement is with the seeming inevitability of sexual difference and heterosexual norms in psycholanalytic feminism. Instead post-positivist epistemologist would agree with criticizing the blindness of the analytic philosopher of religion to his own sexism and ethnocentrism. Jantzen explains this:

> ... In my book I use (with qualifications) a psychoanalytic model to show ... either that specific [Christian] beliefs, or indeed the emphasis upon the centrality of beliefs in general, arise out of projections, fears, or desire for mastery ... while technically this does not confirm or deny the truth of the beliefs themselves, it does put the insistence upon their preservation and justification in a different light ... What is being silenced, what positions of dominance are being reinscribed ...?
>
> [Further she asserts] ... what I am after is a scrutiny of the projections, desires, and fears that underlie beliefs and subject positions. This scrutiny must, to be sure, also be applied to a feminist position[29].

More careful study of Jantzen's feminist position, from the point of view of feminism in post-positivist epistemology, will face a fundamental danger, as well as the significance of, her feminist (philosopher's) ideal of the divine for women. Before commenting further on Jantzen, let us complete the parallel between philosophy of science and philosophy of religion with another significant position, but this time, of a Christian woman working in the field of analytic philosophy of religion.

Women in Christian philosophy of religion

Christian philosopher of religion Marilyn McCord Adams reflects insightfully upon the modelling of religion on scientific methods of inquiry, scientific values and standards of epistemic practice. We see again some of the aforementioned methodological issues, as well as the different respective responses of science and religion to the human need to make sense of ourselves, the world and the reality of

---

[29]   Ibid., p. 89.

our social-material locatedness as western philosophers. In Adams's words, 'In our struggle to survive and flourish, "knowledge is power".'[30] Further,

> Intelligence gives us an advantage relative to other animals ... We can study ourselves, try to discover what patterns of character and forms of social organizations frustrate human life and what make it flourish. Religion and science respond to this need to get our bearings, albeit in different ways. Both draw pictures of the cosmos, offer estimates of human being and its prospects. Both are fruitful with corollary recommendations as to better and worse ways to negotiate life.[31]

But now notice, in the passage which follows, the admission made about the answers we give as philosophers of science and, so too, philosophers of religion:

> ... Nevertheless, in relation to what it would be helpful to know, human cognitive powers are *limited*. Whether individually or collectively, we are inveterate *oversimplifiers*, marginalizing some data in order to come up with tractable systematizations, over time striving for more complexity without sacrificing too much simplicity, only eventually to face such massive misfits as to have to begin again. Idealized scientific method takes the successive approximations approach for granted; its program of testing hypotheses even goes looking for falsifying evidence ... [Religions] too face crises, especially when their accounts are inadequate to handle the very features of life for which they are most needed.[32]

In other words, Adams recognizes correctly that an often debilitating tension arises between, on the one hand, unity and simplicity as epistemological values and, on the other hand, complexity, allowing an openness to truth and its opposite, falsehood, in our philosophical theories about reality.

For a central example, philosophers of religion are expected to say something about evil, 'its nature, source and consequences: how and to what extent it takes root in human beings, whether and how it can be eradicated, how in the midst of it we should conduct ourselves through life'.[33] In the twentieth century a restrictive employment of the epistemological principles of unity and simplicity by philosophers of religion resulted in inadequate 'solutions' to the problem. In Adams' words,

> ... our philosophical propensity for generic solutions – our search for a single explanation that would cover all evils at once – has permitted us to ignore the

---

[30] Marilyn McCord Adams, *Horrendous Evils and the Goodness of God* (Ithaca, NY: Cornell University Press, 1999), p. 1.

[31] Ibid., pp. 1–2.

[32] Ibid., emphasis added.

[33] Ibid., p. 2.

worst evils in particular (what I shall call horrendous evils) and so to avoid confronting the problems they pose.[34]

In particular, analytic philosophers of religion such as William Rowe who debate the logical and evidential problem of evil are, according to Adams (and I strongly agree), '… carried on at too high a level of abstraction. By agreeing to a focus on what Rowe came to label "restricted standard theism", both sides avoided responsibility to a particular tradition'.[35] Nevertheless, a particular understanding of the Christian tradition of philosophical theology is still implied even in this restricted standard theism.

In *Horrendous Evils and the Goodness of God*, Adams steers a middle road through issues of theory and practice, between theories in philosophy of religion which have been modelled on the scientific virtues of unity, simplicity, empirical adequacy, internal coherence, etc, and praxis-orientating solutions to actual suffering. She also steers a difficult path between concern for individual participants in horrendous evil (i.e. horrors in which all integrity is destroyed) and concern for making this lived experience meaningful at a more abstract level of philosophy, or what she calls 'the symbolic level'.[36] In particular, she defends herself against the feminist or social criticism – that her approach would only satisfy the worries of bourgeois individuals. She admits that social systems and economic structures cause massive evils. Yet she poses a serious challenge to an exclusively practical response. She argues that proposals for a global transformation of social structures in order to eradicate evil in the world are likely to fail to respond adequately to individuals who seek to understand real pain and to render meaningful (their own) suffering; a theoretical account of individual participants in horrors is necessary for the meaning-making potential, or integrity, of that person.

It would seem to follow that Adam poses an implicit challenge to *both* Jantzen's total rejection of the social structure, which Jantzen contends reflects the necrophilia (a love of death) of a masculinist imaginary, *and* Jantzen's proposal for a new social imaginary, or 'feminist religious symbolic', which would be life-enhancing and not preoccupied with death like the masculinist symbolic. Yet, would Jantzen's feminist alternative be able to address the particularity of horrendous evils, which evacuates life of any positive meaning? This question is posed, albeit in another form, by Beverley Clack.[37] Although Clack calls herself a post-Christian, non-realist feminist, she would seem to concur with the Christian realist Adams, and not with the feminist Jantzen, on the need to render meaningful the individual experiences of bodily life which are in fact negative, and possibly, horrendous. Put simply, real life involves all degrees of distress, decay and death; the reality of our social and personal lives is not always life-enhancing; and

---

[34]   Ibid., p. 3; see also pp. 26–28, 33, 36f, 195–196, 197–198.

[35]   Ibid., pp. 3, 15; cf. Anderson, *A Feminist Philosophy*, pp. 40–41.

[36]   Ibid., pp. 106–151, 196.

[37]   Clack, 'Embodiment and Feminist Philosophy of Religion', pp. 48–54.

individual participants in evil cannot make their particular experiences meaningful – or regain integrity – by trying to sweep them away as a mere construction, or residue, of the masculinist symbolic.

Let us end this section with two questions, (i) is the influence of feminism on philosophy of religion reflected in the sensitivity to both the actual lived experiences of participants in horrendous evil and the sources of evil in social structures? (ii) Or, in the above case, is Adams merely defensive of her individualist predisposition in the face of more radical criticism?

Plurality and unity: an epistemological challenge

Let us consider feminism in epistemology to see how insight from this branch might be mutually beneficial to feminism in philosophy of religion. In 'Feminism in Epistemology: Pluralism without Postmodernism', Miranda Fricker addresses the philosophical question of 'pluralism', as raised by postmodernism's rejection of unity, especially any unifying perspective on the world. Fricker confronts the competing values of plurality and unity, of resistance to authoritarian uses of reason and acceptance of rational authority. In the end, she concludes that the 'first-order' level of our disagreements and of plurality in practice – where social differences give rise to differences in our everyday perspectives – must remain distinct from the levels of (our) epistemological, ontological and metaphysical claims to unity or agreement.[38] The correct level for plurality is the ground level, while reason seeks unity at an epistemological level where rational authority is not mere authoritarianism. Critical scrutiny of what is given (rational) authority implies an epistemological level of discourse on which there is the possibility of agreement, as well as judgment of what is in fact a terrorist use of reason.

Next, we can apply Fricker's distinction in levels – with the correct, ground level for pluralism – to postmodernism in feminist philosophy of religion. For this application, consider Jantzen. Her feminist position has raised valuable concerns about claims to neutrality in philosophy of religion. In particular, she questions an exclusive preoccupation with the justification of religious belief which tends to reinforce the androcentrism of analytic philosophy of religion as traditionally practised in the Anglophone world. Yet Jantzen has also celebrated the 'postmodern' play of plurality and difference. Unlike Fricker, she assumes that the postmodern rejection of authoritarian uses of reason is correct; she goes no further with the question of rational authority. The danger of rejecting reason which, Fricker correctly points out, is that the postmodern celebration of plurality implies the loss of any rational authority. This means the loss of any rational authority – or credibility – for judging good and bad beliefs, or inclusive, exclusive

---

[38] Miranda Fricker, 'Feminism in Epistemology: Pluralism without Postmodernism', in Fricker and Hornsby (eds), *Cambridge Companion to Feminism in Philosophy*, pp. 159–161.

and hurtful practices. Arguably, realism and the rational authority that enables us to recognize actual injustices are lost at the peril of women and marginalized others. The valuable lesson to be learnt by philosophers of religion from feminism in epistemology is: not to lose the ability to scrutinize beliefs rationally, even feminist belief. As mentioned earlier in her response to Helm, Jantzen encourages a particular sort of scrutiny of belief. Yet a problem remains insofar as Jantzen resists considerations of the epistemology of religious belief.

At the very least the ways in which philosophy's constitutive virtues and standards of epistemic practice are interpreted and employed with or against each other have to be considered in the light of the changing awareness of gender and related historical, material and social mechanisms of oppression. Implied is the critical contention (supported in the present chapter and overall in this book) that knowledge, including justified true belief, cannot be claimed without bringing in ethics – or ethical evaluation and, often unwittingly, a host of potentially damaging assumptions. These include certain constitutive values, or 'virtues', which at first glance appear unproblematic: notably, principles of unity, simplicity, empirical adequacy, internal coherence, external consistency and explanatory power.[39] Ethical norms are also implicit in references to the epistemic *duties* of truth (including self-reflexivity), as well as the fundamental *value* assigned to rational authority and credibility. In turn, scrutiny of these ethical normss which constitute epistemic practices have revealed injustice in the multiple exclusions of knowers by gender which is differentiated by multiple material and social factors such as sexual orientation, race, ethnicity and religion.[40] These exclusions of subjects of knowledge result in epistemic injustice.[41] Ultimately, this can result in the failure to treat women and non-privileged persons as credible knowers, as well as failing to recognize certain forms of knowledge. For example, 'know how' and non-standard forms of practical knowledge as in the 'tales' of illiterate women remain generally unacknowledged by traditional epistemologists.[42]

---

[39]   Helen Longino, *Science as Social Knowledge: Values and Objectivity in Scientific Inquiry* (Princeton, NJ: Princeton University Press, 1990); and Wylie, 'Feminism in Philosophy of Science', pp. 166–184.

[40]   Patricia Williams, *The Alchemy of Race and Rights* (Cambridge, MA: Harvard University Press, 1991); Miranda Fricker, 'Epistemic Oppression and Epistemic Practice', *Canadian Journal of Philosophy*, supplementary volume, *Civilization and Oppression*, edited by Catherine Wilson (1999): 191–210; and Miranda Fricker, 'Feminism in Epistemology: Pluralism without Postmodernism', in Fricker and Hornsby (eds), *The Cambridge Companion to Feminism in Philosophy*, pp. 146–165.

[41]   Fricker, *Epistemic Injustice*.

[42]   Vrinda Dalmiya and Linda Alcoff, 'Are "Old Wives' Tales" Justified?' in Linda Alcoff and Elizabeth Potter (ed.), *Feminist Epistemologies* (London: Routledge, 1993), pp. 217–241.

Epistemic oppression and 'the direction of fit'

In the telling terms of Rae Langton's 'Feminism in Epistemology: Exclusion and Objectification', when it comes to knowledge 'women get left out' and 'women get hurt'. There are sins of both omission and commission. Examples of the former include being left out as subjects of knowledge:

> whether because they lack the knowledge men have, or because they lack knowledge of themselves as women, or because they lack credibility, or because their perspectives on the world are omitted, or because they are excluded by a mistaken traditional conception of knowledge.[43]

Women get left out. Langton's account of the sin of commission is especially insightful for debates about the nature of belief in philosophy of religion. In particular, it enables assessing whether religious beliefs have (deceptively) shaped the way the world is, resulting in the anomalous condition of making the world fit the belief. For example, women who are submissive may confirm the powerful patriarch's belief that women should be left to be submissive. But this is in fact a gender distortion of the potential of real women. It is a myth of their gender that women necessarily have to have inferior social positions and/or their lack of political and material power; the result is women being treated as untrustworthy knowers. When a woman's gender renders her inferior to man, then, is grounded in a false belief about women's nature.

Langton's account helps to explain how it is that women are actively hurt by objectification. This would be a sin of commission: it cannot be remedied simply by letting women in. Appropriating Langton's account of objectification, we can give the particular wrong of objectification sustained scrutiny with regard to ethical ideals and religious beliefs (as well as projections) of contemporary philosophers.[44]

Bear in mind Jantzen's caution against an obsessive preoccupation with the justification of belief; yet let us focus on the construction of belief and belief's relation to the world. Elizabeth Anscombe's original account of 'direction of fit' serves as a useful yardstick; that is, *belief aims to fit the world, while desire aims for the world to fit it*.[45] Langton builds upon Anscombe generating an incisive argument concerning objectification as distinct from objective belief that is true, if it actually fits the world:

> If objectivity is about how mind conforms to world, objectification is about the opposite: objectification is, roughly, about some of the ways in which world

---

[43]   Rae Langton, 'Feminism in Epistemology: Exclusion and Objectification', Fricker and Hornsby (eds), *The Cambridge Companion to Feminism in Philosophy*, p. 134.

[44]   Jantzen, 'What Price Neutrality?', p. 89.

[45]   Elizabeth Anscombe, *Intention* (Oxford: Blackwell, 1957).

conforms to mind. Objectification is a process in which the social world comes to be shaped by perception, desire and belief: a process in which women, for example, are made objects because of men's perceptions and desires and beliefs. To say that women are made objects is to speak in metaphors, albeit familiar ones; but, to make a start, it has something to do with how some men see women.[46]

'How some men see women' could refer to how philosopher of religion Charles Taliaferro, with his ideal observer theory, sees any of the 'extant feminist ethic projects'.[47] However, the ethical problem for feminism is not with the direction of fit for belief, or for desire. Instead it is with the anomalies (i) where belief takes the direction of fit of desire, resulting in (the self-deception of) wishful thinking; (ii) when such thinking begins to shape the world, then objects come to confirm the wish as self-fulfilling belief.

The ideal observer revisited

For a last example, consider how the ideal observer theory, first, links ethical discourse about ideal agency and religious discourse about a God's eye point of view; and, second, how the ideal observer theory assumes an ideal vantage on any feminist ethical project, even ethics built on the rejection of the assumed ideal observer standpoint. First, a question of circularity is immediately raised: if the theory assumes the existence of the very ideal it wishes to justify, then it appears to beg the question of its existence. Moreover, the assumption that a philosopher can achieve the ideal observer position and be omniscient, omni-percipient and impartial.[48] Second, a question of a sin of commission is posed: does the ideal observer theory hurt women by failing to understand the premise of women's ethical thinking? In failing to take on board the feminist rejection of 'detached', ethical thought is likely to be determined by the ideal observer standpoint; the ideal observer could at most merely claim to respect (and endorse) the feminist projects. Seeing feminist ethics from a distance like an object of perception means a failure to recognize the serious challenge posed by the feminist both to the ideal observer's own perception and to the very theory which is supposed to endorse it.

For the fact of the matter, to believe that an ideal agent is omniscient, omnipercipient and impartial does not fit the world. Instead this belief is aimed to fit the direction of the agent's desire for a God's eye view. If the latter is assumed, then desire could gain the power to actively shape the agent's perceptions; if

---

46   Langton, 'Feminism in Epistemology', p. 138.

47   Charles Taliaferro, *Contemporary Philosophy of Religion: An Introduction* (Oxford: Blackwell, 1997), pp. 210, 222.

48   Onora O'Neill, *Bounds of Justice* (Cambridge: Cambridge University Press, 2000), pp. 150–156.

powerful enough this overall conception would shape the social world so that the ideal agent (who, by definition, cannot be an actual individual man, let alone a woman) will shape reality to fit his belief as an ideal observer whose perception determines an idealized, theistic picture of reality. Thus we face the problem of a self-fulfilling belief which threatens to undermine the ideal observer theory.

For her part, Jantzen avoids the harm done by this traditional idealization, or self-fulfilling belief, of the male theist who assumes the reality of an omniscient, omnipercipient and impartial, divine agent as model for the ideal observer; the latter not only confidently claims to ensure the truth of religious belief but serves as the ideal vantage point for moral judgment (for example, of our epistemic and discursive practices). Instead Jantzen proposes a projection of the divine as a gendered ideal for women who seek to become fully themselves, and so divine as 'natals' who are born, finite, but flourish in this life.

However, in fact, Jantzen's feminist proposal is not safe either. Her projection of the divine for women is only a step away from objectification. That is, projection is like wishful thinking, belief arranges itself to desire's direction of fit: the thought is for the world to conform to one's wish/belief. Wishful thinking is more obviously characterized by self-deception insofar as the thought does not become true. For example, belief that 'evil' is only part of the masculinist symbolic remains a wish. This is a self-deception for the one who projects the ideal of a feminist religious symbolic which sees reality as life-enhancing only, but also for those who follow and accept it, while excluding those whose lives fail to fit the desired ideal. Nevertheless, the next step to objectification is dangerously easy: given enough social power from those subjects who follow, the privileged female subjects make their wish a self-fulfilling belief whereby it becomes true at least for those feminists whose life is flourishing. Yet this is precisely the sort of exclusion and objectification which feminism in epistemology aims to eradicate.

Conclusion

After critical reflection upon the ideals and self-images of philosophy of religion, it becomes clear that the ethical and epistemological scrutiny of the gender ideals in philosophy of religion share critical issues with feminism in philosophy more generally. It has perhaps also become clearer why feminism in philosophy of religion has not immediately come to mind when philosophers think of feminism in philosophy. The religious ideals in philosophy of religion, insofar as they support domination of my subject by another, are rejected by feminism's critical thought and norms for change. Yet self-reflexivity as an epistemic virtue and an ethical value can motivate philosophers – and feminists – to scrutinize the nature of their most fundamental beliefs about themselves, their place in the universe, and their relations with others, especially insofar as they are supported (or propped up) by divine ideals. We may have the grounds to argue that feminism in philosophy as well as feminism in theology lack a dimension of self-awareness because both philosophy and theology (admittedly, though, for opposite reasons) have ignored the ideals which are shaped by philosophy of religion. Are there seriously important issues, problems and assumptions confronted by feminism in philosophy of religion that are common to the other branches of philosophy in which feminism has had a crucial role to play? Can these branches of philosophy both be helped by and be mutually informative of feminism as an impetus for change in critical thought and practice? Feminist philosophers of religion would want to answer 'yes' to both questions. Positive answers to these questions by both feminist and non-feminist philosophers would create the new horizon most agreeable to imagining the future for re-visioning gender in philosophy of religion.

Chapter 3
Gendering Theism and Feminism[1]

Introduction: difference feminism and masculinist theism

This chapter will focus on the gendering of theism and feminism in relation to each other. It remains necessary to uncover the process of gendering before it is possible to work out the exact relation of feminism to theism in twentieth and twenty-first century philosophy of religion. The task is to demonstrate how the identities of women and men have been shaped philosophically in relation to the divine. It will become clear that within the implicit process of gendering, male and female subjects in philosophy of religion are generally, but not always related to each other *via* the divine. Mary Daly's feminism will serve as a good, twentieth-century example of the gendering of theism (and, as will be seen later, the re-visioning of gender) from a feminist perspective. Implicit in this chapter is also a focus on theistic practices, not just the methods employed to justify knowledge of God, but also the methods created to access the divine. Today feminism in philosophy of religion continues to manifest itself, notably in exposing gender injustice in the epistemic practices of theism.

Theism and feminism have been treated as opposites. Traditional theists have conceived God as omniscient, omnipotent, omnibenevolent, omnipresent, eternal or everlasting. In contexts where feminist philosophers are informed by Anglo-American object-relations psychology,[2] or Feuerbachian projection theory,[3] this theistic God is read as an ego-ideal for the male subject. According to the feminist of sexual difference, the theistic God is, then, precisely the opposite of what would be the ego-ideal for a female subject.[4] In other words, God as

---

[1]   An earlier version of this chapter appears as 'Feminism', in Stewart Goetz, Victoria Harrison and Charles Taliaferro (eds), *The Routledge Companion to Theism* (New York and London: Routledge, 2012), Chapter 35.

[2]   Daphne Hampson, *After Christianity* (London: SCM Press, 1996) cf. Nancy Chodorow, *Feminism and Psychoanalytic Theory* (New Haven and London: Yale University Press, 1989), pp. 184–189.

[3]   Luce Irigaray, 'Divine Women', *Genealogies and Sexes*, trans. Gillian C. Gill (New York: Columbia University Press, 1993), pp. 55–72; cf. Ludwig Feuerbach, *The Essence of Christianity*, trans. George Eliot (New York and London: Harper Torchbooks, 1957).

[4]   A feminism of sexual difference (or simply, 'difference feminism') is shorthand for the feminist who believes that men and women are distinguished by their biology and other natural features of sex/gender. Difference feminism could be Marxists in distinguishing women as a distinct social and material class, and so different from the class of men.

a 'masculinist'[5] ideal is held to possess *aseity*. He is complete in Himself, not needing to depend on any other being.[6] And then, the sharp contrast emerges between the gendering process constituting sexual difference as feminist and the gendering of theism as masculinist. Distinguished by her psychological gender differences from the male ego-ideal, the female subject's ego-ideal is constituted by this difference feminism with an opposite gender ideal. She is not complete in herself and knows this; she needs to depend on and care for another; so she has precisely the relational capacities necessary for love and morality.

It follows that the sexual-difference feminist at least conceives of gendering as a positive process; her conception of the ego-ideal for a female subject prizes the need for relations with others, especially with the divine. However, when contrasted to masculinist theism, feminists still face a choice of how to interpret their gender's relation to theism. Theism and feminism are either incompatible, requiring that one or the other must be given up, or compatible opposites, requiring one to co-exist alongside the other. When a masculinist divine and a feminist divine exist and are compatible, then the Irigarayan goal of a God for man and a God for woman is achieved.

There is a third alternative, depending on how theism and feminism are conceived. Both feminists and theists could reject the psychological and anthropological interpretations of God; then, neither an ego-ideal nor a projection of human love is necessary. However, since the most prominent trends of feminism in philosophy of religion are driven by the subject-centred interpretations of psychology and anthropology, the two dominant trends in theism and feminism are worth a closer look.

On the one hand, the terms 'theist' and 'feminist' are employed by contemporary philosophers of religion, who follow the French psycholinguistic and Feuerbachian concepts of Irigaray, to describe separate, yet potentially compatible positions. On the other hand, as incompatible opposites, theism or feminism would imply a choice. A feminist philosopher must give up the theistic conception of a God who

---

However, today it is more likely to be assumed that a difference feminist is someone who supports the Irigarayan idea of sexual difference, see Irigaray, 'Divine Women', *Genealogies and Sexes*, pp. 55–72.

[5]   'Masculinist' is a term used to designate 'anti-feminist positions' by Grace M. Jantzen, *Becoming Divine: Towards a Feminist Philosophy of Religion* (Manchester: Manchester University Press, 1998), p. 3. I more or less follow Jantzen's use of masculinist in this chapter.

[6]   Hampson, *After Christianity*, pp. 124–125; and 'That Which Is God', in Gillian Howie and J'annine Jobling (eds), *Women and the Divine: Touching Transcendence* (New York: Palgrave Macmillan, 2009), pp. 174–176. Grace M. Jantzen, 'What's the Difference: Knowledge and Gender in (Post) Modern Philosophy of Religion', in Pamela Sue Anderson and Beverley Clack (eds), *Feminist Philosophy of Religion: Critical Readings* (London: Routledge, 2004), pp. 28–41.

has been conceived to empower men (with the so-called omni-attributes) and not women;[7] or, she must give up her feminism.

French feminist philosophy and theism

If a feminist philosopher is going to escape from the theistic ideal of the male subject who is, in the words of the French existentialist Simone de Beauvoir, 'the essential' (since created in the image of his God), then she must resist becoming 'the inessential'. To become a female subject the Beauvoirian feminist transcends the inessential, goes beyond *en-soi* and beyond being an object, which would have meant being reduced to 'the sex'.[8] The trend in feminist philosophy of religion which builds on, while revising, Beauvoir will be represented in this chapter by the early writings of the American feminist Mary Daly. Daly's later feminism could also be said to come close to Irigaray's attempts to create a feminism of sexual difference.[9]

Despite the diversity of views within feminism, there is some agreement amongst feminists about tackling the sexism which has marred theism. In order to become fully as a subject of philosophy, a woman has to transcend any patriarchal conception of a divine-human and a man-woman hierarchy of demeaning gendered roles and values. In the terms of the French philosopher, Michèle Le Doeuff, the woman philosopher refuses to become 'a kind of nothingness in the eyes of the other'.[10]

So, what about the psychological and anthropological interpretations of women who succumb to their devalued roles in masculinist theism? Irigaray's psycholinguistic reading of Feuerbach's projection theory is a paradigmatic case for maintaining the opposition of theism-feminism. Yet Irigaray also proposes the potential compatibility of a male subject with a God for himself and a female subject with god(dess) for herself. Irigaray's essays 'Divine Women'[11] and 'Toward a Divine in the Feminine'[12] present an ethic of sexual difference for divine women, different from divine men, in the starkest terms. She argues that a God in the

---

[7] Hampson, *After Christianity*, pp. 102, 123–125.

[8] Simone de Beauvoir, *The Second Sex*, trans. Constance Borde and Sheila Malovaney-Chevallier (London: Jonathan Cape, 2009), p. 6.

[9] For background on Irigaray, plus discussion of Daly, see Morny Joy, *Divine Love: Luce Irigaray, Women, Gender and Religion* (Manchester: Manchester University Press, 2006).

[10] Michèle Le Doeuff, *Hipparchia's Choice: An Essay Concerning Women, Philosophy, etc.*, trans. Trista Selous (Oxford: Blackwell, 1991); a slightly revised translation with an Epilogue (2006) by the author (New York: Columbia University Press, 2007), p. 280.

[11] Irigaray, 'Divine Women', pp. 55–72.

[12] Luce Irigaray, 'Toward a Divine in the Feminine', in Gillian Howie and J'annine Jobling (eds), *Women and the Divine: Touching Transcendence* (New York: Palgrave Macmillan, 2009), pp. 13–26.

feminine is equally as necessary as a God in the masculine for becoming fully human and sovereign. Only with their two different and respective ideals can the female and male subjects become completely; each gender can become a subject with her or his own integrity by, first, projecting and, second, reclaiming their own gender ideal; these ideals are norms for their love relations. The obvious question to Irigaray about her theism is: why would a feminist philosopher of religion simply assume that God is (no more than) an ideal for the becoming of a human subject?

One answer is that a feminist philosopher educated according to the European norms of post-Hegelian philosophy – whether of Feuerbach, Nietzsche or Freud – simply assumes that theism plays a concrete role in the ethical, social, sexual and spiritual development of (relations of) love between human subjects. Not unlike the Anglo-American philosopher of religion, the European philosopher of religion begins with an assumption about the God of theism. Generally speaking, the Christian Anglo-American philosopher of religion assumes – and defends – the seventeenth-century philosopher's conception of a single Creator-God who is omniscient, omnipotent, all good, omnipresent, eternal or everlasting, and who is a being that does not depend on any other being for its existence. In contrast, generally the European philosopher of religion assumes the nineteenth-century philosopher's belief that a Father and a Son in God who embrace each other with that intense love, to which natural relations alone inspire, should be replaced with the belief that this natural love and unity is immanent in man himself. A positive reduction of God to man happens by embracing the real life of the family, with an intimate bond of love as naturally moral and divine.

In other words, the conception of theism assumed by philosophers of religion who follow the nineteenth-century philosophies of Feuerbach, Marx and Nietzsche take it for granted that 'God' is replaced with 'man' in the moral and spiritual development of loving human subjects. This is like growing up with a belief in 'Father Christmas' or 'Santa Claus' and eventually replacing it with 'Daddy'. A feminist philosopher in this European tradition would also seek a 'God' who can serve initially as her ideal, so that her 'God' can eventually be replaced by 'woman' (or, mother?). Irigaray insists that both theism and its reversal, which ensure a sexual difference between men and women, are necessary for the future of religion and morality.[13]

It could be argued that the main concern of the present chapter is with feminism in Anglo-American philosophy of religion, not in European philosophy or anthropology of religion. However, when it comes to feminism and theism it may not be easy to maintain a sharp distinction between the feminism(s) in European and in Anglo-American contexts. For example, the first woman philosopher-theologian in the Anglo-American world of philosophy of religion, Mary Daly, challenged Thomist arguments and the conception of a single Creator-God who is omniscient, omnipotent, all good, omnipresent, eternal or everlasting. Daly

---

[13]   Ibid., pp. 13–25.

formulates a, for some decisive, argument against Christian monotheism, drawing on the European traditions of feminism (on Beauvoir), philosophy (on Nietzsche) and theology (on Tillich).

An early example: theism and *Beyond God the Father*

Daly (1928–2010) was one of the first American women to train as a Roman Catholic theologian, completing doctorates both in theology and in philosophy. This philosophical-theological education gave Daly the critical tools both to challenge the God of traditional Christian theism and to propose an alternative to the being of this God. Daly became a controversial feminist; she was criticized for her audacity in proclaiming the sexism of theism and celebrated for her creativity (at least by some feminist 'theists') in eventually formulating a radical lesbian feminist philosophy of liberation/religion. Her initial critique of Christian theism appeared in *Beyond God the Father: Towards a Philosophy of Women's Liberation*[14] where she sought to expose the sexism in theistic doctrines of God as both Father of God the Son and Creator of a paradise in which man would fall from his original perfection when seduced by Eve. Daly criticizes the theistic problems of evil and of divine omnipotence. Claiming to 'exorcize evil from Eve', Daly exposes the sexism at the heart of the theist's solutions to innocent suffering and a free 'human' subject; that is, women's sexually specific suffering is ratified by Eve, while human freedom and divine power are given to the new Adam.

Daly's feminist position in *Beyond God the Father* may not appear radical to our contemporary secular society or to Daly's own later writings. At this early stage, she critically engages with the Christian church and theism. Although, when it appeared, Daly's critique of Christian theism shocked both men and women, she is still rarely studied by contemporary Anglo-American philosophers of religion. Yet she did not go unnoticed by the Roman Catholic authorities who were targeted by her philosophy of women's liberation for their patriarchal hierarchy of values which, she claimed, unfairly oppressed women and hindered women's education.

Daly herself grew up in a Roman Catholic community as the only child of a poor Irish couple. She attended a private liberal arts college for women, the College of Saint Rose in Albany, New York, founded by Roman Catholic Sisters. As Daly records in her 1992 autobiography, although keen to study philosophy, as a woman she could obtain a B.A. only in English from the College of Saint Rose. So, she went to do a PhD in Religion at St Mary's College in Notre Dame, Indiana. After this, she went abroad in order to achieve – finally – her doctorates in theology (1963) and in philosophy (1965) at the University of Fribourg, Switzerland.

At the time, the medieval town of Fribourg had a very traditional Roman Catholic university. Even so, Fribourg allowed Daly possibilities denied to her at

---

[14]   Mary Daly, *Beyond God the Father: Toward a Philosophy of Women's Liberation* (London: The Women's Press Limited, 1986).

Catholic colleges in the States. In particular, she managed to read relatively easily the contemporary European philosophy, especially the existentialist philosophy of Beauvoir, and the liberal theology of Tillich which were popular in Europe during the period 1959–65. In this way, Daly's intellectual and feminist insights were freely cultivated in the European context of radical change, including those proposed by the Second Vatican Council.

In the 1960s, Daly herself would come to considerable public attention in the UK and the USA. In 1963, she was asked by a British publisher to write *The Church and the Second Sex*.[15] Although this publication contains a relatively moderate and tentative argument for gender equality, the controversy generated by *The Church and the Second Sex* prevented Daly's first two-year contract at the Jesuit-run Boston College, Massachusetts, from being renewed. Incredibly, the failure of Boston College to renew Daly's contract became *un cause célèbre* when more than 1500 students at the college and many others in universities across the USA protested, forcing the Board of Boston College to reinstate Daly. As a radical lesbian feminist Daly would continue to face obstacles at the Jesuit-run college. Although she gained tenure and taught at Boston College for more than thirty years, she was in the end forced to retire in 1999. A legal case which was made against Daly's separatist policy of not allowing men to attend her women's studies classes finally forced her into retirement.

Daly is a good case-study of feminism and theism in the Anglo-American world precisely because she is motivated by European philosophy and theology, while her feminist struggle for gender equality supports a radical critique of theism. In particular, she seeks to subvert the theistic ratification of the myth of woman as the Other, that is, the second sex. 'The Second Sex' in the title of Daly's 1968 publication brought to mind Simone de Beauvoir's *Le deuxième sexe* (1949). The similarity between Beauvoir and Daly is noteworthy insofar as each of these feminists insists that women are not born, but become a woman. They either become man's Other or become subjects in their own right. Theistic norms are understood to determine the moral and religious development of the (hu)man subject and his Other. The object of Daly's critique – Christian theism – is both compatible with and is challenged by the existential position that a man's freedom as *pour-soi* required a woman's subordination as *en-soi*. In this way, Beauvoir's philosophical account of the systematic subordination of women in western society and culture by the myth of femininity informs Daly's theological account of the doctrinal subordination of women by the patriarchal theism of 'the Church'.

Yet it is noteworthy that at the early stage in her intellectual development Daly, unlike Beauvoir, engages theologically with Roman Catholicism on feminist grounds. In *Beyond God the Father* she calls for philosophers of religion to rethink the theistic conception of God, especially the divine attributes of omnipotence, immutability and providence. *Beyond God the Father* argues against the immutable, providential power of the God of monotheism. This philosophical argument still

---

    15   Mary Daly, *The Church and the Second Sex* (Boston: Beacon Press, 1968).

holds potential interest for contemporary philosophy of religion. Daly's feminist rethinking of theism draws intelligently on existentialism, while also exhibiting significant knowledge of Thomism. Taken literally, *Beyond God the Father* argues that the fatherhood of God with all his 'omni'-attributes should be transcended, if women are to be liberated from patriarchal oppression. After Daly's use of 'transcendence', this concept will be taken up by later generations of feminist philosophers of religion as an alternative to the concept of an anthropomorphic God.[16]

Daly herself claims to locate her critique of theism 'not merely on the boundary *between* these (male-created) disciplines [of philosophy and theology], but on the boundary *of* both, because it speaks out of the experience of that half of the human species which has been represented in neither discipline'.[17] From this dual-location, Daly proposes new concepts of God and of human consciousness for a philosophy of women's liberation. As she writes, 'The becoming of women implies universal human becoming. It has everything to do with the search for ultimate meaning and reality, which some would call God.'[18] Her transformation of theism aims to allow for 'human becoming', but it was and is not only directed to Roman Catholics or Christian theists, but to the 1960s 'women's revolution' and, it must be said, to contemporary feminist theists.

For Daly, the emancipation from 'God as Father' is liberation from a 'God being male' and so 'male being God'. This emancipation points beyond the idolatries of sexist society and its gender hierarchies. Daly proposes that 'the courage to be' is the key to 'the revelatory power' of the feminist revolution. The freedom for both women and men as subjects to search for ultimate meaning of reality is revelatory in uncovering what some would call a dynamic God. Perhaps Daly's most significant philosophical proposal in her philosophy of women's liberation is that the theistic conception of God can no longer be thought of as a noun. Instead 'God' is a verb. God is 'the most active and dynamic of all [verbs]'. Her conception of becoming has similarities to Beauvoir's existentialism and the role of a dynamic process of freedom in becoming who we are. However,

---

[16] Pamela Sue Anderson, 'Transcendence and Feminist Philosophy: On Avoiding Apotheosis', in Gillian Howie and J'annine Jobling (eds), *Women and the Divine: Touching Transcendence*. New York: Palgrave, 2009, pp. 27–54; Patrice Haynes, 'Transcendence, Materialism and the Re-enchantment of Nature: Toward a Theological Materialism', *Women and the Divine*, pp. 55–78; Mike King, 'Cutting "God" Down to Size: Transcendence and the Feminine', *Women and the Divine*, pp. 153–170. On an idea of 'transcendence incarnate', see Pamela Sue Anderson, 'The Lived Body, Gender and Confidence', in Pamela Sue Anderson (ed.), *New Topics in Feminist Philosophy of Religion: Contestations and Transcendence Incarnate* (Dordrecht; London; New York: Springer, 2010), pp. 163–180. For the most recent Continental philosophical conception of immanent transcendence, see Patrice Haynes, *Immanent Transcendence: Reconfiguring Materialism in Continental Philosophy*, Bloomsbury Studies in Continental Philosophy (London: Continuum, 2012).

[17] Daly, *Beyond God the Father*, p. 6.

[18] Ibid.

this conception of becoming (gendered subjects) was and still is problematic, if fixating bi-gender stereotypes.

In the end, Daly renounces Christianity completely becoming one of the first self-proclaimed post-Christian feminists. Daly replaces Catholic theology with a creative use of language. *Gyn/Ecology: The Meta-Ethics of Radical Feminism* (1978); *Pure Lust: Elemental Feminist Philosophy* (1984); *Outercourse: The Be-Dazzling Voyage* (1993); *Quintessence: Realizing the Archaic Future* (1998) are some of her provocative titles.[19] These are for a radical post-Christian feminism which no longer advocated any form of theism. However, Daly's creative genius in philosophy (of religion) continued to point to deep emotional, psychological and spiritual problems in the lives of women, and indirectly, of men.

New feminist forms of theism

In the second decade of the twentieth century, feminist interventions into philosophical debates about Christian theism continue. However, in contemporary feminist philosophy of religion, the feminist attempts to engage with non-Christian theism have been sharply dismissed.[20] Due to strong resistance, feminist interventions into global theisms are perhaps less persuasive – and certainly less radical – than Daly's early and later interventions into western theism. Anglo-American philosophy of religion has been slow to include Daly as a philosopher of religion, and even slower to recognize the history of 'feminism' in theism.

Certain indications exist that a transformation of the field of philosophy of religion is, however gradually, happening. 'Theism' is slowly being seen in more than Christian forms; and the tweaking of gender-terms and of gendered examples on the fringes of theistic arguments is underway. More radical change would seem to be inevitable, *if* the arguments put forth about 'a future theism' by feminist theologians who follow after Daly such as Daphne Hampson and Grace M. Jantzen are taken seriously. Hampson and Jantzen each tirelessly challenge the philosopher as 'the theistic man-God'. Their descriptions of the deifed male subject of theism stand for all that has been thought to be positive and neutral in philosophy (of religion); they are being shown as far from that. For too long, 'the theist' has been socially and materially located and represented by a particular group of Christian male philosophers. Yet 'he', the Christian philosopher, has

---

[19]   Mary Daly, *Gyn/Ecology: the Meta-Ethics of Radical Feminism* (Boston: Beacon Press, 1978); *Pure Lust: Elemental Feminist Philosophy* (Boston: Beacon Press, 1984); *Outercourse: the Be-Dazzling Voyage* (London: The Women's Press, 1993); *Quintessence: Realizing the Archaic Future* (Boston: Beacon Press, 1998).

[20]   Sarah Coakley, 'Feminism and Analytic Philosophy of Religion', in William J. Wainwright (ed.), *The Oxford Handbook to Philosophy of Religion* (Oxford: Oxford University Press, 2005), p. 512; cf. Anderson, *A Feminist Philosophy of Religion*.

increasingly been forced by political, social and ethical pressures to recognize his gender and the 'male-neutral' perspectives of his theistic beliefs and practices.[21]

Broadly speaking, feminists in philosophy of religion would like the philosopher to see how his relation to, and concept of, 'God' has served as his ego-ideal, excluding all that is not the male ideal. As a kind of nothingness alongside the full purity of the man of reason, the female body has been, in Julia Kristeva's terms, abject, polluted, defiled and devalued.[22] In the history of the philosophy of religion, it is not only the female body, but the female intellect which has been metaphorically and literally associated with the 'other' side of philosophy. In some feminist debates in philosophy of religion, the female way of knowing continues to be associated with the 'soft'-edges of philosophy rather than 'hard core' of (male) philosophy; the latter is represented by the all-powerful being of God whose hard ego-boundaries serve as the male ideal of the subject without dependence on any other. These distorted stereotypical and generally self-deluded images in philosophy are to be, and in some locations have been, addressed. But these are, it must be said, only the tip of an iceberg.

Women like Hampson and Jantzen have attempted to expose the gendered nature of the traditional theist's ways of knowing in philosophy of religion, while questioning 'the master's own tools' within analytic philosophy of religion. Jantzen has proposed an alternative in her 'feminist philosophy of religion'. This is in sharp contrast to a feminist theologian within analytical philosophy of religion such as Sarah Coakley who attempts to gender the field by locating the feminine soft-spots within philosophical texts.[23] The problem with the latter is that Coakley leaves the much deeper dangers of theism and its masculinist injustices untouched.

'Knowing the difference' between surface changes to gender stereotypes and deep shifts aimed at uncovering and alleviating the pernicious injustices of theism has been strongly advocated by Jantzen; her own proposals for an Irigarayan-inspired project of 'becoming divine,' culminates in an Irigarayan-like pantheism.[24] Jantzen is not afraid of bold contentions for women and pantheism as a timely form for a new, broadly construed, 'theism', Jantzen argues that 'the idea of divine embodiment' is not merely 'an adjustment to classical theism'; it is 'a disruption of the dualistic and hierarchical western symbolic'.[25] Her insistence

---

[21] Ibid., p. 13.

[22] Julia Kristeva, *Powers of Horror: An Essay on Abjection*, trans. Leon S. Roudiez (New York: Columbia University Press, 1982), pp. 54–57, 70–79.

[23] Coakley, 'Feminism and Analytic Philosophy of Religion', pp. 494–525.

[24] Grace M. Jantzen, 'What's the Difference: Knowledge and Gender in (Post) Modern Philosophy of Religion', *Religious Studies*, 32 (1996): 431–448. Reprinted in Pamela Sue Anderson and Beverley Clack (eds), *Feminist Philosophy of Religion: Critical Readings* (London: Routledge, 2004), pp. 28–41; and Grace M. Jantzen, 'Feminism and Pantheism', *The Monist: An International Journal of General Philosophical Inquiry*, 80, 2 (April 1997): 266–285. Further discussion of Jantzen's proposals for feminist philosophy of religion and for a feminist pantheism, see Chapter 7 (below).

[25] Ibid., p. 283.

upon pantheism informs her feminist appropriation of Irigaray's 'divine as a horizon of becoming'. For Jantzen, this means 'exploring the embodied, earthed, female divine as the perfection of our subjectivity'.[26] Here she affirms Irigaray's urging that we must be not 'awaiting the god passively, but bringing the god to life through us'.[27]

Similar to Irigaray, but not following French psycholinguistics, Hampson's proposal for a new form of theism draws inspiration from the American development of object-relations psychology concerning women's relational differences to men.[28] Hampson's crucial distinctiveness is evident in her insistence upon a move away from anthropomorphism and from a Feuerbachian projection of either an ideal male self or an ideal female self. Instead Hampson wipes 'the slate clean of an anthropomorphically conceived God, be "he" more or less, powerful', in order to reconceive theism as 'a conviction that there is more to reality than meets the eye; that there are powers on which we may draw; that we are profoundly connected with what is in excess of what we are'.[29] At an early stage in her theistic proposal, Hampson admits that a valid question is what we intend when we use the word 'God'. At later stages, she clearly and confidently employs 'God' in carefully crafted phrases for a future theism. For example, she speaks of her conception of the reality of theism as 'that which is of God'.[30] She also argues that 'On both epistemological and moral grounds it is incumbent upon us to speak otherwise of that love and power which we may truly name 'God'.[31] Hampson tries to carve out the reality of God by attending to the experiences of women and of men who do not identify with the anthropomorphic omni-attributes of the traditional theistic God, but who still *hold onto* the idea of the self's relations to God. Hampson insists that we have misunderstood God because we have based 'God' on a misconception of the self.

'God' has been seen as monadic; this concept has then been projected as an anthropomorphic other, transcendent over us. But our experience suggests a very different understanding as to what it is that God may be. We should be considering the way in which, across its boundaries, the self lies open to that which is beyond itself, such that we are intimately connected with 'God'. We no longer have time for a concept of God as a discrete monad, set over against us in hierarchal fashion, such that God's strength and goodness serve but to show up our weakness and sinfulness.[32]

---

[26]   Ibid.

[27]   Ibid.; cf. Irigaray, Divine Women, p. 63.

[28]   Hampson, *After Christianity*, pp. 213–253; 'That Which Is God', pp. 171–186.

[29]   Hampson, *After Christianity*, p. 253.

[30]   Hampson, 'That Which is God', pp. 171ff.

[31]   Daphne Hampson, 'Searching for God?' in John Cornwell and Michael McGhee (eds), *Philosophers and God: At the Frontiers of Faith and Reason* (London: Continuum, 2009), p. 76.

[32]   Hampson, 'That Which is God', pp. 176–177.

The above passage alone might not appear to say anything about feminism. But behind Hampson's argument for a re-conceptualization of theism is an awareness of feminist arguments such as Daly's against God the Father who as Creator retains all the power, while Eve personifies weakness and sinfulness by leading Adam to fall from a state of perfection. Moreover, Hampson has attended to the history of conceptions of God and to the evidence of religious experiences of that which is beyond and exceeds the self – as something women may have known – but that men have not known insofar as they have conceptualized God as 'above', as eternal, changeless, i.e., like a Platonic form which is completely transcendent of the human body and physical world. Instead, insists Hampson, God must be found through human discernment, not just through openness to the world, but through living in the world, 'to that which is God'.

As a self-declared post-Christian feminist theologian Hampson may not (yet) be known to contemporary philosophers of religion. However, in recent years Hampson's arguments for understanding the non-anthropomorphic reality of God offer much to those feminist philosophers interested in contemporary theism.[33] Hampson conceives a theism which is ethically and epistemologically consistent with gender equality, but without the dangers of projecting ideal male or female attributes onto God, and then, having to retrieve them for oneself.[34] In the end, Hampson aims to render feminism and theism compatible by re-conceiving God.

Feminist 'methods' within theism

The focus of this chapter so far has been largely on conceptions of theism and of feminism as different ways of understanding male and female subjects in relation to the divine. However, feminism in philosophy of religion also manifests itself in its gender assessment of the practices of theism. Theistic practice includes the methods employed to justify theistic beliefs as rational, but also the methods employed to gain access to the divine. Hampson advocates a non-technical method for accessing God through the self's openness and active attention to the reality which is the world and the relations in that world. However, there are feminists in philosophy of religion who push the idea of intimate relations to God much further, advocating sexually specific, or 'gendered', experiences of God as intimacy with the divine.

For example, Coakley advocates that Christian women embrace their 'power in weakness' before God.[35] She works out her feminism within theism and the

---

[33] Hampson, *After Christianity*; 'That Which is God'; 'Searching for God?'; and Hampson 2010.

[34] Hampson, 'That Which is God', pp. 172–178.

[35] Sarah Coakley, '*Kenosis* and Subversion: On the Repression of "Vulnerability" in Christian Feminist Writings', in Daphne Hampson (ed.), *Swallowing A Fishbone? Feminist Theologians Debate Christianity* (London: SPCK, 1996), pp. 82–111.

field of Christian analytical philosophy of religion. She claims to exploit the blind spots in the dominant methods of Anglo-American philosophers of religion for feminist ends.[36] In this process of gendering some of the key core texts in the field, Coakley has examined the arguments for theism presented by William Alston, Richard Swinburne, Alvin Plantinga and Nicholas Wolterstorff with an eye to any significant gendered ways of knowing. She unravels the gendered standpoints concealed in Alston's notion of doxastic practice of Christian devotion, exploits the places in Swinburne's argument for the existence of God where he exposes a soft epistemic centre, say, of reliance on others or on trust, and brings out the elements of vulnerability expressed in Wolterstorff's conception of belief and Plantinga's proper basicality. Her contention is that despite themselves these (male) philosophers bring in what they elsewhere devalue as feminine forms of subjectivity, including trust, vulnerability and suffering. Traces of traditionally feminine qualities indicate places at which feelings, including erotic passion, reveal a bodily relationship between human and divine. Coakley's gendering of our ways of knowing has been revealing and significant for feminist philosophy of religion.

And yet, if the methodological practice of exposing gender soft-spots is extended beyond the practices of a core group of Anglo-American Christian analytic philosophers of religion, the content of gender becomes problematic; that is, what Coakley identifies as gendered properties cannot be easily fixed onto men or onto women outside this social grouping. Moreover, the idea that either men or women in theism should cultivate their weakness, their vulnerability and other soft dimensions of their philosophical virtues for theism and feminism has become increasingly dubious.[37] Coakley's feminist method in assessing theistic practices is undermined by her mistaken assumptions about gender and sweeping generalizations about gendered virtues. Moreover, Coakley advocates no explicit change to the dominant conception of the God of Christian theism in western philosophy of religion. Although to be fair, she does offer a legitimate defence of Christian theism for women and for men. For Christian 'feminists', this may be sufficient.

---

[36] Sarah Coakley, *Powers and Submissions: Spirituality, Philosophy and Gender* (Oxford: Blackwell, 2002), pp. 25–39, 98–105; cf. Pamela Sue Anderson, 'Feminist Theology as Philosophy of Religion', in Susan Franks Parsons (ed.), *The Cambridge Companion to Feminist Theology* (Cambridge: Cambridge University Press, 2002), pp. 40–59.

[37] Pamela Sue Anderson, '"Moralizing" Love in Philosophy of Religion', in Jerald T. Wallulis and Jeremiah Hackett (eds), *Philosophy of Religion for a New Century* (Amsterdam: Kluwer Academic Publishers, 2004), pp. 227–242; Anderson, 'Liberating Love's Capabilities: On the Wisdom of Love', pp. 201–226; Anderson, 'The Lived Body, Gender and Confidence', pp. 163–180.

Nevertheless, if considered more closely by a feminist philosopher, Coakley's theological use of the distinction between the hard, masculine way of knowing and what is said to be the soft epistemic centre of philosophers' texts will appear to keep women and the feminine where masculinist theists want women: that is, in a different sphere which can, at most, inform the male philosopher's 'feminine' side. Coakley's feminist method associates feminine virtues with softness, intimacy and sexuality. Her appeal to women's experiences of gender-specific intimacy with a male God and to the feminine emotional capacities which they can share, even with masculine theists, is provocative. Recognizing gender differences for the theist leads Coakley to advocate sharing characteristically feminine and characteristically masculine qualities between women and men. However, she does not explicitly question whether these feminine 'virtues' of vulnerability and weakness are constructed strictly in relation to and exclusively for access to a God whose very nature depends upon a hierarchy of masculine over feminine virtues.

Coakley claims that Anderson's project in *A Feminist Philosophy of Religion* eclipses 'any intimacy with' the divine.[38] Yet this claim contains an uncritical assumption that 'to intensify intimacy with the known'[39] is an unquestionably positive possibility. No question of self-deception (whether this intimacy is more than narcissism or bad faith) or the dangers of abuse by the other (whether by actual men or by the masculinist projection of omnipotence) are raised when it comes to intimacy with the male God of theism. Moreover, to assume that Anderson eclipses intimacy runs the danger of projecting on to her an unfair intention. To be fair, Anderson should be assessed in relation to her own feminist aim to avoid the real physical and ethical dangers in being a kind of nothingness in the eyes of the other.

Anderson urges every woman to avoid an eclipse of herself by the other, especially to resist the way in which women have both demeaned themselves and been eclipsed by a man's patriarchal God. Beauvoir and Le Doeuff, but also Daly and Irigaray, each expose the pernicious nature of theism which has damaged the nascent female subject by imposing values which not only lack equality for women (to men), but ratify the innocent suffering of women who, like Eve, are 'abjected' precisely because of their knowledge of good and evil.[40] Although neither Beauvoir nor Le Doeuff advocates – as Irigaray does and as the later Daly comes close to – becoming divine (i.e., creating the divine out of a woman's gender), they both speak insightfully, on the one hand, to the problems of a debilitating narcissism

---

[38] Coakley, 'Feminism and Analytic Philosophy of Religion', in Wainwright (ed.), *The Oxford Handbook to Philosophy of Religion*, pp. 516–519.

[39] Ibid., p. 516.

[40] Anderson, 'The Lived Body, Gender and Confidence', pp. 163–180; cf. Julia Kristeva, *Powers of Horror: An Essay on Abjection*, trans. Leon S. Roudiez (New York: Columbia University Press, 1982).

and, on the other hand, of an absolute altruism whereby a woman becomes 'a kind of nothingness' in men's eyes for his use and his abuse.[41]

Without a balance of equality and reciprocity between male and female subjects to ensure the justice of interpersonal relations, theism can easily re-enforce the problem of a self-annihilating mysticism within patriarchal societies. Admittedly, justice is not the only goal of women in contemporary philosophy of religion. Even today some feminist political theorists, feminist psychologists and feminist philosophers would argue that an ethics of care, like an ethics of sexual difference which sustains loving relations, remains in a problematic tension with liberal theories of distributive justice whose goal is equality. The choice between love and justice is not straightforward. An Irigarayan feminism of sexual difference tends to prize love and human relations over formal claims to equality. It is especially difficult for Christian theists simply to dismiss Irigaray's ethics of sexual difference out of fear that love between men and women will eclipse justice and equality. Love, as agape, over equality is traditionally more attractive to Christians.

Yet it is at least arguable that Beauvoir's ethical critique of 'the second sex' anticipates – by almost thirty years – the serious dangers of Irigaray's assumptions concerning the divinized female body as the necessary, other-half of love. Uncovering the pernicious dangers of female narcissism as Beauvoir had seen it within the context of her particular French Catholic upbringing remains important as a form of suspicion, or critique, of both feminist and masculinist theisms. Yet neither Beauvoir nor Daly offers a completely fair picture of theism either. There is little doubt that Beauvoir's own account of Roman Catholic theism, female mysticism and the female-in-love remains limited by her early twentieth-century preoccupation with equality. Jantzen, Hampson and Coakley would each have very different things to say about the female mystic and her desire for intimacy with God.

Nevertheless, female love in Beauvoir is not only undermined by a choice between an annihilation of the body of the female mystic in her love of self/god or a transcendence of the body by the female mystic in her denial of imperfections of being human. Beauvoir offers one positive example of a female mystic: Teresa of Avila avoids paranoia and decisively debilitating narcissism. Teresa's achievement is, according to Beauvoir, due to the situated autonomy and reciprocity of the mystic's practical projects. This kind of mysticism shapes women of action who know very well what goals they have in mind and who lucidly devise means for attaining them. Their visions provide objective images for their certitudes, encouraging practically minded mystics to persist in the paths they have mapped out in detail for themselves.

Disagreements between feminists often rest on the question of feminine and masculine values, virtues or methods. Beauvoir seems to trust the objective methods and practical outcomes of mysticism, while Irigaray, Coakley and

---

[41]   Le Doeuff, *Hipparchia's Choice*, pp. 278–280.

Jantzen (and possibly Hampson) would mistrust such 'objectivity' which has been associated with men by their sexual difference feminism. Instead Coakley and, however different to Coakly, Irigaray would undoubtedly advocate the 'feminist' virtues of holding fast to subjective truth and to emotion-based connectedness.

Conclusion

To end with, perhaps the most quoted – and contentious – statement about women and theism, Irigaray asserts 'The only diabolical thing about women is their lack of a God.'[42] This assertion challenges the form of theism which has excluded or devalued women, leaving them without a god of their own, while deifying men. As seen above, the assumption that women lack a God in their own image is contentious for, and rejected by, some philosophers on both feminist and theistic grounds. Not every feminist philosopher of religion sees theism as a conception of an omniscient, omnipotent, omni-benevolent, omnipresent, eternal or everlasting God whose attributes and *aseity* are merely a projection of an exclusively male ideal. Yet Irigaray is seductively provocative in persuading women, like men, that they need a God(dess) as an ego-ideal for a female subject.

In a positive sense, the Irigarayan critique of Christian theism has helped to expose male supremacy in the form of an exclusively masculinist projection of love relations onto God the Father. Accompanying this critique is Irigaray's imperative that each woman seek a direct relation to her own God. The critical issue is whether 'God' functions as the projection of human gender onto an ideal, while this ideal needs to become both the ground and the goal for a subject's gender identity. This latter assumption could be the crux of the matter. Gender could have functioned in this (possibly positive) manner, in the mind and in the cultures of men globally, and yet to the serious detriment of women. In a negative sense, if Irigaray shows projection of a gender exclusive ideal to be the problem, then it follows that female deification (becoming a gendered subject in the form of her own ideal-divine) may enable women, like men, to achieve both great and diabolical things, e.g., diabolical when it comes to their treatment of the other sex. Granted Irigarayan feminism teaches philosophers of religion that theism should take more seriously the psychological and anthropological critiques of personal relations, especially when theistic philosophers have the power to shape our personal relations and to make claims for concrete life and love. Yet, is becoming divine an unequivocally positive goal for either feminist or masculinist theism? We will return to this question in later chapters.

Without the various philosophical critiques of theism which have been developed within feminism, the danger of failure would remain for the philosopher who holds an uncritical conception of the traditional theistic God. The pernicious failure would be not to hear and/or not to understand the innocent cries of women

---

[42]   Irigaray, *Divine Women*, p. 64.

and of men who have been destroyed by the absolute power, the narrowly defined providence and the exclusive purposes of (sexual) supremacists in the name of their God.

Chapter 4
Philosophy on and off 'the Continent'[1]

Introduction: a divided field

As already recognized when discussing Jantzen and Helm in Chapter 2, 'Continental'[2] is a term used to describe a distinctive approach to doing philosophy (of religion). In Jantzen's case, she identified her own proposals in feminist philosophy of religion with the 'Continental' tradition. Yet the received view has been that Anglo-American philosophers do 'philosophy of religion', or more recently, it has been claimed that analytic philosophers of religion are philosophical theologians – some of whom would liked to be known as 'analytic theologians'.[3] Neither the Continental nor the Anglo-American analytic approach should be thought to give either the whole or the best picture of philosophy of religion. This is a field which continues to grow and expand. At the end of the previous century, a popular reply to the question 'who does "Continental" philosophy of religion?' would have been, 'Jacques Derrida'! Yet today many other names come to mind.

What made Derrida's philosophy 'Continental' or non-analytic is a focus of the present chapter. Which topics in Derrida's writings, would other philosophers in the field recognize as philosophy of religion? This chapter will offer indirect answers to this question through an exploration of an especially relevant philosophical exchange, between Jacques Derrida and A. W. Moore, not long before Derrida's

---

[1]   This chapter draws material from two previously published essays: Pamela Sue Anderson, 'Ineffable Knowledge and Gender', in Philip Goodchild (ed), *Rethinking Philosophy of Religion: Approaches from Continental Philosophy*, series edited by John Caputo (New York: Fordham University Press, 2002), pp. 162–183; and 'Gender and the infinite: On the aspiration to be all there is', *International Journal for Philosophy of Religion*, Issues in Contemporary Philosophy of Religion on the Occasion of the 50th vol., no. 1–3 (December 2001): 191–212.

[2]   For a more recent and extremely helpful account of the changing status of 'Continental' philosophy of religion, see Bruce Ellis Benson, 'Continental Philosophy of Religion', in Paul Copan and Chad Meister (eds), *Philosophy of Religion: Classic and Contemporary Issues* (Malden, Mass: Wiley Blackwell), pp. 231–244.

[3]   A more recent distinction in the field of philosophy of religion, which is in addition to that of Continental and analytic philosophers, aims to distinguish those analytic philosophers of religion who have begun also to call themselves 'analytic theologians'; this distinguished the latter from other Continental philosophical theologians and other philosophers of religion, see the review essay, William Wood, 'On the New Analytic Theology, Or the Road Less Travelled', *Journal of the American Academy of Religion*, 77/4 (December 2009): 941–960.

own death. On this occasion in 1999, Derrida also had an exchange with five other British philosophers. But the present focus is this one exchange at the interface of what has been labelled 'Continental' and 'Anglo-American' (analytic) philosophies on a topic which, as will be argued, is timely for philosophy of religion today: ineffability.

Clearly known as an analytic and Anglo-American philosopher, A. W. Moore took part in 'Arguing with Derrida' and began by making a new distinction concerning two styles of philosophy.[4] Instead of using 'analytic' or 'Continental', Moore proposed the adjective 'conceptual' to describe himself as an Oxford philosopher who was endeavouring to 'argue with' Derrida; and Derrida could be called a 'non-conceptual' philosopher. The change from analytic to conceptual in Moore's self-description helps philosophically to understand the styles of 'arguing with' that brought together these two contemporary philosophers who had been trained philosophically in different geographical locations and with different approaches to doing philosophy.

After stipulating the conceptual and non-conceptual distinction, Moore turns to a topic in conceptual philosophy and, as will be shown here, in both non-conceptual and conceptual philosophy of religion: that is, ineffable knowledge.[5] The present chapter follows this exchange as both an indirect approach to Continental philosophy of religion and an approach on the edge of the analytic philosophy of religion practiced under the label, 'Anglo-American'. Ineffable knowledge will take us to a philosophically significant meeting point for philosophers on and off 'the Continent', as well as for feminist analytic and Continental philosophers.[6] In a manner of speaking, the challenge is to build bridges or, simply, 'to connect'.

An unusual occasion and its upshot

Derrida himself listened and responded to Moore in person.[7] This was an unusual occasion when Derrida bowed to the generous nature of a philosopher who had attempted to find points for the convergence of perspectives which had previously been sharply divided. This occasion was also momentous in the light of certain

---

[4]   A. W. Moore, 'Arguing with Derrida', *Ratio: An International Journal of Analytic Philosophy*, Special Issue, edited by Simon Glendinning, XIII/4 (December 2000): 355–381. On this occasion of revisiting a former debate between a British analytic philosopher and Derrida, see Simon Glendinning, 'Inheriting 'Philosophy': The Case of Austin and Derrida Revisited', *Ratio*, XIII/4 (December 2000): 307 n1.

[5]   A. W. Moore, 'Ineffability and Religion', *European Journal of Philosophy*, 11/2 (2003): 161–176.

[6]   Analytic and Continental philosophers of religion can find further background for this exchange in A. W. Moore, *The Infinite* (London: Routledge, 1990; second edition, with a new Preface, 2001); and *Points of View* (Oxford: Oxford University Press, 1997).

[7]   Jacques Derrida, 'Response to Moore', *Ratio: An International Journal of Analytic Philosophy*, Special Issue, edited by Simon Glendinning, XIII/4 (December 2000): 381–386.

past failures to bridge the philosophical divide between the Continent (notably, France) and Britain. In his response, Derrida alluded to thirty years earlier when both the idea and the reality of an Oxford philosopher arguing with him (Derrida!) had proved impossible.[8] The change in philosophy over those years is what made it possible to imagine new relations and attitudes developing between the French and the British in philosophy.

However, a notable dimension of this momentous occasion that went without question was the gender of the speakers. Perhaps gender did not matter in this performative exchange! Yet it appeared to be a gender exclusive exchange with an all-male list of six conference speakers, confronting Derrida with their broadly similar material and social backgrounds (despite the geographical connotations of the adjectives used to describe their different philosophical approaches). Using a term which was popular in the 1990s, we could call the panel of speakers arguing with Derrida, 'male-neutral'.[9] In other words, the philosophical assumption seemed to be one of arguing from a gender-neutral perspective, yet the maleness was conspicuous from another perspective.

After what might be criticized as a 'male-neutral' exchange between the style of Derrida as non-conceptual philosopher and the style of Moore as conceptual philosopher, my philosophical interest should consider feminist uses of Derrida. Can Derrida, or 'feminist' Derrideans, address the question of gender, notably, in female forms of mysticism?[10] But here I am suggesting new philosophical uses of Moore to address the question of ineffability. Two styles of philosophy, conceptual and non-conceptual, seemingly came together in the Moore-Derrida exchange. In turn, this has made possible, in retrospect, my own feminist reflection

---

[8]   On 'the gulf' made explicit between Continental and analytic philosophers by R. M. Hare and Gilbert Ryle thirty years ago at the time when Derrida wrote '*Différance*', see Simon Glendinning, 'The Ethics of Exclusion: Incorporating the Continent', in Richard Kearney and Mark Dooley (eds), *Questioning Ethics: Contemporary Debates in Philosophy* (London: Routledge, 2000), pp. 120–131. Glendinning makes reference to two papers from that period, confirming this gulf, as well as equating British philosophy with Oxford philosophers, see R. M. Hare, 'A School for Philosophers', *Ratio*, II/2 (1960); Gilbert Ryle, 'Phenomenology versus *The Concept of Mind*', reprinted in Gilbert Ryle, *Collected Papers* (London: Hutchinson, 1971). Also see the contribution to the Special Issue on 'Arguing with Derrida' by Glendinning, 'Inheriting "Philosophy": The Case of Austin and Derrida Revisited', 307–331; cf. Jacques Derrida, '*Différance*' and 'Signature, Event, Context', *Margins of Philosophy*, trans. Alan Bass (Chicago: University of Chicago Press, 1982), pp. 1–28 and 307–330.

[9]   Pamela Sue Anderson, *A Feminist Philosophy of Religion: the Rationality and Myths of Religious Belief* (Oxford: Blackwell, 1998), p. 36.

[10]   Grace M. Jantzen, *Power, Gender and Christian Mysticism* (Cambridge: Cambridge University Press, 1995); Amy Hollywood, *The Soul as Virgin Wife: Mechthild of Magdeburg, Marguerite Porete and Meister Eckhart* (Notre Dame: Notre Dame University Press, 1995); and *Sensible Ecstasy: Sexual Difference and the Demands of History* (Chicago: University of Chicago Press, 2002).

on their male-neutral exchange, on both the style and the content of their thinking. In addition, the current reflection can be further contextualized by locating philosophical theologians either on or off 'the Continent'; two that come to mind are Jean-Luc Marion in France and William Alston in the USA who have written on mysticism and language from two different locations, with two different styles of philosophizing.

So, on the one hand, let us bring in the Continental and feminist philosophers of religion who, in writing on mysticism, have employed the theological term, 'apophatic', to describe the mystical experience of emptying language of content. This experience is often associated with negative theology. Alternatively, the philosophical mystic might claim that the apophatic is simply an inexpressible experience of union with a transcendent being, as in a feeling of an absolute oneness. Apophatic practice can be contrasted to 'cataphatic' practice in meditation and other religious rites. Instead of emptying language of content, the cataphatic fills the practice with expressible content.

Both conceptual and non-conceptual philosophers could give attention to apophatic practice as ineffable or inexpressible (knowledge). Moreover, feminist attention has been given to those women whose mystical experience crosses gender-boundaries and moves toward ineffability.[11] Two non-feminist examples of explicitly Continental approaches to mysticism are the American philosophical theologian Thomas Carlson and the French phenomenologist of religion, Jean-Luc Marion. Carlson and Marion have each concerned themselves with the problem of naming God on the basis of mysticism.[12]

On the other hand, let us bring in the Christian analytic philosophers/theologians and, more generally, Anglo-American philosophers of religion, as well as feminist philosophers writing on ineffability. The feminist philosopher of religion Grace M. Jantzen wrote analytically about Continental philosophers's contributions to discussions of power and gender in Christian mysticism.[13] Similar to Moore's discussions of ineffability, Jantzen is willing to argue with, in Moore's terms, non-conceptual philosophers from a position in analytic philosophy. Yet the most well-known Christian Anglo-American analytic philosopher of religion, writing in the twentieth-century on mysticism and ineffability was the late William Alston.[14]

---

[11]   Kitty Scoular Datta, 'Female Heterologies: Women's Mysticism, Gender-Mixing and the Apophatic', in Heather Walton and Andrew W. Haas (eds), *Self/Same/Other: Re-visioning the Subject in Literature and Theology* (Sheffield: Sheffield Academic Press, 2000), pp. 125–136.

[12]   Thomas A. Carlson, *Indiscretion: Finitude and the Naming of God* (Chicago: University of Chicago Press, 1999); and Jean-Luc Marion, 'In the Name: How to Avoid Speaking of "Negative Theology"', in John D. Caputo and Micheal J. Scanlon (eds), *God, The Gift and Postmodernism* (Bloomington, IN: Indiana University Press, 1999), pp. 20–53.

[13]   Jantzen, *Power, Gender and Christian Mysticism*, pp. 101–109, 278–321; Moore, 'Ineffability and Religion', 161–176; cf. A. W. Moore, *The Infinite* (second edition, London: Routledge, 2001), pp. 186–203; *Points of View*, pp. xii, 75, 142, 146–156, 164, 166, 200.

[14]   William Alston, 'Ineffability', *Philosophical Review*, 65/4 (1956): 506–522.

Although Marion offers an argument directed to Continental philosophers of religion, to avoid negative theology and, especially the 'metaphysics of presence', he also exhibits a similarity to the conceptual philosopher A. W. Moore writing on 'infinite'.[15] Marion contends that the infinite offers a way to talk without saying something about something, and so without the metaphysical commitment to affirmations and negations of truth. Marion illustrates this 'third way' of talking without saying something in a careful reading of the fifth-century philosophical theologian, Pseudo-Denys, who is perhaps better known as Dionysius. According to Marion, the thought of Dionysius has been wrongly reduced to negative theology. Instead as Marion argues, Dionysius can be found to 'speak divine truth as the experience of incomprehension', and not negation as affirmation of what is not. Marion endeavours to articulate his third way in terms of the pragmatic use of language as 'de-nomination'. As will be explained in more detailed, Moore himself might call this 'showing', or talking nonsense. For both Marion and Moore, a third way between effability and ineffability does not give up a commitment to truth, but it gives up 'saying' or denying it. Marion also associates de-nomination with a 'saturated phenomenon', since there is an excess of intuition, saturating the measure of each and every concept.[16]

Despite the different styles in approaching philosophy on and off the Continent, overlapping issues open up the possibility of a new area of philosophical debate concerning the infinite, the ineffable and the mystical. If successful, this area of debate could offer new common ground for philosophers of religion, whether the philosophers are theist or atheist, non-naturalist or naturalist, feminist or non-feminist. This common ground would bring together Anglo-American philosophers of religion and British and French philosophers in an exploration of mysticism and mystical practices, but also other religious practices as forms of ineffable knowledge.

An additional, marked difference in philosophy of religion in the English-speaking world exists between the philosopher's and the theologian's conceptual frameworks. This difference does not just follow the analytic and Continental, or conceptual and non-conceptual, divide. Instead it becomes even more complex when the philosopher is analytic and the theologian is informed by cultural theorists, social historians and psycholinguists who could be either on or off the Continent. The next section will consider the different approaches to contemporary philosophy, as well as the shared concerns for philosophy of religion. The gender issues running through this chapter are gradually coming into play.

---

[15]   Jean-Luc Marion, 'In the Name: How to Avoid Speaking of "Negative Theology"', pp. 20–53; cf. Moore, 'Ineffability and Religion', pp. 161–176; cf. Moore, *The Infinite*, pp. 186–203.

[16]   Marion, 'In the Name', p. 40.

On mysticism and ineffable knowledge

Anglo-American philosophy as apparent in Moore's writings on ineffable knowledge can be far more philosophically nuanced and insightful than evident in the criticisms made of this contemporary style of philosophy by certain Continental and feminist critics such as Jantzen.[17] Despite difficulties due to different approaches, careful study reveals that Continental philosophy shares common concerns with, since influencing crucial strands of, analytic philosophy; and vice versa! Even Derrida himself admitted to being closer to a conceptual philosopher, as defined by Moore, than to the so-called Continental side. Derrida insists, '… there are many misunderstandings of what I am trying to do, and it's perhaps because I am not simply on the "continental" side'.[18]

One of the shared concerns is ineffable knowledge. Consider how, according to Moore, ineffability is 'shown' in 'images of infinitude'. The significance of showing what cannot be said from Moore's philosophical writings is its affinity to the psycholinguistics writings of the highly influential Continental feminist Luce Irigaray.[19] Irigaray, for her part, 'mimes' the ways in which philosophers, as Moore suggests in his exchange with Derrida, 'make play' with images of infinitude. Moore and, I suggest, Irigaray know at some level that this making play involves prescinding the limitations of human finitude. Moore, for his part, identifies Derrida's play with images as one broad area of (the unwitting) attempts to put ineffable knowledge into words which results in nonsense.[20]

In 'Arguing with Derrida' Moore admits that he does not intend to represent analytic as opposed to Continental philosophy. Instead he aims to demonstrate how philosophically nuanced perspectives, or 'styles' of philosophy, can converge. Admittedly there is plenty of resistance to and misunderstanding of, what Moore calls, 'a play with nonsense'.[21] Nevertheless, Moore represents, not just an exception, but an increasing tendency for philosophical concerns to converge, if

---

[17]   For feminist criticism of the infinite in analytic philosophy, see Jantzen, *Power, Gender and Christian Mysticism*, pp. 101–109, 278–321 and 344–345, and *Becoming Divine: Towards a Feminist Philosophy of Religion* (Manchester: Manchester University Press, 1998), pp. 154–155, 177–178.

[18]   Derrida, 'Response to Moore', p. 382.

[19]   Anderson, 'Gender and the Infinite', pp. 193–203. For examples of what might constitute these images of infinitude, see Luce Irigaray, *Elemental Passions*, trans. Joanne Collie and Judith Still (London: The Athlone Press, 1992), pp. 28–29; and Irigaray, 'Place, Interval: A Reading of Aristotle, *Physics* IV', and 'Love of the Same, Love of the Other', in her *An Ethics of Sexual Difference*, trans. Carolyn Burke and Gillian C. Gill (London: The Athlone Press, 1993), pp. 34–58 and 109–110, respectively.

[20]   Moore, 'Arguing with Derrida', pp. 363–365; also, see Moore, *Points of View*, pp. 197–203, 216–219.

[21]   See, for example, the review of *Points of View* by Jerry Fodor, 'Cat's Whiskers', *London Review of Books* (30 October 1997): 16–17, and also the response by Moore, 'Cat's Whiskers', *London Review of Books* (27 November 1997): 8.

at times unwittingly, to cross former divisions. For one thing, both the analytic and the Continental philosopher exhibit a significant awareness of the perspectival nature of philosophical thinking. For another thing, changes in philosophical understandings of science and possibly renewed interest in metaphysical questions (about frameworks of belief, realism, and anti-realism) have encouraged a tendency to dialogue across these former divides.

As indicated already, in 'Arguing with Derrida', Moore introduces himself as a conceptual philosopher rather than an analytic philosopher. So, his philosophical activities are not restricted to the ultimate task of the scientist, i.e. to produce truth alone. Yet, as he admits, both the scientist and the conceptual philosopher are concerned with the affirmation of a true proposition, or its denial. Ultimately, as a conceptual philosopher Moore both seeks clarity for increased understanding and retains a commitment to truth.[22] In Moore's words,

> an ineffable state of knowledge is one that cannot be expressed by means of a truth. It doesn't have content; if you like, it doesn't share content with any truth – where what a truth is … is just a declarative sentence, which is true rather than false. … When someone has ineffable knowledge there is no truth to be stated.[23]

However, crucially, Moore would reject as impossible the conception of either a conceptual philosopher or a natural scientist as someone who *only* affirms truth in the sense of representing what is. Nevertheless, insofar as he intends (theoretically) to produce truth, Moore differs from Derrida. Agreement between them is evident in their, however implicit, quests for understanding; and even possibly in a certain 'commitment' to truth. Derrida admits that insofar as this commitment is not a theoretical matter, but an 'engagement which calls for performative gestures', he also has a commitment to truth: 'if only to question the possibility of truth'.[24] Moreover, Moore is willing to engage with Derrida in a detached way in playing with nonsense. For example, when he puts a word in inverted commas the meaning of the word is waived; in this way, a word that is merely mentioned does not have to have a sense, but neither does it entail talking nonsense.[25] The crucial question for the present chapter is whether this use of inverted commas exhibits a significant possibility for debates not only about ineffable knowledge, but about mysticism.

Aiming to clarify his conceptual task Moore offers a definition of ineffable knowledge, in apparent agreement with Derrida, as 'what resists expression by any *customary* linguistic means; and, more particularly and more pertinently, we can say that it is what resists expression by means of the affirmation of truths'.[26] Moore stresses that ineffable knowledge is *shown*, and so, makes a critical distinction

---

[22] Moore, *Points of View*, pp. 2–3, 28–31.

[23] Moore, 'Arguing with Derrida', p. 276.

[24] Derrida, 'Response to Moore', p. 382.

[25] Moore, 'Arguing With Derrida', pp. 368, 372.

[26] Ibid., p. 362.

between 'know-how' and 'knowing that'. The former can be understood as practical knowledge, while the later has been the concern of analytic philosophers when it comes to (propositional) truth.

Moreover, it is common to hear a feminist epistemologist claim that far too much has been excluded from philosophical conceptions of knowledge in focusing exclusively on propositional truth. For instance, women's practical knowledge has often been dismissed as 'old wives' tales'.[27] In the words of Vrinda Dalmiya and Linda Alcoff,

> Traditional women's beliefs – about childbearing and rearing, herbal medicines, the secrets of good cooking, and such – are generally characterized as 'old wives's tales.' These 'tales' may be interwoven into the very fabric of our daily lives and may even enjoy a certain amount of respect and deference as a useful secret-sharing among women ... [yet] fail to get accorded the honorific status of *knowledge.*[28]

All modes of knowing, according to the traditionalist, can be *said*; we suggest that some knowledge can only be *shown* and other knowledge can only be said in an inherently perspectival language.[29]

Moore himself would seem to recognize the fact that some kinds of philosophical knowledge involve knowing how to do certain things which can be shown, but cannot be put into words.[30] A further question is whether it can only be put into the words of a particular (privileged) perspective within the dominant conceptual scheme. If so, this would seem to be a case of Moore's ineffable knowledge.

Moore's distinction between showing and saying has been worked out with the help of Ludwig Wittgenstein's philosophy. Moore offers a modification, or extension, of the distinction as found in the early work of Wittgenstein. In both *The Infinite* and *Points of View* Moore goes further than (the analytic philosophy of) Wittgenstein to a point at which he meets a Continental philosopher such as Derrida on the question of ineffability.[31] In *The Infinite*, Moore explains, 'there are certain things that can be known though they cannot be put into words'.[32]

> [but t]he full-blown saying/showing distinction, whereby there are things that cannot be said at all, emerges only when I pass from consideration of how

---

[27]   Vrinda Dalmiya and Linda Alcoff, 'Are "Old Wives' Tales" Justified?' in Linda Alcoff and Elizabeth Potter (eds), *Feminist Epistemologies* (London: Routledge, 1993), pp. 217–241.

[28]   Ibid., p. 217.

[29]   Ibid., p. 241.

[30]   Moore, *Points of View*, pp. 156–157.

[31]   Moore, *The Infinite*, pp. 186–200; *Points of View*, pp. xii–xiii, 156–157, 195–213 and 277–278.

[32]   Moore, *The Infinite*, p. 186.

things are in my field of vision to consideration of how things are, full stop – to consideration, in other words, of the world as a whole.[33]

The implicit account (above) of reality and the finitude of vision also resonates with post-Kantian philosophers of religion.[34] Moore himself would seem to make this link (to at least Derrida) by producing nonsense as follows:

> What Derrida (in '*Différance*') is drawing attention to … is something that can never be the subject of any truth. It is that which in some quasi-Kantian way makes possible and precedes the affirmation of any truth. There are clear links here with what each of Frege and Wittgenstein is doing.[35]

Later Moore returns to the problem of contradiction in the above assertion that 'What Derrida is drawing attention to' can never be a subject of any truth.[36] Moore admits this assertion is nonsense. He claims that the assertion, 'what Derrida is drawing attention to can never be a subject of any truth' is self-stultifying. In recognizing this, he both distinguishes himself from Derrida in insisting that the affirmation of truth is an ultimate concern and draws himself into Derrida's play with meaning – albeit Moore remains detached in his play. As Moore explains,

> … Derrida's style of philosophy (unlike conceptual philosophy) does not labour under a restricted conception of what linguistic resources are available to it; in particular, it does not treat affirmation of the truth as its sole primary mode of philosophical expression.[37]

This implies that in order to 'argue with Derrida' Moore must be willing to play with nonsense, while still at pains (as a conceptual philosopher) to avoid self-stultification. He explains how he avoids the latter:

> The first task confronting any conceptual philosopher trying to come to terms with the ineffable is to show how it is possible to affirm truths about the ineffable without belying its very ineffability.[38]

---

[33]   Ibid. For the development of Moore's own account of showing and ineffable knowledge, see Moore, *Points of View*, pp. 186–194.

[34]   Ibid., pp. 203–209, 249–251. Moore's account has an affinity with Paul Ricoeur's Kantian account of the finitude of our points of view in Ricoeur, *Fallible Man*, trans. Charles Kelbley with an Introduction by Walter J. Lowe (New York: Fordham University Press, 1986); and Anderson, 'Gender and the Infinite', pp. 6–8, 13.

[35]   Moore, 'Arguing with Derrida', p. 362.

[36]   Ibid., p. 366.

[37]   Ibid., p. 363.

[38]   Ibid., p. 366.

A second task for any conceptual philosopher who accepts that some things are ineffable is to say what the term 'things' ranges over in this claim.[39]

> The only decent way that I can see of discharging either task is to say that the term 'things' ranges over objects of knowledge. The claim that some things are ineffable is to be understood as the claim that *some states of knowledge cannot be put into words*, or more strictly, that some states of knowledge *do not have any content* (and therefore *do not share any content with any truth*). The knowledge in question is not knowledge that anything is the case. *It is knowledge how to do certain things.* ... knowledge *how to handle concepts* ... there is nothing self-stultifying about discussing somebody's ineffable knowledge how to do something. We can even put into words what is involved in the person's having the knowledge. What we cannot put into words is what the person knows (italics added).[40]

The minimal extent of Moore's agreement on this question with Derrida or, more generally with Continental philosophers since Kant, allows the possibility that Derrida may communicate something ineffable to the conceptual philosopher. Moore claims, 'there is no mystery in the idea of somebody's 'communicating' something ineffable. All that is required for this to happen is that the person exploits language – plays with language – in such a way that other people come to share some of his or her ineffable knowledge'.[41] At the same time, Moore is only willing to play with nonsense, while Derrida ironically seems far more serious about nonsense! The conceptual philosopher remains fully beholden to the truth and to the ultimate task of *producing* true and meaningful linguistic expressions, whereas the Continental philosopher, Derrida, questions the possibility of truth in his play with ineffability.[42] Moreover, Moore remains detached in his play with words, whereas Derrida is serious in engaging with the ineffable. Moore concludes,

> What I hope to have done ... is to give some indication of how it is possible, first, to appropriate resources highlighted in [Derrida's] 'Signature, Event, Context', in order, second, to reckon with ineffable insights afforded by [Derrida's] '*Différance*', while managing at the same time, third, to conform to methodological paradigms of conceptual philosophy. In various senses of the phrase, then ..., this has been an attempt to 'argue with Derrida'.[43]

---

[39]   Moore, 'Arguing with Derrida', p. 367.

[40]   Ibid.

[41]   Ibid., p. 367.

[42]   Ibid., p. 366.

[43]   Ibid., pp. 372–373; cf. Derrida, '*Différance*' and 'Signature, Event, Context', in *Margins of Philosophy*, pp. 1–28, 307–330.

The inverted commas placed around 'argue with Derrida' makes clear Moore's intention to maintain a detached way of playing with Derrida. So, Moore does not aim to produce nonsense, or to engage seriously with it. At most he attempts to 'argue with ...' where the meaning of this is presumably not fixed (i.e. this does not have *a* sense), but neither is it talking nonsense.

The relevant question is what re-visioning gender in philosophy of religion would gain specifically from a Continental philosopher of religion and from Moore's engagement with a particular Continental philosopher? Moore's 'arguing with' Derrida helps us to begin to understand the philosopher's epistemic locatedness. Philosophers have different relations to truth, to meaning and to the conditions necessary for argumentation. Nevertheless, Moore finds common ground in philosophy by recognizing the common issues of ineffable knowledge – and of practical knowledge – and why not, the practical know how of the mystic?

Moore seems to find common ground in Derrida's idea of meaning: the meaning of a word is its infinite potential for iterability in new contexts.[44] Meaning appears to be context dependent. Yet Moore does not give up his commitment to produce something both meaningful and true. In the end, his clear distinctions, as well as an overlap of interest in infinity, between his philosophy and Derrida's can direct us to our next question concerning the infinite and gender.

The infinite and gender: an ancient question

Feminist (analytic) philosopher Sabina Lovibond has explored the association of the unlimited, or infinite, with femaleness beginning in ancient Greek philosophy. From Lovibond we learn that for Pythagorean and Platonic philosophers, 'the infinite' was a term of abuse. It was associated with chaos, matter and femaleness, while the finite was good and associated with order, form and maleness.[45] An early twentieth-century feminism of difference informed by Irigaray proposed a return to the ancient conception of the infinite as female, while reversing its value from bad to good. Strangely, Jantzen criticizes Anglo-American philosophers of religion for the infinite which she insists is male.

Jantzen defends her view of the maleness of the infinite. Yet her defence seems reliant upon inconsistent readings of gender in relation to two central conceptions; that is, the infinite and ineffability. On the one hand, Jantzen insists that the drive for infinity is a masculine or male obsession. On the other hand, she claims that

[44]   Moore, 'Arguing with Derrida', pp. 364–365 and 372.

[45]   Sabina Lovibond, 'An Ancient Theory of Gender: Plato and the Pythagorean Table', in Leonie J. Archer, Susan Fischer and Maria Wyke (eds), *Women in Ancient Societies* (London: Macmillan, 1994), pp. 88–101; and 'Feminism in Ancient Philosophy: The Feminist Stake in Greek Rationalism', in Miranda Fricker and Jennifer Hornsby (eds), *The Cambridge Companion to Feminism in Philosophy* (Cambridge: Cambridge University Press, 2000), pp. 10–28.

male philosophers had associated ineffability (and mysticism) with private, and so, female experience. Apparently then, according to the binary logic which Jantzen aims to reject, the female philosopher would associate male experience with the effable and the limited? If so, Jantzen's own answer is contradictory when it comes to the ineffable and the limited. Jantzen explicitly equates the masculine with the fear of limits on one page, only to present the Pythagorean table of opposites as representative of the binary thinking of western philosophy where the masculine is equated with the limited, not the unlimited.[46] The question is: are men always associated with one side of this binary? Gender theorists might have expected an affirmative answer. Their assumption would, then, be that men are linked to the limited and the effable, while women are associated with the unlimited and the ineffable. However, reality does not support this overly simplistic reading of gender identities and differences.

For her part, Jantzen contends that, while the urge for infinity as limitlessness is a masculine obsession, the ineffable is feminine and lacking (order?) so, it should be rejected, except perhaps in 'naming' God.[47] Jantzen assumes here that, for masculinists, the ineffable is an untrustworthy source of knowledge; and its association with the feminine undermines the knowledge of, in this context, female mystics. For feminists like Jantzen, we must dissociate women from any such conceptual devaluation.

Even if we acknowledge Jantzen's great contributions to debates about gender and Christian mysticism, it is still necessary to ask whether she makes some illegitimate moves between the nuances of her terms. She seems to jump from infinity as a powerful drive to the infinite's association with men and, similarly, jump from the ineffable as a private experience to its association with weakness and women's lack of knowledge. If this is correct, this bi-gender reading of terms is incompatible with the actual readings of the philosophers in the history of the western tradition.

The Pythagoreans serve as a good counter example. If the Pythagoreans did associate both the infinite and the ineffable with women, consider roughly their logic. Women are associated with the infinite, since they are disorderly; and so, they are not philosophical, since philosophers think orderly as another term for rationally. Women are associated with the ineffable, since they represent not truth as the finite, but the infinite; but then, the infinite has not always represented maleness. In this light, something has gone wrong in Jantzen's argument, since she rejects the Pythagorean table of opposites as the source of mistaken gender associations: it created a hierarchy of binary oppositions in which the first term

---

[46]   Jantzen, *Becoming Divine*, pp. 154–156 and 266–268.

[47]   Jantzen, *Becoming Divine*; cf. Jantzen, *Gender, Power and Christian Mysticism*, pp. 278–289. For an admirable defence of ineffability as evidence of mystical experience which is not necessarily a source of injustice to women, see Jerome Gellman, *Mystical Experience of God: A Philosophical Inquiry* (Aldershot, Hampshire: Ashgate Publishing Ltd., 2001), pp. 103–111.

in any pair is male and given greater value, including finite/infinite, order/disorder; and the second term in the pair is assumed to be associated with the female.[48] In sharp contrast, Le Doeuff argues for the case that no possibility of any straightforward extension of gender-dichotomies from the Pythagorean table to men and women with a variety of social and class backgrounds exists.[49]

However, in rejecting the Pythagorean's view of women as associated with the finite, Jantzen in fact rejects precisely what she wants to uphold: the value of the finite (female) as a 'portion of infinity'.[50] Perhaps Jantzen would have countered that her problem with the Pythagoreans is the masculinism in the whole of western philosophy – in which they play an integral and foundational role. Whatever her counter argument, she assumes that masculinism generates an unconscious urge for infinity. Her apparently psychological critique of masculinism is roughly, that men want it and they think they can have it, while women know that they cannot have it. Ultimately, her aim seems to be a reversal of the valuation of gender terms; but it is not clear that feminism should be privileged over masculinism (a question to which we will return).

Questions of the infinite and of ineffable knowledge are generally ignored by analytic philosophers of religion in the twentieth century. In fact, the very gender associated with these concepts could be the very grounds given for ignoring them. But then, the Continental (feminist) philosopher of religion might argue that these issues of gender offer precisely a common ground of debate in analytic and Continental philosophy of religion. Basically both sides tend to ignore gender as a philosophical topic.

Whether writing Continental, analytic, conceptual, or non-conceptual philosophy, each philosopher can be challenged on gender issues concerning conceptions such as infinity and ineffability. But the argument for both gendering and re-visioning gender in philosophy of religion is still not easy to make. A proposal in this chapter is, insofar as the philosopher takes seriously the play of language and imagery in philosophical debates, he or she is in a propitious place to reverse devaluation of feminist concerns and of femaleness. From what has been discussed in this chapter, it would seem to follow that philosophical queries about gender come in at the point where conceptual and non-conceptual (post-Kantian) philosophers meet. This was intimated when discussing ineffable knowledge.

The difficulty which Jantzen's thinking flags up is that, if the infinite cannot be associated strictly with the male or female, then the non-feminist philosopher might argue that the infinite be treated as gender-neutral. The feminist could counter that in claiming this neutrality gender is simply ignored, since it cannot be eradicated. However, this counter-claim fails to recognize that philosophers have bodies and these bodies, including their bodily specific material and social

---

[48]   Jantzen, *Becoming Divine*, pp. 266–270.

[49]   Michèle Le Doeuff, 'Long Hair, Short Ideas', in *The Philosophical Imaginary*, trans. Colin Gordon (London: The Athlone Press, 1989), pp. 113–114.

[50]   Jantzen, 'Becoming Divine', pp. 154–155.

conditions, inevitably gender their grasp of the infinite. The process of gendering and re-visioning should persist, unless it can be shown that there are no new concepts or knowledge to be gained from our fully lived experiences.

In philosophy of religion clarity on the question of beings with or without bodies will flag up a fundamental difference between divine attributes, as traditionally debated, and human attributes.[51] In particular, those human attributes of having a body, yet seeking the infinite, unity, all-knowledge and so on serves as a ground for understanding human and divine relations. Gender is an attribute of each body, since intimately related to human sexuality and sexual relations. We might then ask, if God is transgender. At the same time, we might ask, is there a conscious or unconscious masculinist drive for infinity, that is, to be all-knowing, all-powerful, omnitemporal and without a body? Alternatively, is the place of the infinite a female domain? The feminist pursuit of knowledge of, what has been called, 'the whole framework of the finite', is ironically an urge to find a place in the infinite; and from this place that ineffable knowledge of infinity is to be gained. So, opposing gender or sexual types can only curtail knowledge by bracketing out the experiences of gender of women and men in all their specificities.

Philosophers of religion have generally been more preoccupied with what is far more certain/possible; that is, the finite, order, truth and effable knowledge. Nevertheless, some philosophers will have argued that the greater practical, yet ineffable knowledge of the process of 'knowing how to be finite',[52] has in fact been a domain of female insight – unacknowledged by male philosophers. The lesson seems to be that imposing divisions of gender appear both arbitrary across history and cultures, but ignoring gender altogether inhibits the knowledge of those who are not seen or heard.

For example, as Vrinda Dalmiya and Linda Alcoff also assert:

> There is nothing embarrassingly limited about the midwife's perspectival (and hence partly exclusionary) knowledge; rather, it ensures a higher level of holistic care by taking into account certain perspectival facts that are necessarily beyond the reach of traditional forms of knowledge ...

> ... we suggest that some knowledge can only be *shown*.[53]

The above lines of argument might suggest (to the feminist epistemologist at least) something about ineffable knowledge being shown and gender's association with the knowledge claimed to be 'limited'. In contrast to Jantzen's rejection of ineffable knowledge due to its association by some philosophers with female mysticism (and degradation), the present proposal would insist upon the

---

[51]   Chapter 9 will return to a question of gender in the conception of a divine being without a body, who is also supposed to love and reason.

[52]   Moore, *Points of View*, p. 277.

[53]   Dalmiya and Alcoff, 'Are 'Old Wives' Tales" Justified?' p. 241.

rich complexity of the philosophical question of ineffable knowledge and the philosophical history of its gendering in philosophers' writings. New knowledge rests in yet unexplored dimensions, such as what is beyond, or presupposed by, the finite in current associations with gender. In particular, this complexity renders impossible any straightforward equation of the infinite with masculinism or feminism. Yet considering why the infinite is given this or that gender will give us new understandings for the re-visioning of gender. There is more effable and ineffable knowledge to be gained from the philosophical critique of gender.

Philosophers both on and off the Continent

The complexity of gender associations equally challenges analytic and Continental philosophers alike. Moore's conceptual and non-conceptual philosophers can be challenged by gender, especially by the lack of its acknowledgement. Contemporary philosophers of religion, including feminists on and off the Continent, need not reject either ineffable knowledge as untrustworthy or its association with an urge for infinitude as a refusal to accept boundaries.[54] In making this positive assertion on ineffable knowledge, we move against a current trend to (mis)represent, on the one hand, Anglo-American philosophy as necessarily rejecting the ineffable as a source of knowledge and, on the other hand, Continental philosophy as rejecting ontological or onto-theological questions as a guide to practical knowledge.

Basically, the conclusion to be drawn at this stage is that ineffability and any urge for infinitude, as evident in making play with the infinite, are not merely employed to prescind the philosophical boundaries of men or to exclude and oppress women. To the contrary, ineffability and (female) mysticism raise all sorts of significant ontological, metaphysical and epistemological issues. The danger is to misrepresent philosophers, whether this is Derrida, Moore or other post-Kantian philosophers, in assuming they fit neatly under particular territorial or gender labels. This would inhibit the possible convergence of perspectives which this chapter is at pains to pursue, even if not expecting any final agreement.

An ongoing methodological presupposition of this book is to remain open to a fuller picture of Continental philosophy and its influence since Kant on philosophy on both sides of the English Channel. Another presupposition is to expose the unacknowledged role of gender in timely matters such as ineffable knowledge and mystical practice. Moore's conceptual philosophy demonstrates how it is possible to give the ineffable, a serious and necessary role in epistemology, while also holding firm the critical role of truth and realism in philosophy (of religion). Ineffability is fundamental to discursive practices, i.e. in knowing how to do something with concepts. It is also fundamental to making narrative sense of life – a philosophical concern on both sides of the channel. The role of ineffability is apparent in the philosophical attempt of Ricoeur and of Adriana Cavarero, or even

---

[54] Jantzen, *Becoming Divine*, pp. 154–155.

of Alasdair MacIntyre, in each of their singular attempts to make narrative sense of our lives.[55] Moore himself explicitly claims that 'knowing how to be finite is a paradigm of ineffable knowledge'.[56] This is a highly relevant claim for unravelling the gendered associations and the value hierarchy of finite/infinite, limited/ unlimited, order/disorder, reason/desire, male/female and so on. Knowing how to be finite has potentially decisive implications for those feminist philosophers who claim that the *hubris* of the male philosopher leads to a categorical denial of ineffable as male-gendered knowledge. Undoubtedly certain feminist philosophers will continue to object that ineffable knowledge could only be a contradiction in terms for the masculinist philosopher, and so ineffability's association with femaleness would exclude the topic from any serious philosophical debate.

Nevertheless, it can be argued to the contrary that the epistemic injustice done to women whose practical knowledge has been devalued can be reversed by recognition of their insight in knowing how to be finite as the flip side to a paradigm of ineffable knowledge. This paradigm of knowing how to be finite includes the states of understanding, or practical knowledge, that we each have to various degrees. We might agree that knowing how to employ concepts and to use language, in order to express truth fits the paradigm. Yet in more narrowly realist terms, ineffable states of knowledge are not representations and (so) do not answer to how things are.

Ironically this paradigm of ineffability appears compatible with Derrida's play with words precisely because this does not affirm or deny truth. Derrida is not committed to truth; it depends upon how things are. Moore is a realist and committed to truth, while he also exhibits an awareness of, or interest in, knowledge that does not represent how things are. Moore and Derrida seem to meet as, roughly speaking, realist and anti-realist. Yet, Moore admits that realism cannot exclude knowledge of the process of how we know, especially how we understand a language; items such as words, sentences and so on are part of knowledge, even if there are not words to make sense of the functioning of the non-conceptual. For him, realism must rest upon ineffable knowledge of the process of knowing how to *x*. The implication may be that human understanding depends upon an acceptance of transcendental conditions as a sort of bridge or middle ground between the effable and the ineffable. Nevertheless, it is then perplexing that Moore himself rejects transcendental idealism as the way to make

---

[55]   Adriana Cavarero, *In Spite of Plato: A Feminist Rewriting of Ancient Philosophy* trans. Serena Anderlini-D'Onofrio and Aine O'Healy, with a Foreword by Rosi Braidotti (Cambridge, UK: Polity Press, 1995); *Relating Narratives: Storytelling and Selfhood*, trans. with an introduction by Paul A. Kottman (New York: Routledge, 2000). Alasdair MacIntyre, *After Virtue: A Study in Moral Theory*, second edition (London: Gerald Duckworth & Co. Ltd, 1985), pp. 204–225. Paul Ricoeur, *Oneself as Another*, trans. Kathleen Blamey (Chicago, IL: University of Chicago Press, 1992), pp. 140–168; cf. *Moore, Points of View*, pp. 220ff, and 'Ineffability and Religion', p. 6.

[56]   Moore, *Points of View*, p. 277.

claims to certain knowledge, while setting boundaries for this knowledge (as if the ineffable serves as knowledge's boundary). Perhaps Irigaray's (Kantian) notion of a 'sensible transcendental' has yet to be given the support it might deserve, despite doubts about her realism.[57] Know how, or practical knowledge, may be shown, and we hope that it saves the day for realism and truth.

On a common urge to make play with nonsense

While summarizing the argument so far, let us not forget the role of nonsense. In 'Arguing with Derrida', Moore endeavours to place his own account of ineffable knowledge in relation to Derrida's non-conceptual philosophy. In doing so, Moore reveals a highly important point of contact between the (otherwise) divergent perspectives of Continental and analytic philosophers, and so, between an anti-realist and a realist. To work out how/whether Moore and Derrida (really) find a point of agreement on ineffability and mysticism, let us look more closely at Derrida's response to Moore. Moore suggests that they agree about the role of ineffability.[58] Remarkably and revealingly, Derrida responds with apology for not long ago reading Wittgenstein and, presumably, for not reading those Kantian analytic philosophers such as Moore whose work on ineffability and nonsense owe much to Wittgenstein.

Ironically, Wittgenstein's relation to the content, or nonsense, as set out in his *Tractatus* begins to seem closer to Derrida's relation to nonsense (since he takes it very seriously) than Moore's detached play with nonsense. Nonsense, as defined by Moore, is the result of putting into words what we are shown.[59] And there is a clear convergence of the thought of Derrida and Moore in the play with words. Yet it is not easy to find the more serious and substantial common ground (in Wittgenstein?) between Moore and Derrida. We are still taking Derrida to represent Continental philosophy of religion, while Moore represents his conceptual philosophy.

Now, to make sense of the relation between the conceptual and the non-conceptual Moore takes up a distinction from Wittgenstein, saying and showing, in discussions of ineffable knowledge.[60] In *Points of View*, Moore employs the

---

[57]   Irigaray might offer new insight on Kantian transcendental idealism; cf. Irigaray, 'An Ethics of Sexual Difference', in *An Ethics of Sexual Difference*, pp. 128–189. For a fascinating account of Irigaray's response to Kantian transcendental idealism see Rachel Jones, *Irigaray: Towards a Sexuate Philosophy* (Cambridge, UK: Polity Press, 2011), pp. 114–129; cf. Luce Irigaray, 'Any Theory of the "Subject" Has Always Been Appropriated by the "Masculine"' and 'Paradox A Priori', in *Speculum of the Other Woman*, trans. Gillian C. Gill (Ithaca, NY: Cornell University Press, 1985), pp. 133–146 and 203–213, respectively.

[58]   Derrida, 'Response to Moore', pp. 381–382.

[59]   Moore, *The Infinite*, pp. 186–200; and *Points of View*, pp. 180 n13, 258–259.

[60]   Moore, *The Infinite*, pp. 186–200; *Points of View*, pp. xii–xiii, 156–157, 195–213, 277–278.

formula, '*A* is shown that *x*' as equivalent to *A* has ineffable knowledge, and when an attempt is made to put what *A* knows into words, the result is *x*. According to Moore, whatever words are put in place of *x* will be nonsense or mere verbiage because such states of knowledge are not representations; they do not answer to how things are.[61] To quote Moore,

> Knowing how to be finite … has nothing to answer to. It is knowledge of how to be finite *in accord with our craving for infinitude*. But there is no independent right or wrong about it.[62]

So, this 'knowing how' has nothing to answer to. Yet it is in accord with our craving for infinitude. The craving becomes corrupt when we aspire to be infinite, that is, to be all there is.[63] Moore's account of finitude and infinitude is consistent with Kant and post-Kantian philosophy, in recognizing a boundary to what we (say we) know.[64] Transgression of this boundary renders our aspiration vulnerable; aspiration is an enabling and corrupting power.

Similar to Moore, philosophers on the Continent have also turned to Wittgenstein. Frequently, saying and showing helps to mark out the boundaries of their language and their world. The French philosopher Maurice Blanchot relies on Wittgenstein's say and show distinction to articulate both faith in unity and desire for the impossible as the origin of his mysticism. In *Writing of the Disaster* Blanchot reasons that

> Wittgenstein's 'mysticism',[65] aside from his faith in unity, must come from his believing that one can *show* when one cannot *speak*. But without language, nothing can be shown. And to be silent is still to speak. Silence is impossible. That is why we desire it.[66]

Blanchot's reading of Wittgenstein is that we can 'show' what cannot be said. But this is still speaking (*Le Dire*). Blanchot also links this 'showing' with 'mysticism'. But in Moore's Wittgensteinian terms, any attempt to put what we cannot say into

---

[61]   Ibid.

[62]   Ibid.

[63]   Anderson, 'Gender and the Infinite', pp. 2, 6–9.

[64]   For a recent discussion of metaphors employed to show the 'boundary' (or boundaries) between the knowable and the unknowable in Kant, see Pamela Sue Anderson, 'Metaphors of Spatial Location: Understanding Post-Kantian Space', in Roxana Baiasu, Graham Bird and A. W. Moore (eds), *Contemporary Kantian Metaphysics: New Essays on Space and Time* (New York, NY: Palgrave Macmillan, 2012), pp. 169–196.

[65]   See Ludwig Wittgenstein, *Tractatus Logico-Philosophicus*, trans. D. F. Pears and B. F. McGuinness, with the Introduction by Bertrand Russell (London: Routledge & Kegan Paul, 1961), 6.44, 6.522, 7.

[66]   Maurice Blanchot, *Writing of the Disaster*, trans. Ann Smock (Lincoln, Nebraska: University of Nebraska Press, 1986), pp. 10–11.

language results in speaking nonsense.[67] The question is, then, whether mysticism is both 'shown' and when spoken nonsense. Blanchot (above) comes close to undoing the distinction, and value-hierarchy, of saying and showing; both need 'language'. He asserts that whether mysticism is shown or said it needs language. But he is clear: mysticism is not said. This returns us to the question of mysticism; as proposed earlier, this question exists for both the philosopher and the theologian who focuses on ineffable knowledge, states of knowledge without content or experiences which do not make sense.

Blanchot's references to mysticism, to faith in unity and to the impossible move him seductively close to questions of the divine in philosophy of religion. This is also the case for Blanchot's references to (our Being toward) death. With the question of death we are not far from questions of knowing how to be finite, ineffability and religious rituals about life and death. In both death and mysticism neither the object nor content of knowledge is ever identifiable; hence, we are reminded of Moore's account of ineffable knowledge as without truth and as states without content.[68]

The fascination with mysticism and ineffability is not just about common ground between conceptual and non-conceptual philosophy; it is a ground shared with female mysticism and gender in Christian philosophy of religion. Any connection between mysticism and the showing which is always still a saying could also come into gender debates about male and female mystics. Following, yet going beyond Moore and Blanchot, let us suppose that the language of the female subject who attempts to put (certain) ineffable knowledge into words could in certain instances be called religious as in the case of the female mystic: she might, then, speak nonsense yet show practical knowledge. If so, Jantzen responds that this ineffability, or nonsense, further degrades the female mystic who, she claims, is already relegated to a separate, private sphere of life, blocked from modern epistemology. Can Moore yet shed a more positive light on ineffability?

To appropriate a formula from Moore, we assert that the female subject (A) is shown that x is equivalent to A has ineffable knowledge and when an attempt to put what A knows into language the result is x? According to Moore, x must be nonsense. Yet he admits that one of the things we are shown is that God exists. But then, 'God exists' in the phrase 'We are shown that God exists' is a piece of nonsense. Moreover, his admission that this is a piece of nonsense appears in the wider discussion of human aspiration(s). One aspiration is to crave infinitude (divinity) and another is to be infinite (God); Moore claims that only the latter aspiration, to be infinite, is 'deep, pervasive and corrupt':

---

[67]   Wittgenstein, *Tractatus*, 4.12, 5.62, 6.12 and 6.522; cf. Moore, *Points of View*, pp. 149ff.

[68]   For a study of the analogy between mystical unknowing and the limits of human knowing, negative theology and negative anthropology, see Carlson, *Indiscretion*, pp. 239–262.

the aspiration to be infinite has a different focus. It includes the aspiration to be rational, but includes it as a residue within the distorted aspiration to be (so to speak) rationality itself.

When the craving is distorted, [its] perspectival character is turned in on itself in such a way that the craving becomes an aspiration *that we alone exist.*[69]

> This may be all well and good. Yet ineffable knowledge as nonsense seems unlikely to be the sort of knowledge to enabling us to know how to avoid this deep, pervasive corruption. Nevertheless, it could be that the negative connotations of 'nonsense' should be ignored and the task is to think about the know-how of practical knowledge; this knowledge may not have an object, or make sense, as theoretical knowledge does. The real question is whether women who show mysticism to be a form of practical knowledge, or women who tell 'tales' about human finite experience,[70] are wise in bringing the two aspirations come together.

In 'Ineffability and Religion', Moore argues that 'the language that results from attempting to put our ineffable knowledge into words is very often of a "religious" kind'. This is not to claim that 'attempts to put our ineffable knowledge into words result only in such language; nor, for that matter, that such language results only from attempts to put our ineffable knowledge into words … But there is significant overlap.'[71] He goes on to sketch some of this significant overlap. I can only indicate one area of overlap which seems equally relevant to my discussion. In Moore's words, 'Because the attempt to put our ineffable knowledge into words involves prescinding from our limitations, there is an area in which we make play with images of unlimitedness and infinitude. These are applied in the first instance to ourselves. But then, when combined with our re-awakened self-consciousness about the very limitations from which we have been prescinding, they are extended to a reality beyond us. Eventually they sustain talk of God.'[72] Perhaps this wisdom as both effable and ineffable knowledge can be achieved in (feminist) philosophy of religion. In fact, a unity of aspirations could be, after all, what is meant by the mystic's union with the divine.

To recall a crucial fact at this point, Moore does not intend to produce nonsense. Instead he aspires to produce truth. Yet, if the two aspects of this fact are true, doesn't Moore belie his own gender bias, opting for the sense of effable

---

[69]   Moore, *Points of View*, pp. 275–278.
[70]   On the use and abuse of women telling tales, see Pamela Sue Anderson, '*Des contes dits au féminin: pour une éthique de nouveaux espaces*', in Alban Cain (ed.), *Espaces public, espaces privées* (Cergy-Pontoise, France: Université de Cergy-Pontoise, 2002), pp. 43–52.
[71]   Moore, 'Ineffability and Religion', pp. 161–176.
[72]   Moore, *Points of View*, pp. 277–278.

knowledge, when the female mystics know-how[73] and the wise women's tales fail to produce sense – and so truth! To return to one of our earlier philosophical examples, Irigaray appears willing to produce (what Moore would call) nonsense, in order to gain knowledge of how to be finite. The Irigarayan attempt to mime, in order to disrupt, the texts of female mystics might challenge the negative connotations of nonsense.[74] To speak the mystic's silence, Irigaray makes play with images of infinitude. She mimes a female subject's desire to bring together two human aspirations or, in her terms, the union of the sensible transcendental.[75] But she is bold in affirming divinity and becoming divine. Her boldness could be construed as corrupt. Irigaray *shows* ineffable knowledge in images of female desire, of song and dance, and in other creatively subversive expressions;[76] but she also wants to advocate that we aspire to be divine, infinite.[77] New possibilities for 'expressing' the ineffable include strategies for exploiting language in the play of images in a mystic's text, art or dance. This is similar to what Moore says about Derrida's play with words, it is a manner of exploiting language, showing and not making sense. It should be noted that Jantzen also recognizes the importance of stretching language to represent the 'inexhaustible fecundity' of the divine, and not 'frustrated speechlessness'.[78]

Conclusion

There may be a common core concern in the variety of masculinist, feminist and other philosophical attempts to show what is ineffable. Yet when we add gender to the mix it suddenly becomes clear that values are added to the task: philosophy is called to be serious or playful, sense-making or nonsense-producing, effable or ineffable, rational or corrupt; the values of these terms and their gender seem initially arbitrary; but they matter when it comes to ethics and justice, if not a sort of truth, that is worth having. Certainly, if we follow Moore an urge to orientate our finiteness, in knowing how to be finite, exists and it seems most valuable. However, to exploit this urge, in order to establish a (more) common concern: to

---

[73] Michel Foucault, *The History of Sexuality*, Vol. 1, An Introduction, trans. Robert Hurley (Harmondsworth: Penguin Books, 1979), pp. 92–94.

[74] Luce Irigaray, 'La Mysterique', *Speculum of the Other Woman*, trans. Gillian C. Gill (Ithaca, NY: Cornell University Press, 1985), pp. 191–202. Also see, Amy Hollywood, 'Beauvoir, Irigaray and the Mystical', *Hypatia*, 9 (Fall 1994), 158–185.

[75] Irigaray, 'An Ethics of Sexual Difference' in *An Ethics of Sexual Difference*, pp. 128–129.

[76] Concerning music as an example of expressing the inexpressible, see Moore, *Points of View*, pp. 201–203.

[77] Jantzen, *Gender, Power and Christian Mysticism*, pp. 283, 328–329, 344–346.

[78] Moore, 'Arguing with Derrida', pp. 365, 367, 372. Jantzen, *Power, Gender and Christian Mysticism*, pp. 284, 286.

better orientate our finiteness, we do perhaps need to admit the gendering of our relations.

The variable range of human values is especially problematic when gender comes into the mix. Attributing heterosexual or homosexual, male or female, human or divine to someone inevitably brings in scales of value. These scales develop according to the intersection of (our) gender with variable sexual, racial, religious, ethnic, class categories. To understand the tendencies of women and men to prescind their boundaries and to make play with nonsense is to approach serious matters. The tendency to deny or ignore our materially and socially specific relations has serious, political and ethical implications for humanity, individually and collectively. Yet denial of gender-related categories has seemed to be the status quo in western philosophy. Nevertheless, whether it is a matter of religious, sexual, racial, material or other social relations, gender norms matter for justice, if not truth.

At this point in the chapter, it is almost too late to bring in a French contemporary of Derrida, Michel Foucault. Yet Foucault's account of immanent power could not be more appropriate here. Taking Foucault seriously means accepting that the political is no longer a position of exteriority with respect to personal or social relations. Political positioning read with the help of Foucault helps in knowing how to be finite: power would be recognized as immanent in our lives; hence, in both the content of our knowledge and in how we process that knowledge. If relations of power are immanent in living and thinking, then they have a directly productive role to play in everything, especially in our expressions of ineffable knowledge, including (nonsensical) words and practices of a religious kind.

Whether a conceptual or a non-conceptual philosopher, we can accept with Foucault that power is everywhere. It is, then, necessary to recognize power's intimate connections with both effable and ineffable knowledge. Insofar as the gendered relations of power are integral to the paradigm of ineffable knowledge, they would be expressed in how we make play with images of infinitude. Acceptance of this account of power has its advantages and difficulties. One difficulty is confronting the corrupting relations of power in all expressions of knowledge. One advantage is recognizing the possibilities in a transformation of the power immanent in our relations. Positively, the power for rational change, which circulates in the implicit and explicit networks of the relations shaping our lives, is the common (yet ironic) feature of every form of passion (whether religious or not) and so, in what remains ineffable.

We have seen that conceptual philosophers, along with other contemporary philosophers on and off the Continent, confront a common passion, or urge, and a common problem. They confront an urge to express the inexpressible as ineffable knowledge. This urge shapes practical knowledge as both passive and productive know how. Serious attempts to communicate the ineffable in new ways have become part of the productive project of feminist philosophy today. In particular, Irigaray exemplifies this project. Arguably Irigaray has *shown* that we know we are in-finite:[79] that is, 'that we know we are in-finite' is nonsense, since claiming to be both finite and infinite is self-contradictory. Yet we are shown this ineffable knowledge as we inevitably aspire to be infinite. In other words, the inscrutable desire for infinitude (as finite beings) becomes apparent in, for instance, Irigaray's play with language, but also in claims that we are shown *x*.[80]

In this chapter, ineffable knowledge and gender have raised significant sorts of questions concerning language, reality, understanding, truth and power. These topics offer rich terrain for philosophical analysis and for debates between Continental and analytic philosophers of religion, but also between feminist philosophers and philosophical theologians. The novelty of this work on ineffable knowledge and gender rests in recognizing the ironic, yet necessary tension between the enabling and corrupting power immanent in the material, personal and social relations of men and women. No critical reflection on language, understanding and truth can remain content with traditional answers to the philosophical question of ineffable knowledge. These answers are inadequate insofar as they have failed to acknowledge a necessary tension in our gendered relations to the finite and the infinite, as both corrupting and enabling. Philosophy of religion as practised by both those who aspire to produce truth and those who engage seriously with nonsense can overcome this failure: it can acknowledge this tension as the first step towards new ethical and epistemological relations between women themselves, men themselves, and women and men, of different material and social perspectives.

---

[79] Irigaray, *Elemental Passions*, p. 89.

[80] We are also shown that desire for infinitude is good in motivating us and shaping the *politicized* nature of works of love. Yet there are equally dangers for men and for women in desiring infinitude. On the one hand, the danger is evident in the male aspiration to be infinite. On the other hand, there would seem to be a similar danger in the female aspiration to become divine. Any desire which overwhelms us remains indefinite until embraced *critically*. The fundamental problem lies in the aspiration to be, or become, whether divine men or divine women *all that is*. In aspiring to be or become all, the Other and others are eclipsed. A critical embrace of bodies is meant to change our thinking. It should also challenge our physical, sensual and material relations with the Other and others. However, this sort of transformation, as Irigaray intimates so provocatively concerning sexual difference, involves violence and pain. Cf. Irigaray, *Elemental Passions*, p. 90; and Anderson, 'Gender and the Infinite', pp. 9–12.

Chapter 5
Gendering Love in Philosophy of Religion[1]

The challenge: gendering love and morality

At certain times a philosopher will reflect upon her or his own teaching and writing in philosophy. Such reflection becomes necessary for any attempt to uncover the process of gendering which has been at play in the field of philosophy of religion. In this chapter the task will be to consider the role played by love. The contention is that the identities of women and men have been shaped sexually, socially, spiritually and ethically by philosophical conceptions of love and morality. These two interrelated conceptions would seem to shape gender in philosophy of religion: 'love' is accompanied by 'morality', especially in the contexts of religious communities. Instead of stipulating definitions, let us look to see how love and morality have motivated theory and practice in gendering philosophy of religion.

Love, or what is called 'love', can be distorted and corrupted by the patriarchal domination which men and women have imagined to be sanctioned by the theistic God. Chapter 1 briefly explored Wollstonecraft's criticism of Milton's 'God' who had given man authority over women; and this man-woman relation was modelled on God's authority over man.[2] As explained, the problem that Wollstonecraft finds in Eve's voice from Milton's magisterial poem resounds in the ears of the woman at the heart of this patriarchal tradition in the history of European philosophy. Eve's apparent willing submission to Adam (man) is based upon an analogy to man's submissive obedience to his beloved God. This patriarchal hierarchy of obedience is not easily dismantled. The European Christian tradition still contains conceptions of Eve which merely re-enforce, what was described in Chapter 1 as, 'the hidden obstacle against a woman's own thinking'. This obstacle against women's cognition is repeatedly identified in philosophical texts and in social reality; yet to be able to see the obstacle as patriarchal the woman as a submissive partner must want to, and often be enabled to, recognize it as misogyny. In sharp contrast to this critical account of the decisive problem for feminism of a woman's submission to male authority, the Christian theologian Sarah Coakley – to whom

---

[1]   Material revised for this chapter comes from Pamela Sue Anderson, '"Moralizing" Love in Philosophy of Religion', in Jerald T. Wallulis and Jerald Hackett (eds), *Philosophy of Religion for a New Century* (Dordrecht: Kluwer Academic Publishers, 2004), pp. 227–242.

[2]   Sarah Coakley, *Powers and Submissions: Spirituality, Philosophy and Gender* (Oxford: Blackwell, 2002).

we will return in Chapter 9 – finds power in the right sort of 'submission' to the Christian God.

For centuries, the patriarchal account of the Christian God who, in the minds of those great British authors like Milton, eclipsed a woman's reason and her rights in the name of His (God's) love has determined gender relations in love; and this patriarchal conception of woman has been one of the most pervasive and difficult forms of gender injustice to unravel. Under the domination of an all-powerful love, the idea of perfection loses a sense of correct proportions for perfected divine love or perfecting human love. We will return, in Chapters 8 and 9, to the idea of love's perfection in the philosophy of Iris Murdoch.

In fact, the ideal of an all-powerful, all-knowing God easily becomes a human ideal for, what was called in Chapter 4, the 'corrupt aspiration to be infinite [God]'. As a result, to command love and to perfect love are contradictory. Without the freedom to love and to learn to love, domination and control are not only self and other destructive, but they destroy love itself.[3] When the love between human beings is modelled on the gender ideal of a man aspiring to be God, this (masculine) gender ideal becomes a tragic norm for men whose desire to be all-powerful and all-knowing in love not only destroys the other (woman), but potentially the (man's) self's ability to love and be loved. At the same time as this normative 'man' aims to be God, the normative woman submits to a man-God. Yet her submission also becomes self-destructive, as well as damaging to love itself.

To reverse the gender roles would not result in anything better: a woman aspiring to be divine herself can be trapped by the same model of love that is always, at least potentially, self- and other-destructive. The outcome of this gendering is asymmetrical values and heterosexual love-relations which fail to be – at a minimum – mutually love-enhancing.

The other conception, the second focus in this chapter, is morality. My contention is that moral norms in philosophy of religion motivate the gendering, or shaping of the identities of men and women in love relations. Morality and its close relation to the 'moralizing'[4] of love can become a problem inherent in the process of gendering. 'Morality' – taken roughly as the standard of what *ought* to be done – can motivate human beings in seeking to shape sex/gender relations, in order to perfect them either by themselves or by the measure of a divine ideal of perfection. Further on, we will see how cultivation of love, especially when love is cultivated as a virtue, can provide a non-authoritative reason and a critically constructive moral standard. Nevertheless, the nagging question persists, whether morality in the case of love is, or should be, about making rational judgments and correct reasoning? Gender complicates these matters. Due to the lack of philosophical engagement concerning 'gender', as well as 'love', any answers to philosophical

---

[3]   Pamela Sue Anderson, 'Sacrifice as self-destructive "love": why autonomy should still matter to feminists,' in Julia Meszaros and Johannes Zachhuber (eds), *Sacrifice and Modern Thought* (Oxford: Oxford University Press, 2013).

[4]   Anderson, '"Moralizing" Love in Philosophy of Religion', pp. 227–228, 241–242.

questions about morality and love, motivating the process of gendering, are not straightforward.

Frequently, if asked, or inclined, to make moral judgments about love and gender, along with sexual, racial, plus other social and material relations, we can be quickly confronted by accusations of 'moralizing'. Not only does this immediately have negative connotations, but when moralizing is said to come from either a feminist or a masculinist[5] standpoint on right and wrong, then positions quickly become polarized. An one-sided gender defence of a matter of love also quickly becomes dogmatic. Can a moral judgment, or a well-reasoned argument, about gendering avoid being polarized into dogmatic gender positions, especially on love? The philosopher (or moralizer) would hope so. Yet it is easy to doubt the possibility of rational argumentation when confronted by moral accusations and dogmatic responses. Indeed, the philosopher of gender may find herself in a vicious circle of thought. The problem becomes circular: the more she tries to be self-aware the less she is aware of the other in love (her beloved), the more she tries to be aware of her beloved the less she is self-aware (loving herself). Moralizing about the rights and the wrongs of love can become a trap. Let us see how this has been so, and whether we can do something about it.

Polarized gender positions: on the morality of love

Specific problems in this present context are created by the traditional, often unwitting gendering of human and divine love in philosophy of religion. First, as has been suggested in the paragraphs above, the immorality of one subject dominating another in love manifests itself in relations that fail to be what they ought to be: that is, mutually love-enhancing. But this sense of failure requires justification. Not every Christian philosopher would agree with this account of 'failure' due to the asymmetry of love relations: that asymmetrical relations result in pernicious domination and abuse is contentious. For instance, it could be argued that to have each subject either dominating or obeying another is how God created and commanded heterosexual love relations to be. Even some female psychologists might argue that domination in sexual relations is necessary to satisfy the desires of some men and of some women. Can we agree on 'what ought to be' the nature of gender relations in love? A question for morality is: how ought we treat each other sexually, socially, spiritually and ethically in love? Arguably if consciously gendering love in philosophy of religion we should be able to propose possible justifications of how we ought to act in relation to (i) those of the same, different or similar gender who love us; (ii) those of the same, different or similar gender

---

[5]   'Masculinist' is a term used to designate 'anti-feminist positions' by Grace M. Jantzen, *Becoming Divine: Towards a Feminist Philosophy of Religion* (Manchester: Manchester University Press, 1998), p. 3. I mainly follow Jantzen when using masculinist in this book.

who do not love us; and (iii) those of the same, different or similar gender who we ought to love in return.

Second, a perennial issue for morality and religion emerges with love. Is something loved (good) because God has commanded this thing? Or, does God command something because it is love (good)? The traditional divine command position would say it is the former: it is the loving or good thing to do because God has commanded. Yet to think about gendering in this context it could be philosophically significant to propose that 'love' is not the same as 'good' or, at least, not an absolute 'good'. Instead love is uniquely relational; if perfected love requires reciprocity, then love comes from loving and being loved. Of course, love could start with a personal God who chooses to relate to human beings in love; and divine self-giving love could begin the chain of reciprocal and relational love. If this follows, then to love correctly, as we ought, would be to make reciprocal love relations flourish. Both lover and beloved would, then, manifest mutual love, reciprocally loving oneself and another self.

However, there are many different kinds of love. To name some of those well-known terms distinguished in Greek as *agape*, *eros*, *philia*, these terms for love have come into moral philosophy in order to distinguish the norms of who and how to love. To complicate matters, the traditional moral norms of Christian theism tend to make it contentious to try to argue that gender is not based on biology as our God-given nature, but on personal or social grounds. Nevertheless, love could yet be shown to be merely a matter of the norms for personal love relations as determined by a particular social context. One argument for gendering love in philosophy of religion could be that personal norms depend upon theistic morality and the Christian religion. Whatever the view of love there is a good reason for philosophers of religion to be involved in the process of justifying or not the gendering of love which shapes personal and social relations. The critical and analytical skills of philosophy, if any abilities can, should be able to enhance informed knowledge of love and gender, but also to confront uncritically assumed religious norms for gender. In fact, religious beliefs have tended to determine gender norms; that is, what is or is not moral behaviour within, say, a religious community, or a country can be determined, say, by the 'Church of England' or head(s) of communities.

In light of these contentious matters it is not surprising that when it comes to gender and philosophy of religion, philosophical reasoning is rarely successful in sorting out disagreements over gender's intersection with religion, sexuality, class, race and ethnicity. Instead philosophers have appeared to be much happier claiming gender-neutrality in their argumentation about knowledge, morality and religion. Yet love would be a very strange thing without gender and a very difficult thing to trust without critical reflection. Even when God is said to love no matter a person's gender, love for human beings and between human subjects and a divine being will continue to find it a strange predicament that the omni-being can love without gender: no human being can love exactly as God loves or return the exact same love to God if 'he' is genderless, precisely because gender cannot be separated from our bodily nature, our bodily relations and our positioning in life. Instead human subjects behave in every other love relation, as if informed by the gendered norms of their societies and religions.

Thus we will inevitably have to ask about a disembodied God, or love without a body, as soon as we begin to consider gender and love in philosophy of religion. What determines how we decide whether a judgment is good or bad, right or wrong, when it comes to love relations? Traditionally, 'the Church' in the west has been heard speaking out for or against specific kinds of sexual behaviour, as the authoritative standard for when someone is deviating from previously determined moral norms, or so it is thought. Nevertheless, today from each of the feminist and the masculinist camps, as discussed in Chapter 3, the lines are drawn and sides are taken when it comes to gendering God: it tends to be either the views of difference feminists or masculinist theists which make the judgments, on how gendering determines or not the moral behaviour of women and men. For instance, the sexual difference feminist is like to defend a different voice for women in Christian ethics from that a men. However, as seen already, not all feminist philosophers or feminist ethicists maintain an ethics of sexual difference.

Recall that advocates for a feminist of sexual difference claim a woman becomes fully herself only with the help of a divine ideal in her own gender. According to Irigaray, the best-known advocate of sexual difference, men already have a God who defines their own gender. So Irigaray contends that the traditional Christian model of masculine subjectivity and a man's love is not complete, or ethical, without a 'divine in the feminine' and a woman's love.[6] As also stated in Chapter 3, this feminine divine is meant to give women the ideal for her gender which is what men have had. Irigaray insists that a 'divine in the masculine' has been the ideal for men's gender (in Christian patriarchy). Yet as demonstrated in Chapter 3, not every feminist or masculinist would agree with gendering the divine, in order to create the ideals for one's own sexually specific gender. As will be argued in Chapter 9, domination and abuse seem to be a constant threat for the submissive gender in the love relations which are based upon a divine ideal. Under gender domination, the heterosexual love-relations apparently fit the traditional model of one gender as all-powerful, and, perhaps like the Christian God, all-knowing, while the other gender is submissive. A singular divine who is the gender ideal for 'man' himself to become divine is an interpretation of the traditional Christian picture of patriarchy: God as the ideal for man knows best what it is for man to become divine; and in turn, the man like God knows best what love is for the other gender, woman, who only has to submit – and to suffer – to fulfill her gender ideal.

---

[6]   Luce Irigaray, 'Toward a Divine in the Feminine', in Gillian Howie and J'annine Jobling (eds), *Women and the Divine: Touching Transcendence* (New York: Palgrave Macmillan, 2009), pp. 13–26. Also see Luce Irigaray, 'Divine Women', *Genealogies and Sexes*, trans. Gillian C. Gill (New York: Columbia University Press, 1993), pp. 55–72.

It remains unclear whether a submissive relation of a woman to a man can be undone by following Irigaray's proposal for a divine in the feminine. Try to imagine a woman who successfully becomes divine with a divine in the feminine as her ideal, a very clear sense of the relation between the different genders would seem to be required. Yet, mutually formative male and female relations would seem to be unlikely insofar as the feminine and masculine genders are formed in relation to their own divine ideals and not to each other. The danger with this would be a form of mutual narcissism rather than sadism and masochism.[7] For an alternative to this gendering of love in Irigarayan 'theology' of sexual difference, the present chapter turns to feminist philosophy informed by Enlightenment philosophers. In particular, a later section in this chapter will explore the gendering of love relations by Wollstonecraft. In so doing, it will pick up an issue from Chapter 1, while also bringing in Kant's conception of practical love.[8]

'Moralizing': a problem for pure reason

The writing of *A Feminist Philosophy of Religion* (1998)[9] was motivated by a twofold sense of (i) yearning for love in a heartless world; and (ii) longing to put things in order, arising from a highly specific consciousness of gender injustice. A sense of yearning for love can move women to question religious beliefs which have proven inconsistent with the reality of domination and/or with the perfecting of love. A sense of longing to-put-things-right moves the desires of women and men who have suffered unfairly the painful disorientation of trauma. It seems philosophically right to give order to emotions and to reasons disordered by evil suffered and committed. Arguably, in philosophy of religion, love and morality should come together in trying to give a rational defence for re-ordering things as they ought to be.

Some readers will have already recognized the distinctive Kantian overtones of my critical reflection on love and on the imperative to love and to desire what ought to love and desire. For some non-Kantian, this will sound circular. Nevertheless, love's motivation to do (love) as 'we ought to' love could be correct, while the

---

[7]   For an account which addresses the problems of sadism and masochism in love relations modelled on a French Hegelian self-other struggle, see Pamela Sue Anderson, 'A Story of Love and Death: Exploring space for the philosophical imaginary', in Heather Walton (ed.), *Literature and Theology: New Interdisciplinary Spaces* (Farnham, Surrey: Ashgate Publishing Limited, 2011), pp. 167–186.

[8]   For reception of Kant by philosophers on matters to do with theology and with gender, see Pamela Sue Anderson and Jordan Bell, *Kant and Theology*, Philosophy for Theologians (New York and London: T & T Clark, a division of Continuum International Publishing, 2010).

[9]   Pamela Sue Anderson, *A Feminist Philosophy of Religion: The Rationality and Myths of Religious Belief* (Oxford: Blackwell, 1998).

problem is that any human demand for perfection is bound to be disappointed. Many feminists and other perfectionists suffer a great deal of guilt for not being able to meet the rationally optimum standard, whether in love or in morality. Of course, the masculinist philosopher could diagnose the problem as one of pride: it is sinful or, as we recall, it is hubris to want 'to be (so to speak) rationality itself'.[10] This takes up the point from Chapter 4, where the following view of A. W. Moore was stated:

> When the craving [for infinitude] is distorted, [its] perspectival character is turned in on itself in such a way that the craving becomes an aspiration *that we alone exist* ... It becomes the aspiration to be a complete self-sufficient unconditioned whole, to be that which the craving for infinitude is a craving for.[11]

However, when it comes to generalizing this position as accounting for the sin of pride, a contemporary feminist theologian will undoubtedly – and quickly – object that, under patriarchy, a woman's sin is not one of pride. Instead it is the opposite; if sinful, the problem for the woman dominated by patriarchal gender norms will be that she does not love herself enough!

As mentioned in the first section of this chapter, the challenge is to avoid the trap set for feminists in gendering love and morality. It is not clear where the fault lies. The moralizing trap for women's love is set by two equally unattractive gender alternatives (at least this is unattractive for feminists who do not embrace an 'ethics of sexual difference').[12] This imagery of a trap captures the no-win choice of either becoming divine as women in love or remaining submissive to men in love; it could 'feel' inevitable that feminists moralize about right or wrong, but not advance beyond the choice. If so, it is not surprising that moralizing love has had negative connotations for both feminist and non-feminist philosophers. Most problematic philosophically is that 'moralizing' connotes an imposition of moral judgment onto non-moral phenomena; or the intrusion of moral concerns where they do not rightfully belong. Notwithstanding these connotations, when accused of moralizing, feminist philosophers have tried to turn this negative into something positive. The history of European philosophy supports positive interpretations of moralizing in the sense of making moral sense of love.

For example, Enlightenment philosopher Wollstonecraft, not totally unlike Kant when it comes to the role of reason in love, makes good sense out the moralizing of love. Selecting passages in texts from these two philosophers helps to shift our focus away from that choice of equally unattractive gender roles in love. As clear from Irigarayan feminists debates about difference, 'the feminine'

---

[10] Moore, *Points of View*, p. 276.

[11] Ibid.

[12] For a collection of essays on religion and sexual difference, see Morny Joy, Kathleen O'Grady and Jill Pozon (eds), *French Feminists on Religion: A Reader* (London/New York: Routledge, 2002).

and 'the masculine' are very often seen as battling polarized opposites; this is clearly the case, whether the hierarchy of gender values are merely to be reversed or the two genders are merely separated from each other.

An additional disclaimer should be made before launching into Enlightenment philosophy: it is a fairly popular assumption that Irigarayan and other Christian readings of Enlightenment philosophy generally reject the role of human reason in matters of love and of morality. Sarah Coakley has also seemed to reject Enlightenment philosophy insofar as she returns to medieval theology, although Coakley's rejection is less obvious than that of contemporary Christian theologians who bluntly dismiss Kant for damaging Christian theism and moral theology.[13] Nevertheless, it is worth mentioning Coakley at this stage because of her distinctive vision for a feminist philosophy of religion. Her work on gender is linked to a reading of the body in pre-Enlightenment theology texts; but it also treats gender as a quality of female or male subjectivity. For example, she has pointed out 'soft spots' in the texts of Anglo-American Christian (male) philosophers of religion, in order to tease out dimensions of gender in philosophy of religion which has gone unnoticed. For Coakley, unlike Kant or Wollstonecraft, love and one's relation to divine love is bound to one's passions, gender and practices such as prayer in which female subjects find power in submission to God. One consequent of her view is that Coakley's conception of gender and religious practices are unlikely to be compatible with Kantian feminism or Kantian philosophy of religion. However, the challenge in this chapter is directed to the assumption that the Enlightenment was simply bad for women and for love.

Here it is crucial that we grasp the position of the contemporary Kantian and, generally, 'modern' rather than 'postmodern' thought for feminist philosopher of religion. This crucial if we seek to expose what has been deceptively imposed as authoritative in philosophy of religion which sits uneasily with the Enlightenment.[14]

Beverley Clack has offered more even-handed view of the way through the horns of a dilemma between Anglo-American masculinist philosophy and French feminist philosophy of sexual difference, not blaming the Enlightenment or modern philosophy of religion. Clack remains in the line of Anglo-American feminist philosophy of religion, while being impatient with overly abstract

---

[13]   Sarah Coakley, *Powers and Submissions: Spirituality, Philosophy and Gender* (Oxford: Blackwell, 2002).

[14]   For the dangers with this feminist opposition to the authority of reason as the ground of morality, see Sabina Lovibond, 'The End of Morality', in Kathleen Lennon and Margaret Whitford (eds), *Knowing the Difference: Feminist Perspectives in Epistemology* (London: Routledge, 1994), pp. 63–78. For discussion of reason in modern ethics and epistemology, see Sabina Lovibond, *Ethical Formation* (Cambridge, MA: Harvard University Press, 2002); and Miranda Fricker, 'Feminism in Epistemology: Pluralism without Postmodernism', in Miranda Fricker and Jennifer Hornsby (eds), *The Cambridge Companion to Feminism in Philosophy* (Cambridge: Cambridge University Press, 2000), pp. 146–165.

debates in analytic philosophy of religion on love, sex and death.[15] Clack concerns herself with the practical level of Anglo-American and French feminists which finds common ground on shared issues of gender justice. Feminist philosophers each in their own way can confront the practical side of gendering philosophy of religion. This could be, say, in a practice which would rationally (that is, coherently, consistently, precisely, logically, etc) work out and rightly order actions and passions; but this would be, without giving up the messiness of life, which (masculine) gender practices in philosophy tend to ignore or to smooth out. Epistemic practices in traditional philosophy of religion and religious beliefs have to their own detriment appealed to phenomena and to concerns which transcend bodily life, ignoring moral and other concrete phenomena. The critical question is: could transcendence of bodily life be precisely the problem of sexism in love? One answer is that philosophers who claim to transcend the body in philosophical arguments concerning the traditional theistic God, ignore the gender rendering their claims about love self-defeating. Without awareness of their bodies and gender's intersection with sexuality, religion and so, these philosophers eclipse reason in thinking and acting in their most intimate relations.

However, again as in Chapter 3 questioning the morality of love and gender meets popular debates between masculine theists and difference feminists. But this is a problem for gendering love in philosophy of religion. When sharply opposed feminism and theism appear to be two separate ways of understanding male and female relations to the divine. Crudely speaking, one of these ways is transcendence, the other way is non-transcendent moralizing. Chapter 9 will return to the claim that, crudely speaking, 'masculine theism' is a caricature of Christianity looked at from outside of actual Christian practices; and this is so, precisely on the question of gender. Gendering love in theism involves an omnibenevolent God without a body.[16] Yet men and women inevitably gender love and differentiate who to love and how to love according to factors related to bodily life. A God who is omnipotent, omni-benevolent, omniscient, impassible and sovereign may be beyond moral scrutiny; yet if we are going to talk concretely about love, or concretely about any other topic to do with practical matters, in philosophy of religion, then we have to address questions about God and love just as much as God and time, or God and morality.

In contrast to the masculinist who attempts to transcend bodily life, in order to love by aspiring to be God, the feminist philosopher of religion finds she cannot transcend bodily life but must make 'the personal' and all that goes with it 'political'. Treating morality, in this context, as personal moral philosophy becomes political; and re-visioning gender begins. This political re-visioning aims to block attempts to separate private and public spheres of love and morality. If morality is a matter of practice, it deserves a public (just as much as a philosophical) debate; if this is agreed, then morality does play a role in political life. Yet we

---

[15]   Beverley Clack, *Sex and Death* (Cambridge: Polity Press, 2002).

[16]   For more detailed questions about a 'personal' God 'without a body', see Chapter 9.

need to become clear about whether philosophy (of religion) is political or not. If feminist philosophers make a moral judgment about, or introduce a moral issue concerning, love in philosophy are we imposing morality? One answer would be: not necessarily, if we can talk practically and rationally about gender and love. As long as both moral concerns and philosophy are public, or political, matters then there would be no imposing of morality on something private.

The problem is that pure reason – or, so it seems to some critics of the Enlightenment – led modern philosophers off onto the wrong track on matters of love. Basically, the charge has been that Enlightenment philosophers fail to know how to cultivate love as fully incarnate, since love cannot be known (empirically) to exist through bodies. But this does not necessarily follow. For example, Kant makes a clear distinction between theoretical and practical reasoning. Love is a topic for both pure and practical reason. For instance, the implication here is that love can be learnt as a 'know how', that is, as discussed in Chapter 4 concerning Moore's account of 'ineffable knowledge', to knowing how to love can be shown, but not put into propositional form. A proposition asserting love will not express knowing how to love. And yet, if love was treated as 'nonsense' this only means that the concept, 'love', does not have an object which can be pointed to; it is without sense content, yet we do love. In fact, Kant himself never wrote that bodies cannot practice loving others. Instead according to Kant, love as a 'pathological feeling' can become 'practical', through rational cultivation of the feeling beyond the pathological.[17]

Although there is not space for a detailed defence of Kantian virtue of love here, it should be made clear that neatly abstract examples of the morality of God's love as might be found in contemporary philosophy of religion are not examples which Kant would discuss. On theoretical grounds, Kant could not talk about empirical examples of God who is empirically unknowable. On practical grounds, Kant cultivates love without erasing bodily experiences of love's inevitable messiness and brokenness: the very idea of Kantian morality as an 'ought' not an 'is' reflects the fact that Kant did not assume any human morality could get away from life – from its messiness and concreteness, its natural inclinations and difficulties working out of moral maxims. All of this life is presupposed by the demand of Kantian morality to do what one ought to do. No 'ought' would be necessary if we just did the good or just knew how to love. Morality needs cultivation; it must be practically worked out not empirically known. As Christine Swanton[18] has pointed out, Anglo-American philosophers seem to ignore the fact that in Kant's 'Doctrine of Virtue' he refers to love as one of two 'great moral forces'. To cite Kant:

---

[17]   Kant, *Groundwork of the Metaphysics of Morals*, p. 65 (399); and Kant, *The Metaphysic of Morals*, pp. 159–160 (399–400).

[18]   Christine Swanton, 'Kant's Impartial Virtues of Love', in Lawrence Jost and Julian Wuerth (eds), *Perfecting Virtue: New Essays on Kantian Ethics and Virtue Ethics* (Cambridge: Cambridge University Press, 2011), pp. 241–259.

In speaking of laws of duty (not laws of nature) and, among these, of laws for human beings' external relations with one another, we consider ourselves in a moral (intelligible) world where, by analogy with the physical world, *attraction* and *repulsion* bind together rational beings (on earth). The principle of **mutual love** admonishes them constantly to *come closer* to one another; that of the **respect** they owe one another, to keep themselves *at a distance* from one another; and should one of these great moral forces fail, 'then nothingness (immorality), with gaping throat, would drink up the whole kingdom of (moral) beings like a drop of "water"'.[19]

So, Kant does treat love as not a 'law of nature' but as a necessary 'moral force' which, as a principle, practically admonishes rational beings to come closer together and binds rational beings together 'on earth'. Love could not be more central to Kantian morality in a practical sense: it is a motivating moral force to participate in Kant's whole kingdom of rational beings as ends in themselves, not as mere means.

Enlightenment philosophy: on the authority of reason

In dismissing 'female emotions', contemporary feminists of sexual difference have been known to object to what they see as Wollstonecraft's deep suspicion of emotion. However, this is clearly a harmful dismissal of a great woman thinker who, in 1792, wrote *A Vindication of the Rights of Woman*[20]. Moreover, the danger of not reading any philosophical text, including Wollstonecraft's text, with sensitivity to its precise use of concepts and to its author's own social and political interlocutors will probably always fail to find women writing philosophy before one's own time and with one's own conceptual framework.[21] Instead Wollstonecraft's texts gives every indication of her knowing women of her time, as well as knowing her contemporary philosophical concepts in the texts of her formidable male contemporaries. As already mentioned she knew Milton's account of women in *Paradise Lost*; and she clearly read Rousseau's *Emile* with great care, finding in Rousseau a target to address the issue of gender injustice in the different moral and aesthetic educations of men and women.

Much of the evidence gathered to dismiss Wollstonecraft in fact comes from her argument that women be educated, and follow their reason like in Rousseau's

---

[19] Immanuel Kant, *The Metaphysics of Morals*, trans. and edited by Mary Gregor (Cambridge: Cambridge University Press, 1996), pp. 198–199 [6: 449].

[20] Mary Wollstonecraft, *A Vindication of the Rights of Women*, edited with an Introduction by Miriam Brody (Harmondsworth: Penguin Classics, 1985), pp. 113ff, 142ff, 174, 278.

[21] For careful textual argument on Wollstonecraft and Kant, see Susan Mendus, *Feminism and Emotion* (London: Macmillan, 2000).

argument for moral education. So Wollstonecraft was arguing for women's education and not just for them to follow emotion. However, far from construing emotion as the enemy of reason Enlightenment philosophy can be a source of help in the moralization of love. Careful textual analyses of both Wollstonecraft and Kant reveal highly nuanced accounts of emotion (such as we have seen with love in Kant) as reason's moral complement and not its opposite.

In her personal correspondence to her lover Gilbert Imlay, Wollstonecraft herself becomes a strong advocate of the moral cultivation of love, in bringing this emotion into league with practical reasoning and the laws of duty. In this way, love becomes an object of moral assessment, while lack of practical reasoning is a moral fault. Wollstonecraft clearly and passionately insists that being a slave to a form of love which is simply brute passion is a great moral weakness. Readers can find much more evidence of Wollstonecraft's feminist arguments for the education of women and for the moral cultivation of love in friendship between men and women. Far from dismissing Wollstonecraft, along with the rest of the Enlightenment, philosophers of religion and feminist theologians interested in gender and in love in various forms of friendship and in the different forms of love, could not do much better than read Wollstonecraft. Her insistence on women's education and cultivation of friendship between men and women appears in *A Vindication*, in conjunction with her argument for the need to moralize emotion. Wollstonecraft's arguments could have the effect of undermining the public and private opposition oppressing many women even today.

Admittedly, contemporary feminist philosophers have raised serious questions about Kant surviving feminist critiques of his rationalist philosophy.[22] Yet arguably, the popular postmodern idea that feminists have 'subverted' Enlightenment 'reason' has done untold damage to women's reading of Kant's own texts. It is crucial to recognize a critical distinction between the role of reason as 'authoritative' for morality and 'authoritarian' in imposing moral judgments on men and women. Perhaps (too) often anti-Enlightenment philosophers of religion have read the 'authority' of reason to be only 'authoritarian'. If so, then it is understandable that authoritarian reason has been read as oppressive for women.[23] However, this is still not an excuse for muddling terms; it does not help questions of moral (rational) judgments or the gendering of love, to fail to understand or to make fine distinctions. Basically, this chapter is urging women and any dogmatically anti-Enlightenment philosophers of religion to think beyond what may seem obvious, to recognize that perhaps a certain 'intrusion' when it comes to moral questions about love is inevitable. In fact the proper intrusion of the 'right', as in the just

---

[22]   Sally Sedgwick, 'Can Kant's Ethics Survive the Feminist Critique', in Robin May Schott (ed.), *Feminist Interpretations of Kant* (University Park, PA: Penn State University Press, 1997), pp. 77–100; cf. Mari Mikkola, 'Kant on Moral Agency and Women's Nature', *Kantian Review* (2011): 89–112.

[23]   Lovibond, 'The End of Morality', pp. 66–68; cf. Fricker, 'Feminism in Epistemology: Pluralism without Postmodernism', pp. 146–165.

authority of reason, would be helpful when it comes to trying to tackle gender injustice. The goal, as I see it, would be to avoid oppositional thinking; if the theistic God is 'in control', then we do not need to worry about distinguishing the right authority of human reason.

For example, consider the admonition of Wollstonecraft to her lover Gilbert Imlay:

> The tremendous power who formed this heart must have foreseen that, in a world in which self-interest, in various shapes, is the principal mobile, I had little chance of escaping misery. To the fiat of fate I submit. I am content to be wretched; but I will not be contemptible. Of me you have no cause to complain, but for having had too much regard for you – for having expected a degree of permanent happiness, when you only sought for a momentary gratification.[24]

It seems rational and practically wise to argue that the right authority of reason would force unfaithful lovers to rethink brute passion as that which fails reason's tests of reliability, consistency and constancy. In other words, emotion which is not controlled by reason – though this is not the same as being under oppression or domination of authoritarian uses of reason – reflects a moral fault in failing to be steadfast. In the case of Wollstoncraft, if Imlay only wanted to satisfy momentary gratification, love fails to become habitual, or habituated, as a virtue.

A critical aim of the present chapter – to be picked up again in Chapter 9 – is to argue that careful readings of love in Kant as a moral force and in Wollstonecraft as a moral commitment have significant philosophical implications for practices – including religious practices – but also for debates about human identities and relations, about love and perfecting love. If take seriously, the 'Kantian feminist' would not be a laughable oxymoron. Kant does not just make emotion subservient to reason.[25] Instead, a potentially attractive picture of Kant's reconciliation of reason and emotion can be found in his moralizing of love. Reference has already been made to Kant's *The Metaphysics of Morals* which should be read on love and reason, since his *Groundwork of the Metaphysics of Morals* does not give an adequate picture of his practical philosophy, especially on questions to do with Kantian virtue.[26] The picture in the *Groundwork* is that love, which springs solely from inclination, has no moral worth. It is necessary to learn that Kant builds upon the distinction he makes in the *Groundwork* between pathological and practical love, when in his later *Lectures on Ethics* and *The Metaphysics of Morals*

---

[24]   Mary Wollstonecraft, 'Letters to Imlay', in Marilyn Butler and Janet Todd (eds), *The Works of Mary Wollstonecraft*, vol. 6, LXVII (London: Chatto & Pickering, 1989).

[25]   For notable critique of Kant and Kantian morality, see Bernard Williams, *Ethics and the Limits of Philosophy* (London: Fontana Books, 1985), pp. 55–70, 104.

[26]   Immanuel Kant, *Groundwork of the Metaphysics of Morals*, trans. and edited by H. J. Paton in *The Moral Law* (London: Hutchinson & Co., 1951), pp. 63–65 (original text, 398–399).

he reveals emotion as a presupposition to moral philosophy; this emotion can be cultivated.[27]

Basically, the aim of a Kantian account of love as a moral force, then, would be to unearth morally contentious matters in everyday experience. For example, the Kantian account would consider the contention that love should be universalizable, habitual, reliable and consistent: otherwise it is not rational-moral, but immoral. But even more, to open our minds to the idea that the emotions are morally contentious could give us ground for the rightful intrusion of feminism and philosophy into everyday life, as well as feminism into philosophy of religion. Our relationships of love are especially contentious today, insofar as the gendering of these relationships has begun to re-shape our lived experiences. For instance, to elucidate the ways in which gendering love has followed strictly heterosexual norms reveals how these norms have dominated our interpretations of lived experiences. But is this treating non-heterosexual subjects as Kantian ends-in-themselves? If not, Kantian morality would have to say that the non-heterosexual are not being treated rationally or morally as persons in their own rights. So, it is possible that Wollstonecraft and Kant can each critically inform our gendering of love in philosophy of religion. But 'gendering', in this context, includes an internal critique of morality; and the latter would have to seek to avoid moralizing.[28] In other words, Enlightenment reasoning is not a fixed measure for all moral cases for all times. Instead gendering love should be able to show when and who acts morally. The additional question to be addressed in later chapters is when gendering love requires re-visioning.

Intervention of feminism: on the 'theft' of love

In the late 1990s bell hooks – whose writings, as should have become obvious, have inspired sections of Chapters 1, 6, 8, 9 and 10 of this book, especially on gender's intersectionality – urged feminists to realize how an ethic of love must be part of any political movement. Love should motivate a move toward other gendered subjects across a range of social and material categories.[29] Although before hooks published on love, the Bulgarian-Parisian psychoanalyst Julia Kristeva had also urged that 'tales of love' would, or at least could, give meaning to our lives. This

---

[27]   Immanuel Kant, *Lectures on Ethics* (London: Methuen, 1930), p. 197; and *Metaphysic of Morals*, trans. and edited by Mary Gregor (Cambridge: Cambridge University Press, 1996).

[28]   For further discussion of 'gendering', see Pamela Sue Anderson, 'Autonomy, Vulnerability and Gender', *Feminist Theory,* 4(2) special issue on *Ethical Relations: Agency, Autonomy and Care*, edited by Sasha Roseneil and Linda Hogan (August 2003): 149–164.

[29]   bell hooks, *Wounds of Passion: A Writing Life* (New York: Henry Holt and Co., 1997); and *All About Love: New Visions* (London: The Women's Press, 2000).

includes love in all its forms. In fact, urgency is also heard in Kristeva's own narrative texts as she exposes the 'maladies of our souls'.[30]

> No matter how far back my love memories go, I find it difficult to talk about them. They relate to an exaltation beyond eroticism that is as much inordinate happiness as it is pure suffering; both turn words into passion. The language of love is impossible, inadequate, immediately allusive when one would like it to be most straightforward; … what I shall be discussing here is a sort of philosophy of love … . an infinite quest for rebirths through the experience of love, which is begun again only to be displaced, renewed … [31]

> … satisfying the narcissistic discontent that accompanies the modern crisis of values seems to be at odds with this sort of psychic inquiry, an inquiry that seems necessary for any transformation of subjectivity.

> Psychoanalysis goes against the grain of the modern convenience that calls attention not to the end of the Story of Civilization, but to end of the possibility of *telling a story*.[32]

For Kristeva – as for hooks – the living body is a loving body, and the loving body is a speaking body; but without words and words woven into narratives of love, we are wandering soulless, corpses; and so the figure of Narcissus haunts the works of Kristeva on love. Narcissus is 'an exile, deprived of his psychic space, an extraterrestrial with a prehistory that grounds a longing for love'. Kristeva continues, 'Thanks to Christian elaborations, Narcissus was able to rally, give himself musical and pictural dignity, and move generations on account of his [unwitting] metamorphoses …' into figures of love. Yet today, with the loss of belief in Christian narratives as 'true' in a scientific or empirical sense, Narcissus only 'longs to reinvent love'.[33]

When it comes to gendering as an internal critique of the morality of religion Kristeva's near contemporary, who has been presented as the representative of sexual difference, that is, the Belgian-born, French psycholinguist, Irigaray has

---

[30]　Julia Kristeva, *Tales of Love*, trans. Leon S. Roudiez (New York: Columbia University Press, 1987), p. 1; *New Maladies of the Soul*, trans. Ross Mitchell Guberman (New York: Columbia University Press, 1995), pp. 27ff.

[31]　Kristeva, *Tales of Love*, p. 1.

[32]　Kristeva, *New Maladies of the Soul*, pp. 43–44.

[33]　Kristeva, *Tales of Love*, pp. 382–383. Kristeva portrays this crisis of love and atheism in a novel where persons are metamorphosed into wolves: *The Old Man and the Wolves*, trans. Barbara Bray (New York: Columbia University Press, 1994). For Kristeva's language of exiles in this novel, see Pamela Sue Anderson, 'Writing on Exiles and Excess: Toward a New Form of Subjectivity', in Heather Walton and Andrew Hass (eds), *Self/Same/ Other: Re-visioning the Subject in Literature and Theology* (Sheffield: Sheffield Academic Press, 2000), pp. 106–124.

done perhaps more than any other feminist to evoke and provoke radical thinking on the specifically *sexual* nature of love. In particular, she describes in highly dramatic and poetic terms, the 'theft' of women's love from her own world, her body and her relation to the divine. In Irigaray's words,

> [the female lover] is brought into a world that is not her own so that the male lover may enjoy himself and gain strength for his voyage toward an autistic transcendence. In his quest for a God who is already inscribed but voiceless, does she permit him not to constitute the ethical site of lovemaking? A seducer who is seduced by the gravity of the Other but approaches the female other carelessly, he takes her light to illuminate his path. Without regard for what shines and glistens between them. Whether he wills it or not, knows it or not, he uses this divine light to illuminate reason or the invisibility of the 'god' … and he will have sent her back to darkness. He will have stolen her gaze. And her song.[34]

A Feminist Philosophy of Religion cites the same passage from Irigaray's text to provoke thinking about love in its relations to both divine and human subjects.[35] But 'An Ethics of Memory' turns to focus more constructively upon hooks's attempt to make narrative sense of life.[36] Moving beyond broken promises and lost love, hooks expresses forgiveness in a narrative of new beginnings. The themes of love, new beginnings (natality), promising, forgiving and making narrative sense of life run through the writings of women philosophers in the twentieth-century. From Hannah Arendt to Kristeva, Irigaray, Adriana Cavarero and Jantzen, each of these women in (or, in relation to) philosophy had recognized a common desire or need to try to make sense of the brokenness of our lives.[37] Yet generally speaking this does not mean to suppress love's suffering. Instead,

> To become natals – and mortals – we must be created and creative in love. …
> The yearning to *know* such love renders possible not only our relationships and

---

[34]   Luce Irigaray, *An Ethics of Sexual Difference*, trans. Carolyn Burke and Gillian C. Gill (Ithaca, NY: Cornell University Press, 1993), pp. 209–210.

[35]   Anderson, *A Feminist Philosophy of Religion*, pp. 99–100.

[36]   Pamela Sue Anderson, 'An Ethics of Memory: Promising, Forgiving and Yearning', in Graham Ward (ed.), *Blackwell's Companion to Postmodern Theology* (Oxford: Blackwell, 2001), pp. 231–248.

[37]   See Hannah Arendt, *Love and Saint Augustine*, edited with an Interpretative Essay by Joanna Vecchiarellis Scott and Judith Chelius Stark (Chicago: University of Chicago Press, 1996); *The Human Condition* second edition (Chicago: University of Chicago Press, 1998), pp. 175–192. Julia Kristeva, *Hannah Arendt*, trans. Ross Guberman (New York: Columbia University Press, 2001), especially pp. 40–48, 234–240. Adriana Cavarero, *In Spite of Plato: A Feminist Rewriting of Ancient Philosophy*, trans. Serena Anderlini-D'Onofrio and Aine O'Healy (Cambridge: Polity Press, 1995), pp. xviii, 6–7, 25.

mutual promises, but our suffering in birth, in life, and at the death or loss of another.[38]

A central example of the brokenness of commitment is the marital promise and, similarly, the implicit promises of love involving sexuality. In the failure of such promises we find the loss of love in an acute, personal form.[39] In particular, ethical debates tend to support the view that promises of love, or sexual commitment, cannot be made because in the long term none of us remains the same. We recognize in this reasoning a problem of personal identity. Yet the problem is in a deeper assumption which has intuitive appeal: that only short term promises carry any moral weight. This intuition has been most powerfully stated and impressively defended by Oxford philosopher Derek Parfit.[40] Parfit treats commitment as if an act of prediction: it is a guess at how much I will change and what new knowledge I will have in the future about my self and the person to whom I might make a commitment. Nevertheless, the counter argument has a strong intuitive appeal, too: that a commitment is not a prediction; it is not based upon limited knowledge of a person or of what will be. Instead making a commitment like a promise is an act of intention that is meant to endure; it can remain even as the partners change and gain greater (self)-knowledge of, or in, the future. In other words, a prediction is not the same as, nor can it form an unconditional commitment. A making of a promise is an intention or diachronic (i.e. temporally shaped) act which can endure; this is the distinctive quality of commitment.

Kant himself is well-known for his demonstration of self-consistency in promise keeping.[41] Any popular belief about promises being predictive is conceptually incoherent. The intuitive appeal of the moral worth of short-term promises is grossly misleading, since it misunderstands the nature of a commitment.

Love and commitment in analytic philosophy

This section aims to explore what the 'moralizing' of love in personal commitments offers to debates in analytic philosophy? William Newton-Smith, in 'A Conceptual Investigation of Love', acknowledges that 'concepts like love, which we use

---

[38]   Anderson, 'An Ethics of Memory', p. 242.

[39]   For a conceptual analysis of love involving sexuality that reveals the extent to which such love implies commitment, see William Newton-Smith, 'A Conceptual Investigation of Love', in Alan Montefiore (ed.), *Philosophy and Personal Relations: An Anglo-French Study* (London: Routledge & Kegan Paul Ltd, 1973), pp. 113–136.

[40]   Derek Parfit, 'Later Selves and Moral Principles', in *Philosophy and Personal Relations*, pp. 144–162; and *Reasons and Persons* (Oxford: Oxford University Press, 1984), Chapter 15, 'Personal Identity and Morality'.

[41]   Immanuel Kant, *Critique of Practical Reason*, trans. and edited by Mary Gregor (Cambridge: Cambridge University Press, 1997), pp. 37–44 (5: 42–50).

in describing, explaining and ordering the personal relations of ourselves and others, have received scant attention in the recent Anglo-American philosophical tradition'.[42] In this essay from forty years ago, Newton-Smith makes an interesting contrast between his style of analytic philosophy in addressing love and personal commitment and a French style of existential philosophy on love and personal relations. He turns to Jean-Paul Sartre for his contrast:

> Sartre, when discussing relations with others in *Being and Nothingness,* concludes at the end of something bearing at least a family resemblance to an argument, that it follows from his account of the relation between mind and body that an attempt to love is bound to fail. The acceptance of Sartre's argument would have clear import for someone who regulated his or her sex life according to the principle that sex without love was not permissible. A person who accepted the argument and who was unwilling to adopt a chaste life would seem to be compelled either to violate or to revise his or her principles.[43]

Newton-Smith responds to Sartre's argument. First, he notes its difference from an Anglo-American argument, and second, employs the conceptual tools of analytic philosophy to clarify a concept of love, in order to explore the possible practical bearing of such a concept on our thinking and acting in the context of personal relations. Newton-Smith confines his application of the concept, love, to sexual relations.

Next, Newton-Smith asserts the clear difference of Sartrean philosophy to analytic philosophy. The analytic philosopher describes and clarifies linguistic practices; after the description and clarification of love, a second-order reflection on the concept is analysed in relation to actual practices or common sense. In Newton-Smith's words, '… it is highly unlikely that someone [in this analytic tradition] would argue [as Sartre's seems to] that something which we took, at the level of common sense, to be the case was not in fact the case'. So, analytic (linguistic) philosophers would simply not be able to accept Sartre's argument: 'In the presence of Sartre's strong and counter-intuitive conclusion that love is not possible, it would be argued via paradigm cases that love is indeed possible and that consequently Sartre's account of the relation between mind and body is shown, by *reductio ad absurdum*, to be false.'[44]

Finally, it is noteworthy that the results of Newton-Smith's own conceptual investigation of love are not, however, very significant. He distinguishes 'love-comprising relations' (LCR) and establishes that within these LCRs commitment

---

[42]   Newton-Smith, 'A Conceptual Investigation', p. 113.

[43]   Ibid. In Sartre's account of relations with others, the subject wants to be loved, but there can be no reciprocity, see Jean-Paul Sartre, *Being and Nothingness: An Essay on Phenomenological Ontology*, trans. Hazel Barnes (New York: Philosophical Library, 1956), pp. 361–379, 624–628.

[44]   Newton-Smith, 'A Conceptual Investigation', p. 114.

is important.[45] Reciprocity seems essential. But two conflicting pictures of love emerge: the involuntaristic or romantic picture of love as a feeling or emotion which overcomes, and the voluntaristic picture of love as a deliberate volitional commitment to another; elements of each picture seem to come into LCRs, while different individuals variously stress these elements.[46] In the end, Newton-Smith has, at the very most, clarified some disputes about what love is. His disappointingly thin conclusion is that

> The variability in possible conceptions of love has ruled out the sort of precise and determinate conceptual relations that philosophers are prone to seek. Because of this indeterminacy, how one must (conceptually) think about love drifts imperceptibly into how one does generally think about love.[47]

To add a final, even more pessimistic note Newton-Smith says,

> To show that an analysis of love is relevant to practical dealings in personal relations, would not in any way demonstrate that beneficial results would accrue for the lover or the beloved from the utilization of such knowledge. Ibsenian life lies may be productive of the greater happiness.[48]

In fact, this negative conclusion from a philosophical analysis of the concept of love is unsurprising to readers who find analytic philosophy uninformed when it comes to gender and sexual relations; and Newton-Smith's essay was written forty years ago. Yet we might hope to find a philosopher who will us lead to more constructive discussions of the morality of love.

Martha Nussbaum says something similar to what we have concluded from Newton-Smith, that romantic and sexual love have been excluded from the Anglo-American tradition of moral philosophy.[49] However, contrary to the position which is being argued for here, Nussbaum places the blame – at least in part – on the Enlightenment philosophy of Kant.[50] Any of several counter-arguments to Nussbaum would demonstrate that her assumptions about Kant reflect a failure

---

[45]   Ibid., p. 120.

[46]   Ibid., pp. 128–129. He finds these pictures in Iris Murdoch, *Bruno's Dream* (London: Chatto & Windus, 1969).

[47]   Newton-Smith, 'A Conceptual Investigation', p. 135.

[48]   Ibid.

[49]   Martha Nussbaum, *Love's Knowledge* (Cambridge: Cambridge University Press, 1990), pp. 336ff; and *Upheavals of Thought: The Intelligence of the Emotions* (Cambridge: Cambridge University Press, 2001), pp. 463ff.

[50]   Nussbaum, *Love's Knowledge*, pp. 336–340; and *Upheavals of Thought*, pp. 463–470.

to read at least Kant's account of practical love and his account of love as a great moral force.[51]

Returning to contemporary philosophy of religion, we have already found French feminist reflections on the divine more likely than analytic philosophy to consider love and embodiment. In this sense, it may seem wise in both gendering and re-visioning gender to follow the Continental philosopher who moves on from Sartre. Nevertheless, it is very important to recall how much we have learnt from the conceptual philosophy of A. W. Moore. His philosophy not only takes Kantian morality seriously; but Moore himself is driven by a philosophical desire 'to make sense of things'. His desire is both moral and metaphysical. So we will return to Moore's philosophy again for its contribution to the re-visioning which is being developed for contemporary philosophy of religion. Continental rationalists will come into this discussion, too. However, I won't agree with the picture of Enlightenment philosophy given by Nussbaum, while the picture of analytic philosophy given by Newton-Smith shows how much the field has developed in forty years, especially if the writings of Moore are taken even more seriously than they have been to date.

A Kantian feminism

A last word on Kant for this chapter is necessary. Recall that Kant rejects the view that something is good because God loves, or commands, it. When Kant does refer to moral obligation 'as divine commands', he never gives up the autonomy of morality. According to Kant, we can regard our moral actions as divine commands only because we are (internally) obligated to them; but they are not obligatory simply because they are God's commands.[52] Kant's rejection covers viewing divine commands as whimsical or arbitrary, which I contend is significant for the moralizing, as well as the gendering, of love in philosophy of religion. Remember that gendering is at least in part the internal critique of the philosophical concept of love. Obedience to God's commands would render women as well as human men, servile. Unfree, we would not be able to claim (in Kant's terms) that either the human or the divine agent is moral. Treating actions as moral because they are divine commands would infringe human free will; acting out of fear of punishment could not be a moral motivation. Even more significant in this context is the fact that Kant demonstrates the role of pure practical reason in moralizing the love of humanity. In the *Groundwork*, Kant calls 'practical love' action done for the sake of duty, and not done out of inclination. Kant's *Groundwork* contains the initial

---

[51]   For instance, see Swanton, 'Kant's Impartial Virtues of Love', pp. 241–259.

[52]   Immanuel Kant, *Critique of Pure Reason*, trans. and ed. Paul Guyer and Allen W. Wood (Cambridge: Cambridge University Press, 1998), A 819/B 847, A 771/B 799. Also see A. W. Moore, *Noble in Reason, Infinite in Faculty: Themes and Variations in Kant's Moral and Religious Philosophy* (London: Routledge, 2003), pp. 149–150.

distinction between pathological and practical love, which is based upon his more general distinction between inclination and reason. In his words, '... *practical*, not *pathological*, love [resides] in the will and not in the propensions of feeling, in principles of action and not of melting compassion'.[53]

Later in *The Metaphysics of Morals* Kant introduces a further, crucial distinction between pathological and moral feeling: an original emotion, or feeling, of love exists prior to its moral cultivation. The former, which everyone possesses, is a precondition for the latter. Here is the crucial passage:

> There are certain moral endowments such that anyone lacking them could have no duty to acquire them. They are *moral feeling, conscience, love* of one's neighbor, and *respect* for oneself (*self-esteem*) ... All of them are natural predispositions of the mind for being affected by concepts of duty, antecedent predispositions on the side of *feeling*. ...
>
> ... there can be no duty to have a moral feeling, or to acquire it; instead every human being (as a moral being) has it in him [or her] originally. Obligation with regard to moral feeling can be only to *cultivate* it and to strengthen it through wonder at its inscrutable source.[54]

So, Kantian morality requires feeling that can be cultivated by consciousness of duty. It also requires the equality of rational agents, with feelings and duties. Equal rational agents should carry out moral actions, including acts of love, which are each done for the sake of duty alone. The moralization of love, whether human or divine, depends on reason. A divine being would will what reason requires; insofar as the 'personal' being requires love, God's practical reason is the same as love. Although Kant himself argues for a conception of self-legislation as the ground of morality, it is not difficult to rethink his conception in the contemporary terms of 'relational autonomy'.[55] That is, moral action is carried out by an autonomous agent, i.e. not done in service to arbitrary commands; this agent is also always in relation to other rational agents, whether divine or human; yet only human agents find emotional vulnerability to be a necessary precondition for their own real autonomy, though not for divine love.[56] Again it should be stressed that reason has a crucial role in the moralizing of affection, which means that true affection is

---

[53]   Kant, *Groundwork of the Metaphysics of Morals*, p. 65 (399).

[54]   Kant, *The Metaphysic of Morals*, pp. 159–160 (399–400). This passage provides one piece of textual support for contemporary philosophers who aim to bring Kant into the most recent developments in virtue ethics; cf. Rosalind Hursthouse, *On Virtue Ethics* (Oxford: Oxford University Press, 1999), pp. 91–107, 120.

[55]   Catriona MacKenzie and Natalie Stoljar (eds), *Relational Autonomy: Feminist Perspectives on Autonomy, Agency and the Social Self* (New York: Oxford University Press, 2000).

[56]   Anderson, 'Autonomy, Vulnerability and Gender'.

habitual; despite human vulnerability and failure to be fully rational, reason aims to ensure the reliability and consistency of love; and God serves as Kant's practical ideal: only a divine being is fully rational – hence, reliable and consistent in love.

One problem for Christian theism with the Kantian rejection of the view that divine commands replace human autonomy is the loss of divine sovereignty. Arguably, sovereignty and omnipotence are challenged by the Kantian feminist picture given in this chapter. These divine attributes are brought under question when the philosopher of religion accepts that divine actions must be judged good by consistency with an independent ethical standard of goodness, that is, the moral law. Feminist philosophers can find in Kant support for their rejection of a gender exclusive conception of divine sovereignty and omnipotence. Neither Kant himself nor those concerned with a less gender exclusive conception of God would assume divine neutrality in the omniscient and omni-benevolent grounding of divine power. To follow the commands of an omnipotent God simply because they are the commands of an all-powerful, divine being is, in this context, to be immoral. Kant does conceive a divine being (God) to be supremely rational and wills whatever any rational being wills. The crucial difference between Kant and (other) divine command theorists is that this supreme rationality does not curtail human freedom – just the opposite. Insofar as we are rational, we both can and will be legislating for ourselves, while nevertheless being in relation to other self-legislating rational agents.[57] Granted there is a difference between human and divine rationality: the emotional vulnerability of human beings renders necessary the moralization of love. Yet Kant's moralization of love should never be read as servitude to a divine power. Instead as supremely rational, a divine being would show love out of respect for beings who are rational, yet vulnerable. Here we return to my earlier feminist concern with the right, or just, authority of reason.[58]

Conclusion: gendering love and morality

The previous section in particular attempts to undermine a popular caricature of Kant as an advocate of cold deeds of duty. Each of the previous sections in this chapter are intended to raise awareness of the morality of divine love and how it has been gendered in the texts of modern and contemporary philosophy. A caricature of Kant as a man of cold deeds of duty alone would inhibit the significant role he

---

[57]   Kant, *Critique of Pure Reason*, A 771/B 799; also see A 622/650 and A 814–815/B 842–843. On seeing our 'self-legislation' in a divine light as a mere device, see Moore, *Noble in Reason*. Moore also reconstructs Kant's account of the moral necessity to believe in God, i.e. belief which is hope-sustaining and a meaning-conferring function.

[58]   Lovibond first raised this concern for me, but Fricker develops the Foucauldian question, whether we can ever distinguish between reason as authoritative and as authoritarian, see Fricker, 'Feminism in Epistemology', p. 156; cf. Lovibond, 'The End of Morality', pp. 68–71, 75–76.

actually gives to love. In addressing life's contingencies and vulnerability, without the precondition of the emotions, the attempts of philosophers otherwise as different as Wollstonecraft and Kant to secure the moral realm against the operation of moral bad luck, inconsistency and unreliability, would be unintelligible.

Roughly, human love remains messy and this is the reason why we strive for its cultivation by practical reason. Enlightenment philosophers who advocate, as I've addressed the term, 'moralizing' love with careful attention to the nature of gender and of moral motivation can do a great deal to enrich the field of philosophy of religion in the twenty-first century. This is said, despite radically different readings of love and modern morality by postmodern feminist theorists who seek to subvert the gender exclusivity in philosophy. According to these latter theorists, Kant is no friend of feminists since the authority of reason is an imposition. But the counter-argument is that these postmodern theorists of gender fail to distinguish between the authority of reason and authoritarian reasoning in love and morality.

According to Kant, everyone has the emotion, love, as a necessary precondition of being able to recognize moral duty. The duty to cultivate this emotion as a moral feeling provides a sense in which we may, mutually, motivate ourselves to love; and this will be more than an instruction to perform cold deeds. What is morally objectionable – indeed, false – is the claim that I can do nothing about my emotions. It is wrong to suppress the emotions as negative, but equally wrong to celebrate merely the positive. Instead the task of, in a positive sense, moralizing love is ongoing. Love endures, despite change or discord, between embodied subjects, but the task is to understand love and the difference between practical reasoning and harmful moralizing.

In brief, this chapter concludes with an admonition: we have, to our detriment, missed the significant role of emotion in the reliable use of reason. Yet debates about moralized love in the process of cultivating reason and emotion can still serve as a rich ground for recognizing the role played by gender in both positive and negative forms. If accusations of, in a negative sense, moralizing prevents feminist philosophers from being able to take Kant seriously or to develop the insights of his practical philosophy in particular, then something has gone wrong. Instead I urge caution to avoid gendering Kant as perniciously masculinist and against love. The next chapters will keep in mind this problem in gendering love. A possibility, not yet addressed is to consider re-visioning a regulative ideal of divine love and the morally good as an unachievable yet nevertheless guiding goal. Such a goal inspired and guided the great moral force of love.

Chapter 6
Restoring Faith in Reason[1]

Introduction: sharing concepts

If women and men today are to redeem *truth*, restore *faith* in *reason* and achieve change through *love* and *trust* in others, then we need to take a step back to reflect upon the concepts which currently direct our lives. Similar to Chapter 4, the present chapter owes a significant debt to the conceptual philosophy of A. W. Moore; but this chapter freely appropriates Moore's use of terms and, in particular, his account of 'possessing' a concept. The basic definition of 'a concept' comes from Simon Blackburn. More technical definitions of 'thick' and 'thin' (ethical) concepts comes from Moore whose thinking about thick ethical concepts is informed by Bernard Williams.[2] To enrich the gender and philosophical debates in this chapter, I bring together Moore and Williams along with the writings on faith and reason by the late Pope John Paul II. Finally, the chapter will bring my particular appropriation of conceptual philosophy together with the epistemic practice of bell hooks's 'a writing life'.

If a concept is that which is understood by a term such as predicate, then 'to possess a concept is to be able to deploy a term expressing it in making judgments: the ability connects with such things as recognizing when the term applies, and being able to understand the consequences of its application'.[3] The use of language will show whether a person has or does not have a 'grasp' of a concept; and this use is learnt in a particular human context. The possession of a concept is not only manifest in the ability to recognize which things fall under that concept; it is shown in the ability to apply and misapply a concept, to extend it to new cases, to abandon it in favour of an alternative concept, to invoke the concept in the absence of things to which it applies, and so forth.

---

[1]   An earlier version of this chapter appeared as 'Redeeming Truth, Restoring Faith in Reason: A Feminist Response to the Postmodern Condition of Nihilism', in Laurence Paul Hemming and Susan Frank Parsons (eds), *Redeeming Truth: Considering Faith and Reason* (London: SCM, 2007), pp. 60–84.

[2]   Bernard Williams, *Ethics and the Limits of Philosophy*, second edition with a commentary on the text by A. W. Moore (London: Routledge, 2006), pp. 140–145, 214–216. A. W. Moore, 'Williams on Ethics, Knowledge and Reflection', *Philosophy: The Journal of the Royal Institute of Philosophy*, 78 (2003): 337–354; and A. W. Moore, 'Maxims and Thick Ethical Concepts,' *Ratio*, XIX (June 2006): 129–147.

[3]   Simon Blackburn, *Oxford Concise Dictionary of Philosophy* (Oxford: Oxford University Press, 1994), p. 72.

A certain amount of support for the idea that (Christian) women and men should reflect upon the concepts which direct their lives derives from a reading of the encyclical letter of the late Pope John Paul II on *Faith and Reason*.[4] Admittedly, choosing the late Pope's letter on faith and reason as a source for redeeming truth is an unusual choice to make for re-visioning gender in philosophy of religion. Nevertheless, that particular Pope's realism about human life, his philosophical reflection, as well as his desire for the objectivity of modern philosophy,[5] has stimulated a significant discussion of faith and reason, but also, of self-consciously gendered philosophical conceptions and religious beliefs. The late Pope boldly claims that: 'All men and women ... are in some sense philosophers and have their own philosophical *conceptions with which they direct their lives*'. This translation of this claim follows Janet Martin Soskice's use of an early translation of this encyclical letter which renders 'all men and women', not just 'all men', philosophers.[6]

I would like to explore, by extending to the present context, this Pope's idea that we each have our own philosophical conceptions with which we direct our lives. To re-vision this idea in terms of possessing a concept, consider Moore's idea that 'to possess a concept is to live by it'.[7] Moore employs 'possess' as a term of art.[8] He further clarifies this term with an explanation of what it is 'to grasp a concept in an engaged way'. Grasping a concept in an 'engaged' way can help to 'make sense of' our lives.[9]

I take a certain poetic licence with all of the terms (above). Experimenting freely with possibilities in the art of possessing concepts, I will extend the

---

[4]   *Restoring Faith in Reason*, A New Translation of the Encyclical Letter *Faith and Reason* of Pope John Paul II, together with a commentary and discussion, edited by Laurence Paul Hemming and Susan Frank Parsons (London: SCM Press, 2002).

[5]   Note that this agrees with John Haldane that the Pope, John Paul II's encyclical, *Fides et Ratio*, is not a postmodern text (John Haldane, 'John Paul's philosophy', *The Tablet*, 7 June 2003: 22–23). In the Pope's discussion of the relationship between theology and philosophy, he takes a modern and so, a generous view of philosophical reflection; see *Restoring Faith in Reason*, especially paragraphs 64–65, 68–69, 73 and 75–77.

[6]   Soskice, '*Fides et ratio*: The Postmodern Pope', in Hemming and Parsons (eds), *Restoring Faith in Reason*, p. 294. To compare the early to this more recent translation, see *Restoring Faith in Reason*, p. 51, paragraph 30 which is also quoted in Soskice's footnote, p. 294 n10.

[7]   A. W. Moore, *Noble in Reason, Infinite in Faculty: Themes and Variations on Kant's Moral and Religious Philosophy* (London: Routledge, 2003), p. xv; cf. Pope John Paul II, *Restoring Faith in Reason*, p. 51.

[8]   Ibid., p. 48. Note that this chapter uses Moore's account of grasping a concept which derives from *Noble in Reason*; but in later published work he no longer uses exactly the same terminology about possessing a concept and grasping it in a (dis)engaged way.

[9]   Moore, *Noble in Reason*, pp. xv, 39–51, especially #8. The concepts, which I have in mind include reason, faith and hope; but Moore gives other examples to illustrate what it is to possess a concept and grasp it in an *engaged* way, ibid., pp. 39–40 and 74–78.

application of the concepts of faith and reason, but also trust and truth, to gender debates in philosophy of religion. A close reading of Moore's own philosophical writings on the moral and religious philosophy of Immanuel Kant reveals that Moore himself has an engaged grasp of the concepts of faith and hope; and I suggest this is for reasons of religious commitment. Possession of the concepts of faith, hope and reason creates certain possibilities for 'restoring faith in reason'.[10] However, before I try to suggest more about Moore's own possession of concepts in an 'engaged' way, let us consider the distinction he draws between an engaged and a disengaged grasp of a concept. In his words,

> ... I intend 'possess' in an unusually demanding way.
>
> To convey what I intend I need to draw a distinction. Many concepts, if not all concepts, can be grasped in two ways, an engaged way and a disengaged way. To grasp a concept in the disengaged way is to be able to recognize when the concept would (correctly) be applied, to be able to understand others when they apply it, and so forth. To grasp a concept in the engaged way is not only to be able to do these things, but also to feel sufficiently at home with the concept to be prepared to apply it oneself, where being prepared to apply it oneself means being prepared to apply it not just in overt acts of communication but also in how one thinks about the world and in how one conducts one's affairs. What *this requires*, roughly, is *sharing whatever beliefs, concerns, and values define the outlook that gives application of the concept its point.*
>
> Take the concept of *the Sabbath*. Those who are not Jewish have no difficulty in grasping this concept in the disengaged way. But only a Jewish person recognizing an obligation to keep the Sabbath can grasp the concept in the engaged way. We might say ... that such a person *lives* by the concept.[11]

In an earlier context, Williams himself had explained the difference between someone who possesses an action-guiding concept and 'the sympathetic observer'; the latter can report, anticipate and even take part in a discussion of the use made of the concept relating to religion, for instance, without being ultimately identified with the use of the concept: 'it may not be his'.[12] Moore's account of what it is to possess a concept builds on this.[13] It becomes more and more apparent the debt that Moore owes to Williams. However, what Moore explains with his philosophical account of possession of concepts is not exactly the same as what we can discern to be his own grasp of particular concepts. For example, I am seeking to demonstrate in this chapter that Moore himself grasps certain moral and theological concepts in

---

[10]   Ibid., especially pp. 51–52, 108–112, 166–169 and 170–196.

[11]   Ibid., p. 48; italics added.

[12]   Ibid., p. 142. For Williams's own disengaged use of concepts relating to Christianity, see Bernard Williams, *Shame and Necessity* (Berkeley, California: University of California Press, 1993), pp. 10–12 and 91–95.

[13]   Moore, *Noble in Reason*, pp. 48–57.

an engaged way; In contrast, Williams himself does not have an engaged grasp of any similar Kantian or theological concepts, whether derived from Kant's morality or a more direct product of Christianity. Stated more strongly by Williams about himself and 'most of us':

> Most of us do not have ... traditional religious reasons for thinking that the route from the fifth century B.C. to the present day had to take the course that it did take and, in particular, run through Christianity. ...The overwhelming role of Christianity in the transition from antiquity to the modern world is necessary, in the sense that if we try to subtract it, we cannot think determinately of an alternative history, and we cannot think of people who would be ourselves at all; but while the role of Christianity is in this way necessary, it might not have been.[14]

Thus, for Williams, Christianity is a necessary contingency in making us who we are today. We might say that our lives have been directed by certain concepts which are determinate of our self-understanding, yet contingent in the sense of 'might not have been'. To understand our lives, our personal and social identities, we need to recognize those fundamental concepts, which have shaped our thinking and acting. Even if Christian concepts are necessary for our self-understanding, Williams does not think that Christianity had to be; and in fact, he does not share any Christian concepts, in Moore's terms, in an engaged way. If a sympathetic observer of the use of Christian concepts, Williams would be in a position to say that some of these concepts are false.[15] Yet the crucial point for the present argument is that Williams can only have a disengaged grasp of a Christian concept of faith. Employing Moore's terms, Williams does not share the same beliefs, concerns and values which define the outlook that give the application of a Christian concept of faith its point.[16] So, Williams differs from both Moore and the Pope in not having an engaged grasp of faith, love and redemption; Williams would only have a disengaged grasp of these concepts insofar as he is a sympathetic observer. As for Moore and the Pope, although sharing certain philosophical and theological concepts of modernity, they could not share all of the same Christian concepts, since Moore's Christian outlook is Protestant, not Roman Catholic.

It is most relevant for my argument that, although Moore has a philosophical debt to Williams – whose account of truth will be explored later in this chapter – he is nevertheless unlike Williams in the nature of his engaged grasp of faith and hope.

---

[14]   Ibid., p. 12. The 'us' certainly covers other analytic philosophers, but Williams may assume that 'us' covers other contemporary non-philosophers.

[15]   For a significant, however brief discussion of the possibility of recognizing true and false ethical concepts as a 'sympathetic observer', see Williams, *Ethics and the Limits*, pp. 142–147.

[16]   Moore, *Noble in Reason*, p. 48.

At the same time, Williams and Moore share certain fundamental philosophical concepts: they both grasp reason and, as will be argued, truth in an engaged way.

Modern philosophy: loss of faith in reason

Before discussing the redemption of truth and faith in reason, it is necessary to say something more about the definition of philosophy which is at play. On the one hand, we need to be sensitive to recent changes in the philosopher's self-understanding.[17] The contemporary philosophers's increasing awareness of philosophy's own history and locatedness has been transforming philosophy's self-definition. As has been argued in Chapter 2, feminism in philosophy has increased the growing consciousness of the social and material locatedness of philosophers and philosophy.[18] On the other hand, the particular sort of commitment to 'the truth' conceived as an absolute, or an absolute conception of reality, continues to dominate certain accounts of philosophy and, especially, of philosophical theology.[19] The theologian's commitment to truth has been re-asserted in recent years in direct reaction to current trends of nihilism in philosophy, while the secular changes in philosophy's self-definition have been, often unfairly, blamed for this trend.

Neither of the theological or the philosophical extremes concerning reality and truth can restore faith in reason nor achieve change through love and trust, insofar as these extremes are distortions of truth. In response to this loss of faith in reason's ability to address 'the big questions' about reality, Soskice interprets the Pope's message as an expression of philosophical urgency: '[philosophers, men and women] have contented themselves with philosophical trivia while the *big questions are left unanswered or unaddressed.* The philosophers have made themselves marginal in a world that more than ever needs their honest deliberations, and here we arrive at the nihilism.'[20]

---

[17]   Bernard Williams, 'Philosophy as a Humanistic Discipline', *Philosophy*, 75 (October 2000): 477–496.

[18]   Miranda Fricker and Jennifer Hornsby, 'Introduction', in Fricker and Hornsby (eds), *The Cambridge Companion to Feminism in Philosophy* (Cambridge: Cambridge University Press, 2000), pp. 1–5; and Pamela Sue Anderson, 'Feminism in Philosophy of Religion' in Deane-Peter Baker and Patrick Maxwell (eds), *Explorations in Contemporary Continental Philosophy of Religion* (Amsterdam: Rodopi, 2003), pp. 189–190.

[19]   For examples of this commitment to truth, and at least the possibility of the absolute conception, in philosophy, see A. W. Moore, *Points of View* (Oxford: Oxford University Press, 1997), pp. 74–75, 79, 85–89. On the commitment to truth in philosophical theology, see Pope John Paul II, *Restoring Faith in Reason*, especially pp. 127–129, 135; and Eilert Herms, 'Objective Truth: Relations between Truth and Revelation in the Encyclical *Fides et Ratio*, in *Restoring Faith in Reason*, pp. 206–224. In addition, for Moore's discussion of the nihilistic dangers of Nietzsche's perspectivism, see *Points of View*, pp. 103–114.

[20]   Soskice, '*Fides et ratio*', p. 294.

Ironically, this tension in philosophy between truth and loss of the ability to make sense of things also characterizes two different extremes in contemporary culture. Some followers of the philosophy of Friedrich Nietzsche have been accused of bringing about a culture of nihilism due to their Nietzschean denial of truth; or at least, the denial of truth's unity, simplicity and absoluteness.[21] Yet, as will be seen, Williams discovers another possibility in reading Nietzsche: that is, the affirmation of truthfulness emerges in Nietzsche's critical work on genealogy. Further on in this chapter, we will return to Williams's re-reading of Nietzsche's affirmation of truth.

To stipulate a few more useful definitions at this stage, 'nihilism' will be understood in the contemporary terms of Williams's and Moore's analytic philosophy as 'the loss of any hope of making sense of the world'.[22] 'Making sense of things' can be taken to be one philosophical response to nihilism.[23] In the context of re-visioning gender, it would be helpful, if analytic philosophers and philosophical theologians considered taking 'a feminist standpoint', as a critical perspective, from which women and men can come to grasp new, more inclusive concepts in an engaged way.[24] This feminist standpoint would be both sensitive to the changes in the philosopher's self-definition and informed by recent philosophical writings on socially situated knowledge. It is also informed by feminist writings on the social and material locatedness of both philosophical and theological concepts. The crucial element of this feminist standpoint is the political imperative: that 'everyone must change', if sexist and racist oppression is to be overcome.[25] As bell hooks explains, when a movement for liberation inspires itself chiefly by a hatred of an enemy rather than form a vision of possibility, it begins to defeat itself. So, we need new concepts, like hope, if 'feminism is for everybody'.[26] At this moment in the history of women's liberation when gender

---

[21]   Cf. Pope John Paul II, *Restoring Faith in Reason*; Moore, *Points of View*, pp. 106ff; and Bernard Williams, *Truth and Truthfulness: An Essay in Genealogy* (New York and Oxford: Princeton University Press, 2002), pp. 18–19, 126–128 and 135–140.

[22]   Williams, *Truth and Truthfulness*, pp. 267–269.

[23]   The idea of making sense of things (or, the world) from both Williams (ibid., pp. 232–269) and Moore (*Noble in Reason, Infinite in Faculty*, pp. xvi, 78–81, 87, 171). A potentially fruitful shift in analytic feminist philosophy toward an awareness of the social and material locatedness of our thinking and writing will become apparent when these passages in Williams and Moore are compared (later in this chapter) to bell hooks, *Remembered Rapture: the Writer at Work* (London: The Women's Press, 1999), pp. 12f. Also, see 'Conclusion: from a feminist standpoint' in this chapter.

[24]   On a feminist standpoint, see Pamela Sue Anderson, '"Standpoint": Its Rightful Place in a Realist Epistemology', *Journal of Philosophical Research*, xxvi (2001): 131–154.

[25]   bell hooks, *Feminist Theory: From Margin to Center*, second edition (London: Pluto Press, 2000; first edition, 1988), p. 166.

[26]   This phrase is borrowed from bell hooks, *Feminism is for Everybody: Passionate Politics* (Cambridge, MA: South End Press, 2000).

and its material conditions are seen to be interlinked with social locatedness we need reason, truthfulness, trust and love, if we are to hope for change.

Contrary to some popular beliefs, the dissolution of 'the myth[s] of patriarchy'[27] does not necessarily result in nihilism. In fact, just the reverse is possible, if we learn to grasp the appropriate philosophical concepts of truth, trust/faith and reason in an engaged way. We have an engaged grasp of a concept, if the concept functions in overt acts of communication, as well as in how we think about the world and in how we conduct our affairs. Coming to possess concepts in an engaged way is, admittedly, not going to be a simple matter of learning new concepts or even of coming to employ them. It is crucial to give the determinate content and truth conditions to those concepts which guide our lives.[28] I agree with Moore that knowing how to use a language is a form of art and that knowledge of how it is possible for us to employ concepts correctly remains ineffable. [29]

In 2003, Williams and Moore each published a highly significant book of philosophy which, I propose, can be read as unwitting responses to, what has been called 'postmodern' nihilism. They each explain and develop at least one crucial philosophical concept for this discussion: one concept is truth and the other concept is reason, respectively. In *Truth and Truthfulness: An Essay in Genealogy*,[30] Williams writes in a spirit of creativity, which retrieves Nietzsche as not a denier of truth but an advocate of truthfulness. In *Noble in Reason, Infinite in Faculty: Themes and Variations in Kant's Moral and Religious Philosophy*,[31] Moore creatively weaves his concerns with pure practical reason through Kantian themes and variations on morality, freedom and religion. Moore demonstrates in Kantian terms that we all seek to make ethical sense of things. It seems that Williams and Moore each have sought to make sense of things both individually and collectively.[32] Moore links making sense of things and sharing possession of concepts as follows:

> Sharing possession of a concept is part of sharing a life. An individual, through possession of concepts, is enabled to make sense of things, and more particularly to tell various stories, and more particularly still to tell his or her own story, the

---

[27]   Pamela Sue Anderson, 'Myth and Feminist Philosophy', in Kevin Schilbrack (ed.), *Thinking Through Myths: Philosophical Perspectives* (London: Routledge, 2002), pp. 103–113.

[28]   Williams, *Ethics and the Limits*, pp. 146–151.

[29]   I have agreed with this twofold claim, but began my own work to extend Moore understanding of ineffable knowledge in Pamela Sue Anderson, 'Ineffable Knowledge and Gender' in Philip Goodchild (ed.), *Rethinking Philosophy of Religion: Approaches from Continental Philosophy*, series edited by John Caputo (New York: Fordham University Press, 2002), pp. 162–183.

[30]   Williams, *Truth and Truthfulness*.

[31]   Moore, *Noble in Reason*.

[32]   Williams, *Truth and Truthfulness*, pp. 15, 18, 267–269; Moore, *Points of View*, pp. 106–110; Moore, *Noble in Reason*, pp. 75–76.

telling of which is inseparable from acting it out – from living a life. But so too, a community, through shared possession of concepts, is enabled to make collective sense of things, and more particularly to propagate various stories, and more particularly still to propagate its own story.[33]

Yet, as stated already, Williams does not have an engaged grasp of either Christian or Kantian concepts, while Moore energetically writes variations on Kantian themes, upholding a realm of pure reason, as well as concepts of faith and hope which are compatible with at least one Christian story. It may also be surprising in this light that Kant, Williams and Moore – none of whom are either Roman Catholic philosophers or theologians – came to mind when reading the late Pope's account of a culture characterized by the diremption and, hence weakening, of faith and reason. Yet if we accept this diremption, it undermines both theology and philosophy. This is a crucial reason for connecting the Pope's outlook on philosophical theology to modern analytic philosophy in the present discussion of sharing possession of concepts.

In response to the threat of nihilism, neither the Pope nor Williams calls for a return to the Enlightenment philosophy of Kant with its elevation of human reason to make sense of things. In sharp contrast, Moore finds creative possibilities in variations on Kantian moral and religious themes. Despite this contrast, the Pope's allegiance to modern philosophy comes through his interpretation of Thomas Aquinas; this interpretation brings Aquinas's thinking closer to contemporary philosophical re-readings of Thomistic, Kantian and Christian philosophical theology, especially bringing together Aquinas's accounts of reason and morality with contemporary readings of virtue and Kantian ethics.[34] Williams, too, admits that 'modernity is not just a catastrophic mistake'; and that '… the formative influence of Christianity is something we owe to the way things turned out'.[35] Moreover, Williams showed a personal interest in Moore's work on Kantian reason.[36] There is no doubt in my mind after reading his encyclical that the Pope would be similarly intrigued by Moore's argument that as humans we all have a rational drive to make sense of how things are.[37]

---

[33]   Ibid., p. 75.

[34]   On reason, philosophy and ethics, see Pope John Paul II, *Restoring Faith in Reason*, especially pp. 23–57, 71–81 and 97. Cf. Linda T. Zagzebski, *Virtues of the Mind: An Inquiry into the Nature of Virtue and the Ethical Foundations of Knowledge*, Cambridge: Cambridge University Press, 1996, pp. 18 n11 and 263; Nancy Sherman, *Making a Necessity of Virtue: Aristotle and Kant on Virtue* (Cambridge: Cambridge University Press, 1997); Robert Audi, 'A Liberal Theory of Civic Virtue', *Social Philosophy and Policy*, 15/1 (Winter 1998), especially pp. 155–167; Robert Merrihew Adams, 'Introduction', in Allen Wood and George di Giovanni (eds), *Religion within the Boundaries of Mere Reason and other Writings* (Cambridge: Cambridge University Press, 1998), pp. vii–xxxii.

[35]   Williams, *Shame and Necessity*, pp. 11 and 12.

[36]   Moore, 'Preface', *Noble in Reason*, p. ix.

[37]   Ibid., especially pp. 170–172, 183, and 193.

Moore, as one of the very best analytic philosophers alive today, with an extraordinary ability to argue with both conceptual and non-conceptual philosophers, also bridges philosophies on and off the Continent, exemplifies my idea of restoring faith in reason! Furthermore, consider Moore's selection, in *Noble in Reason*, of an account of 'faith' from Kant's *Lectures on Ethics*:

> We take faith ... to mean that we should do the best that lies in our power, and this in the hope that God, in His goodness and wisdom, will make up for the frailty of our conduct ... [Now] practical faith ... lies in this, that we in no way prescribe anything to God through our will, but resign the matter to His will, and hope that if we have done what lies within our natural capacity, God will repair our frailty and incapacity by means that He knows best.[38]

Insofar as the late Pope's life was directed by concepts of practical reason and faith, I wager that the Pope in question could have agreed with the above statement on faith, while also accepting that our 'natural frailty' is accompanied by hope in God's knowledge and grace. But this shared possession of concepts leads to the extraordinary conclusion that Moore shares with both the Protestant Kant and the Roman Catholic Pope concepts of practical reason and faith, precisely in seeking to make ethical sense of the world.

Noble in Reason does not explicitly discuss truth. However, recall that in Chapter 4 a highly significant characteristic was attributed to the conceptual philosopher: Moore describes the aim of the conceptual, as distinct from the non-conceptual, philosopher that of affirming truth.[39] While in the context of Moore's making *ethical* sense of the world truth does not seem to play a terribly significant role, in the context of Moore's making sense of things truth and truthfulness are philosophical concerns at the heart of his *The Evolution of Modern Metaphysics: Making Sense of Things*.[40] Moreover, truth and truthfulness join up with Moore's own keen metaphysical interest in a group of philosophers: Spinoza, Nietzsche,

---

[38]   Ibid., p. 196; cf. Immanuel Kant, *Lectures on Ethics*, edited by Peter Heath and J. B. Schneewind, trans. Peter Heath (Cambridge: Cambridge University Press, 2001), pp. 106–107; 27: 321–322. Note that Kant himself goes on to distinguish 'fleshy' and 'wise' trust: 'Fleshy trust is when we ourselves determine the worldly ends of our inclinations. ... in order that our trust may coincide with the plan of wisdom, it must be a wise trust, and unconditional, so that we believe in general that God, in His goodness and holiness, will both lend us His aid in regard to acting morally, and also allow us to participate in blessedness' (ibid., pp. 107; 27: 321–322).

[39]   As explained in Chapter 4, Moore describes himself as a conceptual philosopher who aims to affirm truth, see A. W. Moore, 'Arguing with Derrida', *Ratio: An International Journal of Analytic Philosophy*, Special Issue, edited by Simon Glendinning, XIII/4 (December 2000): 357, 366. Moore maintains 'a commitment to a certain paradigm of language use, namely that in which truths are affirmed' (ibid., pp. 365–366).

[40]   A. W. Moore, *The Evolution of Modern Metaphysics: Making Sense of Things* (Cambridge: Cambridge University Press, 2012).

Deleuze and Williams.[41] To address the critical concept of truth more closely and more widely, let us turn directly to the Pope, to Williams and to a feminist theorist, bell hooks. All the while this discussion will remain close to Moore's contribution on faith in reason, on hope, trust and, in the end, truth.

A redemptive practice: writing to tell the truth

The concept of truth appears in the Pope's account of man and woman.[42] His conception of humanity in *Restoring Faith in Reason* depends upon the possession of truth:

> for all that they may evade it, the truth still influences life. Notwithstanding, even when fleeing from it, truth disturbs existence. Life in fact can never be grounded upon doubt, uncertainty or deceit; such an existence would be threatened constantly by fear and anxiety. Man [woman] may be defined, therefore, as *the one who seeks the truth*.[43]

The Pope also adds:

> Man [woman], the one who seeks [the truth], is ... also *the one who lives trusting in others*.[44]

For his part, Williams uncovers the values of truth and a concept of truthfulness in Nietzsche's philosophy, for those philosophers who reject nihilism and resist self-deception:

> Although Nietzsche was keenly alive to what concerns the deniers [of truth], he was an opponent of them. The indifference to truthfulness which they encourage would be for him merely an aspect of nihilism. When he discovered that the values of truth and truthfulness, such as the resistance to self-deception and to comforting mythologies, were not self-justifying and not given simply with the concept of truth ... [He aimed] to see how far the values of truth could be

---

[41]   For evidence of Moore's interest in what these philosophers share (in addition to truth and truthfulness), including a celebration of activity, of a distinctive sort of joy, an affirmation of life and 'metaphysics as a humanistic discipline', see *The Evolution of Modern Metaphysics*, pp. 56–57, 64–65, 371–373, 388, 390–391, 396–398, 545–549, 574–577, 602–604.

[42]   In the light of the earlier point from Soskice concerning gender and translation, I am inclined to be charitable to Pope John Paul II in assuming (with her support) that the Pope's references to man and humanity can also be translated into gender-inclusive terms.

[43]   Pope John Paul II, *Restoring Faith in Reason*, p. 49.

[44]   Ibid., p. 53.

revalued, how they might be understood in a perspective quite different from the Platonic and Christian metaphysics which had provided their principal source in the West up to now.[45]

Williams both affirms and re-values truth following Nietzsche in this twofold task. He goes on to demonstrate that a new genealogical story, not dependent on Christian metaphysics, can be truthful.[46] Affirming the task of philosophy as a search for truth, the Pope also argues that men and women should seek redemption from the old ways of thinking, while re-establishing a trust in each other. The revaluations of truth by Williams and by the Pope connect truthfulness with trust and other virtues, moving the primary philosophical task to everyday truths, while also going beyond the everyday. This means moving the foundation of philosophy away from an epistemology which has been built upon philosophical scepticism about other minds or the existence of an external world.[47] Moreover, Moore's variations on Kant and Williams's variations on Nietzsche, are in substantial agreement with the Pope on the current need for trust. In the case of Moore, this is bound up with faith in reason as a common Kantian sentiment. Moore affirms the value of reason in making sense of things:

> One thing that I have been trying to accomplish … is a way of making sense of things, including our own yearning to make sense of things; that allows us to say, 'Amen' to this sentiment in Kant.[48]

The motivation to make sense of things rests on a yearning bound up with a Kantian concept of hope. At the same time as reason shapes this yearning, it helps to make sense of our lives. Recall that Moore connects the desire to make sense of things with a '*nisus* for rationality'.[49]

At this point 'bell hooks' comes in: she is the contemporary woman writer and feminist theorist who captures a concrete form of the yearning to make sense of things. hooks writes to make sense of her life and of injustice. Her writings add to Moore's *nisus* for rationality the feminist longing for truth and a shared human *telos*, however unattainable. 'bell hooks' is a pen-name deliberately spelled with

---

[45]   Williams, *Truth and Truthfulness*, p. 18; cf. Moore, *The Evolution of Modern Metaphysics*, pp. 388–339.

[46]   Williams, *Truth and Truthfulness*, p. 19; cf. Moore, *The Evolution of Modern Metaphysics*, pp. 393–394.

[47]   On everyday truths, see Williams, *Truth and Truthfulness*, p. 10. For revelation of the significant roles played by 'the virtues of truth', and especially the virtues of accuracy and of sincerity (bound up with the concept of trust), see ibid., pp. 11–12, 35, 83 and Chapters 5–6.

[48]   Moore, *Noble in Reason*, p. 196; *The Evolution of Modern Metaphysics*, pp. 581–588, 595–605.

[49]   Moore, *Noble in Reason*, pp. 183 and 193–196.

a lower case 'b' and a lower case 'h'. Her name is Gloria Watkins; but renaming herself was a deliberate act, marking the beginning of 'a writing life' which had emerged historically out of the life of black slavery. From the 1980s and continuing today, bell hooks has been known as the African-American feminist and cultural critic who emerged at a creative moment in a new wave of feminism. hooks spoke boldly against the racism of white feminism. She spoke the truth and it was heard. Moreover, in writing, hooks seeks to redeem truth 'in the mysterious place where words first come to be "made flesh"', that is, in the place of the everyday where she struggles to learn to trust in others.[50] Her writing is individual and corporeal; it is truthful and powerful.

hooks's self-description captures her own spiritual and ethical practice: hers is literally 'a writing life'.[51] Her practice of writing is distinctive both in making narrative sense of life and in creating a subversive practice; that of 'women telling tales'.[52] For hooks, a writing life becomes not only a means to make sense of one's own life and the world, but a means to create a redemptive practice characterized by truth-telling.[53] In this way, hooks seeks to transform fear – of abuse, of domination, of slavery, of violence … of degradation ending in death – into love. Ultimately, having a desire for communities and communion of love, hooks does overcome nihilism: she evokes a yearning to tell the truth and forgive the past. Her redemptive practice of truth-telling heals wounds and connects each one of us with each other. In fact, recalling Chapter 1, where writing was given a necessary role in re-visioning gender, it was hooks herself who revitalized the words of Virginia Woolf as written to all women, 'I ask you to write more books … for your good and for the good of the world.'[54] So hooks writes books. In doing so, she captures the redemptive practice of writing:

> After what seemed like endless years of journal writing about the past, I wrote a memoir. … It was indeed the culmination of this effort to accept the past and yet surrender its hold on me. This writing was redemptive.

> There are writers who write for fame. And there are writers who write because we need to make sense of the world we live in; writing is a way to clarify, to

---

[50]   hooks, *Remembered Rapture*, p. 130.

[51]   For an example of this practice of writing, see bell hooks, *Wounds of Passion: A Writing Life* (New York: Henry Holt & Company, Owl Press, 1997).

[52]   Pamela Sue Anderson, 'Des contes dits au féminin: pour une éthique de nouveaux espaces', in Alban Cain (ed) *Espace(s) public(s), espace(s) privées*: Enjeux et partages, Université de Cergy-Pontoise CICC (Paris, France: L'Harmattan, 2004), pp. 43–52.

[53]   hooks, *Remembered Rapture*, p. 13.

[54]   These words from Virginia Woolf appear as an epigraph on the otherwise blank page before the 'Contents' in bell hooks, *Remembered Rapture*: '… when I ask you to write more books I am urging you to do what will be for your good and for the good of the world at large'; cf. Woolf, *A Room of One's Own*, p. 99.

interpret, to reinvent. ... We do not write because we must; we always have choice. We write because language is the way we keep a hold on life. ... We communicate to connect, to know community. Even though writing is a solitary act, when I sit with words that I trust will be read by someone, I know that I can never be truly alone.[55]

Her writing also captures the value of truth-telling:

... To make community, we need to be able to know truth, to speak openly and honestly. Truth-telling has to be a spiritual practice for many of us because we live and work in settings where falseness is rewarded, where lies are the norm. Deceit and betrayal destroy the possibility of community.[56]

At this point, let us compare hooks's truth-telling and trust to the claim of Pope John Paul II that: 'man [woman], the one who seeks [the truth], is ... also the one who lives trusting in others'.[57] hooks connects speaking truth to trust, and then, truth and trust to love of justice. Read her dramatic, unequivocal criticism of contemporary culture:

When men and women are loyal to ourselves and others, when we love justice, we understand fully the myriad ways in which lying diminishes and erodes the possibility of meaningful, caring connection, that it stands in the way of love ...

[Today] widespread cultural acceptance of lying is a primary reason many of us will never know love. It is impossible to nurture one's own or another's spiritual growth when the core of one's being and identity is shrouded in secrecy and lies.[58]

The loss of truth renders our culture and nature one of deceit; and this culminates in the loss of the virtues associated with truthfulness for her especially the virtue of love. To confront cultural and personal problems resulting from a lack of truth and the loss of a concept of love, hooks urges us to make sense of things. Unwittingly her project resonates somewhat with the Pope's concepts of trust and truth, but to an even more provocative extent to Moore's making sense of 'the world itself'. Moore writes this in his reconstruction of Kant:

---

[55] hooks, *Remembered Rapture*, pp. 12–13.

[56] Ibid., pp. 120–121.

[57] bell hooks, *All About Love: New Visions* (London: The Women's Press, 2000), pp. 42 and 46.

[58] Ibid., p. 46.

> In th[is] reconstruction, rationality also demands that we seek concepts that
> enables us to make sense. We must realize that the world itself does not make
> sense: we have to make sense of it.[59]

To repeat, the *nisus* for rationality motivates our search for concepts that enable
us to make sense. Although hooks does not explicitly connect her search with
rationality, her yearning to make sense of the world embodies in a profound way
reason's *nisus*.

Remember the opening quotation in this chapter from the Pope that 'All men
and women ... are in some sense philosophers and have their own philosophical
conceptions with which they direct their lives.'[60] Can we say, which 'concepts' we
do – and should – live by? truth? faith? love? reason? and hope in 'sense-making'?
Moore offers a philosophical, dare I say, a 'metaphysical' and not strictly an ethical
answer in this context on Kant:

> We do not and cannot possess our concepts *in vacuo*. We do not and cannot pick
> them up at will. Each individual comes to possess concepts by being immersed
> in a community, and each individual makes his or her contribution to telling
> the stories of these concepts, occasionally by helping to bring them to an end,
> occasionally by helping to initiate them, but most often by simply carrying them
> on.[61]

Moore's own contribution to telling the stories of the concepts we live by is
nowhere better exemplified than in *The Evolution of Modern Metaphysics*.

Pope John Paul II, Williams, Moore and hooks each contribute their own
answers to make up alternatives to twentieth-century cultural forms of nihilism.
Each manages to resist meaninglessness in seeking to make sense of things, and so
giving the ground for coming to truth. Mutual support from very different points
of view poses a challenge for all those women and men who acquiesce to a cultural
nihilism that shrinks from truth. The concept of truth – in telling 'the truth' and in
giving a truthful account – is central to restoring faith in reason.

Reason as authoritative (not authoritarian): truth-telling and trust

As argued above, hooks seeks to restore *faith* in *reason* by learning to trust the
knower of everyday truths. Not only reason, but truth is linked to trust. hooks's
search for truth and meaningful love touches on similar points to those made
already, in other ways, by Moore, Williams and the Pope about reason. The crucial
difference is that all three of these men are respected, treated as authorities, as

---

[59]   Moore, *Noble in Reason*, p. xvi (17).
[60]   Pope John Paul II, *Restoring Faith in Reason*, p. 51.
[61]   Moore, *Noble in Reason*, p. 76.

rational agents and credible knowers. They are authoritative as male thinkers, but their privileged gender roles make them trustworthy. In contrast, if hooks is trusted to tell the truth authoritatively it is as a result of her life-long struggle to write, in order to communicate to others whose lives are not like hers, or like the lives of those who she loves. Ultimately, hooks's struggle has been *to write* to tell the truth, to be heard and to be trusted. For this she needs to be recognized as a knower who is credible and also trustworthy for those at the centre of epistemic practices and for those at the margins of an epistemic community.

Asserting that hooks's social knowledge is credible means that she herself is seen to be trustworthy. Her act of truth-telling intends to shift the grounds of credibility and trustworthiness. Her credible knowledge is true precisely because she is trustworthy; she tells the truth and it is credible! However, these grounds are more often than not, obscured by the biases and injustice of the epistemic practices with which authoritative/authoritarian knowers have asserted 'credible' and 'trustworthy' knowledge. Biased practices are too often the epistemic norm; but such norms exclude. Untrustworthiness is attributed, in order to exclude, 'knowers' from epistemic practices. A mechanism of mistrust at the ground level of our epistemic practices creates its own injustice. Mistrust and epistemic practices of social ignorance together generate formidable conditions for epistemic injustice. This form of injustice is deeply grounded in mechanisms of exclusion of racial, sexual, religious, ethnic differences. In turn, other interlinking, social and material mechanisms of oppression make it seem impossible that the oppression of, in this case, poor black women can be overcome.

Chapter 1 of this book begins by asserting that 'reflective critical openness'[62] is the ethical disposition from which the re-visioning gender in philosophy would be carried out. Here I urge feminist and non-feminist philosophers of religion alike to cultivate this disposition as an intellectual virtue. Cultivating reflective critical openness is to learn to practice a disposition of being openly and critically reflective of social and material markers of all subjects of knowledge; these epistemic markers are only recognized through interaction, imaginative and reflexive thinking. With this threefold process, each of us can realize that how, when and where our epistemic communities have unfairly rendered 'credible' knowers untrustworthy for reasons which are not strictly speaking epistemological. bell hooks has struggled to write and speak words in the language of those women and men whose real-life stories are either not told or not heard. hooks struggles to find and create new concepts which can be heard and understood. But the challenge lies in expressing herself in words which are not socially or materially marked as authoritative, and yet they need to be spoken for the (often awful) truth they express.

---

[62] For my discussion of reflective critical openness as an intellectual virtue, see Pamela Sue Anderson, 'An Epistemological-Ethical Approach to Philosophy of Religion: Learning to Listen', in Pamela Sue Anderson and Beverley Clack (eds), *Feminist Philosophy of Religion: Critical Readings* (London: Routledge, 2004), pp. 87–92.

To illustrate this, imagine the social markers of Gloria Watkins who was born in 1952, poor, a woman and black in rural Kentucky, USA. As hooks herself points out, when 'white folks have a child the first think they want to know is the sex; but when a child is born to a black woman the first thing that is noticed is the skin colour; and then, the sex; colour and sex interlock, determining the child's fate'.[63] Here we have an example of gender interlinking with race, class and sex. In other words, hooks's writing reflects her awareness of gender's intersectionality. In her social reality, colour has mattered when it comes to trustworthiness. Colour mattered when it came to credible knowledge. Domination and injustice inhibit the growth of knowledge, and this prohibits some knowers from knowing they know and being recognized for their knowledge. In this way, it has been all too easy to prevent a woman from knowing she knows. For hooks, the crucial fact is that skin colour is a social and material marker; it has marked out those who can be trusted to tell the truth and those who cannot be trusted. In this manner, our epistemic sensibilities have been prejudiced by external markers; and so, we can see the devastation and loss of truth suffered because of racial markers that have silenced and degraded women and men. We can imagine similar cases of unjust markings which generate and maintain sexism, homophobia, misogyny, and other social and epistemic injustices. The challenge persists to restore faith in reason with truth-telling. A rational yearning for truth-telling is necessary even for hope; credibility and trustworthy also have to be rightfully restored, if change is to take place.

In 1981, Gloria Watkins published her first book, under a penname: *Ain't I a Woman: Black Women and Feminism* by bell hooks. 'bell hooks' quickly became known for this landmark text which challenged the authority of 'the white face of reason'. The concept of truth took on a movement when the woman who asks, 'Ain't I a Woman?' took up the name of Sojourner Truth. With this sojourning of truth, the gender assumptions associated with 'woman', her race, sex, gender and humanity were decisively subverted. *Ain't I a Woman* derives its title question from real life: Isabella Baumfree was a black woman and former slave in 1852 and, at a meeting for women's rights in Akron, Ohio, Baumfree challenges the public view of woman as fragile and timid. Instead she witnesses to the truth of women whose gender is characterized by hard labour. After all she had done as a black woman, she asks, 'ain't I a woman?' Later hooks creates this historical-fictional woman who appears frequently in her own and other feminist literature as an image of transformation and truth-telling. With repeated appearances of Sojourner Truth she becomes a mythical figure in stories of resistance. The story portrays a definite challenge to the dominant concept of a woman as white, fragile and (so) untrustworthy. By treating the ongoing narratives about Sojourner Truth as an inter-text, hooks builds upon a tradition, not only of resistance, but of change. hooks impressively and creatively names truth as *located* in a shared tradition, yet *moving* in the sense of embodied in a sojourner.

---

[63]   hooks, *Feminist Theory*, p. xii.

In her 1981 book, hooks exposes white feminism's blindness to the difference that race makes to what it means to be a woman. As recalled in numerous places here throughout the chapters of *Re-visioning Gender*, hooks's act of writing – many books – is more important than either her historical identity or any details about the author of her life. The woman who writes *Ain't I a Woman?* derives her authority from a distinctive social location and within a matrilinear genealogy, going back to her great grandmother named 'hooks'. Her writing deliberately subverts the concepts which her readers possess, in order to change how they live, think and act.

With her conception of a writing life, bell hooks seeks to make sense of the world. She also explores the nature of truth as, in part, history and, in other part, fiction.[64] However, in using 'fiction' it must be understood that this still is an exploration of *truth*; it is the truth of social reality. The activities of making sense of our lives and of seeking new concepts do not aim to create, or promote, mere fabrications. We do not need to fabricate our traditions. Instead we need to grasp and understand human reality as well as possible. At the same time, in this context, we need to be recognizing how our lives have been shaped by the histories of philosophy and religions. The disciplines in these histories are disciplines which have sought to understand human finitude, as well as our relation to something infinite. The relevance of hooks's writing to philosophy of religion exists in demonstrating that truth, history and its relation to what might be fiction, should matter to philosophers. However, it has to be stressed that, in turning to fiction, or to other literature, we are not turning to fabrications of life. It is just the opposite.

Williams astutely explains how philosophy should use literature and literary examples:

> It is not of course peculiar to [the] sort of inquiry, which aims at historical understanding, that philosophy should be concerned with literature. Even when philosophy is not involved in history, it has to make demands on literature. In seeking a reflective understanding of ethical life, for instance, it quite often takes examples from literature. Why not take examples from life? It is a perfectly good question, and it has a short answer: what philosophers will lay before themselves and their readers as an alternative to literature will not be life, but bad literature.[65]

Williams's idea of philosophers 'seeking a reflective understanding of ethical life' from 'good literature' which captures life, fits nicely with bell hooks's writing life. Her writing as part fiction and part life can provide material for philosophers in developing a reflective understanding of ethical life. hooks also offers philosophers of religion who care about justice the chance to see the gendered

---

[64] bell hooks, *Bone Black: Memories of Girlhood* (New York: Henry Holt Company, 1996), pp. xiv. Also see Anderson, 'Myth and Feminist Philosophy', pp. 101–122.

[65] Williams, *Shame and Necessity,* p. 13.

grounds of epistemic injustice. In this way, she helps us to restore faith in reason which can practically work out the truth of who we are.[66] hooks transforms the ways in which black women are represented in literature, in private and public life, but more than that she challenges philosophers of religion to think about our ethical and epistemic practices. Williams suggests that philosophers require good literature to gain reflective understanding of life. When it comes to re-visioning gender they also require good writing for reflective understanding of gender in our life. hooks's writing is good in the sense of revealing the truth and truthfulness of women's and other marginalized lives.[67] Williams also acknowledges that the practices of human life are both something 'we' *share* as 'local' or 'perspectival' and something 'we' question as no longer straightforwardly 'universal'. In other words, human practices are not universally determined; yet as cultural practices, they reflect a remarkable human evolutionary success. So, the practice of philosophy becomes part of the shared activity of understanding ourselves and our other practices. In this latter sense, the practice of philosophy comes very close to hooks's practice of writing.

In telling her own story, in renaming herself and in re-telling a story of Sojourner Truth, hooks reveals the imaginative power in naming, in creating new realities. At the very same time, she makes sense of the social reality of the personal and communal lives in which she has found herself. Reality becomes more just, the more we are true to who we are. The particularity of each life story matters; it matters to the conception of philosophy being advocated in this chapter; and it matters to the image of gender justice to be developed further in Chapter 8. hooks's concern for life stories, for truth and truthfulness resonates with Williams's proposal that philosophy today should be understood as a 'humanistic discipline'.[68] His use of humanistic implies located within a philosophical history, hooks could be read as participating in this discipline of philosophy by her act of disrupting its history with her insistence on truthfulness about the excluded woman of another race, and the excluded black, poor or non-patriarchal man. She exposes what is false. Here I am reminded of Moore's commitment to truth.

To summarize salient points, hooks's story about a black woman who re-names herself, Sojourner Truth, challenges the false universality of a woman's gender as white, fragile, timid, silent and submissive. She also challenges the dominant and privileged western religious myth about a white man, 'Adam', as representative of 'everyman', while at the same time she subverts the myth of the suffering servant as the god-man who redeems. We will return to these challenges and subversions, in Chapter 10, to demonstrate how our epistemic locatedness grounds religious diversity, gender and philosophy. But the point to retain is that restoring faith in reason has to be accompanied by truth-telling; that is, a willingness to recognizes

---

[66]   For additional use of this mythical figure, see Anderson, 'Myth and Feminist Philosophy', pp. 115–117.

[67]   Williams, 'Philosophy as a Humanistic Discipline', pp. 484–485, 493–496.

[68]   Ibid., pp. 477–496; cf. Moore, *The Evolution of Modern Metaphysics*, pp. 602–604.

the true injustices of gender-blindness and epistemic privilege. Unlike the suffering servant, or Christ-figure, Sojourner Truth represents un-freedom and the reality of false universals which have been obscured by the apotheosis of male saviours.

Ideally, a gender subversive story illustrates the transformative power of telling the truth: the concepts of woman, of human, of a divine man are changed by recognition of the falsehood which fails to fit social reality. In this way, Sojourner Truth gains an epistemic authority, while new social markers and concepts are tried out. This process constitutes the redemptive possibilities of hooks's writing life. The injustice and falsehoods of the past are revealed and surrendered to truth. In this way, the oppressive beliefs about human and woman are to be transformed, enabling the imagination of new concepts – of truth.

Obviously, hooks is not alone in creating new concepts by telling new stories, in order to make sense of the 'we' of humanity. Williams himself writes a genealogical account, in a new 'the State of Nature' story, which makes sense of very basic human needs. Williams reveals the value of this philosophical practice as follows:

> In setting out my own State of Nature story, I shall invoke some very basic human needs and limitations, notably the need of co-operation, and I shall consider ways in which they are related to discovering and telling the truth.
>
> …
>
> The State of Nature story is a fiction, an imaginary genealogy, which proceeds by way of abstract argument from some very general and, I take it, indisputable assumptions about human powers and limitations. In virtue of that, and in line with other examples we have considered, I take it to be an example of philosophy.[69]

This example of philosophy arguably serves a similar purpose to hooks's story of Sojourner Truth. Williams employs a method of genealogy to conceive his 'State of Nature story' which begins with very basic human needs. hooks's founding myth of humanity also begins with the very basic need for freedom. According to Williams, a 'genealogy' is a story that 'tries to explain a cultural phenomenon by describing a way in which it came about, or could have come about, or might be imagined to come about'.[70]

hooks explains the cultural phenomenon of racist oppression (that is, injustice and lack of freedom) by telling a true story about slavery (that is, a pernicious falsehood, a denial of freedom and humanity). Her true story reveals women excluding women; the transgressive concept of a woman excluded by another race of women forces the privileged race to re-vision gender. Williams also employs an imagined developmental story to explain a concept 'by showing ways in which [an

---

[69] Williams, *Truth and Truthfulness*, pp. 38–39.
[70] Ibid., p. 20.

exclusive concept] could have come about in a simplified environment containing certain kinds of human interests or capacities, which, relative to the story, are taken as given'.[71] Williams creates a State of Nature story to establish a primitive ground of truthfulness. As he explains,

> I use a method which I call 'genealogy'. It is a descendant of one of Nietzsche's own methods, but only one kind of descendant among others. Nietzsche himself was fully aware that the critique which he directed against old illusions might call in question some of what he said himself. ... But ... in the end he only defends the idea of there being truths but also gives every sign of thinking that he has uttered some.[72]

Thus, in a Nietzschean spirit, we could conclude that both Williams and hooks seek to utter some truths, which will uncover old illusions, and generate the possibility of a new story. hooks's story also becomes a political narrative of resistance and redemption, in creating something powerfully different from the old myth of patriarchy, which oppressed persons in very specific ways, according to the interlocking factors of race, class, religion, ethnicity and gender. In particular, Sojourner Truth challenges the racist nature of representations, which have conceived sexist oppression in terms of the suffering of white women only, whether in the 1830s or today.[73] hooks's story of a suffering, but strong black female figure, takes on the significance of a new, founding myth in generating a narrative that represents the differences between what a general concept – in this case, woman – signifies within a system of meanings and practices and what the general concept ought to represent; hence, she is suggesting a new concept.

Generally, hooks's writing seeks to make sense of life by generating socially situated knowledge. As hooks explains, 'I write as one committed simultaneously to intellectual life [and to the art of writing], which means that ideas are tools I search out and work with to create different and alternative epistemologies (ways of knowing).'[74] In this art of shaping words and writing to make sense of things which have not been known or trusted, hooks (re)creates and reconfigures the false universal concepts which have made up an arbitrarily fixed myth of humanity.

A rational passion for a shared humanity

As will have become increasingly apparent in the present and other chapters in this book, my thinking about gendering reason and love in philosophy of religion

---

71   Ibid., p. 21.

72   Ibid., p. 18, also see pp. 19, 21–22, 31ff.

73   As in Chapter 1, it is important to make reference to Toni Morrison, *Playing in the Dark: Whiteness and the Literary Imagination* (New York: Vintage Books, 1992).

74   hooks, *Remembered Rapture*, p. 16.

has been decisively shaped by hooks's distinctive conception of yearning for a space in which needs and passions can be shared. Drucilla Cornell also builds upon hooks's idea that, in retelling stories of slavery and oppression, feminist philosophers can generate a new conception of humanity for men and women who genuinely seek to uncover the particular conditions for their own freedom as passionate and sexuate beings.[75] This would be a space where we might imagine one and another's common humanity, in order to create new concepts by which we can live more truthfully. For hooks, knowledge of our shared sentiments is both socially situated and critically engaged, to express this knowledge hooks also creates her novel concept, yearning, which re-appears again and again in various ways in her writing (and in my own writing, thanks to, her concept which I extend to this particular context). hooks describes the initial conception as: 'The shared space and feeling of "yearning" opens up the possibility of common ground where all [our] differences might meet and engage one another.'[76]

hooks's imagination of new possibilities in yearning resonates with, as already suggested in Chapter 5, Moore's account for craving infinitude, but also of initiating new concepts. Again, Moore and Williams agree on the shared activity of philosophy as a humanistic discipline. hooks, Moore and Williams have caused me to reflect on my own understanding of ethical life. Here I am reminded of *A Feminist Philosophy of Religion* where I had expressed a hoped for *telos* in discovering a shared humanity:

> I support an account of … a rational passion named 'yearning', as a vital reality of religion. [in hooks's words,] 'under the heading *Yearning*[77] … I looked for *common* passions, sentiments shared by folks across race, class, gender, and sexual practice, I was struck by the depths of longing in many of us. Those without money long to find a way to get rid of the endless sense of deprivation. Those with money wonder why so much feels so meaningless. … there are many individuals with race, gender, and class privilege who are longing to see the kind of revolutionary change that will end domination and oppression even though [our] lives would be completely and utterly transformed.[78]

The distinctiveness of this yearning reflects in part a global culture that has lost its meaning and in other part a life that is missing its humanity. The unwitting nature in the gendering of philosophy and of our ethical lives has obscured our

---

[75]   Drucilla Cornell, *Beyond Accommodation: Ethical Feminism, Deconstruction and the Law* (London: Routledge, 1991; Oxford: Rowman and Littlefield, 1999); *At the Heart of Freedom: Feminism, Sex and Equality* (Princeton, NJ: Princeton University Press, 1998)

[76]   bell hooks, *Yearning: Race, Gender and Cultural Politics* (Boston: South Bend Press, 1990), pp. 12–13.

[77]   Ibid.

[78]   Pamela Sue Anderson, *A Feminist Philosophy of Religion: The Rationality and Myths of Religious Belief* (Oxford: Blackwell, 1998), p. 22.

vision; we fail to see gender injustices, lacking common passions and shared moral sentiments. Yearning is both a response to and indicative of our human need to make sense of things with new stories of men and women, by which we can live more just and humane lives. The problem which renders necessary the mediating role of stories, as in part fiction and in other part history, is that the concept of humanity and the belief in human freedom, which have played a central role in the western myth of the man of reason, are unimaginable for all women and some men in current, empirical terms. The category 'all women' must cover a range of persons globally who differ economically, materially, socially, personally and in religious, ethnic, racial and sexual terms. The explicitly available concept of humanity, or humankind, in our culture today carries only certain accepted meanings and these disallow human freedom as a genuine possibility for women generally, although it is more likely to become a possibility for particular, privileged women. Precisely how the concept of humanity and our belief in human freedom can inform our practices to enable flourishing is not explicable in the terms of present culture(s). To the degree that the sexist, racist or ethnocentric character of a society itself precludes the possibility that the universal concept of a free human(ity) is adequate for all persons, the problem lies in the nature of knowledge more generally.

Chapter 8 will address the problem of gender injustice. The present chapter has both uncovered an epistemic problem (bound up with the nature of knowledge of gender and truth) and suggested the possibility of grasping new concepts. The problem for women in philosophy is often one of misplaced mistrust.[79] The struggle for less partial knowledge and new, more inclusive concepts necessitates the imagination of the impossible in good stories which aim to undermine the foundational myth of patriarchy. Susan E. Babbitt describes this well: '... in a situation in which certain options are impossible even to dream, the bringing about of the imaginability of such possibilities can be personally empowering, even if such conceivability, as is often the case, itself entails suffering. For if it were to become possible for [the woman excluded on racist and/or sexist grounds] just to *dream* that which in other terms *is*, in fact, impossible, she might have been able to deliberate about herself and eventually to act in ways, and to influence others to act in ways, that expressed the possibility of such a dream.'[80] Also, we need to confront the concept of God – of divine truth – which has re-enforced the mistrust of women and their general exclusion from trustworthiness. An epistemology of hope opens

---

[79]   Onora O'Neill discusses the problem of trustworthiness without trust, demonstrating that unlike misplaced trust, 'misplaced mistrust' cannot be simply eliminated by improving trustworthiness, see O'Neill, *Autonomy and Trust in Bioethics* (Cambridge: Cambridge University Press, 2002), pp. 141–142 and p. 165f. We see this problem of the refusal to trust authority in ethics today; cf. Anderson, 'An Epistemological-Ethical Approach'.

[80]   Susan E. Babbitt, *Impossible Dreams: Rationality, Integrity and Moral Imagination* (Boulder, CO: Westview Press, 1996), p. 195; cf. hooks, *Feminist Theory*, pp. xiv, xv, 5, 165; and Patricia Hill Collins, *Fighting Words: Black Women and the Search for Justice* (Minneapolis, MN: University of Minnesota Press, 1998), pp. 187–191, 198–200, 229–240.

up the possibility of creating and possessing new concepts;yet the possibility will necessarily involve both an ethical and an epistemological struggle.[81] Ultimately, a new concept of hope rests on the willingness of men and women to imagine new possibilities; and perhaps the first stage towards this possibility is the restored faith in reason which has been sought here. Faith, reason and truth are not the enemies of women in philosophy. Instead they remain absolutely necessary for re-visioning gender in philosophy of religion.

A final ethical question arises about the danger in the abuse of the imagination in creating, telling and retelling stories about humanity, women, men and the divine. This issue of abuse is not ultimately intractable. Justice can be brought in as a practical ideal, which critically regulates both the epistemological and the ethical dimensions of our rational passions for the possible.[82] Again, Moore's contention that there is a *nisus* for rationality, which motivates our search for making sense of things, could enable our grasp of a concept of hope shaped by a regulative ideal of justice. Justice does not exist for all of 'us'; hence, it must be hoped for, along with truth and love, from – as I have argued elsewhere – a feminist standpoint.[83] The distinctiveness of this standpoint at this political moment results from a struggle for truth and truthfulness.

Conclusion: from a feminist standpoint

Allowing bell hooks to have a significant role in guiding the critical reflections on restoring faith in reason has enabled us to uncover a struggle to end sexist and racist oppression. But this is an ongoing search aimed at a general cultural transformation which would destroy oppressive relations and eradicate systems of domination. Ultimately, this struggle would seek the dissolution of patriarchy in its various global manifestations.[84] Crucially, this struggling for transformation informs our re-visioning gender in philosophy of religion; the heart of the feminist struggle for gender justice is epistemological and ethical. Philosophers of religion, who actively respond to the argument in this book, are required to understand the complex nature of the struggle, the gendering, the injustice in order, finally, to re-vision gender relations with the tools and skills of philosophy.

---

[81] For an epistemology that resists the dualist danger of making science (or knowledge) an exclusively masculinist domain, and for hope that seeks to include women and men in knowing, whether this is scientific, ethical or spiritual knowledge, see Michele Le Doeuff, *The Sex of Knowing*, trans. Kathleen Hamer and Lorraine Code (New York: Routledge, 2003), pp. 153ff.

[82] For more discussion of the role of practical or regulative ideals, see Pamela Sue Anderson, 'Gender and the Infinite: On the aspiration to be all there is', *International Journal of Philosophy of Religion*, vol. 50 (2001), 191–212.

[83] Anderson, '"Standpoint"', pp. 132–133.

[84] hooks, *Feminist Theory: From Margin to Center*, pp. xiv, 5, 163, 165.

One of the steps in Chapter 5 which has been assumed in the present chapter is to reject the philosophical attempt to view the world as if from standpoint of 'a personal being without a body' (to which Chapter 9 will also return). The preferred alternative at the end of this chapter and in anticipation of the next chapter is a 'feminist standpoint'. In the 1990s, I defined this as 'an epistemologically informed perspective, that is achieved – but not without struggle – as a result of gaining awareness of particular positionings of women within relations of power, determined (but not definitively so) by both material and social reality'.[85] It is from this distinctive, yet open feminist standpoint that this chapter concludes, bearing in mind that, from this standpoint, men and women can possess the concepts of trust, love and justice. But it seems to follow that, if we are to redeem truth and restore faith in reason, these concepts would have to be grasped in an engaged way.[86]

This chapter has arrived at a concept of truth which is located, yet not fixed, as moving in the sense that our knowledge is changing or in process; what was once thought true has been shown to be false; old concepts are being discarded; new possibilities are being opened up, giving new meanings to concepts from which we had often become disengaged in any case. Ideally, the concept of faith would be neither irrational nor determined; and the concept of reason, neither authoritarian nor reductive. Any position that sets reason and faith in opposition can, and should, be collapsed through a struggle to transform thinking which is riddled by doubts about reason and about faith. hooks's strategy in writing is to practice telling the truth; it is also to create a space for critical dialogue which eradicates, however gradually, domination whether by the white masculinist or the white feminist. A space of freedom allows new possibilities and becomes a place for making sense of the world; this socially situated place also provides space for healing wounds and for enabling a renewed trust in others. Yearning for a common humanity goes to the heart of truth, but also to the depths of our embodiment, individually and collectively.

hooks arouses her readers to touch the pleasures of the body, mind and soul. She also exposes the wounds of racist and sexist oppression caused by white male supremacy. hooks performs words in writing, in order to create a place for the transformation of our sexual, social and racial passions. Her act of writing is a gesture of political solidarity in a feminist standpoint that is ever restless; with hooks, there is always a spiritual passion that keeps us on the move, while yearning for a place where all differences fall away; this is the infinitude in which humanity would be united by truth and love. However, the argument of the present chapter is that change, love and trust can only take place gradually by the creation of new possibilities, new beliefs and new concepts with which we can (re)direct our lives.

In particular, the contemporary diremption of faith and reason, of theology and philosophy, runs deep amongst privileged philosophers and philosophical

85   Anderson, '"Standpoint"', p. 145.

86   Also see Patricia Hill Collins, *Fighting Words: Black Women and the Search for Justice* (Minneapolis, MN: University of Minnesota Press, 1998).

theologians. The exception in this chapter has been A. W. Moore who has us looking for shared concepts and new ways to make sense of the world. For those of us with less privilege, but still with a sense of responsibility for our global world, we experience a keen sense of injustice which is often not noticed by a privileged thinker who seems to be reasoning about abstract matters. In addition to sexist oppression, the abstract and absent-minded sort of thinker will not understand the present project of re-visioning gender in philosophy of religion. This means not seeing the wide-ranging injustices which generate global conflicts: injustices of sexual orientation race, ethnicity, class and any other social and material inequalities. A very basic human need for freedom – for freedom to know and to speak truth, and to trust in love – is at the heart of what needs to be transformed in our personal, social and spiritual lives. With hooks, women and men in philosophy can seek new ways to express faith and hope. In making narrative sense of suffering and of finitude, hooks writes to move forward. As she tells it:

> As a writer, I seek that moment of ecstasy when I am dancing with words, moving in a circle of love so complete that like the mystical dervish who dances to be one with the Divine, I move toward the infinite.[87]

The political solidarity represented by hooks's 'circle of love' is implicit in writing from a feminist standpoint. This circle creates a vision of possibility for actual change, remembering that everyone must change, if truth-telling is going to be heard and understood.

In this chapter, the political vision of 'restoring faith in reason' has aimed to resist cultural excesses and divisions, especially the extremes which reject reason completely as always authoritarian or merely reductive. Instead we recognize the way in which reason informs human passions for change as expressed, on the one hand, in the philosophical theologian's faith and hope, and on the other hand, in the philosopher's yearning for truth and trust. The philosopher of religion could share a common passion bringing reason and faith together. Much more could be thought, written and done about love and our all too human vulnerabilities. However, at this point the chapter ends with a twofold claim about philosophy and faith. If we are going to move beyond the cultural conditions of nihilism, then our yearning must bring us together in order to make (better) sense of our world philosophically; and if we aim to complete this sense-making project, then we need to grasp the possibility of understanding faith in relation to the infinite. As only human we are always struggling for this understanding, while we long for infinitude. When it comes to gender justice, the topic of Chapter 8, this longing takes the form of a yearning for the place where wounds are healed and we share a common humanity in a circle of love. The next chapter will focus on the aims of feminist philosophy of religion where reason's role in transformation of the field of philosophy takes a prominent place.

---

[87] hooks, *Remembered Rapture*, p. 38.

Chapter 7
Feminist Philosophy of Religion[1]

Introduction: the feminist aims

This chapter is devoted to feminist philosophy of religion. It begins with the feminist aims which were openly discussed in 2000 by Grace M. Jantzen in an exchange of published letters with me, Pamela Sue Anderson, as author of *A Feminist Philosophy of Religion*.[2] The aims were originally mapped out as three questions for our open correspondence. Consider these in the list below with my three working answers:

1. How do we seek transformation? We re-vision Anglo-American philosophy of religion to address gender injustice.[3] This new vision would come about more easily, if an alternative form of rationality were added to a dominant kind of formal reasoning on theistic matters. This would offer reasons for action which are generative of a life-giving and whole-making philosophy of religion.

2. How do we carry out our critiques? Philosophers of religion in the mainstream are not yet seeking any radically new understanding of gender. In contrast, feminist critiques aim to move forward to embrace the radical

---

[1]   Material in this chapter comes from 'The Urgent Wish: To Be More Life-Giving', in Elaine Graham (ed.), *Grace Jantzen: Redeeming the Present* (Farnham, Surrey: Ashgate Publishing Limited, 2009), pp. 41–54.

[2]   Unfortunately the open correspondence was published in the wrong order. Instead of Anderson's first letter appearing followed by Jantzen's response to this; and then, each of the replies to the other, Anderson's letter and her reply to Jantzen were published together in September 2000 before Jantzen's first letter to Anderson and her subsequent reply to Anderson's second letter. So the September 2000 issue of *Feminist Theology* (25) should be read alongside of the January 2001 issue (26) going from Anderson's first letter and then to Jantzen's and then back to Anderson's reply and Jantzen's. The present chapter takes up crucial points, especially from Jantzen's letter to Anderson concerning *A Feminist Philosophy of Religion: the Rationality and Myths of Religious Belief* (Oxford: Blackwell, 1998); see Grace M. Jantzen, 'Feminist Philosophy of Religion: Open Discussion with Pamela Anderson', *Feminist Theology*, 26 (January 2001): 102–109.

[3]   Harriet A. Harris, 'Feminism', in Paul Copan and Chad Meister (eds), *The Routledge Companion to Philosophy of Religion* (London: Routledge, 2007), pp. 651–660; and Michael Levine, 'Non-theistic Conceptions of God', in Paul Copan and Chad Meister (eds), *The Routledge Companion to Philosophy of Religion* (London: Routledge, 2007), pp. 237–248.

spirit of a life-giving vision for a feminist philosophy of religion. At points this will move philosophers of religion closer to the 'Continent', without giving up conceptual precision, to engage with Paul Ricoeur, Gilles Deleuze, A. W. Moore, Michèle Le Doeuff and Genevieve Lloyd.[4] Each of these particular philosophers takes a critical direction from Spinoza's way of persevering in life and of expressing human nature as finite individual modes acting with and upon others. Feminist philosophy of religion could not do much better than to be able to affirm the power to act rationally, as well as to focus on life. As will be seen in the present chapter, contemporary philosophers influenced by radically new readings of Spinoza have taken the lead in affirming life, by falsifying 'contrary relations' of reason and passion, of mind and body, of men and women; as illusions, these contrary relations undermine an(y) individual's power to act both responsibly and with approbation.

3. What do we do with our sources? We seek to re-vision our source texts, and not be afraid to reject arguments which have been construed, in Jantzen's terms, as death-dealing. For example, in (a feminist) philosophical reading of Spinoza's own and other Spinozist arguments, the positive task is to embrace that which enhances our endeavours to persevere in being, and so, in the life of Spinoza's 'God or Nature' (*deus sive natura*). A significant issue exists here for theism: do we exclude 'God' and say, 'Nature', to avoid any confusion between Spinoza's one substance and the Christian theistic God? I would answer that feminist philosophers of religion could find Spinoza's alternative 'God or Nature' liberatory, since neither would be the personal, transcendent God of masculinist theism as discussed in Chapter 3. So, despite what more traditional theists in the discipline of Anglo-American philosophy of religion have dismissed as the pantheism of Spinoza's one substance, Jantzen encourages (feminist) philosophers of religion to move beyond this dismissive labelling and to be free to discover a creative corporeality.

A crucial feminist challenge in philosophy of religion is to free minds to affirm their bodily life within an ever-greater perfection. Although not a feminist, the European philosopher of religion, Paul Ricoeur puts aside the label 'pantheist' in order to focus on Spinoza's 'ethics', especially the ethical journey (*le trajet éthique*) of the finite mode towards recognition of being a particular individual within a larger whole (*la parcelle d'un grand tout*).[5] So, in the spirit of Spinoza, along with some

---

    [4]   Thanks to Kathryn Bevis, Jennifer Bunker, Adrian Moore and Daniel Whistler who have helped me work through technical terms and ideas from Spinoza's *Ethics*, especially in group discussions of 'Spileuze'. However, any incoherence and confusion on Spinoza are mine.
    [5]   Paul Ricoeur, *L'unique et le singulier*. L'intégrale des entretiens 'Noms de dieux' d'Edmond Blattchen (Brussels Belgium: Alice Editions, 1999), pp. 43–47. Also, see

feminist philosophers of religion and some non-feminist philosophers of religion, the rest of this chapter will argue that each and every individual can move forward in striving for a joyful continuation of bodily existence which expresses, what we might agree is, an intellectual love of either God or Nature.

Life and death

Let us read two assertions concerning the core concepts of life and of death found in the texts of two, at first glance, unrelated philosophers. First is Spinoza and second is Ricoeur. Each of their affirmations of life and of the power to act, as much as to suffer, as responsible and autonomous thinking subjects, will in turn resonate profoundly with the core challenge of Jantzen.[6] The urgent wish of Jantzen was that feminist philosophy of religion become 'more life-giving'. In an attempt to take up this challenge, let us read the following words from Spinoza:

> A free man [sic] thinks of nothing less than of death, and his wisdom is a meditation, not on death, but on life.[7]

Let us read these lines from Ricoeur:

> Power, I will say, affirms itself ... this connection between affirmation and power needs to be emphasized. It governs all the reflexive forms by which a subject can designate him- or herself as the one who can. ... [This] affirmation of a power to act already presents a noteworthy epistemological feature that cannot be proven, demonstrated, but can only be attested ... a confidence in one's own capacity, which can be confirmed only through being exercised and through the approbation others grant to it ... other people may encourage, accompany, assist by having confidence in us – by appeal to responsibility and autonomy.[8]

No doubt, Jantzen would have been intrigued by these quotations, even if she would have carefully qualified their philosophical significance for feminists. I will mainly expand on the first quotation with some appropriations of Spinoza's

---

Amelie Rorty, 'Spinoza on the Pathos of Idolatrous Love and the Hilarity of True Love', in Genevieve Lloyd (ed.), *Feminism and the History of Philosophy* (Oxford: Oxford University Press, 2002), pp. 204–224.

[6] For an early feminist conception of affirming life and acting responsibly, see Simone de Beauvoir, *The Ethics of Ambiguity*, trans. Bernard Frechtman (New York: Citadel Press, 1948), pp. 74–155.

[7] Benedict de Spinoza, *Ethics*, trans. and edited by G. H. R. Parkinson (Oxford: Oxford University Press, 2000), p. 276; Part Four, prop 67.

[8] Paul Ricoeur, 'Autonomy and Vulnerability', *Reflections on The Just*, trans. David Pellauer (Chicago: The University of Chicago Press, 2007), p. 75.

meditations on life, that is, on the power of life, including suggestions concerning confidence in life.

Ricoeur's affinity to Spinoza appears in giving a highly significant role to power in an individual's affirmation of life and approbation of others: affirmation and approbation are required for the confidence to exercise this power to act. Some readers will be aware of the post-Kantian dimension in the reflexive autonomy in which Ricoeur reveals his appropriation of Spinoza. I will place this combination of affirmation, approbation and autonomy in the context of Jantzen's urgent wish for philosophy of religion to become life-giving and whole-making. In particular, I will raise questions about the relation between the individual and the collective in a Spinozist conception of corporate life. To be feminist, as I will suggest, this conception of 'life' not only requires affirmation and approbation, but autonomy. Autonomy takes on a crucial role as a concept, ensuring that the Spinozist *conatus* strives to persevere in an individual's own life, even while acting and re-acting in relation to corporate life. Notice here that it is Ricoeur's hermeneutical method of reading philosophical texts and bodily life which can enable feminist and non-feminist philosophers to discover new interpretations of Spinoza's *Ethics*. The hermeneutical task, in this case, is to enhance the human effort and desire to be.[9]

In 2000, as already explained, Jantzen and I began the open discussion of feminist philosophy of religion focusing on *A Feminist Philosophy of Religion*[10] and on *Becoming Divine*.[11] Our exchange was published as a correspondence in *Feminist Theology* and in her first letter Jantzen writes: 'my book was in press when yours came out, and although we are different in approach we very much share the urgent wish for the discipline to be more life-giving and whole-making'.[12] Since own her death, Jantzen's words, have become more poignant; her rational and passionate insistence that feminist philosophy of religion give life, not death, seemed to prevent any turning back to the harshness of suffering and to the fear of death. Instead Jantzen's writings always push us toward a radical transformation of the Anglo-American discipline of philosophy of religion. In the spirit of Jantzen, feminist philosophers of religion are urged to move forward in their thinking and writing.

The overall argument of the present book is consistent with Jantzen's vision: new ways in which to be bold – that is, more confident in acting rationally and passionately – are found by re-visioning, that is, looking back with fresh eyes. It is important to note that Jantzen commended the conception of 'yearning'

---

[9]   Pamela Sue Anderson, 'On Loss of Confidence: Dissymmetry, Doubt, Deprivation in the Power to Act and (the Power) to Suffer', in Joseph Carlisle, James C. Carter and Daniel Whistler (eds), *Moral Powers, Fragile Beliefs: Essays in Moral and Religious Philosophy* (London and New York: Continuum, 2011), pp. 83–108.

[10]   Anderson, *A Feminist Philosophy of Religion*.

[11]   Grace M. Jantzen, *Becoming Divine: Toward a Feminist Philosophy of Religion* (Manchester, UK: Manchester University Press, 1998).

[12]   Jantzen, 'Feminist Philosophy of Religion: Open Discussion', p. 102.

advocated in my earliest feminist writings.[13] It is possible to see in retrospect that yearning is not only an important thread in feminist philosophy of religion but can be significantly enhanced with an alternative form of rationality. In particular, the reasoning which is inspired by contemporary philosophical appropriations of Spinoza's *conatus* has the potential to enhance yearning as a means of increasing activity in human life. The perseverance in being joined with a yearning for (the infinitude of) life can generate (the) power which we each have to affirm our own existence at the same time as approving of another's. Of course, this form of power in approbation, or mutual recognition, would be risky if it was not wise in the rationalist sense of Spinoza's *Ethics*.

To begin to assess this appropriation of Spinoza's *Ethics* for feminist philosophy of religion, let us imagine how Jantzen herself might have moved forward, if she herself were still alive today. Such an exercise in imagination is absolutely essential for the corporate picture at the heart of Jantzen's feminist vision. This 'corporate' picture has to do with the body of each individual but also the collective body. We know that Spinoza's imagination involves free exercise of 'the affections of the human body'.[14] These affections would be 'ideas' in the sense of images of things, or corporeal traces which impinge on the affected body; but these are passive affections in the mind. As such could they take on the required positive role in the process of, in Jantzen's terms, philosophy becoming 'more whole-making'; that is, feminist philosophy would be characterized by both corporate and corporeal relations.

A critical question arises: would Jantzen's feminist philosophy of religion been able to ensure optimism in corporeal relations? So far in our account of Spinoza we seem to be on shaky grounds, insofar as we restrict ourselves to Spinoza's 'imagining' with 'inadequate ideas' as above. However, Spinoza considers such ideas as passively in the mind and at the very lowest level of knowledge. For Spinoza, an inadequate idea is an idea in his mind which is 'fragmentary and confused': to recall Moore's terms of 'making sense', as discussed in the previous chapter, an inadequate idea 'does not fully make sense to him (*sic*)'; but an adequate idea is an idea actively in his mind that 'does fully make sense to him'.[15] The more the mind's activity increases, the more knowledge and the closer we get to a Spinozist conception of joy. The crucial point for Janzen and other feminist philosophers who try to resist the dominant philosophical dualism of mind and body in contemporary philosophy of religion is that Spinoza has no division between these two. Instead the increase of active ideas in the mind is

---

[13]   For this account of yearning as a rational passion for justice, informed by bell hooks and other feminist accounts of injustice which can only be undone with the transformation of our lives, beliefs and passions, see Anderson, *A Feminist Philosophy of Religion*, pp. 22–23, 174, 241.

[14]   Spinoza, *Ethics*, pp. 132–134, 139; Part Two, prop. 17 scholium.

[15]   A. W. Moore, *The Evolution of Modern Philosophy: Making Sense of Things* (Cambridge: Cambridge University Press, 2012), p. 57.

also an increase in bodily activity and in bodily relations as collective activities of individuals. Yet the decisive question is: are women, like men, part of the corporate joy in a Spinozist affirmation of life and intellectual love of nature? If not, Jantzen's feminist philosophy of religion would leave this sixteenth-century Dutch rationalist philosopher behind.

A joyful love of this life, not death or life beyond death

This section aims to embrace Jantzen's encouragement by actively exploring her love of life. We follow her pursuit of a life-giving philosophy, taking up her response to some of my own points as follows:

1. '[I]f we take seriously your emphasis on feminist standpoint epistemology and especially your very creative use of the concept of yearning, then the aim of feminist philosophy is radicalised in a way that I find highly insightful; and it's this that I find of most value in your book. ... I want to ask you to try to take it further.'[16]

2. 'Take for example your important and subversive idea of thinking from others' lives, 'inventing ourselves as other':[17] the consequences for philosophy of religion are enormous. If we stop valorizing the disembodied "genderless" male subject then we also presumably stop valorizing the disembodied "genderless" male deity: what happens to the concept of God so beloved of the discipline.'[18]

3. 'I think ... that in fact your method of thinking from others' lives is far more radical than your stated aim of offering a supplement to the traditional idea of rationality.'[19]

4. 'To take masculinism ... as you point out, men have historically identified themselves with rationality and have identified women with the body, passion, irrationality and madness. Now, to revision rationality so that it includes passion rather than sees passion as its other is indeed a huge epistemological shift; and I especially like your emphasis that one of its central categories is yearning. ... your lifting up of yearning changes the whole epistemological landscape.'[20] ... what you say about yearning actually destabilizes the [Anglo-American] emphasis on [justifying] beliefs rather than being a supplement to rationality.'[21]

---

[16] Jantzen, 'Feminist Philosophy of Religion: Open Discussion', pp. 102–103.
[17] Anderson, *A Feminist Philosophy of Religion*, p. 165.
[18] Jantzen, 'Feminist Philosophy of Religion: Open Discussion', p. 104.
[19] Ibid.
[20] Ibid.
[21] Ibid., p. 105.

5. '[J]ust think what a difference it would have made to the history of modernity if the philosophy of religion had taken as its emphasis and aim a yearning for beauty or goodness, and fostering their discernment.'[22]
6. '[H]ow is yearning to be fostered, individually and collectively, and what forms of education of desire are appropriate?'[23]

With the above, Jantzen argues for the possibility that yearning could constitute a significantly new and radical conception; but this still needs to be pushed forward.

So, Jantzen's reading of *A Feminist Philosophy of Religion* has inspired me to enhance and develop my earlier conception of yearning. In recent years, I have turned to a distinctive genealogy from Spinoza to Kant, Ricoeur, Gilles Deleuze, Michèle Le Doeuff, Genevieve Lloyd and Moira Gatens. Each of these philosophers guide the working out of an alternative form of rationality which has a critical role to play: it is to educate our emotions and passions. In fact, it now seems surprising that Jantzen herself had not drawn more significant content from Spinoza, Ricoeur, Deleuze, Le Doeuff, Lloyd or Gatens for affirming the power to persevere in being and, even more crucially for Jantzen, for meditation on life, not death. In the concluding pages of *Becoming Divine*, Jantzen admits that she would be willing to explore the possibilities in 'a pantheist symbolic'; Jantzen's distinctive and original vision of 'a symbolic of natality' is worth taking seriously as 'a flourishing of the earth and those who dwell upon it'.[24] Given more time, Jantzen herself might have explored Spinoza's *conatus*. In any case, Jantzen pushes feminist philosophy of religion in this direction.

Jantzen's passion for transformation keeps feminist thinking on the move from Anglo-American and Continental approaches in philosophy of religion. It is my contention that contemporary feminist and Continental appropriations of Spinoza's *conatus* not only shape an alternative form of rationality which can become life-giving and whole-making, but enhance Jantzen's passion for a radically new feminist ethics. What might she have said about Spinoza's *Ethics*? Consistent with her wish that I be even more bold in my treatment of yearning, to call yearning (as in craving infinitude) the essence of religion is not too ambitious. Yet with this ambition, it is still necessary to work out whether a particular religious yearning could bind individuals together ethically to create new corporate and productive relations between bodies, minds and nature. This motivation for corporate relations finds support in what Spinoza's *Ethics* says about *conatus*: it is a rational striving of each individual body to exist fully which becomes the essence of a rationalist ethics. As specific form of yearning, Spinoza's *conatus* binds bodies together in

---

[22] Ibid., p. 106.
[23] Ibid., p. 107.
[24] Jantzen, *Becoming Divine*, p. 275; also pp. 272–275. For more background on the theist's dismissive labelling of Spinoza a 'pantheist', see Levine, 'Non-theistic Conceptions of God', pp. 236–248.

love; and so human beings conceived as parts of a dynamic and interconnected whole.

To go over additional, relevant ground in Spinoza's *Ethics*, *conatus* stands for a thing's endeavour to persevere in being against un-wise passions; and this perseverance becomes a thing's very essence. In the case of those individuals who are human bodies, *conatus* has an intimate connection with reason similar to our earlier discussions of yearning, especially in Chapter 6. Instead of having reason serve, in turning away from harmful passion, as an alternative source of ethical motivation the virtuous mind achieves – according to Spinoza – freedom by bringing its understanding to bear on its own passions, transforming them into active, rational emotions. In Spinoza's terms, if we can be the 'adequate cause' of one of 'the affections of the body' by which the power of acting is 'increased or diminished, helped or hindered', then 'I understand by the emotion an action; otherwise, I understand it to be a passion.'[25]

Spinoza's technical term 'imagination' is like emotion in being driven by *conatus*. The activities of the imagination are caught up in the dynamics of *conatus*, that is, in the movement and impetus of the mind in its struggle to express its nature as 'a finite individual'. The mind's joys and sorrows, its loves and hates, are inseparable from the effort to imagine: 'The mind endeavours to imagine only those things which posit its power of acting.'[26] In his general definition of the emotions, Spinoza describes the passions of the mind as 'confused ideas': 'by which the mind affirms of its body, or of any part of its body, a greater or lesser force of existing than before, and which when being given, the mind itself is determined to thinking this rather than that'.[27] This definition incorporates his understanding of the natures: i) of pleasure as 'a man's [sic] transition from a lesser to a greater perfection',[28] ii) of pain as 'a man's transition from a greater to a lesser perfection', and iii) of desire as 'the very essence of man, in so far as it is conceived as determined to do something from some given affection of itself'.[29] So, pleasure or joy, pain or sadness, and desire are at the core of Spinoza's account of the emotions; pleasure, pain and desire are integrated into what it is to be a passion.

Genevieve Lloyd helpfully expands on Spinoza's definition of the emotions with her account of love, including sexual love. According to Lloyd, 'Spinoza's account makes it impossible to talk of the 'pain' of love'.[30] Instead love is always 'joyful' in Spinoza's sense of this term. His parallel definition of the opposite of love, hate, integrates sadness: 'hate is "sadness associated with an idea of an

---

25   Spinoza, *Ethics*, p. 164f.
26   Ibid., p. 205, Part Three, prop 54.
27   Ibid.; Part Three, General Def.
28   Ibid., p. 213.
29   Ibid., p. 212.
30   Genevieve Lloyd, 'What a Union!' *The Philosophers Magazine*, 29 (2005): 48.

external cause'".[31] Lloyd continues to expand on Spinoza, 'What we may see as the disturbance of love, Spinoza sees rather as our being torn by contrary passions.'[32] Understanding these distinctions must be part of what is meant by Spinoza's use of reason to 'educate' or transform the passions.

According to Lloyd's radical and, for some at least, provocative interpretation of Spinoza, to understand the operations of imagination and its interactions with the emotions is to learn to replace misleading and debilitating illusions with better fictions which help rather than hinder the actions of the mind in which freedom consists.[33] The capacity (*potestas*) to act and not merely to be acted on, to express one's own nature and not merely react to the nature of another is an expression of freedom, but equally of one's power (*potentia*) and so of *conatus*.[34] Spinoza's way to conquer (mis)fortune lies in the use of reason to understand the operations of the imagination and the passions. The power of reason rests in understanding the passions and increasing one's freedom. Again Spinoza's 'imagination' is a first kind of knowledge and as such constitutes a necessary step in the education of the passions. More adequate knowledge comes in understanding the errors or fictions which make up socially embedded illusions. The critical question is: what, if any, role the imagination might play in striving for and achieving intellectual knowledge of God? Roger Scruton, for one, assumes that the imagination indicates a lesser kind of knowledge only.[35] Debilitating fictions are bound up with a lack of knowledge. For example, the fiction of a free will for Spinoza exhibits an awareness of one's actions but an ignorance of their causes. An ability to exercise an ongoing critique of illusion generates the highest exercise of philosophical thought: the mind's understanding of itself as 'eternal' with the love of God or nature as its cause. The latter becomes highly significant in the conclusions of Spinoza's *Ethics*.[36]

---

[31]   Genevieve Lloyd, 'What a Union!' p. 48.

[32]   Ibid. For further, fascinating discussions of sexual love and the way in which bodily pleasures are, for Spinoza, as important for the well-being of the individual as the cultivation of reason, see Alexandre Matheron, 'Spinoza *et la sexualité*', *Giornale Critico della Filosofia Italiana*, 8/4 (1977): 454; Rorty, 'Spinoza on the Pathos of Idolatrous Love', p. 222; and Pamela Sue Anderson, 'Liberating Love's Capabilities: On the Wisdom of Love', in Norman Wirzba and Bruce Ellis Benson (eds), *Transforming Philosophy and Religion: Love's Wisdom* (Indianapolis: Indiana University Press, 2008), pp. 214–220.

[33]   For a different and more conservative reading of Spinoza's account of the imagination, see Roger Scruton, *Spinoza: A Very Short Introduction* (Oxford: Oxford University Press, 2002), pp. 74, 90–91 and 95f.

[34]   On the fine distinctions in Spinoza concerning *potentia* as act, active and actual, i.e., the essence of an individual mode and *potestas* as a capacity for being affected, see Gilles Deleuze, *Spinoza: Practical Philosophy*, trans. Robert Hurley (San Francisco, CA: City Lights Books, 1988), pp. 97–98.

[35]   Scruton, *Spinoza*, pp. 92, 97.

[36]   Spinoza, *Ethics*, pp. 309–316; cf. Moira Gatens and Genevieve Lloyd, *Collective Imaginings: Spinoza, Past and Present* (London: Routledge, 1999), pp. 23–40.

Yet the critical question for this chapter can be put crudely: Has Spinoza's core concept of *conatus* led us to a striving for greater self-understanding which, ultimately, remains self-interestedness and so incompatible with Jantzen's vision of a life-giving and whole-making philosophy? Is an individual's effort to persevere in being directed to a self-sufficiency and detachment from other bodies which would be incompatible with Jantzen's pursuit of whole-making in a feminist philosophy of religion? At a glance some readers might think that Spinoza's endeavour could not be compatible with 'a feminist standpoint epistemology' which aims to 'think from the lives of others', as advocated in *A Feminist Philosophy of Religion* and as Jantzen encouraged.[37] And yet, this is to fail to understand the way in which individual bodies, in Spinozist philosophy, combine in order to create a new body and so a collective life. In order to see this, let us diverge a bit and try to redeem the crucial dimensions of Spinoza's account of *conatus* with certain feminist appropriations of his *Ethics* in the terms of individual bodies and gender politics.

Individuals, bodies and gender politics

This section is bound to consider the relation of the individual and the collective body in Spinoza; but I will do this indirectly by considering the appropriation of Spinoza by feminist philosophers Michèle Le Doeuff, Genevieve Lloyd and Moira Gatens. The critical question already raised at the outset is: how can Spinoza and those who follow him ensure optimism and, ultimately, joy? The answer has to do with negotiating reason so that rationality is shared; this in turn would increase power and so joy.

As already stated, Spinoza's concept of *conatus* is the very essence of finite individuals and closely connected to the imagination. For Spinoza, to be an individual is to be determined to act through the mediation of 'other finite modes', i.e. 'that which is in something else and is conceived through something else';[38] and it is likewise to determine these others. One way to think of Spinoza's mode is a modification of the one substance which makes up all of Nature or 'God'. According to Spinoza's definition, imagination assumes the awareness of our own bodies together with others; so the interaction between bodies essentially involves imagination. Early in the present chapter, instead of awareness of our bodies, Spinoza's own terms were employed, that is, 'affections of the human body'. Bodily awareness is not only readily understood as part of the nature of Spinoza's imagination, but we now recognize that it is also closely bound up with the impetus of *conatus*. It is the nature of bodies and minds, as finite individuals, to struggle in order to persevere in being. Our bodies are not just passively moved by external forces. They have their own motion, or movement in a certain relation

---

[37]   See points 1 and 3 (above). Also, see Jantzen 2001, pp. 102–104; cf. Anderson, *A Feminist Philosophy of Religion*, p. 76f.

[38]   'Editor's Introduction' in Spinoza, *Ethics*, pp. 19–26.

to rest, which is their own characteristic force for existing. However, this force is not something that individuals exert of their own power alone. For an individual to persevere in existence is for it to act and be acted upon in a multiplicity of ways. The more complex the individual body, the more ways in which it can be affected by and affecting other things. The power of the imagination is integral to the continued existence and flourishing of the individual as corporeal. So, to define imagination in terms of bodily awareness is to place imagination at the heart of the story of human well-being and flourishing with one another. We approach the collective dimension of Spinoza's *Ethics* in light of the above understanding of *conatus*, imagination and bodily awareness.

We have returned to the crucial point: the nature of these individual bodies. We seek to understand the way(s) in which they make up a collective and corporeal life. To repeat, Spinoza argues that each body, in fact each thing, has a *conatus* which constitutes its very essence and with which it 'endeavours to persevere in its being'.[39] This is as true of humans as it is of anything else. Yet in more exclusively masculine terms, Spinoza cautions specifically men to avoid pity,[40] since pity is an 'effeminate' or 'womanish' emotion.[41] His sharp distinctive between men and women on this point is clear. In other words, pity is something undergone like a 'woman's emotion' and as such obstructs the transition of passions to actions; it blocks the education of the emotions, and more generally, hinders life's *conatus*. Moore again helpfully clarifies this, 'Each man (*sic*), by his very nature, is driven to preserve his own existence, and his happiness consists in his being able to do just that'.[42] In fact, a man's (sic) essence is determined by *conatus*. 'The *conatus* is, in a way, a *conatus* towards *its own* preservation'.[43] The crucial point is, then, that the *conatus* for a human being is a drive to actualize the human essence to the greatest possible degree: this means a drive to maximize human activity and to minimize human passivity. As Moore explains, 'To have this drive to maximize activity is the very essence, power and virtue of the human being'.[44] This model of maximally active self-preservation and so perseverance in being is also Spinoza's model for freedom and salvation.[45] Thus, Spinoza returns us to the point that a thing is free when it 'exists solely from the necessity of its own nature, and is determined to action by itself alone'.[46] Admittedly, this could sound incompatible

---

[39]   Ibid., p. 171; Part Three props 6 and 7.

[40]   Ibid., p. 185–187f, 217.

[41]   Ibid., p. 253; cf. Genevieve Lloyd, 'The Man of Reason', in Ann Garry and Marilyn Pearsall (eds), *Women, Knowledge and Reality: Explorations in Feminist Philosophy*. Second edition (London: Routledge, 1996), pp. 157–159.

[42]   Moore, *The Evolution of Modern Metaphysics*, p. 55; cf. Spinoza, *Ethics*, pp. 230–233; Part Four, props 3–7.

[43]   Moore, *The Evolution of Modern Metaphysics*, p. 55.

[44]   Ibid., pp. 55; cf. Spinoza, *Ethics*, pp. 231–232 and 241; Part Four, props 4 and 20.

[45]   Spinoza, *Ethics*, pp. 310–311; Part Five prop 36 and Scholium.

[46]   Spinoza, *Ethics*, p. 75; Part One def 7; cf. Moore, *The Evolution of Modern Metaphysics*, p. 55.

with the feminist ethicist who defends 'relational autonomy'. Moreover, these readings of Spinoza have not yet give us a gender-inclusive picture of both corporeal and collective life.

Consider Lloyd's serious feminist criticism of Spinoza's attempt to transcend self-centredness for a corporate life. As a highly influential feminist philosopher herself, and expert on Spinoza's philosophy, Lloyd would have to be carefully listened to, for any feminist appropriation of Spinoza's power to exist and the affirmation of that power of existence. Equally her critical assessment of Spinoza would have to be applied equally to Ricoeur's affirmation of the power of the subject to act – which appeared in as one of two valuable quotations – in the second section of this chapter. Lloyd makes two opposing claims for a feminist re-visioning of Spinoza. On the one hand, it is immediately attractive to a feminist philosopher that Spinoza's rejects the dualism of mind and body where, crudely stated, the body had been given less value – especially in its symbolic association with women – than the mind in previous philosophy, notably in Descartes. On the other hand, Lloyd recognizes the problems remaining implicit in the highly gendered references to man in Spinoza's *Ethics*.[47] Lloyd admits that 'there is indeed much that is appealing and impressive in the picture Spinoza presents ... the transcending of self-centred and hence dependent, jealous love; the pursuit of a detached perception of the truths of himself and his situation, transcending the distortions of his limited, unreflective perspective on things; the location of moral worth in a certain style of perception rather than in the will'.[48] Yet there remains the serious question of a man not only transcending selfish and obsessive love but any individual as the proper object of love. Moreover, the gendered repudiation of pity as weak and effeminate indicates a larger problem (for a Spinozist) with any ethics of compassion or care; and the latter is often thought necessary for feminist ethics.

Michèle Le Doeuff has also voiced her strong objection to Spinoza's deliberate exclusion of women from government, and so the larger sphere of political life, on the basis of woman's natural inferiority and spiritual weakness.[49] Le Doeuff points out that in his very last, however unfinished political treatise, Spinoza makes absolutely clear that a woman's weakness and her potential (sexual) distraction of men from their rational emotional life provide definite grounds for Spinoza's conscious exclusion of women from seventeenth-century political society.[50] In her incisive style, 'Now according to [Spinoza] experience would tend to show that if women are excluded from government and subjected to male authority, it is because [of] a natural weakness of spirit ...';[51] and she cites Spinoza here: 'government by women "has nowhere happened, [therefore] I am fully entitled to

---

[47]   Lloyd, 'The Man of Reason', pp. 155–160.
[48]   Ibid., p. 159.
[49]   Le Doeuff, *Hipparchia's Choice*, p. 168.
[50]   Le Doeuff, *The Sex of Knowing*, pp. 104–106; cf. *Hipparchia's Choice*, p. 206.
[51]   Le Doeuff, *The Sex of Knowing*, p. 104.

assert that women have not the same right as men by nature, but are necessarily inferior to them'".[52]

And yet, once women are seen to have the natural right to cultivate knowledge and be part of any government, then we might find Le Doeuff applauding the education of emotions *à la* Spinoza. It is not clear what a 'natural right' might be in Spinozist's *Ethics*; perhaps the closest thing to this is the human capacity to act rather than merely be acted on or merely undergo such passions as 'pity'. But there is something deeply unwitting about Le Doeuff's own affinity with an ethics of joy: it seems close to Spinoza in terms of its affirmation of life and the power to act, while very critical of Spinoza in so far as he excludes women by conceiving them as weak and inferior. Basically, Le Doeuff exhibits her own pleasure in persevering in existence. Le Doeuff's writings are full of positive expressions for women and men which resonate powerfully with the seventeenth-century tradition of rationalism. Her form of rationality clearly embraces the power to act responsibly and autonomously, while also striving for a joyous contemplation of the life of Nature. Moreover, Le Doeuff's characteristic rationalist vision of a political community in which *women* are *united individually and collectively* – with the one-and-many metaphor of 'the corporate' – could not be that far from a modification of Spinoza's expression of *conatus* which would include women.[53] Basically Le Doeuff makes sure that gender is inclusive by turning a negative into a positive when it comes to a Spinoza's womanish weakness. But can this help more generally our understanding of the relation of individual bodies to collective life? and so, a new corporate body?

In fact Le Doeuff's favourite seventeenth-century female philosopher, Gabrielle Suchon, could have a great deal to do with her close affinity to what Spinoza would identify as 'intuitive knowledge' (*scientia intuitiva*) of 'God'[54]; and Le Doeuff has translated this kind of knowledge in Suchon, 'infused'.[55] But here 'God' does not refer to any personal deity. Rather divinity simply refers to the one substance: Nature in which bodies and minds are working as parts in accord. But infused knowledge is far greater than the inadequate kind of knowledge which we have seen is due to the imagination; Spinoza himself calls the latter a 'first' kind of knowledge. Le Doeuff uncovers Suchon's philosophical writing in order to emphasize forcefully the ethical significance of both women and men in gaining knowledge and so freedom. Similarly, one of Le Doeuff's preferred twentieth-century male philosopher, Gilles Deleuze, actively embraces a highly original

---

[52]   Ibid., p. 105; cf. Benedict de Spinoza, *Tractatus Politicus*, in *The Political Works*, edited and trans. A. G. Wernham (Oxford: Clarendon Press, 1958), p. 443f.

[53]   Le Doeuff, *The Sex of Knowing*, pp. 138–141; 2006, 37–43, 168–170, 206–207, 243.

[54]   Gilles Deleuze, *Spinoza: Practical Philosophy*, trans. Robert Hurley (San Francisco, CA: City Lights Books, 1988), pp. 86–91; Moira Gatens, *Imaginary Bodies: Ethics, Power and Corporeality* (London: Routledge, 1996), pp. 111–113, 117f.

[55]   Le Doeuff, *The Sex of Knowing*, pp. 5–10, 15–24, 33–45.

reading of Spinoza's practical philosophy.[56] Instead of traditional theism we discover in the Spinozist dimensions of Le Doeuff's thinking a form of rationalism which has God or Nature (*deus sive natura*) as its ground: no personal, male-gendered deity is implied, yet a creative corporeality is.

It is helpful to present one last quotation – this time from Deleuze – on Spinoza. Notice Deleuze's unequivocal emphasis on life and the positive affirmation of the power of life, as a way of being, in his philosophical account of Spinoza:

> In the reproach that Hegel will make to Spinoza, that he ignored the negative and its power, lies the glory and innocence of Spinoza, his own discovery. In a world consumed by the negative, he has enough confidence in life, in the power of life, to challenge death, the murderous appetite of men, the rules of good and evil, of the just and the unjust. Enough confidence in life to denounce all the phantoms of the negative. Excommunication, war, tyranny, reaction, men who fight for their enslavement as if it were their freedom – this forms the world in which Spinoza lives ...[57] In Spinoza's thought, life is not an idea, a matter of theory. It is a way of being, one and the same eternal mode in all its attributes. And it is only from this perspective that the geometric method is fully comprehensible. In the *Ethics*, it is in opposition to what Spinoza calls satire; and satire is everything that takes pleasure in the powerlessness and distress of men, everything that feeds on accusations, on malice, on belittlement, on low interpretations, everything that breaks men's spirits ... People have asked whether the *Ethics* should be read in terms of thought or in terms of power (for example, are the attributes powers or concepts?). Actually, there is only one term, Life, that encompasses thought, but conversely this term is encompassed only by thought. Not that life is in thinking, but only the thinker has a potent life, free of guilt and hatred; and only life explains the thinker. ... Spinoza did not believe in hope or even in courage; he believed only in joy, and in vision. He let others live, provided that others let him live. He wanted only to inspire, to waken, to reveal.[58]

In the two quotations above from Deleuze on Spinoza, we find a timely and powerful summation of Spinoza's thought with its distinctive method; non-feminist and feminist philosophers alike will find attractive the unequivocal confidence (above) in a Spinozist way of thinking and living, in a striving to increase or to maximize the power of life. Much of Spinoza's positive vision depends on bodies acting together as a more and more complex body, and

---

[56]   Deleuze, *Spinoza*; and Gilles Deleuze, *Expressionism in Philosophy: Spinoza*, trans. Martin Joughin (New York: Zone Books, 2005); cf. Le Doeuff, *The Sex of Knowing*, pp. 217–220; *Hipparchia's Choice*, pp. 168, 319–321.

[57]   Deleuze, *Spinoza*, p. 13.

[58]   Ibid., p. 14.

ultimately, making one whole (nature).[59] This vision exhibits a strong affinity to Jantzen's profoundly positive framework of life, including her crucial picture of natality, of the new beginnings for women and men as 'natals', not mortals.[60] However, perhaps Spinoza is far more Stoic and rationalist than Jantzen when it comes to life. In his determination to understand things, he produces ethics which is also metaphysics. Spinoza has a splendid vision of intellectual joy, but this requires each individual to be increasing in knowledge, increasing in activity, which makes this a demanding vision. Each of us seeks her or his own part metaphysical truths which cannot be communicated in any other way, except to persevere in the ethical task of sense-makings. We have been reading Spinoza as, then, another philosopher who attempts, in Moore's terms, to make sense of things. Yet, is there a distinctively feminist vision to be found here?

In Spinoza's terms, the human body needs for its preservation very many other bodies by which it is continually regenerated.[61] This is an attractive picture for feminist philosophers of religion who follow after Spinoza, Deleuze, Le Doeuff, Lloyd and Jantzen. Feminist philosophers can be assured that the body is involved in the Spinozist picture. It is what we, our bodies with our minds, can do which determines what counts as living well. Consistent with this Spinozist picture, the more we do rationally and corporately – as opposed to undergo – the better we live together. In particular, 'to love God' is no longer to trust in the benevolent purposes of a transcendent creator – the purposes for which we await satisfaction. Instead it is the mind's joyful recognition of itself as corporate, that is, as part of the unified whole of nature which expresses an intellectual love [of 'God']. Thus the core of love in all its forms is the joy of continued bodily existence. That joy is vulnerable, and yet it is a more sure grounding for our loves than the glorification of unsatisfied desire for a wholly transcendent and disembodied divine.[62]

Conclusion

Let us conclude by returning to the opening questions for feminist philosophy of religion and see what can now be added to the initial answers. (1) How do feminist philosophers of religion seek transformation? We strive to re-vision gender in Anglo-American philosophy of religion and, as a result, to transform oppressive gender relations which have been the cause of epistemic injustice. The new vision for the field would seek to be generative of, in Jantzen's terms, a life-giving and whole-making philosophy of religion.

---

[59]   For a feminist discussion of Spinoza's notion of body, bodies and power, see Moira Gatens, *Imaginary Bodies*, pp. 102–113; cf. Spinoza, *Ethics*, pp. 131–132, Part Two, postulates on the body.

[60]   Jantzen, *Becoming Divine*, Chapters 6 and 10; cf. Harris, 'Feminism', pp. 643–645.

[61]   Spinoza, *Ethics*, p. 131f.

[62]   Ibid., pp. 106–112.

(2) How does feminist philosophy of religion carry out its critiques? Generally, feminist critiques in this field should begin by radically questioning the role and limits of reason in the specific philosophical texts on traditional theism. The feminist critique advocated in this chapter does not oppose formal reasoning or any form of philosophical rationality as masculine to non-rational action or emotion as feminine. Instead a feminist critique is best illustrated in its application to the texts of philosophers; and in this chapter, the critique was applied to some of Spinoza's and Spinozist concepts for 'God' or 'nature'. For the critique to make sense philosophers and feminists must be willing to supplement formal logic and other forms of abstract reasoning with what can be gained from a Spinozist feminist understanding of the affirmation of life. If we seek to understand the concept of *conatus* in the text of, for instance, the Continental philosopher of religion, Paul Ricoeur, we find that the yearning at the heart of feminist philosophy of religion is expressed as the essence of a human striving, what Ricoeur calls, 'the human effort and desire to be'. The role and limits of reason in Ricoeur's hermeneutics of *conatus* appear in his conception of the power to affirm life; this affirmation is limited by human vulnerability, but inspired by a rational capability. The problem with Ricoeur's capable subject as the subject who can affirm life is its lack of explicit locatedness, that is, lacking gender awareness. The Ricoeurian rational-capable subject still needs to be located within the interlinking social and material relations of religion, race, class, ethnicity and sexual orientation which determine gender and its finite vulnerability.

(3) How does feminist philosophy of religion deal with its sources? Feminist philosophers of religion come at old texts with fresh eyes and from a critical direction which is whole-making; that is, they constantly aim to connect author, text and readers in a radical vision of what binds humans together philosophically and spiritually. This critical direction makes possible open engagement with, for instance, a Spinozist *conatus* as found in the texts of the history of philosophy without accepting formerly dismissive labels of Spinoza or a Spinozist as merely 'a pantheist', as if this would make him unworthy of a reading, let alone a re-visioning, in contemporary philosophy of religion. Instead of prohibiting or inhibiting women, but also some men, in the field from direct access to any philosophical text and argument in the history of European philosophy, it encourages women in particular to dialogue with texts and with each other, in order to widen the philosophical canon on life/God, religion and gender in philosophy.

The ongoing feminist challenge for re-visioning gender in philosophy of religion is to free the mind to affirm bodily life within an ever-greater perfection that never reaches its goal, but constantly increases power in love and wisdom. In the spirit, if not the exact argument, of Spinoza each and every individual moves forward in striving for a joyful continuation of bodily existence which expresses, what we might agree is, the shared communication of an intellectual love of *deus sive natura*.

Chapter 8
Gender Justice and Unselfish Attention

Introduction: Murdoch and Weil

The twentieth-century philosopher and novelist Iris Murdoch (1919–99) gains insight for her conception of 'unselfish attention' from the religious and political philosopher Simone Weil (1909–43). Weil's highly original conception of attention focuses on turning the mind towards an object or a subject and, gradually, 'the whole soul' towards the good. Weil's focus is expressed in profound assertions about attention's moral and religious activity as a creative faculty. The intense activity of attention develops as a process in being attracted to 'the good'. 'Extreme attention' is a measure of 'authentic religion'.[1] In *Gravity and Grace* Weil presents the following assertions:

> We ... cure our faults by attention.[2]

> Attention, taken to its highest degree, is the same thing as prayer. It presupposes faith and love.[3]

> If we turn our mind towards the good, it is impossible that little by little the whole soul will not be attracted thereto in spite of itself.[4]

> ... Extreme attention is what constitutes the creative faculty ... The amount of creative genius in any period is strictly in proportion to the amount of extreme attention and thus of authentic religion at that period.[5]

Murdoch brings 'attention' in the sense of the 'mind turned towards the good' into her own account of the human search for beauty and goodness by way of love.[6]

---

[1]   Simone Weil, *Gravity and Grace*, trans. Emma Crawford and Mario von der Ruhr, with an Introduction and Postscript by Gustave Thibon (London and New York: Routledge, 2002), p. 117.

[2]   Ibid., p. 116.

[3]   Ibid., p. 117.

[4]   Ibid.

[5]   Ibid.

[6]   For further background on the role of attention to beauty, attention to the aesthetic nature of images and, more generally, to the role of images and the imagination in philosophy's accounts of theism and nature, see Marije Altorf, *Iris Murdoch and the Art of*

Broadly speaking, informed by Weil and Murdoch, the contention of the present chapter is that unselfish attention becomes pivotal for creating justice in attending to beauty and the good. Together the philosophical contributions of both women writers in (1) attending to the good and (2) un-selfing (or, ridding of selfishness) inform the argument for gender justice in this chapter. However, the chapter also aims to indicate not only the strengths, but the weaknesses, of unselfish attention, especially but not only, for re-visioning gender in philosophy of religion. This will take place by a return to Kant's practical philosophy and to bell hooks's gender and race-sensitive visions of love.

Ultimately, attending to beauty involves a progressive movement from the mind being attracted to a single object or solitary subject to the soul attending to the reality of goodness. This process of attraction and attention has significant relevance for both the 'un-doing' of beauty's objectification in gender stereotypes and the re-visioning of beauty's relation to gender justice. However, the weakness of the Weil-Murdoch conception of unselfish attention for gender justice remains in the great danger of re-enforcing oppressive gender stereotypes with requiring an 'un-selfing', or in Weil's terms a 'decreation' of the self.[7] For example, an oppressive gender stereotype for women, as illustrated in Murdoch's novels, but also as demonstrated in feminist literature, is the sexist claim that women philosophers are best left to 'un-selfing' because this is a woman's natural role as mother and carer.[8]

Before addressing gender criticisms, consider a passage from Murdoch's 'On "God" and "Good"'. Not unlike Weil, attention to, in Murdoch's case, beauty begins a process of attraction; she calls this process a 'spiritual exercise' in 'seeing the real' and, ultimately, in loving the good in spite of other 'selfish' concerns. The role of unselfish attention is presented by Murdoch the following:

> The appreciation of beauty in art or nature is not only (for all its difficulties) the easiest available spiritual exercise; it is also a completely adequate entry into (and not just analogy of) the good life, since it is the checking of selfishness in the interest of seeing the real.
>
> It is important too that great art teaches us how real things can be looked at and loved without being seized and used, without being appropriated into the greedy organism of the self. ... selfish concerns vanish, nothing exists except the things which are seen. Beauty is that which attracts this particular sort of unselfish attention.[9]

Imagining (London: Continuum 2008); and Charles Taliaferro and Jil Evans, *The Image in Mind: Theism, Naturalism and the Imagination* (London: Continuum, 2011).

[7]   Sabina Lovibond, *Iris Murdoch, Gender and Philosophy* (London: Routledge, 2011), pp. 30–32.

[8]   Ibid., especially pp. 3–4, 30–32, 93–98.

[9]   Iris Murdoch, *The Sovereignty of Good* (London: Routledge and Kegan Paul, 1970), pp. 64–65.

The appreciation of beauty (above) in generating a spiritual exercise is like Weil's account of attention in being both creative and appropriately disinterested. These are crucial factors for unselfish attention. Being attracted by beauty in Murdoch has both a Kantian moral sense and a Platonic metaphysical sense. The latter sense derives from Plato's ascent of *eros* (love) towards the good. The former, Kantian sense is that of moral goodness which is learnt as beauty is looked at, 'without being seized and used', in order to cultivate love. (Remember also, from Chapter 5, that mutual love does not possess or use as a mere means; and so it is 'one of the great moral forces' in Kant's *The Metaphysics of Morals*[10]). Thus Murdoch's moral philosophy is clearly informed by Weil's conception of unselfing (or, decreation of the self),[11] but also by her own appropriations of Plato and Kant. For this reason, the present chapter aims to explore crucial elements from Kant on beauty and to consider contemporary appropriations of an ancient (Platonic) allegory of love. The critical argument of this chapter brings gender into a feminist re-visioning of beauty for contemporary philosophy of religion.

On judgments of beauty

The influence of Kant's *Critique of the Power of Judgment*[12] on western conceptions of beauty is apparent in Murdoch, even though in the end her positioning of perfect goodness as the *telos* of a spiritual ascent will seem more Platonic than Kantian. Plato recommends a deliberate ascent away from sensuous nature. The human soul aspires to be united with divine love in the apprehension of truth and so, to become the perfect form of love and goodness. For Murdoch, beauty guides perfection in an ascent towards the good. Although this view is Platonic, Murdoch is not a strict follower of Plato, since she arrives at a conception which has no clear parallel in the latter: that is, unselfish attention.

To understand 'attention' requires a close look at the creative faculty, which we found described by Weil, in the previous section of this chapter. The role and nature of attention in both Weil and Murdoch pick up a Kantian concern in twentieth-century European philosophy for the self's relation to the reality independent of its own (selfish) concerns. Aesthetics meets morality here in seeing reality independent of a preoccupation with self either in attraction to beauty or in attending to the good.

---

[10]   Immanuel Kant, *The Metaphysics of Morals* trans. Mary Gregor (Cambridge: Cambridge University Press, 1996), pp. 198–199 [6: 449].

[11]   Murdoch, *The Sovereignty of Good*, pp. 84–87; cf. Sabina Lovibond, *Iris Murdoch, Gender and Philosophy* (London: Routledge, 2011), pp. 30–32.

[12]   Immanuel Kant, *Critique of the Power of Judgment,* trans. Paul Guyer and Eric Matthews in the Cambridge edition (Cambridge: Cambridge University Press, 2000). I will mainly refer to this later translation of Kant's third *Critique*, unless the earlier translation is better known on a particular point.

Admittedly, for Murdoch, in line with Kantian aesthetics, beauty is assumed to be a property of an object that produces an aesthetic pleasure; this pleasure is a subjective response to a beautiful object often, but not always, in nature. For example, the beauty of a rose produces an aesthetic pleasure. Kant thought other objects, not like roses, beautiful to the degree they 'conform to objects in nature'.[13] A question which Kant addresses in his third *Critique* is whether a subjective response to a beautiful object can be spontaneous and universally communicable.

Some philosophers – like Murdoch (I think) – have argued that pleasurable enjoyment of beautiful artistic creations is not originally spontaneous. Instead this enjoyment needs to be cultivated, bringing together cognition and emotion; and it is this cultivation, as in Murdoch's spiritual exercise, which moves the beautiful into the realm of moral goodness. As already suggested in the quotations from Weil and Murdoch, our creative faculty of attention draws the soul towards goodness; but, arguably, this also is the route to cultivating a great social virtue in both an ancient and a modern sense: that is, justice. Beauty's cultivation involves attending to an object or subject to recognize its beauty. In turn, recognition of the beautiful in an aesthetic judgment has a definite affinity to the development of justice as a moral virtue.[14]

In Kant, the two 'great moral forces', mutual love and respect, are cultivated through practical reasoning. For Murdoch, the affinity between judgments of the beautiful and moral virtue would be apparent in how we learn to make good judgments. To repeat, the spiritual exercise in the mind's attraction to beauty moves the whole soul's attention to the reality of goodness. In this way, moral, aesthetic, religious and political philosophies seem to join up into a single goal. According to Murdoch, virtue achieves truth to the degree that it acquires its distinctive form of perfection; true perfection appears to the goal or *telos*. Moreover, if the appropriation of beauty is a human cognitive capacity, then once beauty is acquired in its true form it would be universally communicable. Ideally, beauty would produce aesthetic pleasure spontaneously in all those human subjects whose cognitive capacities are cultivated for their own perfection.

What is the measure of this perfection? Is there a perfect form of beauty for every natural and created object? Or, is this merely a subjective matter? If the latter, how can we agree about what is beautiful? Is perfection of the human form measured against an aesthetic, moral, or divine standard? Aesthetic judgments of beauty try to bring together a subjective response of aesthetic pleasure with a universal communication of a shared feeling.

Ironically, religion has concerned itself with beauty precisely because of the inability of human beings to recognize or create perfection. Despite our apparent

---

[13]   Immanuel Kant, *Critique of Judgement*, trans. James Creed Meredith (Oxford: Clarendon Press, 1952), pp. 157–167 (paragraphs 42–45).

[14]   Kant, *Critique of the Power of Judgment*, Introduction VII, 193; First Introduction XI, 243–244. Also, Elaine Scarry, *On Beauty and Being Just* (Princeton, NJ: Princeton University Press, 1999).

inability, we desire perfection in virtues: we desire beauty in fair countenance as justice, in human relationships as love and in orderly action as goodness. In various dimensions of human experience, we long for perfect order, just like we crave beauty. If we turn this reasoning around, the philosopher of religion could try to argue that evidence of beauty as perfect order in nature serves to indicate to self-consciously imperfect human beings that a divine creator who is perfect in all aspects is necessary for the perfection otherwise impossible for a human being alone.

Beauty as a concept in western philosophy and theology

As a concept, beauty has a history of meanings and uses. Beauty's meaning changes in relation to the variability of human conceptions of nature, as well as the variability of human values and human identity. This history matters to beauty as a concept and to gender justice. As suggested in the previous section, beauty's use in western political, moral, and religious philosophy links it with the cultivation of virtues as dispositions that can become settled states of character. As with the virtues of political justice, moral goodness and religious love, the real existence of beauty may be doubted, especially as human dispositions are fragile and corruptible. Nevertheless, western philosophers would generally agree that human beings continue to seek to achieve the experience of aesthetic pleasure, as well as other forms of authentic perfection. Although justice, goodness, and love are clearly lacking across the globe, we still seek them (and, I think, not just in the western world).

Both western philosophers and theologians would also agree that human beings have a capacity to create and to recognize, in the sense of the French *reconnaître*, beauty. We gratefully acquire knowledge of what is true, legitimate and proper to one's own nature. So this crucial sense of recognition of beauty in goodness, love and justice resonates with western philosophy and theology, insofar as both disciplines are motivated by moral goodness and perfection in truth.

For an ancient concept of beauty, consider Plato in the historical context of ancient Greek metaphysics. As already mentioned, Plato recommends a deliberate ascent away from sensuous nature; and Murdoch seems to recommend something similar. Roughly, in the Platonic tradition, the human soul aspires to be united with perfect love in the apprehension of truth, in order to reach the perfect form of the Good. Beauty is seen in this perfection. But note that a strictly Platonic account is ultimately inadequate for a contemporary philosopher who is re-visioning gender in beauty.

In particular, feminist philosophers who argue for beauty's necessary relation to sensuous nature find Platonism especially problematic. Perhaps Murdoch anticipates some of these feminist arguments against Platonic love and beauty, even though it has persuasively argued by Sabina Lovibond that Murdoch herself was never a feminist philosopher and at times hostile to the ideas of feminists.

Lovibond valiantly endeavours (and very largely succeeds) to uncover what Murdoch herself contributes (perhaps unwittingly) to the cause of women in philosophy. It must be stressed here that Murdoch's own contributions as a woman philosopher and novelist were part of a world not completely unlike the Anglo-American world of philosophy today: the social imaginary of our world still negatively affects the image, as it did Murdoch's time, of a woman philosopher.[15]

A greater, concrete understanding of the social imaginary when it comes to the image of beauty in contemporary aesthetics, morality and religion could be one way to try to rescue the concept of 'beauty' from still predominantly negative gender associations. For one example of such an attempt, at the beginning of the twenty-first century, Wendy Steiner did a critical study documenting the difficulties resulting from an equation of beauty with the female subject. According to Steiner, beauty's exile as Venus from twentieth-century aesthetic culture – and beauty's troubled relationship with feminists, activists, avant-garde artists and the 'postmodern' – are reflected in a major problem today in beauty's association with the female body, and so, modernist 'taboos'.[16] In other words, the modern figure of the female subject was rejected by postmodern feminism pushing the beautiful out of the centre of aesthetics and politics: speaking of beauty in art came to seem aesthetically and politically retrograde.

However, the thrust of this chapter is that to re-vision beauty, especially in its affinity with seeing things rightly or justly, the woman philosopher could consider more closely judgments of beauty as a form of inter-subjective communication; the task would, then, be to re-vision beauty as an exchange in which finding someone or something beautiful is the possibility of recognizing beauty and communicating beauty to one another. Admittedly, good reasons existed for beauty's exile from (much) twentieth-century experience, including a failure of human self-understanding and spiritual development. A less obvious reason is beauty's close association with the idealized female subject who dominated the western religious imagination – whether in the figure of the Virgin Mary, the fragile innocence of the maternal figure of femininity, or the perfect (sexualized) form of the female body – and alongside this was the beauty of the innocent and suffering body of the God-man, Christ, whose sexuality has been of matter of contemporary debate in queer theology. As feminist consciousness gained a critical edge in twentieth-century societies, so did the recognition that the female or suffering (innocent) body had been objectified, even idolized as an erotic object; and this ran the danger of sadistic and masochistic gender relations being justified in the name of love. The uncritical objectifications of the gendered subject of beauty led to violence and abusive, but also to fixed gender-types which idealized the qualities of a specific race, class and religion. Violence and religious conservatism render gender justice impossible to recognize with any confidence and doubtful to achieve.

---

[15]   Lovibond, *Iris Murdoch, Gender and Philosophy*, pp. 3–7, 84–109.

[16]   Wendy Steiner, *Venus in Exile: The Rejection of Beauty in 20th Century Art* (Chicago: University of Chicago Press, 2001).

The extent of the objectification of gender stereotypes, by both men and women, is evident in the degree to which women's self-image is determined by a culture's fetish of beauty. This is when women do not actually see their own selves in representations of female beauty but are seen in terms of what others think they should look like. Beauty becomes the opposite of anything natural, free, or creative. Instead it is bound up with oppressive images of the female subject. Contemporary aesthetics has not generally treated beauty as a central concern. Yet, it is possible to find serious endeavours to restore beauty to what is still thought to be its rightful place in the pleasurable enjoyment of nature, artistic creations, and human love.

To write about beauty in the history of philosophy is to tell a story about values for human beings. Values, including love (*caritas*), and such acquired virtues such as goodness and justice have been portrayed, as suggested earlier in the retelling of ancient myths, in new representations of relations between men, women, and the divine. Traditionally philosophers and theologians have turned to the poets and the artists of their age to imagine in myth what is not seen yet is experienced. Beauty is only truly seen when human vision, and so lived experiences, are not determined by oppressive ideals and images. Even ancient myths about beauty involve struggle and concealment until ideally, the seeing that attends to another achieves a revelation of truth and goodness.

One ancient myth that has been restored to prominence in contemporary discussions of love, pleasure, and beauty is the story of Psyche and Cupid. *Cupid* is the Latin name of the ancient figure of love, represented in this myth by a male god; *Psyche* is the Greek name for a human soul, represented by the female subject who appears trapped in a beautiful body, alienated from others by their envy of her beauty. Psyche's beauty does not bring happiness, but its opposite. The envy of others causes Psyche to suffer the tricks and trials of human and divine subjects. Then Cupid and Psyche become lovers, and Psyche learns to be trustworthy, face-to-face with love in the presence of beauty. In the end, Psyche becomes divine, loving freely and eternally.[17]

Gendering the beautiful and the sublime

A genealogy of the western concept of beauty should include the gender associated with the beautiful and the sublime at a critical moment in European culture near the end of the eighteenth and beginning of the nineteenth centuries. As already suggested here, this critical moment is apparent in the writings of Kant on the beautiful and the sublime. In the eighteenth century, philosophical accounts included a distinctive gendering of the beautiful as feminine and the sublime as masculine. In addition, the sublime aligned with masculine virtue and beauty with

---

[17]   Carol Gilligan, *The Birth of Pleasure: A New Map of Love* (London: Chatto and Windus, 2002).

feminine virtue meant that the divine was associated with the former, not the latter. Why would the divine be associated with one or the other? God as perfect could fulfil the human desire for fairness of countenance, whether as the beautiful or as the sublime. Philosophical awareness of perfection in nature, including human nature, gives grounds for the existence of a (maximally) great creator of this perfect design. But why would Enlightenment philosophy link the divine with the sublime? Insofar as the divine must represent absolute greatness and perfection, the sublime, as greater than beauty in sensuous nature or in its imitation of nature, is taken to represent inexpressible perfection and greatness.

As discussed in Chapter 1, and mentioned again in Chapter 5, Jean-Jacques Rousseau publishes his eighteenth-century account of moral and aesthetic education in *Émile* (1762) where he draws a sharp distinction between masculine and feminine education. Next, this gendering of moral education is reflected in Kant, *Observations on the Feeling of the Beautiful and the Sublime* (1764). Finally, as already discussed in relation to Rousseau, Wollstonecraft, in *Vindication of the Rights of Woman* (1792), responds critically to this gendering of moral education and the related association of beauty with the female subject. Nevertheless, the following contentious statement and its relevance for Kant's later writings on beauty continues to be debated: 'The fair sex has just as much understanding as the male, but it is a beautiful understanding whereas ours should be a deep understanding, an expression that signifies identity with the sublime.'[18] This gendering of the beautiful as distinct from deep understandings has had negative implications, especially when read alongside Kant's assertion that

> The virtue of a woman is a beautiful virtue. That of the male sex should be a noble
> virtue. Women will avoid the wicked not because it is un-right, but because it is
> ugly; and virtuous actions mean to them such as are morally beautiful. Nothing
> of duty, nothing of compulsion, nothing of obligation![19]

Freed from the constraints of duty by their gender, women are excluded from moral autonomy. In addition, while men have the ability to distance themselves from sensuous nature and move closer to the divine, women remain associated philosophically by their gender to nature. Ultimately, women's beauty as a gift of nature becomes increasingly problematic as science and technology seek to dominate nature as unruly and threatening; by association to nature women's gender is not orderly and nurturing but threatening and unruly.

Clearly, Kant's gendering of beauty in 1764 affected subsequent accounts of moral aesthetic education in profound ways. Moreover, his gendering of the sublime equally affects philosophical accounts of divine greatness as the sublime. In fact, a problematic part of this tradition which genders the beauty and the

---

[18]   Immanuel Kant, *Observations on the Feeling of the Beautiful and the Sublime*, trans. John T. Goldthwait (Berkeley, CA: University of California Press, 1960), p. 78.
[19]   Ibid., p. 81.

sublime persists today. The nineteenth-century German idealist Friedrich Schiller passed on this tradition by re-enforcing the gendered differences of Kant's moral virtues. The twentieth-century French postmodernist Jean-Francois Lyotard ensures that women never can obtain absolute beauty and men transcend chaotic and corrupting (female) nature in the sublime.

Attending to love and beauty

The upshot of Enlightenment aesthetics, including the reaction of some feminist philosophers and Christian theologians to Kant's philosophical theology, his moral philosophy and aesthetics, is evident in the disagreements between modern and postmodern philosophers.[20] Crucially, after Kant's third *Critique,* philosophers represent the sublime as either incomprehensible or monstrous. If human desire and delight go beyond their proper boundaries, then human creation becomes monstrous. At the extreme, the yearning connoisseur of beauty fails tragically to be worthy of the divine or the sublime. Without the mutual exchange between creator and creature, lover and beloved, monstrous forms of creativity manifest human unworthiness. Instead of harmony, integrity, and splendor, the one-sided endeavour to create human beauty results in the monstrous sublime of death and destruction: 'An object is *monstrous* where by its size it defeats the end that forms its concept.'[21]

A mutual exchange of love in beauty should be lifesaving. But this, like a new creation in love, would always only be a fragile intimation of the divine. Yet positive qualities of love and beauty are undermined by the monstrous (sublime). As already anticipated in Chapter 1, this monstrosity is imaginatively represented by the Enlightenment myth of a new Prometheus by Mary Shelley, *Frankenstein* (1818).[22] Shelley's story about a man-made creature explores the tragedy and distortions of a scientific 'man' who replaces divine with human creations, religion with science, and love with technology; the outcome is truly horrific. The Romantic idea of human creativity cannot be sustained without mutual love and justice. These virtues, sustained by something transcendent of both men and women, ensure that creativity does not result in self-destruction by a chaotic and violent nature.

---

[20]   For extensive critical engagement with Kant on women and moral personhood, see Christine Battersby, *The Sublime, Terror and Human Difference* (London: Routledge, 2007), pp. 47–67, 69–70. For a recent feminist defence of Kant, see Mari Mikkola, 'Kant on Moral Agency and Women's Nature', *Kantian Review* (2011): 89–112.

[21]   Kant, *Critique of Judgment*, p. 100; cf. *Critique of the Power of Judgment*, p. 136.

[22]   Mary Shelley, *Frankenstein, or the Modern Prometheus*, edited with Introduction and Notes by Marilyn Butler (Oxford and New York: Oxford University Press, World Classics, 1993).

How do men and women acquire those necessary virtues that are not theirs at birth? One answer is to return to the ancient allegory of love. Its lesson is that we have to be inspired to see the beautiful as something to love; perception of beauty in the beloved that renders her or him desirable is an experience inspired by perfect(ed) love. The allegory represents Cupid with the power to transform humans from mere mortals without erotic aspirations to midwives or, indeed, to philosophers who yearn for what they perceive as good. In this allegory, love is motivated neither by desire nor by beauty perceived independent of love. Instead, the very perception of the beloved as good is dependent on, first of all, the true vision of love. The lover, then, beholds the beautiful countenance of her beloved. This vision of beauty takes the two lovers outside of themselves as subjects.

This ability to see beauty is, to repeat, what Murdoch identifies unselfing. Murdoch's account of seeing beauty not only draws on Kant's account of beauty but crucially, now, on Plato's account of love. Read by Murdoch, Plato also adds to her unique vision of attentiveness to the reality of love and beauty:

It is important too that great art teaches us how real things can be looked at and loved without being seized and used, without being appropriated into the greedy organism of the self. This exercise of *detachment* is difficult and valuable whether the thing contemplated is a human being or the root of a tree or the vibration of a colour or a sound. Unsentimental contemplation of nature exhibits the same quality of detachment: selfish concerns vanish, nothing exists except the things which are seen. Beauty is that which attracts this particular sort of unselfish attention.[23]

Murdoch goes on to explain, 'What counteracts [blinding self-centred aims and images] … is *attention to* reality inspired by, consisting of, love';[24] and '… the most obvious thing in our surroundings which is an occasion for "unselfing" … is beauty'.[25] This occasion for unselfing generates an attitude for seeing beauty in all its colours, shapes, and sizes.[26] Although Murdoch's writing predates the postmodern challenges to the racial and ethnic biases of Anglo-American philosophy, her attitude in seeing beauty can be developed more critically in dialogue with the African-American writer and feminist cultural critic whose contributions have been pivotal through the chapters of this book: that is, bell hooks.

In this context, again bell hooks offers a contemporary voice to the chorus of those who call us to re-vision in philosophy. Like Adrienne Rich, who described re-vision as 'the act of looking back, of seeing with fresh eyes',[27] hooks insists

---

[23]   Murdoch, *The Sovereignty of Good*, p. 65.

[24]   Ibid., italics added.

[25]   Ibid., p. 84.

[26]   For a fuller, contemporary discussion of the role of beauty, the aesthetic and the ethical value of, or desire for, a cognitive and affective unity, as in the turning image of beauty, see Taliaferro and Evans, *The Image in Mind*, especially pp. 11, 38–42, 192–193.

[27]   Adrienne Rich, 'When We Dead Awaken', in Barbara Charlesworth Gelpi and Albert Gelpi (eds), *Adrienne Rich's Poetry and Prose* (New York and London: W. W. Norton and Company, 1991), p. 167.

on the importance, for visions of love, in the act of 'seeing', in a new way. But hooks is unequivocal in asserting that we must *learn* to *see*! Seeing here is material, moral and metaphysical: it is 'heightened awareness and understanding, the intensification of one's capacity to experience reality through the realm of the senses'.[28] In 'An Aesthetic of Blackness: Strange and Oppositional', hooks challenges philosophical conceptions of beauty, include that of Murdoch. hooks contends that beauty's function and purpose cannot be separated from material life, metaphysical perception and, crucially, political passion.[29]

Justice, beauty and a new aesthetic

This section aims to take seriously bell hooks's proposal for 'an aesthetic of blackness'.[30] She proposes that beauty is pictured in the eyes of those women and men who take time to see and pay attention to the social and material locations that shape and colour their perceptions, feelings, and relationships. hooks's awareness of epistemic locations is crucial for re-visioning gender in philosophy of religion. In fact, she captures in her artistic selection of words and her carefully crafted writing the epistemic locatedness which is absolutely decisive for successful understanding gender (in)justice.

hooks claims that 'a radical aesthetic acknowledges that we are constantly changing positions, locations, that our needs and concerns vary, that these diverse directions must correspond with shifts in critical thinking'.[31] Without being able to see in aesthetic, moral and political terms how our own specific material and social locations shape and, with change, re-shape us, we cannot understand the roles gender and race in philosophy of religion. Without being able to see how these locations shape our epistemic practices, in particular, we cannot recognize injustice. Awareness of our epistemic locatedness is necessary to tackle epistemic injustice.

A major contention of the present book, to which I will return in Chapter 10, has been from the outset that we must, if serious about justice and truth, recognize the intersection of gender with race, class, ethnicity, religion and sexual orientation. Gender's political and epistemic roles meet at this intersection. Gender justice cannot even be imagined without this awareness of gender at the intersection of material and social locations. Moreover, a free play of imagination and understanding must accompany our seeing with fresh eyes. Seeing reality, in order to re-vision it, requires that we initially face injustice, from a critical direction.

---

[28] bell hooks, *Yearning: Race, Gender and Cultural Politics* (Boston, MA: South Bend Press, 1990), pp. 111–112.

[29] bell hooks, 'An Aesthetic of Blackness: Strange and Oppositional', in *Yearning*, pp. 103–113.

[30] Ibid.

[31] Ibid., p. 111.

But the next task is to bring about change from within our social and material relations; epistemic norms will have to change when injustice is undermining truth and damaging lives.

To stand the test of time, cultivating the ability to see beauty joins the ability to see and re-vision justice. Here 'justice' means, minimally, equality in fair relationships. To seek justice, we may need to use our imagination. This can be enhanced by returning to old myths, or ancient stories, about human and divine relations, love, beauty and justice, For example, the ancient allegory of love generates – whether in an ancient imaginary or a contemporary social imaginary informed by psychological theories of love and pleasure – the ultimate vision of the human soul, Psyche, becoming divine and immortal in a marital union of equality with the god of love, Cupid, this takes place in the presence of beauty that in turn begets pleasure.[32] This allegory portrays for us the main characters and qualities for re-visioning justice and good human-divine relations for love, life and pleasure.

Consistent with the various stories about love and seeing reality, beauty represents an opportunity for self-revelation and exchanges of power between the self and another. Yet, in everyday reality, beauty remains dangerously bound up with oppressive ideals, images, and symbols. At the same time, this ideals, images and symbols can be reconfigure to create an alternative vision of gender. Religious narratives also create contexts in which divine love can raise the human soul above the death that haunts the natural world. But it is this tension which becomes problematic in human experiences of the natural world, since a spiritual ascent to divine love in the presence of beauty is not an ideal to which human beings can aspire unaided. The difficulty is to see a spiritual ascent in a sensorial descent, rising toward the transcendent even in descending. This imagery recalls Weil's *Gravity and Grace*, assertions from which opened this chapter, where implicit is her highly distinctive idea of a spiritual ascent in a sensorial descent, of rising toward the transcendent in descending, runs through the writing.[33]

The idea of love as perfected

To explore the idea of perfection, let us return to Murdoch's account of love's moral and spiritual existence. In 'The Sovereignty of Good over other concepts', Murdoch explores love's perfection as follows:

> ... when we try perfectly to love what is imperfect our love goes to its object
> via the Good to be purified and made unselfish and just ... Love is ... capable
> of infinite degradation and is the source of our greatest errors; but when [love]

---

[32]   Carol Gilligan, *The Birth of Pleasure: A New Map of Love* (London: Chatto and Windus, 2002).

[33]   Weil, *Gravity and Grace*, p. 150.

is even partially refined it is the energy and passion of the soul in its search for Good, the force that joins us to Good and joins us to the world through Good. Love's existence is the unmistakable sign that we are spiritual creatures, attracted by excellence and made for the Good. It is a reflection of the warmth and light of the sun.[34]

Murdoch's vision of love (above) is undoubtedly Platonic. And yet her vision captures something about the good as moral, aesthetics and spiritual which every woman and man can grasp. This seemingly complex, yet in reality simple, conception of the good is essential for love in all of its forms. In as much as human we are each drawn to love. Clearly the person who learns to love will achieve perfection, according to Murdoch's 'The Sovereignty of the Good over other concepts', by attending to the good.

Yet, despite Murdoch's positive account of 'the sovereignty of the good' the reality of our own stories of love often tends to be much more bleak; goodness much less apparent. Taking a critical distance from Murdoch's concept of perfect love, it can be easily shown that in reality knowledge of the good (as our human *telos*) is not immediately connected with doing the good; and knowledge of love is not immediately connected with loving. The missing factor in connecting knowledge to practice is time. It takes time to acquire virtue, and so, goodness as a moral virtue and as the way to love requires time. Elsewhere I have argued that love within human time must be free to be perfected.[35] The role of time also features in the process of re-vision set out at the beginning of this book. It will be recalled that a forward-looking process of re-visioning gender remains crucial for justice so too for love. It is necessary to see love's knowledge as both acquired over time and shaped by the intersecting social and material factors of gender.

In the temporal process of acquiring greater love, the lovers must each, according to just measures, take part in re-visioning gender. Cognitively informed love would seek to re-vision gender for mutual love relations; and so, love would become, again in Kantian terms, 'a great moral force'.[36] At this point, we should also recall the idea of 'gendering' love (from Chapter 5), where it was argued that love as a moral virtue could not be a spontaneous, non-cognitive occurrence. So, 'falling in love' as an instantaneous or discrete act could not make sense of the process of perfecting love or of unselfish attention to the reality required for

---

[34] Murdoch, 'The Sovereignty of the Good over other concepts', in *The Sovereignty of Good*, p. 103.

[35] Pamela Sue Anderson, 'Love's Knowledge', University Sermon, University Church, High Street, Oxford, UK, delivered 8 March 2003; and 'An Epistemological-Ethical Approach to Philosophy of Religion: Learning to Listen', in Pamela Sue Anderson and Beverley Clack (eds), *Feminist Philosophy of Religion: Critical Readings* (London: Routledge, 2003), pp. 87–102.

[36] Kant, *The Metaphysics of Morals*, 6:449. Also, for the complete quotation from Kant and further discussion, return to Chapter 5 (above).

knowledge of perfect goodness. Instead the goal (*telos*) of mutual love must be the culmination of a process achieving true perfection.[37]

In *All About Love: New Visions*,[38] bell hooks boldly proclaims the possibility of new visions for love. According to her, acquiring love comes through nurturing one another's ethical growth and knowledge. hooks expresses an urgency in our engendering trust rather than mistrust, in order to generate a unity of virtues for the twenty-first century. Her ethical project is timely, but it is also about a spiritual exercise that generates knowledge of the social reality of love. New visions are captured in a poetic manner through the love stories.[39] I submit that stories of love are essential for temporal knowledge of love and, arguably, for 'perfecting love' as both a concept and a reality for contemporary philosophy of religion.

hooks claims to be 'especially fond of' the biblical passage in the first epistle to John; 'There is no fear in love, but perfect love casts out fear' (1 *John* 4: 18). But she adds a social and cultural dimension to her understanding of love casting out fear. Reflecting on her childhood memories of religion and racial tension in 1950s Kentucky, she recalls being shaped by a black Baptist church where

> [F]rom childhood ... I thought of [the repeated use of the word 'perfect'] only in relation to being without fault or defect. Taught to believe that ... to be perfect was always out of human reach, that we were, of necessity, essentially human because we were not perfect but were always bound by the mystery of the body, by our limitations, this call to know a perfect love disturbed me. It seemed a worthy calling, but impossible. That is, until I looked for a deeper, more complex understanding of the word 'perfect' and found a definition emphasizing *the will 'to refine'*.[40]

... [hooks goes on to admit that] we do fear. Fear keeps us from trusting in love.

> Cultures of domination rely on the cultivation of fear as a way to ensure obedience. ... we do not question why we live in states of extreme anxiety and

---

[37] On the unity and cognitive nature of the virtues, see Linda Zagzebski, *Virtues of the Mind: An Inquiry into the Nature of Virtue and the Ethical Foundations of Knowledge* (Cambridge: Cambridge University Press, 1996); Alvin I. Goldman, 'The Unity of Epistemic Virtues', in Linda Zagzebski and Abrol Fairweather (eds), *Virtue Epistemology* (Oxford: Oxford University Press, 2001), pp. 31, 43–48; Martha Nussbaum, *Upheavals of Thought: The Intelligence of the Emotions* (Cambridge: Cambridge University Press, 2001).

[38] bell hooks, *All About Love: New Visions* (London: The Women's Press, 2000).

[39] On the role of stories about love in human time, see Paul Ricoeur, *Oneself as Another*, trans. Kathleen Blamey (Chicago: University of Chicago Press, 1992), pp. 140–145, 152–168; A. W. Moore, *Points of View* (Oxford: Clarendon Press, 1997), pp. 220–236; Richard Kearney, *On Stories* (London: Routledge, 2002), pp. 123–156; Bernard Williams, *Truth and Truthfulness* (Princeton, NJ: Princeton University Press, 2002), pp. 233–269.

[40] hooks, *All About Love*, pp. 92–93 emphasis added.

dread. Fear is the primary force upholding structures of domination. It promotes the desire for separation, the desire not to be known. ... When we choose to love we choose to move against fear ... The choice to love is a choice to connect – to find ourselves in the other.[41]

Obviously, this is not a simple choice; and hooks knows this, too. In fact, she raises a question for us about re-visioning gender in love (to which we will turn in Chapter 9).

Re-visioning gender

Can we learn to re-vision gender in love? To see love and the gender of lovers becomes more and more complicated. Early in this chapter, love was first of all about perception of reality and about a spiritual ascent to love by way of a metaphysical reality of the good. After this, love became a moral question where love as a virtue required cultivation, in order to become perfect goodness. Added to the moral and the metaphysical were the aesthetic and the spiritual which originally appeared in the appreciation of beauty. Eventually, our visions of love require re-visioning as things change over time; and gender is not only connected to changing social and the material conditions, but to more fundamental changes in our philosophical concepts in aesthetics, religion, metaphysics, morality and politics. Again, we are confronted with the complexity of love. Can we possibly retrieve love in its simplicity?

Or perhaps this is not necessary. What is wrong with complexity? Or, why might love in its simplicity be vitally important? No one could deny that in the course of this book, love has gained in stature. Love is clearly more than a vague feeling, more than an emotion or action and, certainly, more than blind obedience to an all-powerful God's commands. Contemporary philosophers of religion continue to question the relation between God and goodness: is something good because God commands it? Or does God command something because it is good? Talking about knowledge of God and the Good may not require – or no longer – require the strong normativity of a divine command. At least this chapter has demonstrated that by considering unselfish attention as the way to moral goodness and aesthetic beauty in Murdoch, there is the possibility that the relation of human and divine love is not a matter of following without question whatever is commanded by (loving) God.

Although hooks is a cultural critic – and not a moral or religious philosopher – she takes a timely stance on the question of love's knowledge: 'Understanding *knowledge* as an essential element of love is vital', in her words, 'the message received from the mass media is that knowledge makes love less compelling;

---

[41]   Ibid., pp. 93–94.

that it is *ignorance* that gives love its erotic transgressive edge'.[42] The idea of sexual or romantic love as nothing more than an expectation of falling in love is, according to Thomas Merton, one of the most destructive ideas in the history of (western) thought. hooks finds support for rejecting a position of ignorance about love from two extremes: from the secular novelist Toni Morrison in her first novel, *The Bluest Eyes*,[43] and from the Roman Catholic author Thomas Merton in his spiritual reflection, 'Love and Need'.[44] Any idea of 'falling in love' suggests, not knowledge of love, but a mixture of fear, fascination, confusion and ignorance, implying that we are not responsible for our actions in love: such love is said to 'happen' like falling by accident. In sharp contrast, learning to love is not so simple. Again we confront the complexity of love which now seems an unpopular idea. Nevertheless, an ethics of love and of loving, requires time and knowledge; the upside of such an ethics is that we are able to be responsibility for our emotions and actions. Love, then, is not treated as a matter of mere passivity or romantic self-interest.

However untimely, Kant has informed the picture which has developed in this chapter. Informing Weil and Murdoch, Kant offers the conditions for gaining practical knowledge of even the most morally contentious aspects of love in our daily lives by urging that the 'right' authority of reason plays a critical role in shaping our emotions.[45] Reason has a critical part to play in human and divine love: practical reason needs to guide re-visioning gender in love relations.[46] As argued in Chapter 5, gendering as an internal critique of our practices (of love) exposes the fairly rigid western norms of masculinity and femininity. Gendered norms of reason have dominated the interpretation of our love relationships and so our sexual desires. Reason has played a critical role in shaping love, our practices, norms and desires. It is my conviction that Enlightenment moral philosophers still have something to offer contemporary philosophers of religion on love and on reason. In an age, when a pervasive postmodern scepticism about moral values seems to undermine the authority of reason, Kant and Enlightenment conceptions

---

[42]   Ibid., pp. 94–95 emphasis added.

[43]   Toni Morrison, *The Bluest Eyes* (New York: Pocket Books, 1970).

[44]   Thomas Merton, 'Love and Need', in Naomi Burton Stone and Brother Patrick Hart (eds), *Love and Liking* (Harvest Books, 2002); cf. hooks, *All About Love*, pp. 170–171.

[45]   Immanuel Kant, *Groundwork of the Metaphysics of Morals*, trans. and edited Mary Gregor, Introduction by Christine M. Korsgaard (Cambridge: Cambridge University Press, 1998); *Lectures on Ethics*, edited by Peter Heath and J. B. Schneewind, trans. Peter Heath (Cambridge: Cambridge University Press, 2001); and *Metaphysic of Morals*. For further critical reflection on the general exclusion of 'the point of view of love' in Anglo-American moral philosophy, see Martha Nussbaum, 'Steerforth's Arm: Love and the Moral Point of View'. in *Love's Knowledge*, pp. 335–364. Note that Nussbaum would disagree with my reading of Kant's point(s) of view on love but offers relevant observations on the moral point of view, Adam Smith, *The Theory of Moral Sentiments*, edited by D. D. Raphael and A. L. Macfie (Oxford, 1976).

[46]   Kant, *Lectures on Ethics*, pp. 155–160; *The Metaphysics of Morals*, p. 180.

of love and of reason (to which I will return in Chapter 9) have knowledge to offer for re-visioning gender.

In bringing emotion under the control of the will, Kant has been said to advocate nothing more than cold deeds done for the sake of duty alone. Kant does write that love which springs solely from natural inclination has no moral worth.[47] But, as noted previously, Kant also distinguishes practical love from pathological love; the latter is mere emotion, or feeling, which is not under the control of reason, so not consistent, reliable and habitual; as such it is either non-ethical or unethical, but it can become moral or immoral. For Kant, sexual desire in particular is pathological, not practical love. At the same time, Kant accounts for how love may be given – as a natural feeling – but its knowledge must still be acquired as moral feeling which includes practical love.[48] So, if we take a look at the bigger picture which Kant sketches across his various writings on ethics and virtue, a potentially attractive, yet still demanding account of Kant's reconciliation of reason and emotion can be found in practical love.[49] At the very least a re-visioning of ethics, love and gender has the opportunity of changing the historical upshot of Kant's writings. It can offer new critical debates about gender justice and unselfish attention.

More generally, Enlightenment men and women, especially someone like Mary Wollstonecraft who along with Kant may have been dismissed by postmodern critics, still have a considerable amount to insight to offer us on gender (both negative and positive possibilities to re-vision gender). Kant's later writings could have a critical affinity to love in Weil and in Murdoch. In particular, for Kant, a natural predisposition for love should be the presupposition of moral philosophy; this predisposition for love can be cultivated as practical love, that is, as a moral virtue. Cultivated as a virtue, love aims to be habitual, reliable and consistent. The aim of a loving disposition also implies that we seek the right sort of knowledge for practical love.[50]

In light of the above, we can see how bell hooks comes close to Kant's practical reasoning, especially in her twenty-first century criticisms of contemporary culture. For hooks, love cultivated as a moral virtue would have certain essential cognitive qualities. hooks's criticism of romantic love applies precisely to a lack of practical reasoning and cognition most evident in the ignorance of 'falling in love'. She claims

---

[47]   Kant, *Groundwork*, pp. 12–18.

[48]   Kant, *Metaphysic of Morals*, pp. 159–160.

[49]   Kant, *Lectures on Ethics*, pp. 155–160, 177–184; *The Metaphysic of Morals*, pp. 159–162, 178–80 and 198f. For an original account of 'pure reason' in Kant's moral and religious philosophy which includes valuable discussions of the role of 'non-rational forces', e.g. our emotions, in making sense of things, see A. W. Moore, *Noble in Reason, Infinite in Faculty* (London: Routledge, 2003), especially pp. 129–130 on love.

[50]   Nancy Sherman, *Making a Necessity of Virtue: Aristotle and Kant on Virtue* (Cambridge: Cambridge University Press, 1997), pp. 136–182.

... the mass media ... would have us believe, women are the architects and the planners [of romance]. Everyone likes to imagine that women are romantics, sentimental about love, that men follow where women lead. Even in non-heterosexual relationships, the paradigms of leader and follower often prevail, with one person assuming the role deemed feminine and another the designated masculine role. No doubt it was someone playing the role of leader who conjured up the notion that we 'fall in love', that we lack choice and decision when choosing a partner because when the chemistry is present, when the click is there, it just happens – it overwhelms – it takes control.

... If you do not know what you feel, then it is difficult to choose love; it is better to fall. Then you do not have to be responsible for your actions.[51]

In this account, hooks brings to mind a certain patriarchal reading of Eve's seduction of Adam; that is, the woman leads the man to fall by seducing him to go against a divine command; paradise and innocence are lost by Eve's pathological desire blinding Adam. But, of course, I *could* propose a different, however contentious reading, which Le Doeuff finds in Gabrielle Suchon (1631–1703) and develops for contemporary feminist philosophers, that sees Eve as the first moral philosopher, in seeking knowledge of good and evil, right and wrong.[52] Eve's curiosity in particular should be encouraged as the first sign of a philosophical virtue; and so we begin a re-visioning of gender with Eve.

Conclusion

To conclude, this chapter on gender justice and unselfish attention has been ambitious and made huge claims on behalf of beauty, love and reason. The chapter travels across a great deal of space to address the twofold question of beauty in unselfish attention, perfected love and truth in gender justice. Right from the start of this chapter, the two women philosophers, Weil and Murdoch, have us thinking about the self's role in attending to beauty and goodness; aesthetic and

---

[51]   hooks, *All About Love*, p. 171.

[52]   Gabrielle Suchon, *Traité de la morale et de la politique* (Lyon: B. Vignieu, 1693), II, pp. 3, 5–7, 174, 191; *A Woman Who Defends All the Persons of Her Sex: Selected Philosophical and Moral Writings*, edited and trans. Domna C. Stanton and Rebecca M. Wilkin (Chicago: University of Chicago Press, 2010), pp. 44–45, 51, 168–169. Cf. Michèle Le Doeuff, 'Suchon', in Edward Craig (ed.), *The Routledge Encyclopedia of Philosophy* 9 (London: Routledge, 1998), pp. 211–213; *Hipparchia's Choice: An Essay Concerning Women, Philosophy, Etc.*, trans. Trista Selous, second English edition with an Epilogue (2006) by the author (New York: Columbia University Press, 2007), pp. 94, 116, 206, 213, 314; *The Sex of Knowing*, trans. Lorraine Code and Kathryn Hamer (London and New York: Routledge, 2003), pp. 33–39; and Anderson, 'An Epistemological-Ethical Approach to Philosophy of Religion: Learning to Listen', pp. 87–102.

moral subjects of attention too is the question of justice; and nothing better than love could demonstrate the need for a spiritual exercise, in order to achieve the true mutuality which would motivate our search for justice. Learning how to see beauty which attracts what Murdoch conceives as unselfish attention. It seems that in fact the pair, beauty and unselfish attention, are the two necessary features of any guide to perceiving gender injustice and also, for re-visioning injustice into justice through love.

Although we cannot put it into words, love's perfection seems to be the ultimate vision for justice in our gender relations. Yet this vision is perhaps arrived at indirectly. New vision is something brought about by reconfiguring old myths and other narratives about gender relations, human and divine beings who have the capacity to bring about new life, beauty in pleasure. The old texts of myth and allegory, which have endured alongside the concepts of great philosophers and the doctrines of great theologians, can still teach us how to find new visions of love. Passivity is, in light of philosophical thinkers and actors, the opposite of what love's knowledge requires.

In this chapter reference has been made to Gilligan who attempts to create a new vision of love on the basis of her psychological study of intimate human relationships. It is fair to say that Gilligan endeavours, in the terms of the present book, to re-vision an ancient myth about the birth of pleasure in beauty; her stated aim is to re-locate the shared feelings that shape love; but she also attempts to re-vision gender roles.[53] Of course, the success of using this myth to achieve gender justice has yet to be assessed; but the tools for this are here.

Resisting any merely passive attitude to love, Murdoch writes beautifully about 'the energy ... of the soul' in love, as follows:

> when love is even partially refined it is *the energy and passion* of the soul in its search for Good ... Love's existence is the unmistakable sign that we are spiritual creatures, attracted by excellence and made for the Good.[54]

After reading these words it is easy to say that, surely, perfected love must be both our spiritual goal and our moral guide as we seek to refine what lacks perfection, what lacks constancy, reliability, trust, respect, faith, hope and justice. Love is complex, but as we have seen in Murdoch, the concept of 'the Good' represents a unified goal for the ascent of love. Or, we might argue that for Murdoch a unity of virtues, connected by love, shape the stories we read and write about human lives.

In the end, we face a challenge: to discover if unselfish attention to specifically located injustices can serve as a guide to re-visioning love and reason; and the next chapter will attempt to meet this challenge.

---

[53] Gilligan, *The Birth of Pleasure: A New Map of Love.*

[54] Murdoch, 'The Sovereignty of the Good over other concepts', p. 103 emphasis added.

Chapter 9
Re-visioning Love and Reason[1]

Setting the scene: a question of incarnation and gender

The critical point of departure for this chapter is the philosophical coherence of theism, In particular, can it be coherently held both that the theistic God is 'without a body'[2] (and so, apparently, without a gender) and that this same God has a *personal* relation to human persons who not only reason and love *in a body*, but whose love, if not reason, are shaped by *gender*. In other words, the issue of a personal God having a 'dis-incarnate'[3] attribute and its implications for both gendering and re-visioning gender in contemporary philosophy of religion are wide-ranging. So, I take as the focus a practical question for re-visioning gender: in what sense, if any, does this dominant conception of a God who is without a body[4] inform our bodily practices as men and women? An answer to the latter question will have ethical implications which will guide our re-visioning of love and reason in philosophy of religion.

Chapter 4 raised a contentious feminist criticism of a 'masculinist' drive for infinity: that a masculine-gendered drive is reflected in a man's desire to be God, that is, to be infinite. But now, if bodies are finite and God is not, then this desire would be to escape the body's limitations to be God. Escaping the body is something which feminist philosophers have argued women not only would be less likely to think possible but, given their role in reproduction, women would also be less free to try to do this. Chapter 5 raised the issue of whether love and gender can be attributed to a being without a body. The present chapter is returning to this question of gender and the traditional theistic conception of God who is without a body, but also exploring the more practical issue of incarnation in philosophical texts and bodily practices. The core argument is that an adequate answer to the question of gender will depend upon re-visioning love and reason in philosophy of religion. Attempting an answer involves trying to make sense of a divine being's relation to gender and to human bodily practices.

---

[1]   Material in this chapter comes from 'Divinity, Incarnation and Inter-subjectivity: On Ethical Formation and Spiritual Practice', *Philosophy Compass*, 1/3 (2006): 335–356.

[2]   Richard Swinburne, *The Existence of God*, revised edn (Oxford: Clarendon Press, 1991), p. 8.

[3]   Iris Murdoch, *Metaphysics as A Guide to Morals* (London: Penguin Books, 1993), pp. 202, 248–249; cf. Fionola Meredith, *Experiencing the Postmetaphysical Self: Between Hermeneutics and Deconstruction* (London: Sage, 2005), pp. 112, 128, 156.

[4]   Swinburne, *The Existence of God*, p. 8.

To begin clarifying this issue concerning the God of traditional theism who is, in Richard Swinburne's words, 'without a body',[5] the question is not whether merely to reject theism because of a possible contradiction in the conception of a personal God without a body. Instead, the point is to question whether 'clear-headed'[6] thinking can avoid any gender-bias in the traditional philosophical arguments for Christian theism, especially when terms such as person, action and love, along with adjectives like personal, incorporeal, loving, and the pronouns he, his and him are all applied to God. T. J. Mawson claims that 'no sensible theist has ever thought that God really did have a gender'.[7] Mawson himself admits that in referring to God as a person we must employ either 'he' or 'she'; and he chooses the former, maintaining that as long as one is clearheaded no patriarchal bias is implied. Mawson also insists that God's personhood is essential, while 'his' gender is accidental. Yet, in the present context, more clarity is needed to work out the way(s) in which this sharp separation of personhood and gender in the divine works in practice. Allow me to raise a series of rhetorical questions concerning a personal God who has the traditional omni-attributes but no gender.

First of all, how ought self-consciously gendered persons relate to a genderless personal God called 'He' (or, for that matter 'She')? It is doubtful that we can eliminate gender from our thinking about any (other) person or personal relationship. So, how do we imagine eliminating gender from a personal being to whom we relate and to whom we refer as 'he' or 'she'. Even if God is the one exception as the personal being without a gender, if there is no philosophical discussion of gender's role in the ethical formation of human persons, then how do we know what it would mean for human persons to relate to a personal being, God, who is independent of gender? Gender could be something which gendered persons aspire to be without, say, in seeking a God's eye point of view. However, it is not clear in this aspiration whether something is missing in having a gender as human or in not having a gender as divine.

Second, there are a range of related questions about what it is to be without gender as a personal being. Do some personal beings other than God not have a gender? Or, do some personal beings have more or less gender? Are some personal beings closer to God's genderless state than others? Presumably gender has to have some status in God's plan for human beings. If more or less gender privileges some human beings over others, it must be possible for philosophers to attempt to justify God for allowing this inequality and those differences within the human race. If gender difference is not an issue between human beings and a divine being, then perhaps there are significant gender differences between human beings and other beings which need justification.

---

[5] Ibid.

[6] T. J. Mawson, *Belief in God: An Introduction to the Philosophy of Religion* (Oxford University Press, 2005), p. 19.

[7] Ibid.

Third, the claim that no sensible theist ever thought that God did have a gender makes me wonder whether less value is given to all personal beings with a gender than a personal being without gender. Or, do we give less value to personal beings with one or other gender? This extends to questions about other human persons with a different gender from our own. Are differently gendered persons better or worse than me in some highly specific way because of their gender? If so, God's omni-benevolence may be called into question when it comes to the creation of differently valued beings according to their gender. If gender, or a certain gender, makes a human person good or bad, rational or irrational, strong or weak, and so on, do these differences tell us something about God's omnibenevolence, his omnipotence or omniscience? Or, do we dismiss these questions by assuming that God created gender in the manner, some believe, he created time? If so, we live with gender just as we live in time and space.

Finally, the spatial-temporal identities of men and of women as masculine, feminine or transgender must matter to God's omni-benevolence. If He has not intervened to sort out injustices related to gender, then why not? Is this the result of, in terms of Christian doctrine, 'the fall'? Perhaps a Christian would agree that we would not have sex or gender if 'the fall' did not result in our suffering from the sins of the first created couple of human beings. If the large variety of gender constructions are unequally valued, then should gender be part of the problem of moral evil as an inequality to be eliminated? Some people will suffer more than others due to their gender identities. Are those transgendered persons who suffer excessively at the hands of gender-blind persons who have exclusively normative views of heterosexuality, marriage and procreation innocent?

Perhaps some philosophers will find that a good solution to these sets of questions, for women in Christian philosophy of religion, is offered by Luce Irigaray's ethics of sexual difference. Irigaray argues that women need a god of their own, as an ideal for their becoming perfectly according to their own gender, just as men have a god of their own (God the Father and the Son as ideals) for becoming perfectly according to their own gender. But then, more philosophical questions arise here. Are each of us responsible for our gender? If so, should we, like Irigaray, seek to create, project and retrieve a God in our own gender that can serve in defining our identities as women, just as men have (created?) a God who serves in this way for them. If so, it would seem to follow that philosophers would actively discuss the role of gender in their ethical, religious and epistemic practices. Gender may be what gives us our moral identity, integrity and sovereignty as persons with a sexually specific nature.

Charles Taliaferro presents an alternative position to either Irigaray's gods with genders or Mawson's God without gender. Taliaferro both maintains theism and seeks to avoid sexism by describing God's personal nature in terms of divine passability with 'an interior and comprehensive account of divine omnipresence and goodness'[8]. In other words, Taliaferro recognizes there is a problem with theism that might create a gender-bias or sexism. For this reason, Taliaferro should be applauded for his endeavour to work out how a sensible theist could think that God might have been given a gender when the use of 'He' for God re-enforces sexism; and the only way to find out if God has a gender is to work out what we think of gender and what we think of God.

To find out more about gender in this chapter, I return to a more extensive exploration of love and reason than found in Chapters 5 and 6 by assessing our philosophical texts and practices. Ultimately, I would hope that re-visioning love and reason will address the question of gender in philosophy of religion; that is, it will become a bit clearer why a sensible theist might like to ask about gender and theism. Love and reason will be explored as two concepts with deep roots in the fixed identities of gender.

Re-visioning love and reason in this chapter will, then, require that we consider a failure of gender justice and its implications for the rational argumentation in philosophy of religion. Focusing on a failure to question the coherence of God as both personal and without a body or a gender I will suggest some of the implications of a body-less and gender-less conception of God for our ethical formations.[9] Christian philosophers of religion could assume that ethical formation takes place as each individual being fully embodies the life which she or he is given by God; yet this also assumes a process of gender formation wed to the fact that every human being is an 'incarnation'; that is, each human being is incarnate in 'a very particular body'[10]; and this incarnation inevitably involves a normative formation of gender. Without the gendering of human-human and divine-human relations it would seem to be impossible to talk adequately about incarnation or incarnate love. This talk would involve gendering human relations to God, even if it could be demonstrated that God's gender does not matter.

It seems to follow that historically gendering and re-visioning gender are and have been (however, unwittingly) integral to philosophy of religion and, in particular, to what was addressed to different degrees in Chapters 4 and 6; that is, a human longing to make sense of things, to produce and tell the truth, includes making sense of our bodily life and personal relations; the truth of the gendering

---

[8]   Charles Taliaferro, *Consciousness and the Mind of God* (Cambridge: Cambridge University Press, 1994).

[9]   For a challenge to the ethical formation in philosophy of religion as abstract yet incompatible with non-Christian formations, although here it is directed at western liberal feminism, see Saba Mahmood, *Politics of Piety: The Islamic Revival and the Feminist Subject* (Princeton, NJ: Princeton University Press, 2005), especially pp. 27, 28 n48–n49, 29–39 and 161ff.

[10]   Hannah Bacon, 'A Very Particular Body: Assessing the Doctrine of Incarnation for Affirming the Sacramentality of Female Embodiment', in Gillian Howie and J'annine Jobling (eds), *Women and the Divine: Touching Transcendence* (New York: Palgrave, 2009), pp. 227–251.

of these relations needs to be told for the sake of justice and redemption of wrong practices. Remember A. W. Moore admits that as a conceptual philosopher, he both seeks clarity for increased understanding and retains a commitment to truth.[11] Similarly, bell hooks writes to increase her understanding of life but also to redeem truth. Moreover, in Chapter 7, we found that Spinoza and Spinozist rationalists encourage us to increase understanding and so, increase the joyful continuation of existence in this life. The present chapter assumes we need to make sense of both love and reason as two necessary human capacities which are, nevertheless, part of our gendered incarnation; and after trying to make sense of love and reason, we approach their re-visioning in line with gender justice.

So, some sense of 'incarnation', being in a very particular body, has a fundamental and necessary role in making sense of the world, whether a believer in the Christian incarnation or not. Being in a very particular body, while reasoning and loving, will never square with a bracketing of the body, or with trying to imagine a love without a body. For example, philosophical practices, such as reflective critical openness requires a particular body and other bodies. As I have discussed previously, reflective critical openness aims to address concrete questions, reflectively, imaginatively and relationally.[12] Understanding bodily matters is essential for a human life as necessarily incarnate. To demonstrate the philosophical significance of reflective understanding of the human body in being incarnate, it is necessary not only to look at the two concepts, love and reason, but to place them in the context of spiritual and epistemic practices. Religious life and philosophical activity both require human beings who can practice love and reason. Arguably, an additional requirement of these practices is that believers and philosophers cultivate a certain sense of intersubjectivity. We need to connect to other subjectivities and to recognize the constraints of (patriarchal) gender formations. Only after this, can re-visioning gender in philosophy of religion take up a critical direction.

To repeat words which have helped to inspire the overall argument of this book, 'the act of looking back, of seeing with fresh eyes, of entering an old text from a new critical direction ... [this] is for women more than a chapter of cultural history: it is an act of survival'.[13] The 'critical direction' taken in the texts of philosophy of religion sees with fresh eyes the patriarchal relations which have eclipsed love and/or reduced reason's role. Without love and reason, human lives are dis-ordered, certain women and men suffer as a result of sexual abusive and

---

[11] Moore, *Points of View*, pp. 2–3, 28–31; cf. Chapter 4.

[12] Pamela Sue Anderson, 'An Epistemological-Ethical Approach to Philosophy of Religion: Learning to Listen', in Pamela Sue Anderson and Beverley Clack (eds), *Feminist Philosophy of Religion: Critical Readings* (London: Routledge, 2004), pp. 89–92, 98–99.

[13] Adrienne Rich, 'When We Dead Awaken', in Barbara Charlesworth Gelpi and Albert Gelpi (eds), *Adrienne Rich's Poetry and Prose* (New York and London: W. W. Norton & Company, 1991), p. 167.

oppressive relations. Without love and reason, the expansive, human longing to persevere in being comes under threat.

As a spur for taking a new critical direction with the idea of 'incarnation', this chapter also aims to re-vision love and reason, by looking back at – seeing with fresh eyes – the relatively new texts in and related to *Feminist Philosophy of Religion: Critical Readings*.[14] In her book review of this collection of critical readings, Susan Durber reasons that if the core theistic belief of the contemporary philosopher is assumed to represent belief in a Protestant God, then it seems 'absurd' to conceive this God as, strictly speaking, disembodied. Nevertheless, this assumption that the Protestant God is a god without a body has served as the basis for feminist critiques of theism. As discussed in Chapter 3, the gendering implicit in traditional theism has been a reason for some feminists to reject Protestant forms of philosophical theology; and for some of these feminists to find in Roman Catholic theology a better alternative for women who seek to reconfigure the feminist potential in the bodily imagery of a virgin mother, her divine son and the father God.

As will be become clear Durber is perfectly correct in her review article to raise the issue of absurdity. What appears to be the core object for the feminist critique of traditional philosophy of religion – that of an omni-being without a body – is, in Durber's own words, 'little more than a caricature of Christianity'.[15] However, although correct that this is seemingly a caricature, Christian analytic philosophy of religion, including more recent forms of analytic theology, maintains that this is the correct picture of a rationally justified Christian theistic God; and the God of Christian analytic philosophy of religion is the ground for approaching Christian doctrines as analytic theology.[16]

The present intention is, nevertheless, to redirect both feminist critics and the (masculinist) theistic philosopher to an exploration of what Durber could mean by the actual Protestant 'practice of faith', especially those practices seeking the liberation of women.[17] Durber raises two especially relevant topics for the project of a contemporary (feminist) philosophy of religion: first, the role of incarnation in ethical formation;[18] and, second, the role of the practice of incarnational faith in shaping our emotional and cognitive dispositions. In this way, her criticism becomes a good starting point for my constructive reflections on incarnation and the embodied spiritual practices which give concrete form to our intersubjectivity.

---

[14]   Susan Durber, 'Book Review: *Feminist Philosophy of Religion: Critical Readings*', in *Literature and Theology* 18/4 (December 2004): 493–495; cf. Anderson and Clack (eds), *Feminist Philosophy of Religion*.

[15]   Durber, 'Book Review', p. 494.

[16]   William Wood, 'On the New Analytic Theology, Or the Road Less Travelled', *Journal of the American Academy of Religion*, 77/4 (December 2009): 941–960.

[17]   Durber, 'Book Review', pp. 494–495.

[18]   Sabina Lovibond, *Ethical Formation* (Cambridge, MA: Harvard University Press, 2002), pp. 9–11, 159, 161–164 and 170–171, n58, 173.

Although the object of feminist critique in philosophy of religion has tended to be a disembodied idea of God and a disembodied faith, feminist philosophers of religion have not generally admitted that this is a reductive picture of the Protestant God; nor have they admitted the lack of any explicit consideration of the actual practices of faith which accompany this picture. Instead, so far the most explicit feminist alternative to traditional theism has been the generation of an embodied divinity out of female subjectivity as in Luce Irigaray's imagery of women 'becoming divine'.[19] On this topic, I need to be careful to avoid the creation of another caricature: that of becoming divine. Yet without some such critical contrast it is difficult to find a precise place to open up the debates concerning divinity between feminist and masculinist analytic philosophers of religion. In this case, the critical focus of what might be caricatured as analytic masculinism and Continental feminism has excluded, for instance, the relevant ways in which contemporary Protestant or other Christian (say, Orthodox) practices of faith exhibit that which is incarnate, or embodied, in their form(s) of theism.

Thus, it is in this light and for these reasons that I aim to sketch a new conceptual framework of what could be an alternative philosophical focus for feminist philosophy of religion today. This framework will draw upon certain philosophical accounts of incarnation which are indebted to the philosophy of Iris Murdoch, especially the feminist philosophical reading of Murdoch by Fionola Meredith. In addition, the account of ethical formation in the context of the spiritual and ritual practices which both shape and are dependent upon bodily, emotional and cognitive dispositions will be informed by Amy Hollywood's significant interventions into feminist philosophy of religion. The texts of both Meredith and Hollywood are in the book reviewed by Durber, *Feminist Philosophy of Religion*.

The focus on feminist philosophers of religion in this chapter will turn away from any exclusive Irigarayan preoccupation with female embodied subjectivity in becoming divine. Instead I will argue that a more productive focus for both women and men would be intersubjectivity and the cognitive-emotional shaping of our collective historical experience.[20] This focus would have to bear in mind

---

[19] Luce Irigaray, 'Divine Women', *Sexes and Genealogies*, trans. Gillian C. Gill (New York: Columbia University Press, 1993), pp. 55–72; Grace M. Jantzen, *Becoming Divine: Towards A Feminist Philosophy of Religion* (Manchester: Manchester University Press, 1998); and Tina Beattie, 'Redeeming Mary: The Potential of Marian Symbolism for Feminist Philosophy of Religion', in Anderson and Clack (eds), *Feminist Philosophy of Religion*, pp. 107–122.

[20] For a recent example of this, see Mark Wynn, *Emotional Experience and Religious Understanding: Integrating Perception, Conception and Feeling* (Cambridge: Cambridge University Press, 2005). For a constructive engagement with feminist criticisms concerning the ideal attributes of the theistic God, to include affective points of view, see Charles Taliaferro, 'The God's Eye Point of View: A Divine Ethic', in Harriet A. Harris and Christopher J. Insole (eds), *Faith and Philosophical Analysis: The Impact of Analytical Philosophy on the Philosophy of Religion* (Aldershot, Hants: Ashgate Publishing Limited, 2005), pp. 76–84.

that each woman is uniquely formed and gendered – as are men – by various intellectual, spiritual and bodily practices.

A brief sketch: key feminist figures

My proposal for an alternative focus in feminist philosophy of religion is threefold and will be outlined in this brief sketch. First of all, I will begin with an argument against a poststructuralist dis-incarnation of individual subjects. Although French poststructuralism has shaped an earlier stage of feminism in philosophy and in critical social theory, with certain significantly good repercussions, it is my contention that poststructuralism also led women philosophers of religion to a dead-end when it comes to actual historical experiences; that is, to an abstract point ultimately lacking incarnation and intersubjectivity.[21] Oddly, on this point, both poststructuralist (or, non-conceptual) and analytic (or, conceptional) philosophers tended unwittingly to agree. This is in confirmed by the way in which Irigaray's poststructuralist conception of texts, 'embodying' the female divine, can be paired as sexually different (heterosexually speaking, the opposite) to the male divine in the texts of traditional Christian theism. This is especially noticeable where the aim has been to change philosophy of religion by focusing upon Irigaray's feminism of sexual difference. Instead of giving value to a woman's collective historical experience, alongside of her incarnation as a singular ethical subject, difference feminists seem to have eclipsed a productive discursive engagement with past, present and future, including actual women and actual men in the past, whether religious, philosophical or both.

Although Saba Mahmood is informed by the poststructuralist philosophers, Michel Foucault and Judith Butler, she establishes a critical distance from abstract, atemporal, sweeping or vague appropriations of subjects in texts which tends to populate poststructuralist texts.[22] Instead, in her highly specific reading of the practices of piety in contemporary Islam, Mahmood studies actual practices and stipulates that tradition is discursive

> pedagogical practices articulate a conceptual relationship with the past, through an engagement with a set of foundational texts … commentaries thereon, and the conduct of exemplary figures. Tradition, in this sense, may be conceived as a particular modality of Foucault's discursive formation in which reflection upon the past is a constitutive condition for understanding and reformulation of the present and the future.[23]

---

[21]   For her sustained argument in this regard, see Fionola Meredith, *Experiencing the Postmetaphysical Self: Between Hermeneutics and Deconstruction* (London: Sage, 2005).

[22]   Mahmood, *Politics of Piety*, pp. 95–98 and 113–117.

[23]   Ibid., p. 115.

Thus, tradition is

> ... a mode of discursive engagement ... one effect of which is the creation of sensibilities and embodied capacities (of reason, affect, and volition) that in turn are conditions for the tradition's reproduction.[24]

As the French philosopher Michèle Le Doeuff has further insisted in rejecting the difference feminism of Irigaray, in particular, each woman needs to recognize herself in the context of collective historical experience[25] – that is, not in total isolation or in linguistic abstractions, but within a discursive tradition mediated by written and verbal texts. Furthermore, I contend that the failure to recognize her singular place in a discursive tradition leaves a woman unable to generate the necessary cognitive and emotional dispositions for intersubjectivity.

Second, I will turn to Le Doeuff's criticism of contemporary French feminists who advocate sexual difference to the exclusion of reciprocal equality for each and every human being. The notable advocate of difference feminism is, as already discussed in Chapter 3, the psycholinguistic poststructuralist Irigaray.[26] Le Doeuff and her predecessor Simone de Beauvoir can help us to avoid two ethical extremes which plague poststructuralism. There is the ethical danger for woman, on the one hand, of an extreme altruism and, on the other hand, of a debilitating narcissism; each ultimately render the ethical perspective of intersubjectivity impossible. In turn, the lack of intersubjectivity renders impossible the sort of love and mutual recognition required for the justice sought by women and gender-sensitive men. Le Doeuff encourages the recognition of a fundamental fact: that each woman is part of a collective history. It is this collectivity which shapes either wittingly or unwittingly our bodily and spiritual dispositions as ethical subjects. Without awareness of this ethical formation by way of a collectivity, women cannot begin to cultivate the appropriate spiritual dispositions, including hope, love and joy in their liberation.

Finally, I will turn to Amy Hollywood's courageous and well-informed endeavour to introduce feminist philosophers of religion to contemporary accounts of subject formation via certain bodily and ritual practices.[27] Crucially Hollywood

---

[24] Ibid.

[25] Michèle Le Doeuff, *Hipparchia's Choice: An Essay Concerning Women, Philosophy, etc.* trans. Trista Selous (New York: Columbia University Press, 2007), pp. 126–133, 193–194 and 224–230.

[26] On the significance of Le Doeuff's philosophy and Irigaray's poststructuralism for feminist philosophy of religion, see Pamela Sue Anderson, *A Feminist Philosophy of Religion: Rationality and Myths of Religious Belief* (Oxford: Blackwell, 1998), pp. 9–11, 50–53 and 98–123.

[27] Amy Hollywood, 'Performativity, Citationality, Ritualization', *History of Religions* 42 (2002): 93–115; and 'Practice, Belief and Feminist Philosophy of Religion', in Anderson and Clack (eds), *Feminist Philosophy of Religion*, pp. 225–240.

encourages and guides feminist philosophers of religion to turn from an exclusive focus upon religious *belief* to focus upon ritual and bodily *practice*. In particular, her idea of a formative practice, deriving from the Ancient Greek concept of *askesis*, is extremely useful. For instance, this concept allows me to build upon my own earlier feminist critique of ethical positions, including a certain form of Kantian formalism, which have excluded emotional and spiritual formation from their discussions.

With the help of the above figures in contemporary philosophy, I eagerly set out in subsequent sections of this chapter to build upon writers of contemporary feminist and non-feminist philosophy, while taking seriously Durber's criticism of absurdity. But rather than absurdity, I find an unhealthy irony in the philosophical conception of a disembodied idea of the traditional theistic God being replaced with a feminist conception of female subjectivity modelled upon the traditional Roman Catholic imagery which has shaped female bodily dispositions – those most often associated with patriarchy. For example, Tina Beattie unearths an implicit Mariology in an Irigarayan conception of female subjectivity, in order to reconfigure Roman Catholicism to be compatible with difference feminism.[28] So far I would contend that in general terms both the (Protestant) analytic philosopher's disembodied idea and the (Catholic) feminist's embodied alternative have developed to the detriment of any practically and critically informed process of ethical formation across religious divisions.[29] To counter this, we seem to need a philosophical reshaping of our bodily and spiritual dispositions informed by the lived experiences of women and men.

It is important to bear in mind an argument, which I developed elsewhere, that we, humans, cannot on our own become divine (at least in the Irigarayan 'philosophical' sense), whether incarnate in a female or male body.[30] Furthermore, Sarah Coakley's claim that my own project for a feminist philosophy of religion eclipses 'any intimacy with the divine' should be seen in relation to my attempt to avoid the ethical danger of being, in Le Doeuff's words, 'a nothingness in the eyes of the other'.[31] I sought to avoid an eclipse of oneself by the other, especially to avoid the way in which women have been eclipsed by a patriarchal God.

---

[28]   Beattie, 'Redeeming Mary', pp. 107–122.

[29]   On this critical process, see Lovibond, *Ethical Formation*, especially the third and final part, 'Counter-Teleology', pp. 138–194.

[30]   Pamela Sue Anderson, 'Death and/as Woman: Ambiguity and Ambivalence in the Philosophical Imaginary', (unpublished) Lecture Delivered to Colloquium 1, 'Women Dying: Victims, Suicides, Mourning', Arts & Humanities Research Council Project on Representations of Women and Death in German Literature, Art and Media after 1500, Trinity College, University of Oxford, 5 January 2006.

[31]   For critical assessment of Irigaray's imperative that 'we become divine', see Pamela Sue Anderson, 'Transcendence and Feminist Philosophy: On Avoiding Apotheosis', in Gillian Howie and J'annine Jobling (eds), *Women and the Divine: Touching Transcendence* (New York: Palgrave, 2009), pp. 27–54.

On the basis of the above, rather complex sketch, let us turn to assess critically feminist claims concerning subjectivity, divinity and incarnation. We can, then, consider my rather ambitious proposal for an alternative conception of the feminist philosopher's task in philosophy of religion: that is, to focus on the roles of incarnation and intersubjectivity, in forming the emotional and cognitive dispositions of ethical subjects. This means an ethical formation, by way of the appropriate bodily and spiritual practices, for re-visioning love and reason. But note that I do not, at this stage in the philosophical and theological development of my own thinking, propose a new conception of divinity. Instead I suggest that this might emerge once we grasp, first, our incarnation in the terms of our bodily formation as ethical subjects and, next, the spiritual practices which express our intersubjectivity.

Gender, philosophy and divinity

For the sake of argument, let us grant that the main target of feminist and other criticisms of twentieth-century philosophy of religion has been the apparently disembodied divinity represented by the God of classical theism. Notably, there is Richard Swinburne's well-known conception of the theistic God as 'something like a person without a body (i.e., a spirit) who is eternal, free, able to do anything, knows everything, is perfectly good, is the proper object of human worship and obedience, the creator and sustainer of the universe'.[32]

As contended repeatedly by feminist philosophers in the twentieth century, 'woman' in the western tradition of philosophy has been associated with the body, bodily fluids and all of the ambivalence which is attached to conceiving a new life, giving birth, living out a life, dying, grieving and yearning for love and justice. In turn, this association of woman with the body and incarnation has excluded her from the ethical subject formation which is practiced in analytic philosophy, especially that of the 'man of reason' or the hero who transcends his body in great acts of courage. Generally, western analytic philosophers have defined their epistemic and ethical practices by achieving a rigorous clarity, certainty and unequivocal truth; and often this has led to, or been read as, opposing themselves to the ambiguity, ambivalence and, generally, messiness associated with embodiment and the female sex and gender. Basically, the implication of a discursive tradition of philosophy which has sought unambiguous truth and rationality in all of its best ideas and arguments has – even if unwittingly – excluded women who have been associated with and bound to embodied activities, from the formative position of 'philosopher' and 'man of duty'.

This admittedly sweeping sketch of an argument concerning woman's exclusion from western philosophy has to be clearly in the mind, in order to see the point of

---

[32]   Richard Swinburne, *The Coherence of Theism* (Oxford: Clarendon Press, 1977), p. 1.

re-visioning gender in philosophy of religion. One prominent response of feminist philosophers to their exclusion from philosophy has been to object to formulating philosophical conceptions exclusively as disembodied ideas, unassociated with real lived experiences and the various sorts of ambivalence which this generates. Consider again the feminist writings of Jantzen and Clack who each in their own manner has sought to address the deep ambivalence of lived bodily experiences.[33] For these feminists in philosophy, once the philosophical conception of God is assumed, or accepted, to be a disembodied idea 'he' becomes the first object of their feminist critiques of philosophical theism.

This traditional theistic conception of God has also been a serious obstacle for women outside of philosophy to entering the field of contemporary philosophy of religion. Recognizing this as an obstacle is not only a problem for women, but for those practitioners of the Protestant faith who Durber has in mind. Again we can see an irony for those intellectuals and others with an interest in religion or in Christian theology (rather than Anglo-American analytic philosophy of religion) who find that the theistic belief at the core of analytic philosophy of religion remains so unrelated to real life, death, sexuality, love or other often ambiguous emotions such as grief and compassion; many contemporary theologians see no practical point in doing analytic philosophy of religion, except as exercises in logical argumentation. Moreover, to exclude embodiment in this way from the conception of the theistic God appears self-defeating to the religious practitioner; or, as some would contend, this makes the philosophical debates irrelevant to religious faith.

Nevertheless, philosophers are not typically bothered by criticisms of practical irrelevance; that is, they may not be interested qua philosophers in the bodily and spiritual practices related to living and dying. Instead, it is arguably true that the analytic philosopher of religion is only really concerned with the ideas and arguments about God's existence and possibly, with the doctrines of the Christian God, if an analytic theologian, too. But if the philosopher is concerned not with religious practices or spiritual dispositions themselves, then it could be argued that the issue in this chapter about the ethical formation of gendered persons is not one for philosophy of religion. And yet notwithstanding the legitimate defences made by analytic philosophers of religion who uphold the rigour and purity of their philosophical discipline, this interface between philosophy as religious and as rigorous – which is perhaps in reality a false opposition – has become a fruitful domain for the debates of feminist philosophers who are keen to bring embodiment, especially life, love and death, as well as the ethical issues related to these, into philosophy of religion.

Unsurprisingly Anglo-American analytic philosophers have often found irrelevance in the source and nature of some of the strongest feminist critiques

---

[33]   Jantzen, *Becoming Divine*; Beverley Clack, *Sex and Death* (Cambridge: Polity Press, 2002); and Hanneke Canters and Grace M. Jantzen, *Forever Fluid: A Reading of Luce Irigaray's Elemental Passions* (Manchester: Manchester University Press, 2005).

of western philosophy of religion. In particular, replacing the traditional theistic conception of God as 'without a body' with sexual content, not from Protestant theology, but from French poststructuralism and from 'feminist' Mariology and associated imagery, has not made dialogue between feminist and non-feminist philosophers of religion easy. Anglo-American philosophers of religion might be surprised that some of the strongest terms for feminist dissent from the God of the philosophers has not come from Protestant critiques of patriarchy or from the unambiguous fields of scientific and analytic philosophy. Instead, Roman Catholic theologians have appropriated Irigaray's ethics of sexual difference for their exclusively heterosexual doctrines of Christian sexual ethics and gender. So however dense, difficult and ambiguous the terms of the French poststructuralist philosophers, they had had a profound impact upon feminist and non-feminist theologians at least within certain traditions. Thus, it is here that Irigaray has become the feminist poststructuralist figure *par excellence* in the minds of sexual difference feminists and Roman Catholic theologians who haveappropriated her ethics of sexual difference, especially the role given to the Virgin Mary, to support their exclusively heterosexual doctrines of Christian moral theology.

The ambiguity over whether poststructuralist philosophers are conservative or transformative when it comes to gender, sexuality and female embodiment proves to be the difficulty and obstacle to serious philosophical exchanges between the feminism of sexual difference and other contemporary feminist philosophies (of religion), but not between the former and the masculinism of traditional analytic philosophy of religion.[34] Yet, as I see it, the problem with the feminism of sexual difference and the masculinism of traditional theism is re-enforcing highly traditional norms of heterosexuality, as well as a lack of awareness of gender's intersectionality; gender's intersection with sexuality, religion, race and class render gender highly variable and complex: there cannot be only two sharply differentiated genders as everywhere evident in global relations today.

Essentially, Irigaray's attraction for Roman Catholic theology is in helping to position them against homosexuality and for reproductive sex within the family (only) for procreative reasons. Admittedly, there is often a cavalier appropriation of her attempts to retell the Christian story of salvation with a significant role being given to the suffering of female embodiment, the divine incarnation in a woman's body and the virginity of the mother of God.[35] Nevertheless, the Irigarayan reconfigurations of Mary's story and her relation to God, of female embodiment and of traditional female imagery have brought together in creative

---

[34] For an example of this mutual incomprehension between masculinism and feminism, see Paul Helm, 'The Indispensability of Belief to Religion', *Religious Studies*, 37 (2001): 75–86; Grace M. Jantzen, 'What Price Neutrality? A Reply to Paul Helm', *Religious Studies*, 37 (2001): 87–91.

[35] For references and an account of Irigaray's 'mariology', see Tina Beattie, *God's Mother, Eve's Advocate* (London: Continuum Press, 2002), pp. 23–39, 42–44, 103–105, 184–189 and 193 n66.

and impressive ways Roman Catholic theology and sexual difference feminism. Obviously, the theologians and the feminists who are re-visioning gender, sexuality and the divine according to the role given by Irigaray to Mary, virginity, maternity, birth, life and death are less likely to be Christian Protestant feminist philosophers. It is the secular feminist and the non-Catholic philosopher who equally and rightly question Irigarayan reconfiguration of Mary as the mother of God in the name of women's liberation. Put bluntly, these philosophers are baffled by Irigarayan 'feminist' theology. In fact, we can legitimately ask whether or not the Anglo-American feminist philosopher of religion who follows Irigaray with her philosophy of the feminine divine, as distinct from the masculine divine, has created more bafflement concerning the very nature of this so-called 'feminist' project in philosophy of religion.[36]

The present chapter cannot attempt more than to point to the very different styles of ethical formation of gendered subjects within feminist philosophy, French philosophical theology and Anglo-American philosophy of religion. The main thread and consistent concern is to continue to develop a feminist critique of exclusively male conceptions of gender and divinity in philosophy on and off the Continent.

Permit me a brief account of the received position on the feminist critique of gender and divinity in philosophy of religion as it stands at the moment.[37] Due to the lack of maternal or feminine symbolism in the dominant Anglo-American conception of God and the intellectual debates which surround this conception, a central target of feminists has been that which has remained at the heart of Protestant Christianity. This is the all-powerful, all-knowing, all-good, all-wise, eternal, personal, Father, God without a body. It is, then, not difficult to understand how a prominent feminist alternative to this disembodied God in Anglo-American philosophy became the embodied subjectivity and the spiritual dispositions implicit in the female imagery and ritual devotion of certain Christian mystical practices, especially those identifying with the incarnate Son of God or the virgin Mother of God.[38] It is precisely such embodied dispositions which have been provocatively reconfigured in the psycholinguistic categories of Irigarayan theology and of what some would call 'feminist philosophy of religion'.[39] Yet, this is not the re-visioning which is anticipated in the present chapter.

---

[36] For assessing the dangers and possibilities of Irigarayan 'logic', see Canters and Jantzen, *Forever Fluid*.

[37] For the philosophical terms of feminist debates about divinity and gender in contemporary philosophy of religion, see Grace M. Jantzen, Harriet A. Harris, Tina Beattie, Heather Walton, Melissa Raphael and Beverley Clack, in Anderson and Clack (eds), *Feminist Philosophy of Religion: Critical Readings*, especially pp. 28–41, 73–86, 107–122, 123–135, 136–150, and 183–196, respectively.

[38] Beattie, *God's Mother, Eve's Advocate*; and Hollywood, 'Practice, Belief and Feminist Philosophy of Religion', pp. 229–237.

[39] For support of this point, see Beattie, 'Redeeming Mary', pp. 107–122.

At this point let us return to Durber's criticism of the debates in feminist philosophy of religion. The position criticized as the absurd or ironic 'Protestantism' of Anglo-American analytic philosophy of religion, along with the alternative offered by the feminist philosophers of religion who have been informed by Irigarayan feminism, have distorted the reality of actual Christian (certainly Protestant) beliefs and their practices. Thus the choice is stark between a masculine (disembodied) God and a feminine (embodied) divine; and this division in the gendering of traditional theism and of difference feminism was already anticipated in Chapter 3. Nevertheless, the popularity of Irigaray's sexually provocative writings and of her Irigarayan-influenced feminism is proof enough to suggest that absurdity and crudeness of gendering have been risked in order for Irigarayan feminist philosophers of religion to seek to transform the analytic discipline of philosophy. For what it is worth, this popularity of a feminine divine is significant enough to admit that the Irigarayan alternatives to philosophy of religion respond to something missing in the analytic philosopher's traditional God. Durber clearly picks up on a reason for choosing Irigaray's god over and against the disembodied God, yet Durber correctly muses about what went wrong in the ethical formation of Protestant analytic philosophers of religion. In her words,

> how absurd that a faith founded on the Incarnation became so much a faith of disembodied ideas. ... [positively, she insists] that Protestants are also concerned with the practice of faith (faith not being synonymous with thought) and, sometimes notably, with the overturning of patriarchy and the liberation of women.[40]

So there is no question that feminist and non-feminist philosophers of religion should carefully reflect upon the current situation for both traditional and feminist philosophy of religion. Yet let us do so!

An interlude: on method

A decisive methodological problem needs to be admitted in so-to-speak tackling analytic philosophy of religion head on, and not via Irigarayan psycholinguistics of female and male sexualities. Without a doubt feminist philosophers have been unfair in attacks on mere caricatures which might have been taken to constitute the masculinism of philosophy of religion. Feminist philosophers have been dismissive of the (caricatured) white male analytic philosophers of religion often with the assumption that this implies rejection of Protestant Christianity full stop.[41] To be fair to the feminist intervention, this reductive focus may have

---

[40] Durber, 'Book Review', pp. 493–495.

[41] See Jantzen, *Becoming Divine*, especially pp. 18–33; and Beattie, 'Redeeming Mary', pp. 107–122.

been necessary at an initial stage in the transformation of the oppressive aspects of an exclusively patriarchal philosophy of religion, especially when clarity was essential to make feminist voices heard and understood. But not all feminists have given up reason for 'fluid' logic and female morphology. Instead there are plenty of feminist philosophers who know that different forms of reasoning are essential for many different epistemic, ethical and spiritual practices.

Yet the necessity of finding argumentational clarity can explain – and possibly justify – why the easiest and strongest criticisms by feminists of philosophy of religion on the grounds of gender may have been, or at least may have sounded very like, caricatures of actual positions and of epistemic practices. However enough contemporary women philosophers should have achieved sufficient authority, at least if their philosophical writings have been taken seriously, to be able to articulate more accurate and nuanced arguments for re-visioning love and reason, as two topics that have been strongly gendered both by analytic philosophy and by feminist philosophy of religion in the twentieth-century. This more nuanced thinking for re-visioning gender would imply being able, if desired and as reasonable, to uphold actual practices of faith. It is for this reason that Durber's criticisms have been given more attention than might have been expected in this chapter. Basically, the message from Durber is that philosophers can and should consider actual (in this case) Protestant practices of women and non-patriarchal men, alongside other spiritual and bodily practices as material for philosophical debates.

Suppose that feminist philosophers of religion are ready to listen to the new voices of women philosophers and faith-practitioners. They (We) can, then, move gradually away from what has been an exclusive preoccupation with theoretical issues concerning religious belief as opposed to practice. We should be able to recognize the serious possibilities in the latter's contribution to philosophical debates about the traditional Christian theism of Anglo-American philosophy of religion, without eclipsing other possibilities for conceptions of divinity, subject formation and incarnate experience(s). Any exclusive strategy in the rethinking of religion in philosophical terms only distorts the potential of philosophy of religion for feminist and non-feminist philosophers alike.

In fact, a philosophical tendency to caricature an opponent in order to make strong one's own case in philosophy of religion can also be explained (if not excused) to some degree by the philosophers of religion to whom feminists have expressed their objections and by the moment in which we find ourselves. The tradition has characterized its positions in philosophy of religion with extremely precise terms and logical rigour in order to ensure a strong position: this is a tradition that has been defended and attacked with exactitude. Unfortunately, the implication of this rigour can be the reduction and so distortion of the positions attacked and defended; and the fact that this danger remains in my own writing in the field gives me even more reason to try to transform it.

For feminist philosophers of religion at this moment of transition and creativity in the field, I would like to maintain that philosophical positions concerning love, reason and gender need not be held with obsessive tenacity; neither women nor men need resort to reductive distortions of their own or an opponent's position. Today progress should mean avoiding caricatures of either masculinist or feminist beliefs, but especially avoiding practices which seek to justify religious belief to the harm or detriment of the sexual or spiritual relations and the religious or non-religious positions taken by women and men on matters of love and of reason. Let us resist further distortions of oppositions and conflicts. That distorted interpretations of opposing positions persist in the projects of feminist and non-feminist philosophers of religion alike would seem to say more about the insecurity of these philosophers than about anything either male or female in their projects.

Incarnation, subjectivity and intersubjectivity

The previous sections have urged philosophers to take seriously the ethical and spiritual significance of incarnation for the sake of our vision of reason and of love. Durber has reminded us about the practice(s) of faith which the philosophers of religion would do well to consider. It is, therefore, appropriate to turn, once more, to the woman philosopher who we have already discussed on goodness, beauty and love; that is, Iris Murdoch. But this time we turn to her work on incarnation, including the incarnation of goodness and love. Exciting new work on Murdoch, her philosophy and gender has been published by Sabina Lovibond, since this chapter was first written.[42] Nevertheless, Murdoch as discussed earlier, as informed by , A. W. Moore, is further informed here by Fionola Meredith. In their different ways, Meredith and Moore critically draw on Murdoch's rich accounts of incarnation.[43] Meredith reminds us that Murdoch responded to French poststructuralism, finding it just as empty, abstract and 'dis-incarnate' as feminist philosophers of religion have found the analytic conception of the traditional theistic God. Consider Murdoch's words about Derridaen poststructuralism:

> Something is lost, the existing incarnate individual with his [her] real particular life of thoughts and perceptions and moral living.[44]

---

[42] Sabina Lovibond, *Iris Murdoch, Gender and Philosophy* (London: Routledge, 2011).

[43] See A. W. Moore, *Points of View* (Oxford: Oxford University Press, 1997), especially Chapter 11. Fionola Meredith, 'A PostMetaphysical Approach to Female Subjectivity: Between Deconstruction and Hermeneutics', in Anderson and Clack (eds), *Feminist Philosophy of Religion*, Chapter 4; and *Experiencing the Postmetaphysical Self*, especially Chapters 3, 4 and 5.

[44] Meredith, *Experiencing the Postmetaphysical Self*, p. 112; and Murdoch, *Metaphysics as A Guide to Morals*, pp. 202, also, pp. 185–216.

Murdoch argues specifically against the French Continental philosopher, with whom we found Moore 'arguing' in Chapter 4, Jacques Derrida. Murdoch reasons about Derrida's play with concepts, presence/absence, as follows:

> An inability to be fully present is something which we often feel. We move about in time in all sorts of strange ways which are also entirely familiar. We 'live in memory', we anticipate and plan, we discover unconscious wishes, we 'sum up' in spoken thoughts processes of mental stuff which we could not describe or temporally analyse in detail, our mental life is time-textured, and a certain mastery of time is required for living and in various sophisticated forms of living well. But our time-adventures return to and are based in presence and encounter. These concepts, experience, consciousness, presence, cannot be arbitrarily excluded from philosophical discussion.[45]

Murdoch's helpful and insightful, however secular, account of incarnation brings to mind the singularity of the human subject who is nevertheless embedded in experience, in temporal life, in a process of learning to live well with others. Her words encourage us to re-vision love and reason fully present in 'our time-adventures' (above). So, we might say like Moore did of himself, that Murdoch is a conceptual philosopher for whom truth and reality matter. Moreover, Murdoch points to the very serious role of incarnation, especially for her understanding of love as the incarnation of goodness.

In *Metaphysics as a Guide to Morals*, Murdoch not only 'argues against' Derrida for his loss of 'presence and encounter', or this might be called conceptual philosophy, but she recalls a topic from her own earlier lectures in *The Sovereignty of Good* that of perfection.[46] Her argument engages Anselm, Descartes and Kant concerning the idea of perfection: 'We *experience* both the reality of perfection and its distance from us.'[47] Murdoch's claim holds significance for our ethical and spiritual practices insofar as these latter seek to make manifest the real as an idea embodied in us. Simone Weil's apparent spiritual influence on Murdoch's ethics derives from the former's *attending to* the Christian idea of a god becoming incarnate in a human body. In the end, Murdoch is clearly one woman philosopher trained in the early part of the twentieth-century in Oxford who raises the critical issue of incarnation at the interface of ethics, religion and metaphysics. Accepting an inevitable ambiguity, she nevertheless encourages philosophical reflection upon the relationship between bodily practices and perfect goodness essentially for encountering presence in intersubjectivity.[48]

---

[45]   Murdoch, *Metaphysics as A Guide to Morals*, p. 212; cf. Murdoch, *The Sovereignty of Good*.

[46]   Murdoch, *The Sovereignty of Good*.

[47]   Murdoch, *Metaphysics as a Guide to Morals*, p. 508.

[48]   Murdoch, *The Sovereignty*, p. 77f; and *Metaphysics as a Guide to Morals*, p. 279f and 504–512.

In fact, Murdoch picks up some of her concern with incarnation and (un) selfing not only from Weil, but also from Jean-Paul Sartre. It would be worthwhile to pick up this thread to the individual subject, consciousness, immanent life.[49] We can follow this thread from Murdoch back to debates about Sartre's existentialism, but also forward, to the feminist writings of Simone de Beauvoir; and later, to Beauvoir's feminist influence on both Le Doeuff and Irigaray. In other words, this takes us to questions of the self, raising such issues as whether the self should be un-doing herself for the sake of the other or whether the self should turn in on herself in debilitating forms of female narcissism. For her part, Beauvoir criticizes heavily the female narcissist who sees nothing of the other; but bear in mind she also criticizes the female mystic's love for her God and the female lover who loses herself in her beloved. In Beauvoir's words,

> One can understand the intoxication that permeates the heart of the narcissist when all of heaven becomes her mirror; her deified image is infinite like God Himself, it will never disappear; and at the same time she feels in her burning, palpitating and love-drowned breast her soul created, redeemed and cherished by the adoring Father; it is her double, it is she herself she is embracing, infinitely magnified by God's mediation.[50]

So, Beauvoir recognizes the danger of being seduced like the above mystic by her own identity. This mystic's lacerated desire to be all there is would appear to end tragically in either narcissism or nihilism. As for Le Doeuff, although not speaking about divinity and incarnation, like Beauvoir she inspires caution on the question of woman's subjectivity; and Le Doeuff, as mentioned in earlier chapters, objects strongly to the feminism of sexual difference, chastising any 'feminism' which would return women to an idea of female apotheosis, that is, of becoming divine women. Le Doeuff is a feminist philosopher who takes reason, rationality, wit and a Deleuzian sort of joy very seriously. Unlike Irigaray both Beauvoir and Le Doeuff argue for equality and reciprocal relations, ushering in justice and reason, not the sovereignty of sexual difference. Granted this is not a simple contrast, yet Beauvoir and Le Doeuff each recognize serious ethical dangers for the formation of the nascent female subject in twentieth-century societies due to an ongoing lack of equality. Neither advocates – as Irigaray does – becoming divine, or creating the divine out of a woman's gender, but they both speak insightfully, on the one hand, to the problems of a debilitating narcissism and, on the other hand, of an

---

[49]   For new work on a philosophy of life, focusing on Le Doeuff's rejection of the French Hegelian philosophy of the other, see Pamela Sue Anderson, 'Believing in this life: French philosophy after Beauvoir, in Steven Shakespeare and Katharine Sarah Moody (eds), *Intensities: Philosophy, Religion and the Affirmation of Life* (Farnham, Surrey: Ashgate Publishing Limited, 2012).

[50]   Simone de Beauvoir, *The Second Sex*, complete and unabridged, trans. Constance Borde and Sheila Malovaney-Chevallier (London: Jonathan Cape, 2009), p. 730.

absolute altruism whereby a woman becomes 'a nothingness in the eyes of the other' (again, this is Le Doeuff's voice).[51]

Gendering women as selfless subjects for philosophy of religion may be attractive to Murdoch, but her incarnation of goodness as 'un-selfing' would not immediately pass the test for a feminist re-visioning gender; just the opposite. Murdoch seems to go down the wrong track in the gendering of a female subject compatible with patriarchy. The result is a woman's incomprehensible selfless self-giving. So, Murdoch's idea of incarnation starts well, until her gendering of women becomes very much that of the patriarchal man's conception of femininity. This is in sharp contrast to the hopeful and joyful perseverance in being, which is advocated by the ethics of Le Doeuff, [52] Lloyd, Gatens and other Spinozist rationalists. Imagine, if following the latter, being a part of nature, increasingly in understanding of human passions, especially self-love, and striving for a shared love of humanity.

The above said against Murdoch's doctrine of un-selfing, we did find in Chapter 8 that her work on goodness, love and beauty gives us hope for the cultivation of virtue which could yet avoid the extremes of narcissism and absolute altruism. Beauvoir herself is not easy to interpret when it comes to self-other relations. Consider a contrast of Beauvoir to Irigaray on the gendering of mysticism.

On the one hand, there is little doubt that Beauvoir's own account of religion, mysticism and the female lover remains limited by her distinctively twentieth-century preoccupation with female narcissism and with her Sartrean assumptions concerning the paranoid, nascent subject. Uncovering narcissism is important as a form of suspicion or critique, but clearly not a completely fair picture of every female mystic or her desire. Beauvoir only sees the choice between an annihilation of the body of the female mystic in her love of self/god or a transcendence of the body by the female mystic. Her notable example of a mystic who avoids paranoid or decisively debilitating narcissism is Teresa of Avila. According to Beauvoir, Teresa achieves a situated autonomy and reciprocity in her practical projects. The latter sort of mystic represents, in Beauvoir's words, 'There are women of action … who are well aware of the goals they set themselves and who lucidly invent the means to reach them: their revelations merely give an objective form to their certainties; they encourage them to take paths they have carefully planned.'[53] This

---

[51] Le Doeuff, *Hipparchia's Choice*, p. 280.

[52] Ibid., pp. 278–279.

[53] Beauvoir, *The Second Sex*, p. 733; cf. Amy Hollyood, *Sensible Ecstasy: Mysticism, Sexual Difference and the Demands of History* (Chicago: University of Chicago Press, 2002), pp. 130–135. Beauvoir's reading should be compared to Irigaray's later reading of Teresa of Avila, representing female mysticism as a transcendence that operates through immanence, in Luce Irigaray, *'La Mystérique'*, in her *Speculum of the Other Woman*, trans. Gillian C. Gill (Ithaca, New York: Cornell University Press, 1985), pp. 191–202; also reprinted *'La Mystérique'*, in Morny Joy, Kathleen O'Grady and Judith L. Poxon (eds), *French Feminists on Religion: A Reader* (London: Routledge, 2002), pp. 28–39.

latter, positive practical assertion about certain women mystics, or saints, could equally be developed in terms of cultivating cognitive or spiritual dispositions informing certain ethical practices.

On the other hand, Irigaray develops her own account of a 'sensible transcendental', that is, the sensible as the condition for redeeming and transforming a woman's body. Transcendence in immanence is her ideal; the sensible transcendental is an embodied place where subjectivity can be revalued.[54] As already discussed (and criticized), Irigaray tries to give new value to the Christian narrative of salvation, that is, to give sexually specific value to the female body in realizing the significance of the Christian God's incarnation. God becomes incarnate in and through a woman's body; Irigaray suggests provocatively that when God becomes flesh (a) woman's complete desire can be recognized; her joy is complete and her body becomes divinized. However, this ideal remains problematic: neither fixed nor completely thinkable; its full meaning is constantly deferred, never achieved by any actual, virgin mother.[55] Of course, this is the point at which Beattie builds her constructive theological argument concerning the gendered imagery of the Church as female, as Christ's bride, along with the absolutely central role of Mary's body in God's incarnation.[56]

In other words, the ethical dangers of this Irigarayan ideal include the impossibility of ever fixing or applying this concept of an incarnation to re-visioning the divine-human subject who suffers, and yet achieves perfect joy, in and through a woman's body. Once, or if, this concept is fixed, without a perpetual deferral of its meaning and use, we will find ourselves back in a position similar to that criticized by Beauvoir in the imprisonment of the female:

> Ecstasies, visions and dialogues with God, this interior experience is sufficient for some women. Others feel the need to communicate it to the world through acts.[57]

> Mystical fervor, like love and even narcissism, can be integrated into active and independent lives. But in themselves these attempts at individual salvation can only result in failures; either the woman establishes a relation with an unreal: her

---

[54]   For a postcolonial critique of Irigaray's sensible transcendental, see Mary L. Keller 'Divine Women and the Nehanda Mhondoro: Strengths and Limitations of the Sensible Transcendental in a Post-Colonial World of Religious Women', in Morny Joy, Kathleen O'Grady and Judith L. Pozon (eds), *Religion in French Feminist Thought: Critical Perspectives* (London: Routledge, 2003), pp. 68–82.

[55]   On incarnation in the history of Christianity, and specifically on the contentious implications of any recognition (whether by Beauvoir or Irigaray) of 'the salvific power of the body and of femininity insofar as it is identified with human beings bodily nature', see Hollywood, *Sensible Ecstasy*, pp. 198–203.

[56]   For a fuller picture of her argument, see Beattie, *God's Mother, Eve's Advocate*.

[57]   Beauvoir, *The Second Sex*, p. 733.

double or God; or she creates an unreal relation with a real being; in any case she has no grasp on the world; she does not escape her subjectivity; her freedom remains mystified; there is only one way of accomplishing it authentically: it is to project it by a positive action into human society.[58]

Beauvoir finds freedom not in obsessive love of self, of a man or of God. Instead a woman's re-visioning of her own gender takes place through positive action, through practices which are rationally planned and carried out.

So, Irigaray's predecessor Beauvoir limits the extent of our liberation as solitary women.[59] The becoming of female subjectivity is limited by what Beauvoir sees as the 'failure' or 'unreal' effort at an individual transformation. Her account of extreme forms of female mysticism also uncovers the tension between two conceptions of recognizing the self and the other; this tension is *between* recognizing oneself as the Other in relation to man-God who is the Subject *and* collapsing the rightful boundaries that distinguish self and other. These equally unattractive alternatives for the female subject and her desire in these relations to the male subject and his desire appear to be (i) domination with narcissism or (ii) annihilation with absolute altruism. The hope is that a third possibility emerges with the ethically significant challenge of mutual recognition between subjects in love and in justice.[60]

In the context of feminist critiques of subjects who are supposedly disembodied, or dis-incarnate, autonomy, as in the ambiguous liberty already mentioned, cannot mean strictly speaking separation or independence from others.[61] Instead, women only seem to recognize their autonomy insofar as they recognize that each of us is beside herself in relationship to other women, past and present. In Le Doeuff's words, 'we need to inherit from [other women] (as they really were)' and so our autonomy must be understood to be a collective historical experience.[62] It is important to repeat and stress that, in Beauvoir's words, our political liberation can only be collective.

---

[58]   Ibid., pp. 733–734.

[59]   For a transgressive reading of the solitary figure of Antigone which undoes gender, notably masculine sovereignty, see Judith Butler, *Antigone's Claim: Kinship Between Life and Death* (New York: Columbia University Press, 2000), pp. 8–11 and 23.

[60]   Butler demonstrates how Hegel reads Antigone as a figure without (sexual) desire and so lacking any possibility of recognition in love and justice, see Butler, *Antigone's Claim*, pp. 11–13.

[61]   For a critical reading of theories of the autonomous subject, see Mahmood, *Politics of Piety*, especially Chapter 1: 'The Subject of Freedom', pp. 1–39.

[62]   Le Doeuff, *Hipparchia's Choice*, pp. 128 and 243, respectively.

The infinite and human rationality

At this late stage, we would do well to pick up another philosophical thread concerning rationality. The philosophical question of the nature of rationality, and reason, at work in philosophy of religion has remained implicit through this book. In the short twentieth-century history of feminist ethics, a well-known feminist, or 'feminine', critique was applied to reason in order to propose some distinctively feminine concept of care, love or relationality. In contrast, the overall argument of this book assumes that it is reason, reasons for action and rationality which connects each and every woman and man as uniquely gendered subjects. Earlier we rejected any reductive notion of the 'man of reason'; but 'he' can still haunt the feminist consciousness which feels certain that philosophy and reason are in fact only games or faculties to be exercised by men. However, the main vision in this book is not leading us to oppose feminine to masculine. Instead as found for instance, in Chapters 4 and 6, A. W. Moore makes very useful, fine distinctions which help to articulate the human relation to the infinite; such distinctions are crucial. Additional, new distinctions concerning the concepts we live by enable us to understand how the concepts of faith and reason can both function together, in order to restore faith in reason and to create truth-telling as a redemptive practice. We have seen that the philosophical thread which connects faith, reason, truth and epistemic practices of truth-telling also connects human finitude to the infinite.[63]

In contradistinction to the above arguments Irigaray's characteristic style of miming the male philosopher, Ludwig Feuerbach, asserts that the 'core of our destiny … [is] to generate the human, the divine, with us and among us'.[64] This assertion might be acceptable, if it is interpreted as a claim about the incarnation of the reality of an idea of perfect goodness, among human, female and male subjects. If so, Irigaray could better help her readers with more concrete everyday, socially and materially specific examples of this destiny. No actual historical examples support her claim to the destiny of generating the human and the divine, except for the incarnation of Christ and the immaculate conception of Mary. But the latter are not helpful examples for those who do not accept the Christian story as actually happening to anyone; and even if the divine incarnation and conception did happen, this is not a very helpful story for women who can never be virgin mothers, or for men who choose not to emulate Christ's sacrifice, since for non-divine humans it would be a self-destructive form of 'love'.[65]

---

[63]   I began to elucidate this thread in Pamela Sue Anderson, 'Gender and the Infinite: On the aspiration to be all there is', *International Journal for Philosophy of Religion*, 50 (2001): 191–212.

[64]   Irigaray, 'Divine Women', p. 60; cf. Ludwig Feuerbach, *The Essence of Christianity*, trans. George Eliot (Buffalo, NY: Prometheus Books, 1989).

[65]   Pamela Sue Anderson, 'Sacrifice as self-destructive "love"; why autonomy should still matter to feminists', in Julia Meszaros and Johnannes Zachhuber (eds), *Sacrifice and Modern Thought* (Oxford: Oxford University Press, 2013).

Basically, Irigaray is not clear about the concrete sense in which God, the divine or divinity, can be created out of a gender; nor is it clear, if possible, how a divinity which can be created out of a gender would help women in their becoming gendered subjects. Perhaps there is some sort of help to woman in (her) giving female gendered qualities to 'a god(dess)'. But why not avoid this Feuerbachian projection of a divine in her gender onto a female god? The alternative proposed in this chapter is to find a significant form of intersubjectivity which comes close to the poetic idea that the human-divine is incarnate in and with us as a collective of corporeal bodies joined by love and reason. Remember in Chapter 6, we saw how bell hooks, along with Moore and Williams, critically express the yearning for justice or infinitude.

Avoiding the problems associated with the how or why of Irigaray's Feuerbachian generation of the divine, I have elsewhere argued that we cannot on our own become divine, but we can understand our desire to be divine. To support this, I have turned to a very different account – from Irigaray's miming of Feuerbach – of our relation to the infinite and to finitude. In response to Irigaray's perplexing claim about 'man' that 'if he has no existence in his gender, he lacks his relation to the infinite and, in fact, to finiteness'[66] dare I say that gender makes us human, not divine? Or is this alternative merely a new and unhelpful Kantian antinomy?[67] Consider a more helpful reading of human finitude's relation to the infinite. With this, we will again recall the debt to Murdoch.[68]

From each of Murdoch and Moore there emerges the sobering recognition that we are finite, and yet as rational beings we still desire, or crave, the infinite. This rational desire moves us closer to a metaphysical craving found in Kant.[69] At the same time, this recognition of finitude means that Irigaray's insistence on becoming divine, or 'becoming infinitely'[70] is undermined by our own *hubris* in aspiring to be infinite, however differently as woman or as man. In Murdoch's own terms, the threat is 'a relentless egoism' and a reminder of the negative form of narcissism which has haunted modern moral philosophy. We are still dangerously close to succumbing to this modern moral danger. Le Doeuff senses the same danger when she struggles to draw a fine line between a woman who only un-finds the self she has been and the woman who both un-finds past constraints on herself and finds herself in dialogue with another thinker or actor on a level of equality and reciprocity.[71] It is significant here that Moore ends his account of the human

---

66   Irigaray, 'Divine Women', p. 61.

67   For the problematic role of antinomy has played in feminist epistemology, see Andrea Nye, *Feminism and Modern Philosophy: An Introduction* (London: Routledge, 2004), pp. 130–139.

68   Anderson, 'Gender and the Infinite', pp. 191–212.

69   Immanuel Kant, *Critique of Pure Reason*, trans. Norman Kemp Smith (London: Macmillan), pp. 575–603; cf. Nye, *Feminism and Modern Philosophy*, pp. 130–139.

70   Irigaray, 'Divine Women', p. 61.

71   Le Doeuff, *Hipparchia's Choice*, pp. 206–207.

aspiration to *be* infinite in inertia rather than expansion of subjectivity. He, then, offers a helpful remedy for this particular inertia: to distinguish carefully between a negative and a positive aspiration, resting upon a fine distinction between what we are (reality) and what we hope for (an ideal). A Kantian use of regulative ideals can also keep our rational cravings in check.

Consider a sobering account of the characteristically human aspiration to be infinite, recognizing at a most fundamental level an equivalent danger for women as for men.[72] In the words of Moore,

> Our craving for infinitude has a perspectival character corresponding to the point of view from which alone we exist ... When the craving is distorted, this perspectival character is turned in on itself in such a way that the craving becomes an aspiration *that we alone exist*, – or, in its most distorted form, that the subject alone exists. It becomes the aspiration to be a complete self-sufficient unconditioned whole, to be that which the craving for infinitude is a craving for. Whereas the incorrupt craving for infinitude would be essentially expansive, leading the subject to try to situate itself within the infinite whole, the aspiration to be infinite is essentially inert, leading the subject to try to situate the infinite whole within itself. And, again by its own lights, it (the aspiration to be infinite) is bad. There is an irrationality in wanting to be that which makes anything rational. It is a revolt, and an offence, against that which truly makes anything rational: rationality itself.

> ... [Yet] It is not as if, by means of some simple resolution, we can stop aspiring to be infinite, any more than we can, by means of some simple resolution, eliminate evil. Our aspiration is something that we have to *come to terms with*.[73]

It is the crucial distinction between the essentially expansive craving, or, as I would say, yearning 'for infinitude' and the aspiration 'to be infinite' as essentially inert that we ought to embrace. This would replace any claim to a sovereign liberty or supreme power. When the human craving becomes an aspiration *that we alone exist* – or, in its most distorted form, that the subject alone exists – we face the negative extremes of either hubris or narcissism; hence, there is corruption of truth, goodness and reason.

Consider an example to clarify this use of a Kantian distinction. Moore's fine distinction can help us with the obscurity concerning the reality of the divine (conceived in terms of regulative principles) which is encountered by Hollywood in her reading of *A Feminist Philosophy of Religion*. This use of the distinction between reality and the ideal is not correctly understood or explained as a rejection

---

[72]   I have illustrated how this corrupt aspiration takes on distinctively gendered forms when bringing Moore's account to bear on Jantzen, see Anderson, 'Gender and the Infinite', pp. 192–207.

[73]   Moore, *Points of View*, pp. 275–276.

of both realism and belief in the existence of any ideal of a (female) divine.[74] Instead it needs to be made clear that the task is to embrace the antinomical nature of our knowledge of reality by employing regulative principles to avoid outright contradiction or debilitating inconsistencies. To give Moore's account of these principles,

> Regulative ideals are concepts like that of perfection. We can never realize them, but we can come ever closer to realizing them and ought continually to strive to do so. To this end we may enjoin ourselves to proceed *as if* we could realize them. To enjoin ourselves to proceed as if we could realize a regulative ideal is to frame what Kant calls a regulative principle. A regulative principle is any rule for directing our behaviour in accord with the supposition that some concept, which cannot in fact be applied to reality, can be.[75]

With this clarification in mind, consider the question of the nature of the existence of the divine in Murdoch's provocative claims as follows:

> God does not and cannot exist. *But what led us to conceive of him does exist* and is constantly experienced and pictured.[76] That is, real as an Idea, and is also *incarnate in* knowledge and work and love. This is the true idea of *incarnation*,[77] and is not something obscure. We experience both the reality of perfection and its distance away, and this leads us to place our idea of it outside the world of existent being as something of a different unique and special sort. ... If we read these images aright they are not only enlightening and profound but amount to a statement of *a belief which most people unreflectively hold.*[78]

In this passage, we can glimpse an antinomy in Murdoch's own account: that is, she holds in tension both God's non-existence as an empirical object and the reality of an idea of perfection as incarnate[79] in our knowledge, our action and our attention (to reality).

---

[74]   For example, I think that there is some misunderstanding in a passage in Hollywood, 'Practice, Belief and Feminist Philosophy of Religion', pp. 226–228. And yet, as will be seen below, Hollywood also provides the tools, after Kant, to integrate desire and reason, emotion and cognition, into the ethical formation of subjects via bodily and spiritual practices.

[75]   Moore, *Points of View*, p. 249.

[76]   For a helpful gloss on this, see Ibid., p. 278.

[77]   Compare this idea of incarnation to the concern raised by Durber, 'Book Review'.

[78]   Murdoch, *Metaphysics as a Guide to Morals*, p. 508, emphasis added.

[79]   Incarnation could be discussed further in the terms of 'an intimacy with the known', see Coakley, 'Feminism and Analytic Philosophy of Religion', pp. 516–518. Also see Sarah Coakley, *Powers and Submissions: Spirituality, Philosophy and Gender* (Oxford: Blackwell, 2002).

With this antinomical structure in mind, we can understand Moore's distinction concerning the ontological argument:

> There are those ... who have thought that, on one way of making sense of the claim that God exists, it admits of an ontological proof: existence is a perfection that God cannot lack. Others, not always intentionally, have suggested that, on the same way of making sense of the claim that God exists, it admits of an ontological disproof: existence is an imperfection that God cannot have. As it were there is no such 'thing' as God: God is too big for mere existence.[80]

Yet Moore agrees that what leads us to conceive of God does exist: the reality of the idea of perfection is implicit in *a striving for greater perfection*, or in Moore's terms, *a craving for infinitude*. This constitutes our striving for perfect goodness, truth and love which, nevertheless, remain beyond our spatial-temporal existence. In other words, this argument acknowledges our desire to be infinite, or our 'becoming infinitely' in Irigaray's terms;[81] but equally and crucially it also supports the fact that neither man nor woman as individual subjects can be infinite or become divine in any form by their own will. As human beings we yearn for perfect rationality, but we continue to confront antinomy. In this case, the antinomy rests in the experience of both the reality of perfection and its distance away from us.

Bodily practices and ethical formation

In this penultimate section of Chapter 9, the question is no longer about becoming divine or aspiring to be infinite. Instead philosophers of religion are being urged to take seriously the ethical danger of an absolute altruism. We have already found this to be described by Le Doeuff as a woman becoming nothingness in the eyes of the other whose own nature is eclipsed by unequal positioning of subjects in dialogue.[82] This danger takes on major significance for those feminist philosophers of religion who think autonomously for the sake of a woman's own identity. Autonomous thinking is at the heart of women's subject formation as ethical selves. Subject formation also returns us to an idea from Mahmood, quoted earlier in this chapter, of tradition as a discursive process. Mahmood conceives tradition, to be precise as 'a mode of discursive engagement', but also the effect of this engagement is 'the creation of sensibilities and embodied capacities'.[83] In this light, a woman's subject formation becomes a matter of cultivating bodily and spiritual dispositions by way of social and collective practices.

---

[80] Moore, *Points of View*, p. 277.
[81] Irigaray, 'Divine Women', p. 61.
[82] Le Doeuff, *Hipparchia's Choice*, p. 280.
[83] Mahmood, *Politics of Piety*, p. 115.

According to Murdoch, it is by 'un-doing' in the sense of eliminating self-deception that one's vision of reality is free to perceive the real as the genuine object, or, even better subject, of love; but she adds that this un-doing should not leave the self 'denuded'.[84] Attempts to confront a contradiction in trying both 'to unself' and 'to self' in specific, concrete situations have highly significant implications for philosophical critiques of ethics, religion and moral psychology, but also serious implications for spiritual as well as cognitive and emotional dispositions such as love.[85] Un-selfing does not end in what Murdoch also rejects as the 'denuded' self. Instead the ethical self is clothed with a virtuous (or vicious) disposition; this is the measure of its practical wisdom.[86] Once again we find that ethical and social practices are necessary, if we are to gain wisdom and so, cultivate loving dispositions which are attentive to others. With the topic of love, we move naturally from subject formation to intersubjectivity.

Intersubjectivity is not merely about establishing an emotional connection. Crucially, as subjects we share reasons for actions; such reasons motivate our actions, but they also involve risk in struggling to recognize the shared ground of reasons and passions. Le Doeuff recognizes certain dangers for those subjects whose identities and relationships are undermined by philosophical practices of exclusion. Yet with the question of a common human passion, we move towards replacing the concepts of subjectivity and of divinity with intersubjectivity; here we are close to Le Doeuff's collective historical experience.[87] The ultimate goal of a woman's philosophical search for intersubjectivity is to find reasons for shared actions with an ultimate *telos*, even if this is ultimately unreachable. The *telos* emerges as two subjects find themselves in dialogue about an ethical issue; or two subjects find themselves in love; or, possibly as subjects we share a guiding ideal. It is this rationality of projects which emerge through interaction that also makes

---

[84]   Murdoch, *The Sovereignty of Good*, p. 47. On how a woman 'unfinds herself' through exile from her social identity, see Le Doeuff, *Hipparchia's Choice*, p. 206; cf. Judith Butler, 'Beside Oneself: On the Limits of Sexual Freedom', *Undoing Gender* (London: Routledge, 2004), pp. 19–39.

[85]   If we follow Le Doeuff's argument, then this multiplicity of specific concrete situations of (un)selfing would be most evident in the times and places in history when and where women's 'identity' in reality make up 'a collective disarray,' see Le Doeuff, *Hipparchia's Choice*, p. 207.

[86]   For the image of a 'wiser lover' as opposed to a denuded self, see the conclusion to this essay and Murdoch, *The Sovereignty of Good*, p. 47. For a theological inquiry concerning 'the place' of wisdom, see Paul Fiddes, 'The quest for a place which is "not-a-place": the hiddenness of God and the presence of God', in Oliver Davies and Denys Turner (eds), *Silence and the Word: Negative Theology and Incarnation* (Cambridge: Cambridge University Press, 2002), pp. 35–60.

[87]   Le Doeuff, *Hipparchia's Choice*, pp. 128–133 and 243. For her more recent account of the means by which institutions perpetuate male-dominated spaces of knowledge and knowing, see Michèle Le Doeuff, *The Sex of Knowing*, trans. Kathryn Hamer and Lorraine Code (London: Routledge, 2003).

possible an intersubjectivity. This is not a subjectivity turned back on itself but an intersubjectivity that ensures the realism of our reasons and our loves.

As explained in previous chapters, this re-visioning is indebted to bell hooks and to Adrienne Rich. In addition, the political dimension of a longing to share passions and create ways to enhance our common humanity has been powerfully developed in the twenty-first-century writings of Judith Butler, notably, in 'Longing for Recognition'.[88] To recall bell hooks's words,

> there are many individuals with race, gender, and class privilege who are longing to see the kind of revolutionary change that will end domination and oppression even though their lives would be completely and utterly transformed.[89]

This revolutionary longing can unite subjects across gender, sexual, racial and class divides. Yet the active quality of a longing for recognition retains both the realism and the risk of inter-subjectivity. Risk derives from the ambivalence of human embodiment, sliding from good to evil, from justice and beauty to oppression and death.

Amy Hollywood's conception of aesthetic and spiritual practices of religious women helps feminist philosophers recognize, with illustrations from the history of Christian mysticism, how – and why – ethical and spiritual dispositions have shaped women and men as they have in relation to the ambivalence of human embodiment. Hollywood conceives a positive ethical formation, or a formative practice (*askesis*), as follows:

> ... one becomes a certain kind of person, responds bodily, affectively and intellectually in certain ways, and comes to hold certain beliefs by engaging in certain prescribed behaviors.

> ... in the later Middle Ages ... women did find ways to associate their suffering bodies and souls with that of Christ, other contemporary practices and discourses suggest that at least some men mistrusted these identifications and argued that women should identify, not with Christ on the cross, but with Mary at the foot of the cross. Often couched in terms of concern for the danger done to women's bodies by their excessive suffering and asceticism.

---

[88] Butler, 'Longing for Recognition', *Undong Gender*, pp. 131–151. It should be noted that the women philosophers under discussion, including Beauvoir, Irigaray, Le Doeuff, Butler and bell hooks each engaging critically with twentieth-century re-readings of Hegel's paradigm of master and slave relations, including this as a problematic paradigm for husband and wife relations, in which one subject dominates the other. For Beauvoir's Hegelian background, see Nancy Bauer, *Simone de Beauvoir, Philosophy, & Feminism* (New York: Columbia University Press, 2001).

[89] hooks, *Yearning*, pp. 12–13.

> … Thus we can see the ways in which prescriptions for bodily and meditative practice can both depend on and shape gender ideologies.[90]

Hollywood's examples from the writings by and reports of medieval women and men can be read as part of a collective historical experience in philosophy of religion.

Conclusion

It is crucial to my argument that the tradition of philosophy is discursive: that is, it engages critically with the reading of the texts which make up the collective historical experience of not only men, but women. Reason works through texts as much as in life to develop a collective consciousness across recorded history and contemporary cultures; we share passions and learn new practices. To be able to re-vision love and reason it has been first necessary to recognize the intense gendering of the imagery, narrative, and un-thought elements in the texts of philosophy and religion. The gendering of deeply embodied dispositions, that is, of emotions, desires and beliefs about life become apparent in the critical analysis of historical texts by individual men and women. Philosophical vigilance is necessary here: we need to pay critical attention to expressions of doubt and longing; these expressions shape us individually but also join us together.

In generating distinctively collective practices of loving and reasoning across former barriers, we discover the conditions for understanding and reformulating a discursive tradition in 'contemporary philosophy of religion'. Re-visioning gender in philosophy takes place as we come together in solitude and in dialogue with the texts of women and men who motivate us to give expression to their loves and their longings. The ethical formations of subjects take place as we see with fresh eyes and struggle to change ourselves in relation to nature and to all those who share that nature with us. Incarnation and inter-subjectivity are assumed as the two requirements for being bodied and for being able to share across the boundaries of gender, religion, race and class; we share incarnate passions, but we also share intersubjective reasons for actions. Philosophy of religion needs to include the passions and the reasons which motivate and guide, respectively, our practically worked out projects. In this light, philosophers of religion have a twofold task: to confront and, as need be, to transform the oppressive ways we have, or have not, been constituted emotionally and cognitively by a discursive tradition which, nevertheless, holds the possibility for a positive ethical formation of subjects in and through our spiritual practices.

---

[90]   Hollywood, 'Practice, Belief in Feminist Philosophy of Religion', pp. 233–240.

Chapter 10
Epistemic Locatedness:
Diversity and Gender[1]

Introduction

This book began with a critical exploration of the myths of patriarchy. These are the myths and associated imagery which have inhibited and often prohibited women from writing philosophy and theology. Even when women's education enabled them to write, it was thought to be simply beyond women's cognitive ability to create ideas of their own about the divine, the human and divine-human, or even human-human, relations. Women who acquired knowledge of good and evil were also feared, especially when they were associated with patriarchal religious myths about Eve or Lilith. The Christian imagery of 'the fall' has tied women to the 'evils' of sexual seduction, inordinate desire and sinfulness. In the extreme case, a woman is equated with the impurities of her flesh, and her 'sex' with the stain of original sin. Eve's seduction of Adam who represents every man has made sinless men not only fear the desire of and for women, but blame her sex for its power to seduce him to sin. The blaming of woman for all that has gone wrong in life can, then, take many forms and not least of all abuse and rape. But the disinheritance of women's philosophical ideas and contributions to philosophical theology is another kind of abuse; women have been the knowers who were never acknowledged as knowing, the thinkers with novel ideas which were taken from them to give status and credibility to husbands, lovers and heads of house as, in a colloquial label, 'the boss'. In this way, tackling myths of patriarchy which have been embedded in religions and in philosophy was absolutely necessary as a prerequisite to re-visioning gender in philosophy of religion.

Le Doeuff has called the space in philosophical texts where we find stories about men and women, myths about divine and human, imagery and asides about male omniscience and female humility, 'the philosophical imaginary'. We are indebted to Le Doeuff for demonstrating so well what has been thought to be peripheral to the rigour of rational argumentation is in fact necessary for that rigour and rational coherence. This is the place in which women appear and support even the most self-sufficient philosopher: he has needed her to admire his work, to

---

[1] An earlier version of Chapter 10 appears as 'A Feminist Perspective', in Chad Meister (ed.), *The Oxford Handbook of Religious Diversity* (Oxford: Oxford University Press, 2011), pp. 405–420.

correct his mistakes and to disappear as necessary like the ink in the margins of his texts.

A generic feature of patriarchy's myths has always been the configuration, in the terms of Donna Haraway, 'humanity's face' as 'the face of man'. Haraway contends that

> Feminist humanity must have another shape, other gestures; but, I believe, we must have feminist figures of humanity. They cannot be man or woman; they cannot be the human as historical narrative has staged that generic universal.[2]

In the course of this book it has become readily apparent that gender can never be understood without an awareness of our material and social conditioning and, in turn, this raises the question of our epistemic locatedness. Gender necessarily intersects with religion, race, ethnicity, class, sexual orientations; this intersectionality marks each human subject socially and materially; as a result, the gender of the subject of knowledge plays a crucial role in determining epistemic norms. Here it is not only 'religion' as a generic term, but religions as intersecting factors in gender identities which *must* be considered, if we are to understand how the gendering of our epistemic norms shape debates about religious diversity. The '*must*' in the previous sentence would apply insofar as the philosopher is concerned with epistemic justice. The present chapter approaches the question of epistemic norms for gender and religion indirectly by considering the relationship between feminist identity and religious diversity debates in contemporary philosophy of religion. In turn, these debates will reveal the critical role of our epistemic locatedness in how we reason about our most fundamental values, including those of goodness, God and love.

Even if a philosopher is unconcerned about justice, disagreements over religious diversity in philosophy of religion are as unavoidable in the twenty-first century, as the role that gender plays in negotiating human identity (or identities) across a globally diverse world. So, a simple concern for clarity and coherence should also be enough to motivate a philosopher of religion to consider the question of gender identity and religious diversity. The next section will consider a feminist perspective on this question.

A feminist on religious diversity

A feminist perspective on religious diversity goes to the very heart of the movement and waves of feminism(s); and it faces an inherent paradox of identity and diversity. A feminist claims an identity. Yet it remains unclear how we identify

---

2   Donna Haraway, 'Ecce Homo, Ain't (Ar'n't) I a Woman, and Inappropriate/d Others: The Human in a Post-Humanist Landscape', in Judith Butler and Joan Scott (eds), *Feminists Theorize the Political* (New York: Routledge, 1996), p. 88.

a woman or a man as 'a feminist'. At the same time as identity is both necessary and problematic, diversity is the reality generated from the differences between individual women and between groups of women. The questions of identity and its relation to diversity feed the ongoing debates about women and their relations to, or differences from, men but also about their relations to other women, and men's relations to men.

Ongoing disagreement on the 'nature' of gender and gender's intersection with other social and material variables is found in and between religions due to diverse beliefs about human beings generally. So an extremely complex dimension of religious diversity is constituted by the various assumptions about women and men inherent within a religion and between religions. These assumptions vary partly because differences of race, ethnicity, sexual orientation, class conditioning render gender a cultural variable. Even when a particular religion has assumed that gender is based on a shared, universal (human) nature and a fixed sexual orientation, it can conceal essentially contestable assumptions about women; their gender and sex are difficult, if not impossible to distinguish. At the same time, gender identity and diversity are intimately linked to religious norms; in other words, we have the complicated intersections of gender with religious conditioning. The latter conditioning is apparent in the former assumptions about the human situation or, as Haraway says, 'humanity's face' has been the face of man; as we have seen with some feminist philosophers of religion such as Mary Daly: God's face has been equally the face of man's ideal.

Moreover, when it comes to debates about religious diversity, a significant common issue for our global world is the question of the salvation, liberation or fulfilment of human beings. Religious diversity raises a question about what is or is not shared by religions. Generally speaking, each religion gives its own often conflicting (as compared to another religion's) answers to, 'what is wrong with humanity, how can we solve the problem?' A feminist perspective raises a similar question to this one about humanity; but the feminist will also ask the more gender-critical question which exposes the gender-bias of the dominant conception of the human situation as the humanity-problem of religions. This bias emerges in the exclusion, in some form or other, of women as the obstacle to 'human' (when it is really about man's) salvation, liberation or other ultimate fulfilment. A religion's solution to the human problem has (often) required the separation of man from woman, insofar as she has been variously construed as the source of sin, bodily defilement, inordinate desire or worse.

So a feminist perspective, its paradox of identity and diversity, contains domains interlinking with gender, including the social domains in a religiously diverse world; intersectional nature of gender characterizes the human situation, its problem and solution. The question of religious diversity alongside the intersectionality of gender raises the philosophical question of truth. This could be the truth on which a religion establishes its practices and beliefs. But this is also the 'truth' that will be essentially contested[3] by what was identified in the concluding section of Chapter 6, a feminist standpoint.

Of course, a 'feminist' standpoint is not the same as a 'feminine' perspective; the latter may or may not be feminist, depending on 'who' (which subject), or which religion, defines 'the feminine'. Religions also disagree on whether or not femininity is determined by nature and/or by culture. Religions differ on this question of nature or culture as much, if not more, than feminists who have different perspectives on the matter. The fact that our conception of femininity depends on the question of gender and/or sex tends to obscure the truth.

For purposes of clarity, it will be assumed in this concluding chapter that what distinguishes 'a feminist perspective' is its political focus for women: to expose the falsehoods about women and those relations that denigrate and/or oppress humanity. For example, a feminist might seek to eliminate the false beliefs about gender in the Christian religion; the oppressive structure of male privilege – known as Christian patriarchy – extends its gender-deception to racism, homophobia, ethno-centrism, age-ism and so on. The paradox of identity and diversity renders any feminist perspective on religious diversity a matter of truth; but, in this context, truth is complex and requires teasing out. As will become more apparent, the crucial epistemic norm in debates about feminisms and religions cannot be simplicity. Instead, if truth is to be sought for a feminist perspective on religious diversity, then the epistemic norms must be flexible enough to include the complexity of the diverse relations of men to women, but also of men to socially and/or materially different men and women to socially and/or materially different women. Truth is necessary any time a feminist asks whether human relations involve inhuman or unjust treatment due to gender differences; this includes relations of privileged men both to women and to less privileged men; of patriarchal women both to non-privileged men and other less priviledged women, etc.

Epistemic issues are at the cutting edge of feminist debates in the twenty-first century;[4] and they are integral to the present paradox. On the one hand, a feminist perspective is not able to avoid – at least not for long – confronting diversity. Arguably, religious diversity is one of the most significant reasons for a large and diverse range of assumptions about women and gender; and this diversity inevitably feeds into the complexity of a feminist perspective. So, religions have had a great role to play in constituting our gender relations, knowledge and understanding. On the other hand, a feminist perspective has to assume an identity that will ensure its own coherence as a politics *for women*. So, questions of truth about gender, like religious truth claims about the human situation, cannot avoid epistemic issues of

---

[3]   W. B. Gallie, 'Essentially Contested Concepts', *Proceedings of the Aristotelian Society*, 56 (1955–56), pp. 167–198; Alan Montefiore, 'A Note Concerning "Essentially Contestable" Concepts', unpublished paper, 2011.

[4]   Alison Assiter, *Revisiting Universalism* (New York: Palgrave Macmillan, 2003), Chapters 6–8; Miranda Fricker, *Epistemic Injustice: Power and the Ethics of Knowing* (Oxford: Oxford University Press, 2007), pp. 147ff.

simplicity and complexity; universality and individuality; particular and general; equality and difference. If false beliefs of a certain kind are endemic in a society due to its systems of religious belief, the epistemic inertia – that is, the resistance to recognizing and giving up false beliefs – will be very powerful indeed.[5]

Even though diversity renders impossible one and only one feminist perspective, it can still be argued that a feminist at a minimum makes some universal claim about women (for instance, a claim about the minimal needs of all women), transcending the gender-relations of different religions. The quotation from Haraway in the introductory section of this chapter captures a widely embraced feminist view that (i) in the past 'humanity' has not been gender-neutral but has been 'the face of man'; and that (ii) 'feminist figures of humanity' cannot be a woman or a man.[6] Instead of a fixed-gender, these feminist 'figures' could represent the political problem of truth for religious diversity: that is, we must have more than one feminist figure of humanity precisely because of our epistemic locatedness and the intersectionality of gender across religions.

Religious diversity: a matter of truth

The philosophical question is whether truth can be plural. Can truth inhabit the different figures of humanity constituting the diversity of religions? It could be argued that the truth of humanity's situation is independent of the contingent 'truths' about gender within diverse religions. Yet (how) can the truth of a feminist perspective on religious diversity be independent of our figures of the human? It would be simple if we could choose one configuration of humanity; but at least for a feminist, it is an urgent concern of truth and justice that the gender of 'the human' differs, often unwittingly, according to religion and the gender-differentials of race, class, ethnicity, sexual orientation – each of which feed into social and material conditioning.

It is not unproblematic to make a descriptive claim about the complexity of gender due to the embedded nature of systems of religious beliefs, including diverse beliefs about women, in our different social worlds. Religious, like cultural, configurations of humanity and the human are necessarily plural; and with this plurality goes the diversity of gender. Again, the example of Haraway is helpful to illustrate that figures of humanity could be unproblematic, if merely descriptive of human diversity. This description of human diversity could also suggest that we cannot capture the complete truth about humanity from any one location or from any one gender position. The point of the example would, then, be that as soon as we equate humanity with man or woman, we reduce and distort the truth.

---

[5]   Neil C. Manson, 'Epistemic Inertia and Epistemic Isolationism', *Journal of Applied Philosophy*, 26/3 (2009): 294–298.

[6]   Haraway, 'Ecce Homo, Ain't (Ar'n't) I a Woman, and Inappropriate/d Others', p. 86.

In the following, Haraway's focus is both epistemological and ethical and as such, offers a ground for feminist politics:

> My focus is the figure of a broken and suffering humanity, signifying – in ambiguity, contradiction, stolen symbolism, and unending chains of non-innocent translation – a possible hope. But also signifying an unending series of mimetic and counterfeit events implicated in the great genocides and holocausts of ancient and modern history. But, it is the very non-originality, mimesis, mockery, and brokenness that draw me to this figure and its mutants.[7]

This feminist picture of 'non-originality' in the changing figures of 'a broken and suffering humanity' poses a serious challenge to those philosophers of religious diversity who, on the basis of their rationally justified or warranted religious beliefs, insist upon an 'objective' and 'exclusive' view of what it is to be human (and to believe in God). A feminist philosopher like Haraway and those who agree with her would not only question the gender-neutrality that has been assumed in some of the strongest claims of contemporary religious philosophers to truth, but point to the suffering (for instance, 'the genocides and holocausts'), that indicate the brokenness of human reality due to the blind privileging of one race, religion, class, ethnicity or sexual orientation. This is not a picture of a certain truth, or of a confident hope, in the salvation of humanity. Instead, Haraway's reconfiguration(s) of hope in a broken and suffering humanity could not be more different to the confident assurance of human salvation in the traditional Christian theism of a religious exclusivist like Alvin Plantinga. And yet both Plantinga and Haraway raise a serious matter of truth.

Plantinga presents the problem of religious diversity in terms of truth without any comment on the gender of the human being. But he clearly assumes something about the nature of the human in the second of his two major claims for the exclusivity of religious belief.[8] His gender assumption about the 'divine' is clear; God must be a father since Plantinga refers to 'his' divine son. The philosopher of religion John Hick similarly does not raise any question of gender, assuming male-'neutrality', in discussing religious diversity; but surely gender-bias as much as gender-constructions add to the problems of religious identity. Are women, figures of the human or of the divine, the same in any way across religions? Although Hick

---

[7]   Haraway, 'Ecce Homo, Ain't (Ar'n't) I a Woman, and Inappropriate/d Others', p. 87; cf. Pamela Sue Anderson, 'Myth and Feminist Philosophy', in Kevin Schilbrack (ed.), *Thinking Through Myths: Philosophical Perspectives* (New York and London: Routledge, 2002), pp. 112–118.

[8]   Alvin Plantinga, 'Pluralism: A Defense of Religious Exclusivism', in Thomas Senor (ed.), *The Rationality of Belief and the Plurality of Faith* (Ithaca, NY: Cornell University Press, 1995); reprinted in Chad Meister (ed.), *The Philosophy of Religion Reader* (New York and London: Routledge, 2008), pp. 41–42.

supports a plurality of religions rather than the exclusivist position of Plantinga on religious truth, the former agrees that

> in contemporary philosophy of religion it is customary to use the tripartite distinction between exclusivism, inclusivism, and pluralism. ... note that the entire discussion [of religious diversity] can be conducted in terms of truth claims or salvation claims or both.[9]

In light of the strength and popularity of Plantinga's philosophical defence of one religion and one truth, let us consider his account of exclusivism.

Religious exclusivism: dangerous truth and gender-blindness

In some circles, a more positive label for a position similar to religious exclusivism in its rejection of a so-called liberal political view of universally shared norms or, simply universals that transcend the particularities of diverse forms of religious traditions, is 'particularism'. The critical relation between universalism and particularism is helpfully addressed by a feminist philosopher, Alison Assiter; but she argues for revisiting universalism in ethics and epistemology.[10] In sharp contrast, we have Plantinga's position which he names for himself as follows:

> There are several possible reactions to awareness of religious diversity. One is to continue to believe what you have all along believed; you learn about this diversity but continue to believe, that is, take to be true, such propositions as (1) [The world was created by God, an almighty, all-knowing, and perfectly good personal being (one that holds beliefs; has aims, plans, and intentions; and can act to accomplish these aims).] and (2) [Human beings require salvation, and God has provided a unique way of salvation through the incarnation, life, sacrificial death, and resurrection of his divine son.] consequently taking to be false any beliefs, religious or otherwise, that are incompatible with (1) and (2). Following current practice, I call this *exclusivism*; the exclusivist holds that the tenets or some of the tenets of one religion – Christianity, let's say – are in fact true; he adds, naturally enough, that any propositions, including other religious beliefs, that are incompatible with those tenets are false.[11]

---

9   John Hick, 'Religious Pluralism', in Chad Meister and Paul Copan (eds), *The Routledge Companion to Philosophy of Religion* (New York and London: Routledge, 2007), p. 216. For an account of different forms of religious inclusivism, see Joseph Runzo, 'Religious Pluralism', in Paul Copan and Chad Meister (eds), *Philosophy of Religion: Classic and Contemporary Issues* (Oxford: Blackwell Publishing, 2008), pp. 51–66.

10   Assiter, *Revisiting Universalism*, pp. 4–5, 109–110.

11   Plantinga, 'Pluralism: A Defense', p. 42.

Even without any discussion of the gender-blind assumptions in the propositions above, the epistemic structure that is fixed by the 'truth' of Plantinaga's own religious (Christian) exclusivism only allow for one truth and every other claim to truth, whether exclusivist, particularist or, even, universalist would be false. The epistemic injustice of this system would seem to render the religious exclusivist truth 'unjust' from the start.

However, if Plantinga contended that justice is always on the side of the exclusivist truth, then the next line of questioning could go as follows. What are the epistemic pathways for the formation of the religious exclusivist's beliefs about, as in the block quotation above, 'God' and 'the unique way of salvation' for (some) human beings? How can the religious exclusivist justify 'his' religious knowledge or, as Plantinga might say, 'warrant' Christian belief rationally to the philosopher who does not share the Christian 'faith'? Insisting that certain kinds of beliefs – or, belief-like attitudes to Plantinga's propositions (1) and (2) above – must be maintained does not appear to allow for a dogmatic fideist assertion. This line of questioning aims to suggest that fundamental questions of truth are blocked by the epistemic structure of this debate by the religious exclusivist control of the truth. This suggestion is re-enforced by the fact that contrary to otherwise good evidence, such as found in the conflicting truth claims of epistemologists holding different religious beliefs, the Christian exclusivist renders (his) core beliefs, in its structure of religious beliefs, exempt from revision or question.

In this light, Plantinga's religious exclusivist must also assume that people with, or without, Christian faith are separated from each other by a moral partition; those with faith know the truth and are saved. But this underpins an arguably pernicious assumption about the variation of moral status within the human species. In turn, this assumption of moral status creates an epistemic inertia to prevent the questioning of basic religious beliefs. For instance, this epistemic situation would reinforce the teaching (of a child) that there are serious penalties – horrific and eternal – for a lack of faith. Paradoxically, the obstacles to truth in a position of religious exclusivism are not only serious ethically, but are at the level of epistemic concerns which otherwise would be a preoccupation of such philosophers of religion as Plantinga. The question is why this epistemic blindness is not recognized in its full extent, including the distinctive implications of certain core beliefs for women.

A strange sort of epistemic blindness allows a serious variability in the moral status of humans who differ according to faith, or lack of faith. And this blindness is extended to gender, especially to the gender-blindness perpetuated by a religious upbringing that protects certain sources of pernicious epistemic inertia. The problem for the religious exclusivist is that this inertia – along with a range of false beliefs – might only be recognized by learning to see from the point of view of the excluded.

For instance, Fatima Mernissi illustrates how conservative religious men either force or allow women in Islamic societies with serious economic and gender inequalities to maintain deceptively strange practices – on the basis of false religious beliefs about gender and relevant biological facts – in order to secure the male status required by the norms of their patriarchal society. In her example, men must control, or think that they control, 'the movements of women related to him by blood or by marriage, and by forbidding them any contact with male strangers'.[12] The contentious religious norm is a bride's virginity in Islam (but the same norm, though in a different religious context might be upheld by a Roman Catholic or other conservative Christians). To maintain a religious belief about the rightness of this norm, the contemporary (Islamic) woman may go to great lengths to deceive, with the help of modern technology, her future husband. As Mernissi explains, 'artifices of the most up-to-date medical technology are placed at the service of the age-old imperatives of the patriarchal family' when it comes to upholding the role of virginity in patriarchal societies where some forms of modernization are completely acceptable.[13] The deception is telling in this passage:

> It is no secret that when some marriages are consummated, the virginity of the bride is artificial . ... young women ... resort to a minor operation on the eve of their wedding in order to erase the traces of pre-marital experience. Before embarking on the traditional ceremonies of virginal modesty and patriarchal innocence, the young woman has to get a sympathetic doctor to wreak a magical transformation.[14]

A combination of out-dated religious beliefs about female sexuality and no understanding between the sexes not only undermines religious claims to truth, but perpetuates violence and often tragic outcomes of a failure of contemporary religions to counteract the epistemic inertia posed by religious assumptions concerning women, men and the human situation.

Myth and imagination in pursuit of truth

To tackle these false beliefs and contradictory practices, I have (already) put forward a feminist argument for employing imaginative variations, or a disruptive miming, of traditional myths, especially mythical configurations of women's relations to men, family, private and public social norms.[15] The point of such mimesis is to expose sexism (which intersects with gender, race and other social and material mechanisms) coming to recognize, by contrast to what has been

---

[12]   Fatima Mernissi, *Women's Rebellion and Islamic Memory* (London: Zed Books Ltd. 1996), p. 34.

[13]   Ibid., p. 35.

[14]   Ibid., p. 34.

[15]   Anderson, *A Feminist Philosophy of Religion*, pp. 78–83, 128–129, 135ff; Assiter, *Revisiting Universalism*, pp. 93–96, 102–108.

assumed, the truth that has been hidden. This feminist argument for introducing myth and mimesis into contemporary philosophy of religion has been met by a lack of understanding on behalf of those analytic philosophers of religion who find truth only in the rigour, clarity and gender-neutrality of their arguments rather than in being able to discover 'truth' through the imagining of real figures of a broken and suffering humanity.[16] Whether recognized by traditional philosophers of religion or not, the social and moral epistemology deriving from engagement with recent philosophical debates, say, in feminist epistemology, continues to give support to the idea that myth can have a productive role.[17] Miming myths can help both in coming to see the problems of gender injustice in the context of religious diversity and in imagining new possibilities for perennial myths of gender. Arguably the most sexist of myths can be exposed and reconfigured, in order to tackle the gender-blindness which is most resistant to change in debates about religious exclusivism, inclusivism and pluralism.

Yet worryingly gender injustice can persist, often in another form, even when history forces women and men to bring about a transformation in gender identity. We might show how the religious exclusivist's conception of the truth about women and men can merely be used to shift the object of his or her abuse by shifting the object of their beliefs, for example, about sin and human salvation. When this happens, then gender and racial injustice will still be ratified in the name of religious truth.

Not unlike the exercise of miming myths disruptively, we can turn to narrative interpretations of historical instances which lend themselves to more than one level of interpretation. Consider the role of narrative interpretations in an example of how a religious exclusivist perception of the truth about female gender is transformed on one level; but on another level, a narrative reveals how the same exclusivist merely shifts the object of his sadistic misogyny by shifting the object of his belief. Both the gendering and the continuing violence associated with religious-based misogyny depend upon social and material variables determining the lives of men and women. As seen in Chapter 6, the intersection of gender, race and religion shaping both the nature of transformation and the reasons for ongoing violence are creatively developed in the narratives making up bell hooks's first publication, *Ain't I a Woman?*[18]

---

[16]   Sarah Coakley, 'Feminism and Analytic Philosophy of Religion', in William Wainwright (ed.), *The Oxford Handbook to Philosophy of Religion* (Oxford: Oxford University Press, 2005), pp. 512–516.

[17]   Anderson, 'Myth and Feminist Philosophy', pp. 112–122; Seyla Benhabib, *The Claims of Culture: Equality and Diversity in the Global Era* (New York: Princeton University Press, 2002), pp. 97, 100–104; Assiter, *Revisiting Universalism*, pp. 93, 109–110, 114–125, 128–145; Fricker, *Epistemic Injustice*, pp. 131–151.

[18]   For an earlier discussion of the mythical figure of Sojourner Truth, see Anderson, 'Myth and Feminist Philosophy', pp. 115–118; cf. hooks *Ain't I a Woman?*, pp. 159–160.

hooks also illustrates in graphic details, a specific, nineteenth-century Christian transformation in the gendering of women in the USA. Religion and gender intersected initially changing the perception of a white woman from being a guilty, sinful sexual temptress to becoming an innocent, virtuous (virtually) sexless goddess. But hooks makes clear that this gendering of a white woman as a 'goddess rather than sinner' was not the whole story. The gendering of black women took place as at the same time as the 'virtuous, pure, innocent, not sexual and worldly' white woman emerged: the black woman becomes the sexual temptress, or Jezebel.[19] In fact, hooks suggested that an economic shift in white Christian lives which resulted in the misogyny and suffering of white women being shifted onto black women.[20] Yet this is still not the whole story because it was also a shift in religious beliefs about sin that renders the non-white woman as the female temptress. So gender not only intersects with race but with religion, transforming the gender of black women as socially and materially marked for severe and persistent violence. At the extreme, religious exclusivist claims to truth about (some 'Christian') women can actually re-enforce epistemic injustice rather than be the grounds for challenging sexual and racial abuse.

Ain't I a Woman? works on many levels of interrelated narratives, of history and myth, of race and class, of gender and sex, of religion and slavery. Crucial for re-visioning gender in philosophy of religion is hooks's ability to portray in narratives the intersectionality of gender and race, gender and religion. Her portraits raise the question of epistemic locatedness and its relevance for telling the truth about violence.[21] In her narratives, we see how material and social locations can either protect or fail to protect a woman. This would be equally the case for a man who suffers unjust treatment on the grounds of race, class or sexual orientation. hooks graphically shows us how a woman can suffer epistemic injustice which is unaltered by the 'rational' justification of truth claims by a religious exclusivist. For instance, a Christian fundamentalist with misogynist beliefs finds an object for abuse justifying sexual violence so to speak 'rationally', while retaining racist and sexist myths concerning their object or subject of abuse. In this way. the myths of gender, race and religion have wittingly or not accompanied the Christian system of religious beliefs, even as this system varies from a fundamentalist to a more liberal construal of Christianity.

Ain't I a Woman? bristles with pain, insight and irony, exposing the truth of Christian misogyny and its historical embeddedness in the American institutions of religion and slavery. In hooks's words, 'In fundamentalist Christian teaching woman was portrayed as an evil sexual temptress, the bringer of sin into the world. Sexual lust originated with her and men were merely the victims of her wanton

---

[19] Ibid., p. 31.

[20] Ibid.

[21] Kimberlé Crenshaw, 'Mapping the Margins: Intersectionality, Identity Politics, and Violence against Women of Color', *Stanford Law Review*, 43 (1991): 1241–1279.

power.'[22] hooks captures a Christian practice of projecting sin and inordinate desire onto women which culminated in the projection of hatred of all sexuality onto the enslaved black woman. The urgency in re-visioning gender in philosophy of religion is nowhere more justified than in hooks's argument that the epitome of brokenness and suffering becomes the heart of the sexist-racist myth about the human problem of sin; the myth's solution is salvation for those men who punish and destroy the dangerous object of their desires.

With clear theological, social, material and personal reasons, hooks offers white women an explanation for why they would allow other women to suffer in their place for sins which neither groups of women had committed. Sin was merely attributed to one gender and race by those in power who lived in fear so tortured others. The process of reconfiguring the anti-woman myth into the anti-black-woman myth is the flip side to the supposed solution to the problem of humanity: men are saved from sin by punishing the figure of a sinner, and so protecting themselves from evil and damnation.

However, this chapter began with the confident claim that truth matters and so, too, does justice. If so, then philosophers of religion must ask questions about epistemic injustice and the dangers of being blind to gender biases. Christian religion like any other religion is suspectible to atrocities done in the name of innocence and virtue. 'Truth' cannot only be an outcome of rigorous argument, it requires understanding of the social and personal biases of gender-blind men and of sexist-racist women to their own sexual violence and injustice. It is not clear why religious smugness, as in (over)confidence in one's personal salvation, has stood for truth. But philosophers of religion have the analytical, critical and practical tools to address questions of injustice parading as truth and of violence concealing its agency.

Diversity and a prophetic voice

The feminist message in western debates about religions has often been prophetic. In the spirit of biblical prophets, a voice calls for justice and righteousness condemning those men and 'their white women' who fail to recognize and atone for their evil acts and shocking misogyny. Unsurprisingly, feminists from various religious perspectives, whether Hindu, Buddhist, Jewish, Muslim or Christian (in its various forms), have voiced their concerns about gender injustice on issues of diversity within and outside of a religion.[23] But consider Rita Gross's telling reflection on western feminism's legacy in the appropriation of diverse religions:

---

[22]   hooks, *Ain't I a Woman?*, p. 29.

[23]   For examples, see ibid., pp. 108–113; Mernissi, *Women's Rebellion and Islamic Memory*, pp. 92–108; Martha Nussbaum, 'Religion and Women's Human Rights', *Sex and Social Justice* (Oxford: Oxford University Press, 1999), pp. 82–84; Saba Mahmood, *Politics of Piety: The Islamic Revival and the Feminist Subject* (New York: Princeton

Western feminism clearly was in continuity with the prophetic stream found in the Hebrew Bible, and, to a lesser extent in my view, in the New Testament. There is no similar stream in Buddhist thought. [Its] social ethic takes a form different from active confrontation with injustice and calls for reform of the social-political order. ... I am especially interested in what might result from a serious conversation between the Buddhist emphasis on compassion and the Christian prophetic emphasis on justice and righteousness.

... [But] Buddhists' reactions to [this] caught me by surprise. [Their] distaste for the prophetic voice itself, claims that it is strident and oppressive, that it promotes intolerance, self-righteousness, and sometimes violence.[24]

Clearly personal appropriations of the 'emphasis' of different religions do not lessen the conflict of diverse religious truth-claims. But when Rosemary Radford Ruether responds to Gross (as above), she proposes a different conceptualization of relations between diverse religions:

Unlike Rita, who was first a Christian who then converted to Judaism before finding her primary identity in Buddhism, I have not journeyed through affiliation with several religions. But I have explored a number of religions, starting with the ancient Near Eastern and Greek religious worlds, and then Judaism, Buddhism and Islam. ... In my explorations of religious world views, I have come to think of three major paradigms of religion: first, sacralization of nature, seen in seasonal and life cycles; second, prophetic, historical religions; and third, contemplative religions of inward transformation. There may be more paradigms than these, or other ways of naming them, but these are what I have identified. ... With new challenges, people may desire to renew one of the paradigms that has faded from the tradition of their upbringing.[25]

From the above, it is clear that Ruether and Gross each approach religious diversity from a (woman's) perspective that is highly personal and seriously committed to the truth found by and for herself in a particular religion that is seen as modifiable with insights from other religions. Each woman's autobiography is shaped in large part by her own distinctive reflections on different religions. However, the philosophical problem with this is that the personal nature of these reflections

---

University Press, 2005), pp. 104–117; Dorota Filipczak, *Unheroic Heroines: The Portrayal of Women in the Writings of Margaret Laurence* (Lodz, Poland: Wydawnictwo Uniwersytetu Lodzkiego, 2007), pp. 349–381.

[24]   Rita M. Gross and Rosemary Radford Ruether, *Religious Feminism and the Future of the Planet: A Buddhist-Christian Conversation* (New York: Continuum, 2001), pp. 164–165.

[25]   Gross and Reuther, *Religious Feminism*, p. 183.

may avoid the more difficult, ethical and epistemological questions of truth; these questions, however unanswerable, are necessary for a feminist politics – at least as conceived so far here.

Saba Mahmood is equally eager to voice her feminist concern for contemporary women's personal and social commitments to a traditional religion. The focus of Mahmood's concern is the Islamic practice of piety. However, she is keenly attentive to and highly critical of the politics of the contemporary liberal feminist. Mahmood argues against the dominant western, liberal feminist interpretations of women's relation to diverse religious practices, insisting that not all women are motivated by a desire for freedom, or by the subversion of traditional religious norms. Another example of the diverse motivations on a religious matter for women in Islam is *l'affaire du foulard* in France that reflects the complexity of 'truth' in an ongoing political situation of conflicting cultural, personal and religious norms.[26]

It needs to be stressed that Mahmood's original reading of Islamic women's politics is contentious for contemporary feminism and for liberal political theory generally. She illustrates brilliantly how a specific women's religious movement in Cairo, Egypt, significantly reconfigures the gendered practice of Islamic pedagogy and the social institution of mosques; and, crucially, she demonstrates that this particular women's movement cannot be based upon the liberal woman's freedom of choice. Instead she reveals how these particular Egyptian women desire submission to certain religious norms. To make sense of this desire as something different to a 'deplorable passivity and docility',[27] Mahmood attends to 'the specific logic of the discourse of piety', insisting that 'an appeal to understanding the coherence of a discursive tradition is neither to justify that tradition, nor to argue for some irreducible essentialism or cultural relativism'.[28] In other words, Mahmood's account of the ways in which women 'inhabit' the norms of a religion assumes a critique (that she finds in the feminist-queer theory of Judith Butler) of human agency understood in terms of a liberal political subject. The significant point is that Mahmood exposes the conflicting range of feminist perspectives on religions and gender justice. Unlike Martha Nussbaum, Mahmood does not draw on the well-known liberal feminist politics of religion and women's human rights);[29] and unlike Mernissi, Mahmood does not uncover the ways in which 'Islamic' women have subverted patriarchal norms in rebelling against oppressive gender practices. These different liberal, socialist and cultural (embodied and embedded) feminist politics generate a diverse range of feminist relations to religions. Nevertheless, a common concern for the *actual needs* and *practices of*

---

[26] For details of this example, read in terms of diversity in our 'global era' see Benhabib, *Claims of Culture*, pp. 94–104.

[27] Mahmood, *Politics of Piety*, p. 15.

[28] Ibid., p. 17.

[29] Martha Nussbaum, 'Religion and Women's Human Rights', *Sex and Social Justice* (Oxford: Oxford University Press, 1999), pp. 81–117.

women in the context of their religious traditions may be enough to give a feminist perspective an identity, while still allowing for religious diversity.

Epistemic norms

Women who have actually struggled for their own bodily integrity, their human dignity, their cognitive ability, their rational capabilities, their equal moral status, and/or their sexual difference may *understand* the seriousness of the personal and political debates about religious diversity better than those non-feminist philosophers of religion who offer an 'objective' account of diversity – whether in exclusive, inclusive or pluralist terms. Nevertheless, from the preceding sections, it is undeniable that truth matters to a feminist perspective; it matters just as much as, and at times more than, the truth claims of a religious exclusivist. Critical assessment of a religious commitment confronts a similar paradox of identity and diversity in aiming to bind diverse individuals and communities together. Religion binds individuals into communities both in shared ritual practices and in belief-motivated thinking and acting, while the relation of individual and community informs 'understanding feminism':

> The problem of differences among and within women provides a rich understanding of the complexity of individual identities and the complexity of group interactions … [I]t is emblematic of the necessity for feminist theory and practice to build complexity and the salience of intersecting oppressions into its core.[30]

At this point it is possible to answer some questions. How do the categories developed in discussions of religious diversity, notably those of religious exclusivism, inclusivism and pluralism, inform a feminist perspective on religious diversity?[31] Can a feminist perspective be inclusivist, exclusivist, pluralist or something else? A feminist perspective could force a defender of the truth of religious diversity to consider a different set of epistemic norms; that is, to make sense of the diversity of religions, while also uncovering a politics that is both *for* women and *against* the degrading myths of gender embedded in the systems of religious belief most resistant to change and self-criticism.

In the history of twentieth-century feminism alone, women's recognition of the interlinking of gender oppression with other mechanism of oppression has

---

[30]   Peta Bowden and Jane Mummery, *Understanding Feminism* (Stocksfield: Acumen Publishing Limited, 2009), p. 121.

[31]   A current argument on religious diversity against religious 'pluralism' as opposed to the positions of either exclusivism or inclusivism, see Jonathan L. Kvanvig, 'Religious Pluralism and the Buridan's Ass Paradox', *European Journal for Philosophy of Religion*, 1/1 (Spring 2009): 1–26.

forced some feminists to include in their projects resistance to all forms of social marginalization and exclusion. The result is that to have sufficient conditions for covering injustices against all kinds of women 'a feminist perspective' must include the 'how' and 'why' of feminist resistance to religious forms of gender exclusion, whether these are on the grounds of race, sexuality, ethnicity, class or other material and social differences. However, Mahmood offers a highly significant critical, dissenting voice in her exception to sweeping forms of resistance (by feminists) that fail to understand highly specific forms of women's religious practice.

Generally, without critical-imaginative exposure of the mythology of Christian misogyny and its destructive focus on enslaved black women, a feminist perspective on religions could have remained misguided and exclusionary. Without struggling constantly to distinguish and to understand reality from a feminist perspective, sexism could be easily shifted from one woman, or a group of women, to another. Prior to the generation of feminists enlightened by hooks, Mernissi and Mahmood, a feminist perspective could largely have neglected the challenge of race, class, sexual orientation and ethnicity to the white-privileged beliefs about women, but also the beliefs of women who simply accept the myths and the configurations of sin and salvation built on the exclusion of (some) women for the sake of other privileged women and men.

Prior to the 1980s and continuing today, much feminist attention focuses on the concrete problems of social oppression and embodiment, but this attention could also be revolutionized by use of the imagination to expose the myths and truth hidden by historical narratives that have excluded the distinctive reality of women's sexually or racially specific lives. hooks, Mernissi, Mahmood and other so-called 'third-wave' feminists, who are not merely concerned with liberal forms of equality and free choice (that is, so-called first-wave feminist concerns), or the sexual difference between women and men (that is, so-called second-wave feminist concerns), have transformed accounts of gender roles, knowledge and understanding.[32] This transformation includes confronting the diversity within a religion (for example, Christianity; Islam; Judaism) and between other global religions (for instance, Christianity-Judaism-Islam and Buddhism-Taoism-Confucian).

Conclusion

This chapter has aimed to capture the highly significant, critical and imaginative challenge of third-wave feminism in the question of epistemic locatedness, diversity and gender. A prophetic voice speaks clearly through this chapter; and this is only modified by the search for a critical feminist figure. As Haraway correctly asserts:

---

[32]   Anderson, 'Feminism and Patriarchy', pp. 816–817 n6.

the title of bell hooks's provocative 1981 book, echoing Sojourner Truth, *Ain't
I a Woman?*, bristles with irony as the identity of 'woman' is both claimed and
deconstructed simultaneously.[33]

Personified in bell hooks's figure of a 'woman' is the question of truth but also
of diversity and justice. A black woman dares to raise this question in hooks's
title (above) in a historical context of a women's rights movement where she was
forbidden to speak; this black woman forces the other (white) women present to
see and to hear the truth spoken; the renaming of this black woman as 'Sojourner
Truth' takes on the status of myth.[34] In this manner, historical-mythical imagination
produces the critical ground for a re-visioning of gender shaped by intersecting
relations with other social and material variables such as race, religion, sexual
orientation, class and so on. If we assume that religions themselves are structures
of both gender oppression and gender liberation, then whatever the different
religious claim about (the reality of) gender, of who we are as humans, as men and
as women, must be both variable and critical. The critical point is that religions
make claims about the human situation, the 'human' problem and its solution.
In so doing, they make implicit claims about gender; whether this means that
humanity is gender-neutral, or exclusive to men as essentially a different sex/
gender to women matters. Gender varies for both men and women, individually
and collectively, as well a between one another. Yet the question is whether a
suffering humanity the inclusive figure that we need to imagine and embrace?
Thinking beyond suffering and oppression remains a crucial feature of feminist
philosophy of religion as has been re-visioned in this book.

The question of religious diversity has, nevertheless, raised a timely feminist
issue which is not new: the face of humanity can no longer be the face of one
particular man. The often unwitting gender claims of every religion, especially
those embedded in myths of religious belief, continue to shape gender relations,
knowledge and understanding. The dangers of falsehoods about gender are the
exclusion, degradation and horrific treatment of individual women or specific
groups of women and some men, in the name of religious truth. Insofar as 'to
accept a religion' is to embrace some particular and connected account of the
human situation, its problem and solution, to accept 'a feminist perspective on
diversity and gender' is to embrace some account of what justice and truth would
mean for any gendered location. A range of feminists writing on religions enables
access to the myths about women and/or their sexuality, centrally, in Christian,
Jewish, Muslim, Buddhist, and Hindu contexts.

A crucial feature of feminism is the struggle both *against* reductively sexist
accounts of women's religious practices and *for* inclusive personal-social

---

[33] Haraway, 'Ecce Homo, Ain't (Ar'n't) I a Woman, and Inappropriate/d Others',
p. 93; cf. hooks, *Ain't I a Woman?*, pp. 3, 159–160; and Anderson, 'Myth and Feminist
Philosophy', pp. 115–116.
[34] See footnote 18 (above).

transformation of reality and its depiction insofar as false beliefs have obscured the truth about our lives as women and men. Too often religions have implicitly or explicitly justified the inordinate suffering of women due to sexist violence in this life with the hope for salvation in the next life. In contrast to the religious exclusivist, inclusivist and pluralist who each in their own way claims a soteriological truth about an afterlife, a feminist perspective more often than not allows for religiously diverse solutions to 'the so-called human problem', in order to expose obstacles to truth in this life. These obstacles include the epistemic norms that obscure the ways in which false beliefs and practices continue to denigrate women and non-privileged men with violence and abuse.

Ultimately, a feminist perspective on our epistemic locatedness seeks to re-vision the gender of every woman and every man so that gender relations can meet minimally just conditions for bodily integrity, personal dignity and social life, in which the natural needs of individual women and men, and those they love, can be met. Re-visioning gender in contemporary philosophy of religion is an individual and collective process; and this book has endeavoured to make this process move forward by elucidating the philosopher's reason, love and epistemic locatedness and by gradually changing the field.

Bibliography

Adams, Marilyn McCord, *Horrendous Evils and the Goodness of God* (Ithaca, NY: Cornell University Press, 1999).

Adams, Robert Merrihew Adams, 'Introduction', in Allen Wood and George di Giovanni (eds), *Religion within the Boundaries of Mere Reason and other Writings* (Cambridge: Cambridge University Press, 1998), pp. vii–xxxii.

Alcoff, Linda and Potter, Elizabeth (eds), *Feminist Epistemologies* (London: Routledge, 1993).

Altorf, Marije, *Iris Murdoch and the Art of Imagining.* Continuum Series in British Philosophy (London: Continuum, 2008).

Anderson, Pamela Sue, *A Feminist Philosophy of Religion: the Rationality and Myths of Religious Belief* (Oxford: Blackwell, 1998).

Anderson, Pamela Sue, 'Correspondence with Grace Jantzen', *Feminist Theology*, 25 (September 2000): 112–119.

Anderson, Pamela Sue, 'Writing on Exiles and Excess: Toward a New Form of Subjectivity', in Heather Walton and Andrew Hass (eds), *Self/Same/Other: Re-visioning the Subject in Literature and Theology* (Sheffield: Sheffield Academic Press, 2000), pp. 106–124.

Anderson, Pamela Sue, 'An Ethics of Memory: Promising, Forgiving and Yearning', in Graham Ward (ed.), *Blackwell's Companion to Postmodern Theology* (Oxford: Blackwell, 2001), pp. 231–248.

Anderson, Pamela Sue, 'Gender and the infinite: On the aspiration to be all there is', *International Journal for Philosophy of Religion*, Issues in Contemporary Philosophy of Religion on the Occasion of the 50th vol., no. 1–3 (December 2001): 191–212.

Anderson, Pamela Sue, 'Standpoint: Its Rightful Place in a Realist Epistemology', *Journal of Philosophical Research*, xxvi (2001): 131–154.

Anderson, Pamela Sue, 'Feminist Theology as Philosophy of Religion', in Susan Frank Parsons (ed.), *The Cambridge Companion to Feminist Theology* (Cambridge: Cambridge University Press, 2002), pp. 40–59.

Anderson, Pamela Sue, 'Ineffable Knowledge and Gender', in Philip Goodchild (ed.), *Rethinking Philosophy of Religion: Approaches from Continental Philosophy* (New York: Fordham University Press, 2002), pp. 162–183.

Anderson, Pamela Sue, 'Myth and Feminist Philosophy', in Kevin Schilbrack (ed.), *Thinking Through Myths: Philosophical Perspectives* (New York and London: Routledge, 2002), pp. 101–120.

Anderson, Pamela Sue, 'Autonomy, Vulnerability and Gender', *Feminist Theory,* 4(2) special issue on Ethical Relations: Agency, Autonomy and Care, edited by Sasha Roseneil and Linda Hogan (August 2003): 149–164.

Anderson, Pamela Sue, 'An Epistemological-Ethical Approach to Philosophy of Religion: Learning to Listen', in Pamela Sue Anderson and Beverley Clack (eds), *Feminist Philosophy of Religion: Critical Readings* (London: Routledge, 2004), pp. 87–102.

Anderson, Pamela Sue, 'Des contes dits au féminin: pour une éthique de nouveaux espaces', in Alban Cain (ed.), *Espace(s) public(s), espace(s) privées*: Enjeux et partages, Université de Cergy-Pontoise CICC (Paris, France: L'Harmattan, 2004), pp. 43–52.

Anderson, Pamela Sue, '"Moralizing" Love in Philosophy of Religion', in Jerald T. Wallulis and Jeremiah Hackett (eds), *Philosophy of Religion for a New Century* (Amsterdam: Kluwer Academic Publishers, 2004), pp. 227–242.

Anderson, Pamela Sue, 'What's Wrong with the God's Eye Point of View: A Constructive Feminist Critique of the Ideal Observer Theory', in Harriet A. Harris and Christopher J. Insole (eds), *Faith and Philosophical Analysis: A Critical Look at the Impact of Analytical Philosophy on the Philosophy of Religion* (Aldershot, Hampshire: Ashgate Publishing Ltd, 2005), pp. 85–99.

Anderson, Pamela Sue, 'Divinity, Incarnation and Inter-subjectivity: On Ethical Formation and Spiritual Practice', *Philosophy Compass*, 1/3 (2006): 335–356; 10.111/j 1747-9991.2006.00025.x.

Anderson, Pamela Sue, 'Feminism and Patriarchy', in Andrew Hass, Elizabeth Jay and David Jasper (eds), *The Oxford Handbook to English Literature and Theology* (Oxford: Oxford University Press, 2007), pp. 810–828.

Anderson, Pamela Sue, 'Feminist Philosophy of Religion', in Paul Copan and Chad V. Meister (eds), *Philosophy of Religion: Classic and Contemporary Issues* (Oxford: Blackwell Publishing, 2007), pp. 389–410.

Anderson, Pamela Sue, 'Redeeming Truth, Restoring Faith in Reason: A Feminist Response to the Post-modern Condition of Nihilism', in Laurence Paul Hemming and Susan Frank Parsons (eds), *Redeeming Truth: Considering Faith and Reason* (London: SCM Press, 2007), pp. 60–84.

Anderson, Pamela Sue, 'Feminism in Philosophy of Religion', in Chad Meister (ed.), *The Philosophy of Religion Reader* (London: Routledge, 2008), pp. 655–670.

Anderson, Pamela Sue, 'Liberating Love's Capabilities: On the Wisdom of Love', in Norman Wirzba and Bruce Ellis Benson (eds), *Transforming Philosophy and Religion: Love's Wisdom* (Indianapolis: Indiana University Press, 2008), pp. 201–226.

Anderson, Pamela Sue, 'Transcendence and Feminist Philosophy: On Avoiding Apotheosis', in Gillian Howie and J'annine Jobling (eds), *Women and the Divine: Touching Transcendence* (New York: Palgrave, 2009), pp. 27–54.

Anderson, Pamela Sue, 'The Urgent Wish: To Be More Life-Giving', in Elaine Graham (ed.), *Grace Jantzen: Redeeming the Present* (Farnham, Surrey: Ashgate Publishing Limited, 2009), pp. 41–54.

Anderson, Pamela Sue, 'The Lived Body, Gender and Confidence', in Pamela Sue Anderson (ed.), *New Topics in Feminist Philosophy of Religion: Contestations and Transcendence Incarnate* (Dordrecht; London; New York: Springer, 2010), pp. 163–180.

Anderson, Pamela Sue, 'A Feminist Perspective', in Chad Meister (ed.), *The Oxford Handbook of Religious Diversity* (Oxford: Oxford University Press, 2011), pp. 405–420.

Anderson, Pamela Sue, 'On Loss of Confidence: Dissymmetry, Doubt, Deprivation in the Power to Act and (the Power) to Suffer', in Joseph Carlisle, James C. Carter and Daniel Whistler (eds), *Moral Powers, Fragile Beliefs: Essays in Moral and Religious Philosophy* (London and New York: Continuum, 2011), pp. 83–108.

Anderson, Pamela Sue, 'A Story of Love and Death: Exploring space for the philosophical imaginary', in Heather Walton (ed.), *Literature and Theology: New Interdisciplinary Spaces* (Farnham, Surrey: Ashgate Publishing Limited, 2011), pp. 167–186.

Anderson, Pamela Sue, 'Believing in this life: French philosophy after Beauvoir', in Steven Shakespeare and Katharine Sarah Moody (eds), *Intensities: Philosophy, Religion and the Affirmation of Life* (Farnham, Surrey: Ashgate Publishing Limited, 2012).

Anderson, Pamela Sue, 'Metaphors of Spatial Location: Understanding Post-Kantian Space', in Roxana Baiasu, Graham Bird and A. W. Moore (eds), *Contemporary Kantian Metaphysics: New Essays on Space and Time* (New York, NY: Palgrave Macmillan, 2012), pp. 169–196.

Anderson, Pamela Sue, 'Sacrifice as self-destructive "love": why autonomy should still matter to feminists', in Julia Meszaros and Johannes Zachhuber (eds), *Sacrifice and Modern Thought* (Oxford: Oxford University Press, 2013).

Anderson, Pamela Sue and Bell, Jordan, *Kant and Theology*, Continuum Philosophy for Theologians series (New York and London: T & T Clark, a division of Continuum International Publishing, 2010).

Anderson, Pamela Sue and Harris, Harriet A. (eds), *Women's Philosophy Review*, Special Edition: 'Philosophy of Religion', 29 (2002).

Anscombe, Elizabeth, *Intention* (Oxford: Blackwell, 1957).

Antonio, Diane, 'The Flesh of All That Is: Merleau-Ponty, Irigaray and Julian's "Showings"', *Sophia*, 40/1 (December 2001): 47–65.

Apuleius, *The Golden Ass or Metamorphoses* trans. E. J. Kenney (Harmondsworth: Penguin, 1998).

Arendt, Hannah, *Love and Saint Augustine*, edited with an Interpretative Essay by Joanna Vecchiarellis Scott and Judith Chelius Stark (Chicago: University of Chicago Press, 1996).

Arendt, Hannah, *The Human Condition* second edition (Chicago: University of Chicago Press, 1998), pp. 175–92.

Assiter, Alison, *Revisiting Universalism* (New York: Palgrave Macmillan, 2003).

Astell, Mary, *A Serious Proposal to the Ladies* (London: R. Wilkin, 1694).

Astell, Mary, *Some Reflections on Marriage* [1700] (London: Wm. Parker, 1730).

Astell, Mary and Norris, John, *Letters Concerning the Love of God, Between the Author of the Proposal to the Ladies and Mr John Norris* (London: John Norris, 1695).

Audi, Robert, 'A Liberal Theory of Civic Virtue', *Social Philosophy and Policy*, 15/1 (Winter 1998): 155–167.

Babbitt, Susan E., *Impossible Dreams: Rationality, Integrity and Moral Imagination* (Boulder, CO: Westview Press, 1996).

Bacon, Hannah, 'A Very Particular Body: Assessing the Doctrine of Incarnation for Affirming the Sacramentality of Female Embodiment', in Gillian Howie and J'annine Jobling (eds), *Women and the Divine: Touching Transcendence* (New York: Palgrave, 2009), pp. 227–251.

Barrett, Michèle (ed.), 'Introduction', *Virginia Woolf: Women and Writing* (London: The Women's Press, 1979).

Battersby, Christine, *The Sublime, Terror and Human Difference* (London: Routledge, 2007).

Bauer, Nancy, *Simone de Beauvoir, Philosophy, & Feminism* (New York: Columbia University Press, 2001).

Beattie, Tina, *God's Mother, Eve's Advocate* (London: Continuum Press, 2002).

Beattie, Tina, 'Redeeming Mary: The Potential of Marian Symbolism for Feminist Philosophy of Religion', in Pamela Sue Anderson and Beverley Clack (eds), *Feminist Philosophy of Religion: Critical Readings* (London: Routledge, 2004), pp. 107–122.

Beauvoir, Simone de, *The Ethics of Ambiguity*, trans. Bernard Frechtman (New York: Citadel Press, 1948).

Beauvoir, Simone de, *The Second Sex*, complete and unabridged, trans. Constance Borde and Sheila Malovaney-Chevallier (London: Jonathan Cape, 2009).

Behn, Aphra, *Oroonoko, or the Royal Slave*, in *The Histories and Novels of the Late Ingenious Mrs. Behn* [1688] In One Volume (London: S. Briscoe, 1696).

Benhabib, Seyla, *The Claims of Culture: Equality and Diversity in the Global Era* (New York: Princeton University Press, 2002).

Benson, Bruce Ellis, 'Continental Philosophy of Religion', in Paul Copan and Chad Meister (eds), *Philosophy of Religion: Classic and Contemporary Issues* (Malden, Mass: Wiley Blackwell, 2007), pp. 231–244.

Blanchot, Maurice, *Writing of the Disaster*, trans. Ann Smock (Lincoln, Nebraska: University of Nebraska Press, 1986).

Bowden, Peta and Mummery, Jane, *Understanding Feminism* (Stocksfield: Acumen Publishing Limited, 2009).

Burke, Edmund, *A Philosophical Enquiry into the Origin of Our Ideas of the Sublime and Beautiful* [1757], edited by Adam Phillips (Oxford: Oxford University Press, 1990).

Butler, Judith, *Gender Trouble: Feminism and the Subversion of Identity* (New York and London: Routledge, 1990).

Butler, Judith, *Antigone's Claim: Kinship Between Life and Death* (New York: Columbia University Press, 2000).

Butler, Judith, *Precarious Life: The Powers of Mourning and Violence.* (London: Verso, 2006).

Canters, Hanneke and Jantzen, Grace M., *Forever Fluid: A Reading of Luce Irigaray's Elemental Passions* (Manchester: Manchester University Press, 2005).

Carlson, Thomas A., *Indiscretion: Finitude and the Naming of God* (Chicago: University of Chicago Press, 1999).

Cavarero, Adriana, *In Spite of Plato: A Feminist Rewriting of Ancient Philosophy*, trans. Serena Anderlini-D'Onofrio and Aine O'Healy, with a Foreword by Rosi Braidotti (Cambridge, UK: Polity Press, 1995).

Cavarero, Adriana, *Relating Narratives: Storytelling and Selfhood*, trans. with an introduction by Paul A. Kottman (New York: Routledge, 2000).

Chodorow, Nancy, *Feminism and Psychoanalytic Theory* (New Haven: Yale University Press, 1989).

Clack, Beverley, 'Embodiment and Feminist Philosophy of Religion', *Women's Philosophy Review*, 29, Special Edition: 'Philosophy of Religion' edited by Pamela Sue Anderson and Harriet A. Harris (2002): 46–63.

Clack, Beverley, *Sex and Death* (Cambridge: Polity Press, 2002).

Clément, Catherine and Kristeva, Julia, *The Feminine and the Sacred*, trans. Jane Marie Todd (New York: Columbia University Press; London: Palgrave, 2001).

Coakley, Sarah, '*Kenosis* and Subversion: On the Repression of "Vulnerability" in Christian Feminist Writings', in D. Hampson (ed.), *Swallowing A Fishbone? Feminist Theologians Debate Christianity* (London: SPCK, 1996), pp. 82–111.

Coakley, Sarah, *Powers and Submissions: Spirituality, Philosophy and Gender* (Oxford: Blackwell, 2002).

Coakley, Sarah, 'Feminism and Analytic Philosophy of Religion,' in William J. Wainwright (ed.), *The Oxford Handbook to Philosophy of Religion* (Oxford: Oxford University Press, 2005), pp. 494–525.

Cockburn, Catherine, 'Answer to a question in *The Gentleman's Magazine*' and 'Remarks upon an Inquiry into the origins of human appetites and affections', in Mary Warnock (ed.), *Women Philosophers* (London: J. M. Dent, Everyman, 1996), pp. xxxvii, 29–36.

Collins, Patricia Hill, *Fighting Words: Black Women and the Search for Justice* (Minneapolis, MN: University of Minnesota Press, 1998).

Conway, Anne, *The Principles of the Most Ancient and Modern Philosophy* [1670; 1690], edited by Peter Loptson (The Hague, Netherlands: Martin Mijhoff, 1982); and *The Principles of the Most Ancient and Modern Philosophy,* edited by Allison Coudert and Taylor Corse (Cambridge: Cambridge University Press, 1996).

Cornell, Drucilla, *Beyond Accommodation: Ethical Feminism, Deconstruction and the Law* (London: Routledge, 1991; Oxford: Rowman and Littlefield, 1999).

Cornell, Drucilla, *At the Heart of Freedom: Feminism, Sex and Equality* (Princeton, NJ: Princeton University Press, 1998).

Crenshaw, Kimberlé, 'Mapping the Margins: Intersectionality, Identity Politics, and Violence against Women of Color', *Stanford Law Review*, 43 (1991): 1241–1279.

Crenshaw, Kimberlé, *On Intersectionality: The Essential Writings of Kimberlé Crenshaw* (New York, NY: The New Press, 2012).

Dalmiya, Vrinda and Alcoff, Linda, 'Are "Old Wives' Tales" Justified?' in Linda Alcoff and Elizabeth Potter (ed.), *Feminist Epistemologies* (London: Routledge, 1993), pp. 217–241.

Daly, Mary, *The Church and the Second Sex* (Boston: Beacon Press, 1968).

Daly, Mary, *Gyn/Ecology: The Meta-Ethics of Radical Feminism* (Boston: Beacon Press, 1978).

Daly, Mary, *Pure Lust: Elemental Feminist Philosophy* (Boston: Beacon Press, 1984).

Daly, Mary, *Beyond God the Father: Toward a Philosophy of Women's Liberation*, second edition (London: The Women's Press Limited, 1986).

Daly, Mary, *Outercourse: The Be-Dazzling Voyage* (London: The Women's Press, 1993).

Daly, Mary, *Quintessence; Realizing the Archaic Future* (Boston: Beacon Press, 1998).

Deleuze, Gilles, *Spinoza: Practical Philosophy*, trans. Robert Hurley (San Francisco, CA: City Lights Books, 1988).

Deleuze, Gilles, *Expressionism in Philosophy: Spinoza*, trans. Martin Joughin (New York: Zone Books, 2005).

Delphy, Christine, *Close to Home: A Materialist Analysis of Women's Oppression*, translated and edited by Diana Leonard (London: Hutchinson, 1984).

Derrida, Jacques, '*Différance*' and 'Signature, Event, Context', *Margins of Philosophy*, trans. Alan Bass (Chicago: University of Chicago Press, 1982), pp. 1–28 and 307–330.

Derrida, Jacques, 'Response to Moore', *Ratio: An International Journal of Analytic Philosophy*, Special Issue, edited by Simon Glendinning, XIII/4 (December 2000): 381–386.

Deutscher, Penelope, *Yielding Gender: Feminism, Deconstruction and the History of Philosophy* (London: Routledge, 1997).

Doniger, Wendy, 'Medical and Mythical Constructions of the Body in Hindu Texts', in Sarah Coakley (ed.), *Religion and the Body* (Cambridge: Cambridge University Press, 1998), pp. 167–184.

Durber, Susan, 'Book Review: *Feminist Philosophy of Religion: Critical Readings*', *Literature and Theology*, 18/4 (December 2004): 493–495.

Feuerbach, Ludwig, *The Essence of Christianity*, trans. George Eliot (New York and London: Harper Torchbooks, 1957).

Fiddes, Paul, 'The quest for a place which is "not-a-place": the hiddenness of God and the presence of God', in Oliver Davies and Denys Turner (eds), *Silence and the Word: Negative Theology and Incarnation* (Cambridge: Cambridge University Press, 2002), pp. 35–60.

Fiddes, Paul, 'The Sublime and the Beautiful: Intersections between Theology and Literature', in Heather Walton (ed.), *Literature and Theology: New Interdisciplinary Spaces* (Farnham, Surrey: Ashgate Publishing Limited, 2011), pp. 127–152.

Filipczak, Dorota, 'Autonomy and Female Spirituality in a Polish Context: Divining a Self', in Pamela Sue Anderson and Beverley Clack (eds), *Feminist Philosophy of Religion: Critical Readings* (London: Routledge, 2004), pp. 210–222.

Filipczak, Dorota, *Unheroic Heroines: The Portrayal of Women in the Writings of Margaret Laurence* (Lodz, Poland: Wydawnictwo Uniwersytetu Lodzkiego, 2007).

Filipczak, Dorota, 'Is Literature Any Help in Liberating Eve and Mary?' in Pamela Sue Anderson (ed.), *New Topics in Feminist Philosophy of Religion: Contestation and Transcendence Incarnate* (Dordrecht, New York and London, 2010), pp. 117–126.

Foucault, Michel, *The History of Sexuality*, vol. 1, *An Introduction*, trans. Robert Hurley (Harmondsworth, Middlesex: Penguin Books, 1979).

Fricker, Miranda, 'Epistemic Oppression and Epistemic Practice', *Canadian Journal of Philosophy*, supplementary volume, *Civilization and Oppression*, edited by Catherine Wilson (1999): 191–210.

Fricker, Miranda, 'Feminism in Epistemology: Pluralism without Postmodernism', in Miranda Fricker and Jennifer Hornsby (eds), *The Cambridge Companion to Feminism in Philosophy* (Cambridge: Cambridge University Press, 2000), pp. 146–165.

Fricker, Miranda, *Epistemic Injustice: Power and the Ethics of Knowing* (Oxford: Oxford University Press, 2007).

Fricker, Miranda and Hornsby, Jennifer, 'Introduction', in Fricker and Hornsby (eds), *The Cambridge Companion to Feminism in Philosophy* (Cambridge: Cambridge University Press, 2000), pp. 1–5.

Gamble, Sarah (ed.), *The Routledge Companion to Feminism and Post-Feminism* (London: Routledge, 2001).

Garry, Ann and Pearsall, Marilyn (eds), *Women, Knowledge and Reality: Explorations in Feminist Philosophy* (second edition, London: Routledge, 1996).

Gatens, Moira, *Imaginary Bodies: Ethics, Power and Corporeality* (London: Routledge, 1996).

Gatens, Moira and Lloyd, Genevieve, *Collective Imaginings: Spinoza, Past and Present* (London: Routledge, 1999).

Gellman, Jerome, *Mystical Experience of God: A Philosophical Inquiry* (Aldershot, Hampshire: Ashgate Publishing Ltd., 2001).

Gilligan, Carol, *The Birth of Pleasure: A New Map of Love* (London: Chatto and Windus, 2002).

Gilman, Charlotte Perkins, *The Yellow Wallpaper* [1892] (London: Virago Press, 1981).

Glendinning, Simon, 'The Ethics of Exclusion: Incorporating the Continent', in Richard Kearney and Mark Dooley (eds), *Questioning Ethics: Contemporary Debates in Philosophy* (London: Routledge, 2000), pp. 120–123.

Glendinning, Simon, 'Inheriting "Philosophy": The Case of Austin and Derrida Revisited', *Ratio: An International Journal of Philosophy*, XIII/4 (December 2000): 307–331.

Godwin, William, *Memoirs of the Author of a Vindication of the Rights of Woman* [1798], edited with an Introduction by Pamela Clemit and Gina Luria Walker (Ontario, Canada: Broadview Press, 2001).

Goetz, Stewart, Harrison, Victoria and Taliaferro, Charles (eds), *The Routledge Companion to Theism* (New York and London: Routledge, 2012).

Goldman, Alvin I., 'The Unity of Epistemic Virtues', in Linda Zagzebski and Abrol Fairweather (eds), *Virtue Epistemology* (Oxford: Oxford University Press, 2001).

Goodchild, Philip (eds), *Rethinking Philosophy of Religion: Approaches from Continental Philosophy*, series edited by John Caputo (New York: Fordham University Press, 2002).

Grace, Daphne, *The Woman in the Muslim Mask: Veiling and Identity in Postcolonial Literature* (London: Pluto Press, 2004).

Grimshaw, Jean, 'Autonomy and Identity in Feminist Thinking', in Morwenna Griffiths and Margaret Whitford (eds), *Feminist Perspectives in Philosophy* (Bloomington: Indiana University Press, 1986), pp. 90–108.

Gross, Rita M. and Ruether, Rosemary Radford, *Religious Feminism and the Future of the Planet: A Buddhist-Christian Conversation* (New York: Continuum, 2001).

Haldane, John, 'John Paul's philosophy', *The Tablet*, 7 (June 2003): 22–23.

Hampson, Daphne, *After Christianity* (London: SCM Press, 1996).

Hampson, Daphne, 'Searching for God?' in John Cornwell and Michael McGhee (eds), *Philosophers and God: At the Frontiers of Faith and Reason* (London: Continuum, 2009), pp. 63–76.

Hampson, Daphne, 'That Which Is God', in G. Howie and J. Jobling (eds), *Women and the Divine: Touching Transcendence* (New York: Palgrave Macmillan, 2009), pp. 171–186.

Hampson, Daphne, 'Kant and the Present', in P. S. Anderson (ed.), *New Topics in Feminist Philosophy of Religion: Contestations and Transcendence Incarnate* (Dordrecht, London and New York: Springer, 2010), pp. 147–162.

Haraway, Donna, 'Ecce Homo, Ain't (Ar'n't) I a Woman, and Inappropriate/d Others: The Human in a Post-Humanist Landscape', in Judith Butler and Joan Scott (eds), *Feminists Theorize the Political* (New York: Routledge, 1996), pp. 86–100.

Hare, R. M., 'A School for Philosophers', *Ratio*, II/2 (1960).

Harris, Harriet A., 'Feminism', in Paul Copan and Chad Meister (eds), *The Routledge Companion to Philosophy of Religion* (London: Routledge, 2007), pp. 651–660.

Haynes, Patrice, 'Transcendence, Materialism and the Re-enchantment of Nature: Toward a Theological Materialism', in Gillian Howie and J'annine Jobling (eds), *Women and the Divine: Touching Transcendence* (New York: Palgrave, 2009), pp. 55–78.

Haynes, Patrice, *Immanent Transcendence: Reconfiguring Materialism in Continental Philosophy*, Bloomsbury Studies in Continental Philosophy (London: Continuum, 2012).

Heilbrun, Carolyn G., *Writing a Woman's Life* (London: The Women's Press Ltd., 1989).

Helm, Paul, 'The Indispensability of Belief to Religion', *Religious Studies*, 37 (2001): 75–86.

Hemming, Laurence Paul and Parsons, Susan Frank (eds), *Redeeming Truth: Considering Faith and Reason* (London: SCM, 2007).

Hick, John, 'Religious Pluralism', in Chad Meister and Paul Copan (eds), *The Routledge Companion to Philosophy of Religion* (New York and London: Routledge, 2008), pp. 216–225.

Hollywood, Amy, 'Beauvoir, Irigaray and the Mystical', *Hypatia*, 9 (Fall 1994): 158–185.

Hollywood, Amy, *The Soul as Virgin Wife: Mechthild of Magdeburg, Marguerite Porete and Meister Eckhart* (Notre Dame: Notre Dame University Press, 1995).

Hollywood, Amy, 'Performativity, Citationality, Ritualization', *History of Religions*, 42 (2002): 93–115.

Hollywood, Amy, *Sensible Ecstasy: Sexual Difference and the Demands of History* (Chicago: University of Chicago Press, 2002).

Hollywood, Amy, 'Practice, Belief and Feminist Philosophy of Religion', in Pamela Sue Anderson and Beverley Clack (eds), *Feminist Philosophy of Religion: Critical Readings* (London: Routledge, 2004), pp. 225–240.

hooks, bell, *Ain't I a Woman? black women and feminism* (Boston, MA: South End Press, 1981).

hooks, bell, *Feminist Theory: From Margin to Center*, second edition (London: Pluto Press, 2000; first edition, 1988).

hooks, bell, *Yearning: Race, Gender and Cultural Politics* (Boston: South Bend Press, 1990).

hooks, bell, *Bone Black: Memories of Girlhood* (New York: Henry Holt Company, 1996).

hooks, bell, *Wounds of Passion: A Writing Life* (New York: Henry Holt & Company, Owl Press, 1997).

hooks, bell, *Remembered Rapture: The Writer at Work* (London: The Women's Press, 1999).

hooks, bell, *All About Love: New Visions* (London: The Women's Press, 2000).

hooks, bell, *Feminism is for Everybody: Passionate Politics* (Cambridge, MA: South End Press, 2000).

Howie, Gillian, 'Feminist Generations: The Maternal Order and Mythic Time', in *Luce Irigaray: Teaching*, edited by Luce Irigaray with Mary Green (New York and London: Continuum, 2008), pp. 103–112.

Irigaray, Luce, *Speculum of the Other Woman*, trans. Gillian C. Gill (Ithaca, NY: Cornell University Press, 1985).

Irigaray, Luce, *Marine Lover of Friedrich Nietzsche*, trans. Gillian C. Gill (New York: Columbia University Press, 1991).

Irigaray, Luce, *Elemental Passions*, trans. Joanne Collie and Judith Still (London: The Athlone Press, 1992).

Irigaray, Luce, *An Ethics of Sexual Difference*, trans. Carolyn Burke and Gillian C. Gill (London: The Athlone Press, 1993).

Irigaray, Luce, 'Divine Women,' *Genealogies and Sexes*, trans. Gillian C. Gill (New York: Columbia University Press, 1993), pp. 55–72.

Irigaray, Luce, 'Toward a Divine in the Feminine', in Gillian Howie and J'annine Jobling (eds), *Women and the Divine: Touching Transcendence* (New York: Palgrave Macmillan, 2009), pp. 13–26.

Jaggar, Alison M., *Feminist Politics and Human Nature* (Totowa, New Jersey: Rowman & Littlefield Publishers, Inc., 1983).

Jaggar, Alison, 'Feminism in Ethics: Moral Justification', in Miranda Fricker and Jennifer Hornsby (eds), *The Cambridge Companion to Feminism in Philosophy* (Cambridge: Cambridge University Press, 2000), pp. 225–244.

James, Susan, 'The Power of Spinoza: Feminist Contentions. Susan James Talks to Genevieve Lloyd and Moira Gatens', *Women's Philosophy Reviews*, 9 (Autumn, 1998): 6–28.

Jantzen, Grace M., *Power, Gender and Christian Mysticism* (Cambridge: Cambridge University Press, 1995).

Jantzen, Grace M., 'What's the Difference: Knowledge and Gender in (Post) Modern Philosophy of Religion', *Religious Studies*, 32 (1996): 431–448. Reprinted in Pamela Sue Anderson and Beverley Clack (eds), *Feminist Philosophy of Religion: Critical Readings* (London: Routledge, 2004), pp. 28–41.

Jantzen, Grace M., 'Feminism and Pantheism', *The Monist: An International Journal of General Philosophical Inquiry*, 80, 2 (April 1997): 266–285.

Jantzen, Grace M., *Becoming Divine: Towards A Feminist Philosophy of Religion* (Manchester: Manchester University Press, 1998).

Jantzen, Grace M., 'Feminist Philosophy of Religion: Open Discussion with Pamela Anderson', *Feminist Theology*, 26 (January 2001): 102–109.

Jantzen, Grace M., 'What Price Neutrality? A Reply to Paul Helm', *Religious Studies*, 37 (2001): 87–91.

Jones, Rachel, *Irigaray: Towards a Sexuate Philosophy* (Cambridge, UK: Polity Press, 2011).

Joy, Morny, *Divine Love: Luce Irigaray, Women, Gender and Religion* (Manchester: Manchester University Press, 2006).

Joy, Morny and Neumaier-Dargyay, Eva K. (eds), *Gender, Genre and Religion: Feminist Reflections* (Waterloo, Ontario, Canada: Wilfrid Laurier University Press, 1995).

Joy, Morny, O'Grady Kathleen and Poxon, Judith L. (eds), *French Feminists on Religion: A Reader* (London: Routledge, 2002).

Joy, Morny, O'Grady Kathleen and Poxon, Judith L. (eds), *Religion in French Feminist Thought: Critical Perspectives* (London: Routledge, 2003).

Julian of Norwich, *Revelations of Divine Love*, trans. Elizabeth Spearing with an Introduction and Notes by A. C. Spearing (London: Penguin Books Ltd., 1998).

Kant, Immanuel, *Critique of Pure Reason*, trans. Norman Kemp Smith (London: Macmillan, 1950).

Kant, Immanuel, *Critique of Judgement*, trans. James Creed Meredith (Oxford: Clarendon Press, 1952); and *Critique of the Power of Judgment*, trans. Paul Guyer and Eric Matthews in the Cambridge edition (Cambridge: Cambridge University Press, 2000).

Kant, Immanuel, *Observations on the Feeling of the Beautiful and the Sublime*, trans. John T. Goldthwait (Berkeley, CA: University of California Press, 1960).

Kant, Immanuel, *The Metaphysics of Morals*, trans. and edited by Mary Gregor (Cambridge: Cambridge University Press, 1996).

Kant, Immanuel, *Groundwork of the Metaphysics of Morals*, trans. and edited by Mary Gregor, Introduction by Christine M. Korsgaard (Cambridge: Cambridge University Press, 1998).

Kant, Immanuel, *Lectures on Ethics*, edited by Peter Heath and J. B. Schneewind, trans. Peter Heath (Cambridge: Cambridge University Press, 2001).

Kearney, Richard, *On Stories* (London: Routledge, 2002).

Keller, Mary L., 'Divine Women and the Nehanda Mhondoro: Strengths and Limitations of the Sensible Transcendental in a Post-Colonial World of Religious Women', in Morny Joy, Kathleen O'Grady and Judith L. Pozon (eds), *Religion in French Feminist Thought: Critical Perspectives* (London: Routledge, 2003), pp. 68–82.

King, Mike, 'Cutting "God" Down to Size: Transcendence and the Feminine', in Gillian Howie and J'annine Jobling (eds), *Women and the Divine: Touching Transcendence* (New York: Palgrave, 2009), pp. 153–170.

Kristeva, Julia, *Powers of Horror: An Essay on Abjection*, trans. Leon S. Roudiez (New York: Columbia University Press, 1982).

Kristeva, Julia, *Tales of Love*, trans. Leon S. Roudiez (New York: Columbia University Press, 1987).

Kristeva, Julia, *The Old Man and the Wolves*, trans. Barbara Bray (New York: Columbia University Press, 1994).

Kristeva, Julia, *New Maladies of the Soul*, trans. Ross Mitchell Guberman (New York: Columbia University Press, 1995).

Kristeva, Julia, *Hannah Arendt*, trans. Ross Guberman (New York: Columbia University Press, 2001).

Kvanvig, Jonathan L., 'Religious Pluralism and the Buridan's Ass Paradox', *European Journal for Philosophy of Religion*, 1/1 (Spring 2009): 1–26.

Langton, Rae, 'Feminism in Epistemology: Exclusion and Objectification', in Miranda Fricker and Jennifer Hornsby (eds), *The Cambridge Companion to Feminism in Philosophy* (Cambridge: Cambridge University Press, 2000), pp. 127–145.

Le Doeuff, Michèle, *The Philosophical Imaginary*, trans. Colin Gordon (London: The Athlone Press, 1989; New York and London: Continuum, 2002).

Le Doeuff, Michèle, *Hipparchia's Choice: An Essay Concerning Women, Philosophy, Etc.*, trans. Trista Selous (Oxford: Blackwell, 1991); a slightly revised translation with 'Epilogue (2006)' by the author (New York: Columbia University Press, 2007).

Le Doeuff, Michèle, 'Suchon', in Edward Craig (ed.), *The Routledge Encyclopedia of Philosophy* 9 (London: Routledge, 1998), pp. 211–213.

Le Doeuff, Michèle, *The Sex of Knowing*, trans. Lorraine Code and Kathryn Hamer (London and New York: Routledge, 2003).

Lee, Hermione, *Virginia Woolf* (London: Vintage, 1997).

Lerner, Gerda, *The Creation of Feminist Consciousness: From the Middle Ages to Eighteen-Seventy* (New York: Oxford University Press, 1993).

Levine, Michael, 'Non-theistic Conceptions of God', in Paul Copan and Chad Meister (eds), *The Routledge Companion to Philosophy of Religion* (London: Routledge, 2007), pp. 237–248.

Lloyd, Genevieve, *The Man of Reason: 'Male' and 'Female' in Western Philosophy* (London: Routledge, 1993).

Lloyd, Genevieve, *Part of Nature: Self-Knowledge in Spinoza's Ethics* (Ithaca, New York: Cornell University Press, 1994).

Lloyd, Genevieve, 'The Man of Reason', in Garry, Ann and Pearsall, Marilyn (eds), *Women, Knowledge and Reality: Explorations in Feminist Philosophy*, second edition (London: Routledge, 1996), pp. 149–165.

Lloyd, Genevieve, 'Feminism in History of Philosophy: Appropriating the Past', in Miranda Fricker and Jennifer Hornsby (eds), *The Cambridge Companion to Feminism in Philosophy* (Cambridge: Cambridge University Press, 2000), pp. 245–263.

Lloyd, Genevieve, 'What a Union!', *The Philosophers Magazine*, 29 (2005): 45–48.

Longino, Helen, *Science as Social Knowledge: Values and Objectivity in Scientific Inquiry* (Princeton, NJ: Princeton University Press, 1990).

Lovibond, Sabina, 'An Ancient Theory of Gender: Plato and the Pythagorean Table', in Leonie J. Archer, Susan Fischer and Maria Wyke (eds), *Women in Ancient Societies* (London: Macmillan, 1994), pp. 88–101.

Lovibond, Sabina, 'The End of Morality', in Kathleen Lennon and Margaret Whitford (eds), *Knowing the Difference: Feminist Perspectives in Epistemology* (London: Routledge, 1994), pp. 63–78.

Lovibond, Sabina, 'Feminism in Ancient Philosophy: The Feminist Stake in Greek Rationalism', in Miranda Fricker and Jennifer Hornsby (eds), *The Cambridge Companion to Feminism in Philosophy* (Cambridge: Cambridge University Press, 2000), pp. 10–28.

Lovibond, Sabina, *Ethical Formation* (Cambridge, MA: Harvard University Press, 2002).

Lovibond, Sabina, *Iris Murdoch, Gender and Philosophy* (London: Routledge, 2011).

McCall, Leslie, 'The Complexity of Intersectionality', *Signs*, 30, 3 (Spring 2005): 1771–1800.

MacIntyre, Alasdair, *After Virtue: A Study in Moral Theory*, second edition (London: Gerald Duckworth & Co. Ltd, 1985).

McNay, Lois, *Against Recognition* (Cambridge: Polity Press, 2008).

Mahmood, Saba, *Politics of Piety: The Islamic Revival and the Feminist Subject* (New York: Princeton University Press, 2005).

Manson, Neil C., 'Epistemic Inertia and Epistemic Isolationism', *Journal of Applied Philosophy*, 26/3 (2009): 291–298.

Marion, Jean-Luc, 'In the Name: How to Avoid Speaking of "Negative Theology"', in John D. Caputo and Micheal J. Scanlon (eds), *God, The Gift and Postmodernism* (Bloomington, IN: Indiana University Press, 1999).

Marks, Elaine and de Courtivron, Isabelle (eds), *New French Feminisms: An Anthology* (Hemel Hempstead, Hertfordshire: Harvester Wheatsheaf, 1980).

Mason, Rebecca, 'Two Kinds of Unknowing', *Hypatia: A Journal of Feminist Philosophy*, 26, 2 (Spring 2011): 294–307.

Matheron, Alexandre, *Individu et société chez Spinoza* (Paris: Minuit, 1969).

Matheron, Alexandre, 'Spinoza *et la sexualité*', *Giornale Critico della Filosofia Italiana*, 8/4 (1977): 436–457.

Mawson, T. J., *Belief in God: An Introduction to the Philosophy of Religion* (Oxford: Oxford University Press, 2005).

Mendus, Susan, *Feminism and Emotion* (London: Macmillan, 2000).

Meredith, Fionola, 'A Post-Metaphysical Approach to Female Subjectivity: Between Deconstruction and Hermeneutics', in Pamela Sue Anderson and Beverley Clack (eds), *Feminist Philosophy of Religion: Critical Readings* (London: Routledge, 2004), pp. 54–72.

Meredith, Fionola, *Experiencing the Post-metaphysical Self: Between Hermeneutics and Deconstruction* (London: Sage, 2005).

Mernissi, Fatima, *Women's Rebellion and Islamic Memory* (London: Zed Books Ltd., 1996).

Merton, Thomas, 'Love and Need', in Naomi Burton Stone and Brother Patrick Hart (eds), *Love and Liking* (Harvest Books, 2002).

Mikkola, Mari, 'Kant on Moral Agency and Women's Nature', *Kantian Review* (2011): 89–112.

Millett, Kate, *Sexual Politics* (London: Virago, 1977).

Milton, John, 'Paradise Lost', in *John Milton: The Major Works*, edited with an Introduction and Notes by Stephen Orgel and Jonathan Goldberg. Oxford World's Classics (Oxford: Oxford University Press, 2003), pp. 355–618.

Moi, Toril, *Sexual/Textual Politics: Feminist Literary Theory* (London and New York: Routledge, 1988).

Montefiore Alan (ed.), *Philosophy and Personal Relations: An Anglo-French Study* (London: Routledge & Kegan Paul Ltd, 1973).

Montefiore, Alan, 'A Note Concerning "Essentially Contestable" Concepts', unpublished paper, 2011.

Moore, A. W., *The Infinite* (London: Routledge, 1990; second edition, with a new Preface, 2001).

Moore, A. W., *Points of View* (Oxford: Oxford University Press, 1997).

Moore, A. W., 'Arguing with Derrida', *Ratio: An International Journal of Analytic Philosophy*, Special Issue, edited by Simon Glendinning, XIII/4 (December 2000): 355–381.

Moore, A. W., 'Ineffability and Religion', *European Journal of Philosophy*, 11/2 (2003): 161–176.

Moore, A. W., *Noble in Reason, Infinite in Faculty: Themes and Variations on Kant's Moral and Religious Philosophy* (London: Routledge, 2003).

Moore, A. W., 'Williams on Ethics, Knowledge and Reflection', *Philosophy: The Journal of the Royal Institute of Philosophy*, 78 (2003): 337–354.

Moore, A. W., 'Maxims and Thick Ethical Concepts,' *Ratio*, XIX (June 2006): 129–147.

Moore, A. W., *The Evolution of Modern Metaphysics: Making Sense of Things* (Cambridge: Cambridge University Press, 2012).

More, Hannah, *Strictures on the Modern System of Female Education with a View to the Principles and Conduct Prevalent Among Women of Rank and Fortune* (Philadelphia, PA: Thomas Dobson, 1800).

Morrison, Toni, *The Bluest Eyes* (New York: Pocket Books, 1970).

Morrison, Toni, *Playing in the Dark: Whiteness and the Literary Imagination* (New York: Vintage Books, A Division of Random House, 1993).

Mukta, Parita, *Shard of Memory: Woven Lives in Four Generations* (London: Weidenfeld and Nicolson, 2002).

Murdoch, Iris, *The Sovereignty of Good* (London: Routledge & Kegan Paul, 1970).

Murdoch, Iris, *Metaphysics as A Guide to Morals* (London: Penguin Books, 1993).

Newton-Smith, William, 'A Conceptual Investigation of Love', in Alan Montefiore (ed.), *Philosophy and Personal Relations: An Anglo-French Study* (London: Routledge & Kegan Paul Ltd, 1973), pp. 113–136.

Nussbaum, Martha, 'Religion and Women's Human Rights', *Sex and Social Justice* (Oxford: Oxford University Press, 1999), pp. 81–117.

Nussbaum, Martha, *Upheavals of Thought: The Intelligence of the Emotions* (Cambridge: Cambridge University Press, 2001).

Nye, Andrea, *Feminism and Modern Philosophy: An Introduction* (London: Routledge, 2004).

O'Neill, Onora, *Bounds of Justice* (Cambridge: Cambridge University Press, 2000).

O'Neill, Onora, *Autonomy and Trust in Bioethics* (Cambridge: Cambridge University Press, 2002).

Parfit, Derek, 'Later Selves and Moral Principles', in Alan Montefiore (ed.), *Philosophy and Personal Relations: An Anglo-French Study* (London: Routledge & Kegan Paul Ltd, 1973), pp. 144–162.

Parfit, Derek, *Reasons and Persons* (Oxford: Oxford University Press, 1984).

Paton, Paul (ed.), *Deleuze: A Critical Reader* (Oxford: Blackwell Publishing, 1996).

Pizan, Christine de, *The Book of the City of Ladies*, trans. with An Introduction and Notes by Rosalind Brown-Grant (Harmondsworth: Penguin Books Ltd., 1999); *The Boke of the Cyte of Ladyes* (London: Henry Pepwell, 1521).

Plantinga, Alvin, 'Pluralism: A Defense of Religious Exclusivism', in Thomas Senor (ed.), *The Rationality of Belief and the Plurality of Faith*, Ithaca, NY: Cornell University Press, 1995); reprinted in *The Philosophy of Religion Reader*, ed. Chad Meister (New York and London: Routledge, 2008), pp. 40–59.

Plato, *Symposium*, trans. Alexander Nehamas and Paul Woodruff (Indianapolis, Ind., 1989).

Pope John Paul II, *Restoring Faith in Reason*, A New Translation of the Encyclical Letter *Faith and Reason*, together with a commentary and discussion, edited by Laurence Paul Hemming and Susan Frank Parsons (London: SCM Press, 2002).

Quine, Willard van Orman, *From a Logical Point of View: Logico-Philosophical Essays* (New York: Harper & Row, 1953).

Rich, Adrienne, 'When We Dead Awaken: Writing as Re-vision', *College English*, 34, 1, 'Women Writing and Teaching' (October 1972): 18–30; reprinted in Barbara Charlesworth Gelpi and Albert Gelpi (eds), *Adrienne Rich's Poetry and Prose* (New York and London: W. W. Norton and Company, 1991), pp. 166–177.

Rich, Adrienne, *Diving into the Wreck* (New York: W. W. Norton & Company, Inc., 1973).

Rich, Adrienne, *Of Woman Born: Motherhood as Experience and Institution* (New York and London: W. W. Norton & Company, 1995).

Ricoeur, Paul, *Fallible Man*, trans. Charles Kelbley with an Introduction by Walter J. Lowe (New York: Fordham University Press, 1986).

Ricoeur, Paul, *Oneself as Another*, trans. Kathleen Blamey (Chicago, IL: University of Chicago Press, 1992).

Ricoeur, Paul, *L'unique et le singulier*, L'intégrale des entretiens 'Noms de dieux', d'Edmond Blattchen (Brussels, Belgium: Alice Editions, 1999).

Ricoeur, Paul, 'Autonomy and Vulnerability', in *Reflections on The Just*, trans. David Pellauer (Chicago: The University of Chicago Press, 2007), pp. 72–90.

Rorty, Amelie, 'Spinoza on the Pathos of Idolatrous Love and the Hilarity of True Love', in Genevieve Lloyd (ed.), *Feminism and the History of Philosophy* (Oxford: Oxford University Press, 2002), pp. 204–226.

Runzo, Joseph, 'Religious Pluralism', Paul Copan and Chad Meister (eds), *Philosophy of Religion: Classic and Contemporary Issues* (Oxford: Blackwell Publishing, 2008), pp. 51–66.

Ryle, Gilbert, 'Phenomenology versus *The Concept of Mind*', reprinted in Gilbert Ryle, *Collected Papers* (London: Hutchinson, 1971).

Sanders, Valerie, 'First Wave Feminism', in Sarah Gamble (ed.), *The Routledge Companion to Feminism and Postfeminism* (London: Routledge, 2001), pp. 16–28.

Sartre, Jean-Paul, *Being and Nothingness: An Essay on Phenomenological Ontology*, trans. Hazel Barnes (New York: Philosophical Library, 1956).

Scarry, Elaine, *On Beauty and Being Just* (Princeton, NJ: Princeton University Press, 1999).

Scoular Datta, Kitty, 'Female Heterologies: Women's Mysticism, Gender-Mixing and the Apophatic', in Heather Walton and Andrew W. Haas (eds), *Self/Same/Other: Re-visioning the Subject in Literature and Theology* (Sheffield: Sheffield Academic Press, 2000), pp. 125–136.

Scruton, Roger, *Spinoza: A Very Short Introduction* (Oxford: Oxford University Press, 2002).

Sedgwick, Sally, 'Can Kant's Ethics Survive the Feminist Critique', in Robin May Schott (ed.), *Feminist Interpretations of Kant* (University Park, PA: Penn State University Press, 1997), pp. 77–100.

Shelley, Mary, *Frankenstein, or the Modern Prometheus*, edited with Introduction and Notes by Marilyn Butler (Oxford and New York: Oxford University Press, World Classics, [1818] 1993).

Sherman, Nancy, *Making a Necessity of Virtue: Aristotle and Kant on Virtue* (Cambridge: Cambridge University Press, 1997).

Soskice, Janet Martin, 'Love and Attention', in Michael McGhee (ed.), *Philosophy, Religion and the Spiritual Life* (Cambridge: Cambridge University Press, 1992), pp. 59–72. Reprinted in Pamela Sue Anderson and Beverley Clack (eds), *Feminist Philosophy of Religion: Critical Readings* (London: Routledge, 2004), pp. 199–209.

Soskice, Janet Martin, '*Fides et ratio*: The Postmodern Pope' in Laurence Paul Hemnning and Susan Frank Parsons (eds), *Redeeming Truth: Considering Faith and Reason* (London: SCM, 2007).

Spinoza, Benedict de, *Tractatus Politicus*, in *The Political Works*, trans. and edited by A. G. Wernham (Oxford: Clarendon Press, 1958).

Spinoza, Benedict de, *Ethics* [1677], edited and trans. G. H. R. Parkinson (Oxford: Oxford University Press, 2000).

Steiner, Wendy, *Venus in Exile: the Rejection of Beauty in Twentieth-Century Art* (Chicago: University of Chicago Press, 2001).

Suchon, Gabrielle, *Traité de la morale et de la politique* (Lyon: B. Vignieu, 1693).

Suchon, Gabrielle, *A Woman Who Defends All the Persons of Her Sex: Selected Philosophical and Moral Writings*, edited and trans. Domna C. Stanton and Rebecca M. Wilkin (Chicago: University of Chicago Press, 2010).

Swanton, Christine, 'Kant's Impartial Virtues of Love', in Lawrence Jost and Julian Wuerth (eds), *Perfecting Virtue: New Essays on Kantian Ethics and Virtue Ethics* (Cambridge: Cambridge University Press, 2011), pp. 241–259.

Swinburne, Richard, *The Coherence of Theism* (Oxford: Clarendon Press, 1977).

Swinburne, Richard, *The Existence of God*, revised edition (Oxford: Clarendon Press, 1991).

Taliaferro, Charles, *Contemporary Philosophy of Religion: An Introduction* (Oxford: Blackwell, 1997).

Taliaferro, Charles, 'The God's Eye Point of View: A Divine Ethic', in Harriet A. Harris and Christopher J. Insole (eds), *Faith and Philosophical Analysis: The Impact of Analytical Philosophy on the Philosophy of Religion* (Aldershot, Hants: Ashgate Publishing Limited, 2005), pp. 76–84.

Taliaferro, Charles and Evans, Jil, *The Image in Mind: Theism, Naturalism and the Imagination*, Continuum Series in Philosophy of Religion (London: Continuum, 2011).

Taliaferro, Charles and Teply, Alison (eds), *Cambridge Platonist Spirituality* (Mahwah, New Jersey: Paulist Press, 2004).

Warner, Marina, 'Monstrous Mothers: Women On Top', *Six Myths of Our Time* (London: Vintage Books, A Division of Random House, 1994).

Warnock, Mary (ed.), *Women Philosophers* (London: J. M. Dent, Everyman, 1996).

Waugh, Patricia, *Feminine Fictions: Revisiting the Postmodern* (London: Routledge, 1989).

Weil, Simone, *Gravity and Grace*, trans. Emma Crawford and Mario von der Ruhr, with an Introduction and Postscript by Gustave Thibon (London and New York: Routledge, 2002).

Weil, Simone, *Letter to a Priest*, trans. A. F. Wills with an introduction by Mario von der Ruhr (London and New York: Routledge, 2002).

West, David, *Reason and Sexuality in Western Thought* (Cambridge: Polity Press, 2005).

Whitford, Margaret, 'The Feminist Philosopher: A Contradiction in Terms?' *Women: A Cultural Review*, 3/2 (Autumn 1992): 111–120.

Williams, Bernard, *Shame and Necessity* (Berkeley, California: University of California Press, 1993).

Williams, Bernard, 'Philosophy as a Humanistic Discipline', *Philosophy*, 75/294 (October 2000): 477–496.

Williams, Bernard, *Truth and Truthfulness: An Essay in Genealogy* (New York and Oxford: Princeton University Press, 2002).

Williams, Bernard, *Ethics and the Limits of Philosophy*, second edition with a commentary on the text by A. W. Moore (London: Routledge, 2006).

Williams, Patricia, *The Alchemy of Race and Rights* (Cambridge, MA: Harvard University Press, 1991).

Wittgenstein, Ludwig, *Tractatus Logico-Philosophicus*, trans. D. F. Pears and B. F. McGuinness, with the Introduction by Bertrand Russell (London: Routledge & Kegan Paul, 1961).

Wollstonecraft, Mary, 'Letters to Imlay', in Marilyn Butler and Janet Todd (eds), *The Works of Mary Wollstonecraft*, vol. 6, LXVII (London: Chatto & Pickering, 1989).

Wollstonecraft, Mary, *A Vindication of the Rights of Woman* [1792], edited with an Introduction by Miriam Brody (Harmondsworth: Penguin Books Ltd, 1992).

Wood, William, 'On the New Analytic Theology, Or the Road Less Travelled', *Journal of the American Academy of Religion*, 77/4 (December 2009): 941–960.

Woolf, Virginia, *The Letters of Virginia Woolf* (1888–1912), vol. 1, edited by Nigel Nicolson and Joanne T. Trautmann (London: Hogarth Press, 1975).

Woolf, Virginia, *Mrs Dalloway* [1925] (Harmondsworth: Penguin, 1992).

Woolf, Virginia, *The Voyage Out* [1915] (Harmondsworth: Penguin, 1992).

Woolf, Virginia, *The Waves* [1938], biographical Preface by Frank Kermode, edited with an Introduction and Notes by Gillian Beer (Oxford: Oxford World's Classics, Oxford University Press, 1992).

Woolf, Virginia, *Orlando* [1928] (Harmondsworth: Penguin, 1993).

Woolf, Virginia, *A Room of One's Own* [1929] and *Three Guineas* [1938], and 'Professions for Women' [1931] edited with an Introduction and Notes by Michèle Barrett and Appendix (Harmondsworth: Penguin, 1993).

Woolf, Virginia, *To the Lighthouse* [1927] (Harmondsworth: Penguin, 1993).

Wylie, Alison, 'Feminism in Philosophy of Science: Making Sense of Contingency and Constraint', in Miranda Fricker and Jennifer Hornsby (eds), *The Cambridge Companion to Feminism in Philosophy* (Cambridge: Cambridge University Press, 2000), pp. 166–184.

Wynn, Mark, *Emotional Experience and Religious Understanding: Integrating Perception, Conception and Feeling* (Cambridge: Cambridge University Press, 2005).

Zack, Naomi, 'Can Third Wave Feminism Be Inclusive? Intersectionality, Its Problems and New Directions', in Linda Martin Alcoff and Eva Feder Kittay (eds), *The Blackwell Guide to Feminist Philosophy* (Oxford: Blackwell Publishing, 2007), pp. 193–207.

Zagzebski, Linda T., *Virtues of the Mind: An Inquiry into the Nature of Virtue and the Ethical Foundations of Knowledge* (Cambridge: Cambridge University Press, 1996).

Index